THE BATTLE FOR THE BBC

THE
BATTLE
FOR THE
BBC

A British Broadcasting Conspiracy?

STEVEN BARNETT
& ANDREW CURRY

AURUM PRESS

First published 1994 by Aurum Press Limited
25 Bedford Avenue, London WC1B 3AT

A catalogue record for this book is available from the British Library

ISBN 1 85410 285 0

10 9 8 7 6 5 4 3 2 1
1998 1997 1996 1995 1994

Designed by Don Macpherson
Typeset by Computerset Ltd, Harmondsworth
Printed in Great Britain by Hartnolls Ltd, Bodmin

PICTURE CREDITS

CONTENTS

FOR JOANNA
(who will one day know what her mother put up with)

FOR SUE

PREFACE

The decade from 1984 to 1994 has, even by BBC standards, been an extraordinary one. As an institution at the heart of British public life, the BBC has been embroiled in conflict before, but never so often and never for such a sustained period. Those ten years have raised some fascinating questions which go beyond the BBC itself: about organisational change, the conduct of journalism, issues of management, the concept of public service and the survival of public institutions in a hostile political environment.

In writing this book, we have tried to do two things. First, to offer a narrative history of the unfolding events of those years: the debates that took place, the positions taken by significant players, the process of decision making, the compromises that were made, the deals that were struck. And, second, to go beyond the narrative to tackle some of the difficult issues mentioned above. It has not been an easy task because, in writing what is essentially a contemporary history, we are dealing with events which are still unclear and with people who have positions or arguments they still wish to defend. It is all too recent to expect considered and objective reflection from everyone involved. We have not had access to confidential internal documents, minutes of meetings, memos, unpublished drafts, or any of the other written material that would form the basis of a detailed and truly accurate history (with two exceptions: we have seen the minutes of the second governors' meeting on *Real Lives*, and all the Task Force reports). Perhaps in thirty years' time, when sensitive material is declassified and there are no reputations at stake, someone will tell the full story.

In the meantime, we have had to rely on two kinds of sources. The first is material in the public domain: autobiographies, histories, speeches, annual reports, government documents, Hansard, press cuttings. We have made liberal use of all of these, but they alone cannot provide the background or the thinking which has made the BBC's last ten years so traumatic and so fascinating. Much of the book therefore rests on the numerous interviews and private conversations we have had over a two-year period with a range of people: BBC managers past and present; BBC producers past and present; government ministers and their advisers; producers in ITV companies and the independent sector; journalists; academics; consultants; and friends in other private and public sector industries.

Our narrative is essentially chronological, but some chapters focus on particular 'themes' as they arise. Chapter 1 is a simple introduction to what is at stake: what role does the BBC fulfil and why should it matter what happens to it? Chapters 2 and 3 cover the period leading up to Alasdair Milne's dismissal as Director General in 1987. This is not new ground, although we have used some new material. But it helps to understand the historical context and, in particular, the traumas of Milne's last two years in office. Much of what followed stems from that. Chapter 4 describes the battle for Milne's succession and what was at stake. Chapter 5 is the story of perhaps the biggest – and most underestimated – factor in the upheavals that followed: the rise of the independents. Chapter 6 is the story of John Birt's arrival, his impact on BBC journalism and the repercussions. Chapter 7 tackles another unsung area: the financial and resource problems of a large, creative organisation in a competitive environment. Chapter 8 is the story of 1988–9, the BBC's most vulnerable and embattled period, when it was under the most intense political and competitive pressure. Chapter 9 looks at the roots of an issue which has suddenly taken on enormous importance: the BBC's commercial activities, and the contradictions that were inherent in them. Chapter 10 describes the period leading up to Michael Checkland's one-year extension, and looks in particular at the governors' role. Chapter 11 describes the delicate political manoeuvring around the Green Paper on the BBC's future, and the BBC's response. Chapter 12 looks at the origins, workings, and the problems of the BBC's new internal market – Producer Choice. Chapter 13 is the story of John Birt's baptism of fire in 1993, his first year as Director General. Chapter 14 covers the BBC's launch of its new commercial ambitions, the parliamentary inquiries leading up to the White Paper and the publication of the White Paper itself.

The story is a complicated one and, at times, we have broken with the strict chronological sequence in order to follow through one particular theme or argument before returning to the main narrative. The reader may, therefore, find it helpful from time to time to refer to the Chronology which follows immediately after the end of the main text.

We end with two chapters looking, respectively, backwards and forwards. Chapter 15 is an overview of the battle, with some conclusions about its lessons for the future. In particular, it looks at the repercussions for public institutions of some of the fashionable organisational changes that have swept through the public sector over the last few years. Chapter 16 examines some of the principles underlying the BBC's existence, and the factors that will determine its survival. It makes some recommendations for what we believe to be essential reforms if the BBC is to remain a significant and independent cultural presence.

The BBC itself has been mildly schizophrenic in its attitude towards our venture. It has not in the past had particularly happy experiences as a result of granting access to people wanting to write about it. It suffers from the same dilemma as most public institutions: principles of accountability dictate that it should open its doors to licence payers, but no organisation could withstand scrutiny of every crevice of its operating procedures. Over the last few months we have received a great deal of help and cooperation, particularly in the arrangement of background interviews with a few senior BBC managers. At the beginning, though, there was a marked reluctance.

This was partly because writing books on the BBC seemed at one stage to be becoming an industry in itself. We wrote, inevitably, in June 1993 to the current Director General, John Birt, asking for interviews, an invitation which he courteously declined. He felt it would be unfair to favour one invitation over all the others which he and his colleagues had also refused.

At least he replied to our letter. At the same time, we wrote to six of the governors, chosen to represent a mix of opinion and length of service. Letters went to the Chairman, Marmaduke Hussey; the Vice-Chairman, Lord Barnett; Sir Kenneth Bloomfield; Shahwar Sadeque; Bill Jordan; and Keith Oates. We received one response: a letter from Keith Oates' secretary which read, 'The BBC have asked that all such enquiries be decided by the Corporation. May I suggest, if you have not done so already, that you contact them direct.'

One of the themes in our book is the confusion which surrounds the role of BBC governors, but their constitutional position is clear. The governors *are* the BBC; the most cursory reading of the BBC charter should have made clear that it is a nonsense for them to talk about referring letters to the Corporation. Although the governors do not emerge from our book with great credit, this is a symptom rather than an effect of their indifference to our inquiries.

Governors aside, a lot of people were generous with their time and patience. Some of them are listed below, others have preferred to remain anonymous. In all, we have interviewed or spoken informally to over one hundred people in the last two years, and owe a debt of gratitude to all of them. In our attempt to create a faithful picture, we have tried not to rely on the memory or interpretations of single individuals, although sometimes this has been inevitable. We have rarely quoted dialogue directly, because few memories are precise enough to remember exact words. We have, however, tried to convey a flavour of some of the more dramatic or critical moments.

We are indebted to all of those who have helped us. Particular thanks go to:

Rod Allen, Helen Baehr, Kenneth Baker, Sophie Balhetchet, Nils Blythe, Michael Bunce, Andrew Cartmel, Sir Michael Checkland, Bill Cotton, Luke Crawley, Michael Crick, Jonathan Davis, David Docherty, Sir Paul Fox, Professor Ivor Gaber, Peter Goodwin, Michael Grade, David Graham, Ian Hargreaves, Nicholas Hellen, Georgina Henry, James Hogan, Chris Hopson, Peter Ibbotson, Philippa Johnson, Anne Laking, Stewart Lansley, Nick McCarthy, Kim McCroddan, Laurie McMahon, Lewis Marks, Pam Mills, Alasdair Milne, Janet Morgan,

Cresta Norris, Richard Paterson, Ian Phillips, Jonathan Powell, Gillian Reynolds, John Roberts, Anthony Rose, Andrew Sharp, Colin Shaw, Ros Sloboda, Anthony Smith, Raymond Snoddy, Lynne Stringer, Jane Thynne, Mark Tully, Vicky Wegg-Prosser, Gerry Wells, Brian Wenham, John Wilson and John Woodward.

Thanks are also due to all those who gave us valuable insights but have preferred not to be named.

Special thanks must go to Jan Merson for wading through pages of interview transcripts, and to Marion Sumerfield for her pursuit of the illustrations.

Thanks also to the library staff at the Independent Television Commission, the Royal Television Society and Goldsmiths College. And also to the 'faceless bureaucrats' (their words) in the BBC's corporate affairs department.

Our publishers, Aurum Press, have been a model of support and patience throughout. Piers Burnett and Sheila Murphy, in particular, have offered invaluable editorial advice and assistance from the beginning. We thank them for taking us on, keeping faith through each missed deadline, and for turning manuscript into book so quickly. Thanks also to our agent Bill Hamilton at A.M. Heath who helped with the synopsis and started the ball rolling.

Finally, none of this would have been possible without the support of our wives and families who have had to endure the marathon phone calls, endless faxes and late night vigils. In the Barnett household, eternal thanks to Alexandra for doing more than her share of weekend baby-minding and nappy-changing; and to Clare for the extra hours and deciphering of convoluted answerphone messages. In the Curry household, only Sue's unstinting support and encouragement made it possible to finish the job.

As always, we must remain responsible for errors of fact, interpretation, or controversy. We have tried to keep mistakes to a minimum and apologise for any that escaped us.

Steven Barnett
Andrew Curry
July 1994

CHAPTER ONE
THE LEGACY

The MacTaggart Lecture, the traditional curtain-raiser to the Edinburgh International Television Festival, is a prominent public occasion. The audience includes anyone who aspires to be anyone in Britain's small and incestuous broadcasting community and, falling as it does on the Friday preceding August Bank Holiday, the occasion is virtually guaranteed coverage in the press on a weekend which is usually desperately slack for news. In 1992 the speaker was Michael Grade, the Chief Executive of Channel 4 Television; his subject was the BBC and, in particular, the effect of the policies of its governors and management on the Corporation over the preceding five years. Grade's critique of these policies was forthright:

> I am reminded of a quote from the late Val Parnell when asked what action he proposed to take to prop up his ailing chain of music halls. . . . He replied: 'We shall close Liverpool Empire and if that works, we'll close them all.'

He was particularly scathing about the marketplace language which he believed had come to pervade all discussion of the BBC of the 90s:

> The BBC was never meant to be a business. It was set up all those years ago to be a centre of excellence in broadcasting. . . . It has earned its place in the hearts and minds of British viewers and listeners by being a great cultural institution, a patron and purveyor of information, education and popular entertainment. In short, a spending organisation dedicated to public service.

The emergence, scale and influence of that cultural institution is one of the most fascinating stories of twentieth-century Britain. Its significance was symbolised as much by the fact of Grade's speech as by its content: in what other country, in the market-obsessed, highly competitive world of the post-communist 90s, would the head of one broadcasting institution attack a direct competitor for – in his view – not doing its job well enough? True, there was, as always in the broadcasting industry, a personality factor – Grade himself had applied for the top BBC job and had quit the Corporation after a major row with the man he was implicitly condemning. But his deep-seated sense of affection and concern for the institution was manifest, and is still shared by thousands of fellow (and competing) broadcasters. It extends way beyond the

United Kingdom to almost every country in the world where the BBC can still sit comfortably alongside Manchester United, The Beatles and William Shakespeare as one of Britain's cultural icons.

That the BBC achieved such status was no accident, although its evolution into one of the world's most influential cultural bodies was not inevitable. It started in the autumn of 1922 when an unemployed 33-year-old civil engineer applied for a job as General Manager of the British Broadcasting Company Ltd, recently formed by a group of wireless manufacturers who had to provide some programmes to sell their new-fangled crystal sets. Although John Reith knew nothing about radio he got the job. He started with a staff of four and a free hand, and the first broadcast went out on 14 November 1922. Following two government inquiries in swift succession – the Sykes Committee in 1923 and the Crawford Committee in 1926 – this private company became a public corporation funded by a licence fee levied on all wireless owners on 1 January 1927. Neither the licence fee nor the establishment of a public corporation were foregone conclusions. Sykes considered advertising, but rejected it on economic rather than cultural grounds: it would distort competition by allowing large firms access to the airwaves at the expense of smaller firms without the means to buy expensive airtime. And the Crawford Committee's recommendation for a 'Public Commission operating in the Public Interest' was a notion very much in tune with the political climate of the times.

In the straitened circumstances of Britain in the 1920s, support for unrestrained free-market liberalism had dwindled. As the historian Jean Seaton has written:

> There was a widespread dissatisfaction with the *ad hoc* nature of industrial competition. Even in the 1920s, during the first post-war slump, there was a sense that there must be alternative ways to manage the distribution of resources.

Water and electricity were now administered as public corporations, and World War I had produced a number of civil servants well versed in both the philosophy and the practice of centralised control. Seaton quotes the economist Lincoln Gorden as recording that, by the 1920s, 'public boards had become all the rage'. The BBC was a creature of the times. But its constitutional status also owed much to that civil engineer, who inspired confidence in his ability to run this new public monopoly. The Crawford Committee praised the company and its staff for having 'raised the service to a degree which reflects high credit on British efficiency and enterprise'. Both the government and the wireless manufacturers were happy to entrust the new BBC to John Reith. Reith, for his part, wanted to ensure that his new charge would not become a propaganda tool for politicians, for whom he had little respect, and was proud of the new status granted to his company. He wrote in the 1927 *Handbook*: 'The Royal Academy and the Bank of England function under

Royal Charter. So does the BBC. It is no Department of State.'

By the time of Grade's speech 65 years later, the British Broadcasting Corporation ran two national television channels, five national radio stations, 39 local radio stations, and a worldwide radio service, and its programmes had been shown on virtually every television service in the world. It had won an international reputation, and had served as the model for new public broadcasting initiatives throughout the world. In Britain, by any yardstick, its sheer weight and presence remained enormous even in the so-called multi-channel era of the mid-1990s. Nationally, it is responsible for close to two-fifths of all new television production in the UK; it employs more than two-fifths of those involved in television and radio production; its television programmes consistently attract more than two-fifths of the total television audience, and its radio programmes over half of all radio listeners. (By contrast, NHK in Japan, the only public broadcaster which employs more people, has a much smaller share of the audience.) The combination of all these things – of programmes, of employment, of audience share – means that the complicated knot of values which have come to be embodied in the BBC have exerted a profound influence on British cultural and political life on a number of different levels.

The first and most basic level is programmes and the people who make them. Those who have chosen to work in British broadcasting have done so principally for creative rather than commercial reasons; historically the industry has offered a good living rather than a lavish one. (It is only recently that some executives have become millionaires on the back of their shareholdings in successful ITV companies.) For many – probably most – of those working for it, getting a job at the BBC has been a matter of personal achievement and great pride; in career terms the BBC has exemplified a trade-off between creative opportunity and lower salary levels – no-one joins the BBC to get rich. The private sector is still largely staffed by exiles from the Corporation, many of whom retain a peculiar loyalty and affection not just for their ex-employer but for its practices and philosophies, and view the BBC as something of an *alma mater*.

Such loyalty is founded on values which represent a social rather than a commercial view of the purpose of broadcasting. Those broadcasters who derive their income from advertisers and sponsors must deliver a commercially attractive schedule – usually low-risk, high-rating programmes which will appeal to as many high-spending viewers as possible. Those dependent on customers' subscriptions must provide services for which those customers are willing to pay a premium, typically movies and sport which have a disproportionately high value to viewers. In a system driven entirely by outright competition for commercial revenue, ratings impose a tyranny which allows little scope for the creative or the original, the unexpected or the challenging. The BBC has always been a public space for those people in the industry who wish to make the highest quality radio and television programmes simply because they hope their audiences will find them stimulating.

It is this environment which has produced some of the most enthralling moments in radio and television history. Whether it be programmes, series or personalities, two generations of British citizens have grown up with aspirations, fantasies and heroes inspired by the BBC across the whole range of broadcasting output. In comedy, the success stories have ranged from *Educating Archie* to *Steptoe and Son* to *Monty Python's Flying Circus* and, most recently, *One Foot in the Grave*. In drama, there were the Wednesday Plays of the 1970s, around which viewers would plan their social lives; costume dramas like *I, Claudius* and *Middlemarch* or popular serials like *The Forsyte Saga* and *Casualty*. In sport, *Match of the Day*'s soccer highlights became the focal point of Saturday night viewing for nearly two decades, while the introduction of commercial television made barely a dent in the BBC's role as the eyes and ears of British television sport. When both ITV and BBC showed the FA Cup Final simultaneously, the BBC consistently won the ratings battle by two to one. In news and current affairs, it was a trusted and authoritative voice and the guarantor of impartial coverage. For the latest news in times of national crisis, it was and remains the first instinct of most people to turn to BBC radio or television. Two generations of children were raised on *Uncle Mac's Children's Favourites*, *Watch with Mother* and *Blue Peter*, and still talk about their relative merits. From factual series like Kenneth Clark's *Civilisation* and Bronowski's *Ascent of Man* to David Attenborough's wildlife programmes and attempts to popularise science in *Tomorrow's World*, the BBC succeeded in making a vast range of material accessible and watchable to every owner of a television set in Britain.

The reputation of the BBC's programmes rested on its ability to attract extraordinary personalities and exceptional talent. Somehow, this single institution bred journalists like Charles Wheeler and Joan Bakewell, playwrights like Dennis Potter, Harold Pinter and Alan Bennett, directors like Ken Loach, comedy writers like Johnny Speight, comedians like John Cleese, Ronnie Barker and Victoria Wood, commentators like John Arlott, Dan Maskell and Bill Maclaren, disc jockeys like John Peel and Jimmy Savile, as well as popular entertainment figures like David Frost and Noel Edmonds. These were men and women of extraordinary talent who were themselves happy to acknowledge the decisive role of an organisational environment which could give them the space, the freedom and the security in which to flourish. Partly, it was an environment based on intangible notions of public service, quality and commitment. But a vital ingredient was the acceptance of risk: the ability to experiment with new ideas which might take time to establish an audience, the willingness to persevere with series which a commercial channel would typically axe if the first few programmes failed to capture a significant audience. Risk was not confined to individual programmes. There was risk in terms of programme types ('genres') or particular formats which would struggle to find a place in a commercial environment: the single play, religious programmes, arts documentaries or educational children's programmes will never be money-spinners. And there was risk in terms of scheduling, that mystical television art of determining what programmes are placed where, on what day and at what time. In an aggressively commercial schedule, current affairs and factual programmes are rarely granted a mid-evening prime-time slot. Adventurous scheduling allows for the possibility that people will happen upon new, unfamiliar material – programmes in which they will become happily immersed although no market researcher could ever have forecast a demand for them.

But the BBC's influence on broadcasting extends beyond its own programmes. Through its training schemes – in journalism, in studio management, in technical skills or in programme production – it makes an investment not just for itself but for the nation's skills base. At another level, it affects the programmes made by its competitors. The oft-quoted phrase, that British television is the best in the world, may be testimony to a certain British insularity and smugness, but it also reflects an undeniable truth: that, over forty years of commercial competition, the BBC's values have permeated its competitors. As a result, viewers in Britain have enjoyed a greater range and variety throughout their television service than almost anywhere else in the world. In a memorable passage in his Edinburgh speech, Michael Grade explained why:

> Commercial broadcasters invest in programming up to a level sufficient – but not beyond – to achieve the audiences necessary to attract revenue. . . . Where you have strong, benchmark public service television channels driven to produce excellent, home-grown programming for domestic audiences, then all television has to aspire to the same quality in order to compete and gain share of viewing. In Britain this is certainly true and I have always said that it is the BBC which keeps us all honest.

Finally, there is a level of influence which reaches beyond the confines of the broadcast media, to the roots of British culture and British society. The BBC's five symphony orchestras make a major contribution to maintaining Britain's reputation for excellence in classical music, and the Proms have become an institution in their own right. The Reith Lectures can still be relied upon to trigger intellectual debate in the columns and letter pages of the broadsheet press. The BBC played a major role in the creation of the Open University. Its broadcasters, from Brian Redhead and Jeremy Paxman to Delia Smith and the panel of *Gardener's Question Time*, have become national figures. By providing a television platform, it can generate interest in and support for minority interests – be they sporting or otherwise: who would have imagined, before the arrival of *One Man and His Dog* or *The Antiques Roadshow*, that sheepdog trials or antique collecting were the stuff of mainstream television? The BBC can clear schedules and provide airtime for major public events, whether they are tense parliamentary debates, funerals of major public figures, the state opening of Parliament, moments of national drama or crisis, charity concerts or royal occasions. Its journalism can abide by news values which are not dictated by the need to capture and keep large audiences, often at the expense of foreign stories or political analysis. It does not need to create any artificial sense of heightened drama in the quest for ratings. It has, as Alan Bennett once put it, performed the task of introducing the nation to itself, and has in the process become one of the foremost cultural institutions in the world.

This has not been achieved without conflict. Because it has become so intimately woven into the fabric of British social and political life, the BBC has always attracted opprobrium as well as praise, and has always been prone to internal struggles which have sometimes seeped into the open. But its purpose, and very existence, have never been as consistently threatened as they were between the mid-1980s and the mid-1990s. In government, in Whitehall, in think-tanks and in Broadcasting House itself, questions were being asked that went to the heart of the role of public broadcasting in a modern society. Should the BBC be restricted to an elitist role, simply making all those high-minded programmes which the burgeoning commercial sector could not cope with? Should it bother with orchestras? Should it maintain a significant production base of employees with craft skills, or simply draw on the pool of freelance talent like its competitors? What is its role, if any, in preserving some sense of a shared British identity, and therefore securing at all costs the rights to national sporting events like Wimbledon, the FA Cup and test matches? Is there any place on the BBC for audience-grabbing soap operas or quiz shows? Such questions had always been implicit, but in the cost-conscious, competitive and highly politicised atmosphere of the 80s they became the subject of open, and heated, debate.

As a result, the past decade has been the most traumatic and unpredictable in the Corporation's history. The battles that are recorded here reflected not just a fluctuating debate on the continuing role and relevance of the BBC, but the political and ideological struggles that were at the same time remoulding other parts of British society. An enormous number of protagonists were involved, ranging from the government, to the governors of the BBC, its management, the independent production sector, satellite broadcasters, and high-profile individuals like Grade. It was not a straightforward battle between heroes and villains, although often portrayed in the press as such. But the conflict was real enough. Perhaps because of the BBC's highly visible place in British life, the values which those protagonists brought to the debate reflected their wider perspectives on British society. The BBC became a crucible in which a whole nexus of related issues about economics, about politics, about

culture, business, public policy, even the idea of being British, were being held
to the flame. From the vantage point of Alasdair Milne's seat in the Director
General's office in 1985, this might have all seemed a little far-fetched. But he
had had ample warning that all was not well.

CHAPTER TWO
THE BATTLEGROUND

The BBC of the mid-1980s was in most respects similar to the BBC of the late 1950s. The successful programme makers of the 50s, 60s and 70s had risen through the ranks and were now in charge. Under its Director General, Alasdair Milne, the Corporation's character and culture were not far removed from that of the institution in which he had started his career as a general trainee thirty years earlier. It was still a large and fairly bureaucratic organisation, with arcane internal financial structures; it trained much of the industry, and held on to many of the best people; and it competed with its commercial rivals across the entire spectrum of programmes. (Indeed, the most obvious difference between the BBC of the late 1950s and that of the mid-1980s was that, with the advent of local radio and daytime television, the range across which it competed was greater than ever before.) Above all, it still used the language of public service, a language that was perceived as arrogant and unresponsive by its critics on the right. But the rest of the world had moved on. The right was now firmly in political control, and there were promises of new technologies which would deliver dozens, perhaps hundreds, of new TV channels and radio stations. If the BBC was to keep pace with the times, something would have to give.

Milne's career had been that of a model BBC programme maker. He had been Deputy Editor, then Editor, of the acclaimed *Tonight* programme in the 60s, and had moved steadily up the ladder, from Controller BBC Scotland to Director of Programmes and then Managing Director of BBC Television. By 1981, when it was time to find a successor to the retiring Director General, Ian Trethowan, Milne had been thoroughly groomed for the job. There were almost no dissenting voices. On 10 December 1981, following a fairly undemanding interview, he was told that the job was his; the following July he took office as the BBC's tenth Director General.

Milne took over at a bad time. The job of DG had always been fraught, and success depended on a number of factors: adequate income, reasonable relations with the main political parties, a cooperative and sympathetic Board of Governors, stability in the broadcasting industry, and a general acceptance of the BBC's aims and role among British society at large. Milne took over at a time when none of these could be taken for granted. The BBC suddenly seemed to be vulnerable.

Of all these factors, the political environment and relations with government have overwhelmingly been the most important. The government of the day has three levers with which it can, if it chooses, exert pressure on the BBC: through setting the level of the annual licence fee, historically done at three-year intervals; through appointment of the twelve governors, including both Chairman and Vice-Chairman, for five-year terms; and through renewal of the BBC Charter and its accompanying Licence and Agreement, which together define the BBC's constitution and terms of reference (historically, renewal has usually been for a ten-year period). Ultimately the government could go further: break up the BBC, change its funding, privatise it, or abolish it altogether. It also has the power to appoint Royal Commissions or committees of inquiry, although historically these have generally been open-ended exercises to explore policy options. The Beveridge Committee (1951), the Pilkington Committee (1962) and the Annan Committee (1977) were all set up in advance of allocating a new television channel and renewing the BBC's charter. In short, any government can, if it so wishes, find some means of sticking an influential oar into the Corporation's affairs; since its very first broadcast, it had never been advisable for the Corporation to get too far on the wrong side of government.

In fact, the history of the BBC is studded with examples both of government attempts to influence and intimidate, and of a succession of BBC compromises intended to maintain some kind of distance. The pattern was established during the General Strike of May 1926, in the midst of the BBC's conversion from private company to public corporation. With the closure of virtually every newspaper in the country, radio suddenly acquired enormous significance and the Chancellor of the Exchequer, Winston Churchill, was keen to exploit it as a propaganda weapon. Reith argued vehemently against Churchill, but at the same time made it clear that the BBC was 'for the government in the crisis'. Although Reith's view prevailed, the BBC was still prevented from allowing any trade unionist or even the leader of the Labour opposition to speak. What the BBC broadcast was not propaganda, but it was a selective view of the truth.

In 1935, when broadcasts by the communist Harry Pollitt and the fascist Oswald Mosley were planned, the Foreign Office was not prepared to tolerate a communist on air. But nor did it want to be seen to issue a direct prohibition (as a government is entitled to do under the BBC Charter). Instead, the Postmaster-General reminded Reith that the licence fee was shortly due for renewal, and the government made it quite clear it would not countenance any mention of its own interference. Both broadcasts were abandoned without any reference to government pressure.

By the time of World War II, then, the BBC's vaunted independence had been established, but on a basis of enlightened compromise rather than determined resistance. The arrangement guaranteed survival, but it created precedents which were to resonate for the next sixty years – and particularly during the 1980s and 90s. In the words of Jean Seaton,

> It made the BBC vulnerable to bullying. At various times, it was implied
> that the licence fee might not be allowed to rise, or even that the
> Corporation's licence to broadcast might be terminated. As a result, the
> most important constraint came to be the Corporation's anxiety to pre-
> empt the threats.

The most blatant example of government intimidation came during the
Suez crisis of 1956, when the BBC proved that it could make a stand. Prime
Minister Anthony Eden had asked for a ministerial broadcast on 3 November
to explain Britain's military intervention in Egypt. An *aide-memoire*, agreed
between the political parties in 1947, had established that the opposition had a
right of reply to government statements if they were 'controversial'. The
opposition Labour Party in 1956 was vehemently opposed to military intervention, and immediately asked for an opportunity to reply; the government
argued that, with the country in effect at war, this was not appropriate. With
the parties deadlocked, it was left to the BBC to decide what to do.

The BBC had little hesitation in offering the opposition leader, Hugh
Gaitskell, his right to reply, which he exercised the following day. Eden was
furious. His fury was compounded when the BBC would not censor its
Overseas Service reports of newspaper editorials criticising government
actions. Eden's Press Secretary recorded years later that 'innumerable
schemes to discipline the BBC' were discussed, and some reports had Eden
working out ways in which the government could simply take it over. In the
end, he settled for a token revenge: the budget of External Services was cut by
£1 million.

The 60s saw the pace of government intervention increase and the first
instance of a Chairman appointed by the government with the deliberate intention of controlling a 'troublesome' Director General. In November 1962 the
BBC introduced political satire to British screens when *That Was the Week,
That Was* arrived with a bevy of talented writers and performers, who poked
some acerbic fun at the establishment – particularly the incumbent
Conservative government. Telephoned by an excited press for his reaction
after the first edition, the Postmaster-General, Reginald Bevins, promised
icily, 'I'm going to do something about it.' But the Prime Minister, Harold
Macmillan, was more robust. Bevins returned to his desk to find a note from
Macmillan saying simply 'Oh no you're not.'

Two years later, an overtly political request from the new opposition leader
Harold Wilson *was* implemented – and may have changed the course of the
1964 general election. Wilson had discovered that the BBC was planning to
show a repeat of the enormously popular comedy *Steptoe and Son* in the early
evening of election day. He was convinced this essentially working-class sitcom might prejudice the Labour vote and asked the Director General, Hugh

Greene, to move it to 9.00 pm, after the polls had closed. Greene agreed. According to Greene's biographer, Michael Tracey, Wilson was effusive in his thanks, saying, 'That will be worth a dozen or more seats to me.' Labour won the election by four seats.

Towards the end of that decade, however, the BBC had become highly influential and Greene had himself become a controversial figure. Wilson, in particular, was concerned about the power being wielded by a single individual and used one of the other levers available to governments to control the BBC: he appointed an equally strong-minded Chairman to curb Greene's perceived excesses. The ex-Conservative minister and former 'Radio Doctor', Lord Hill, was appointed Chairman in September 1967, with the desired effect: ten months later Hugh Greene announced his retirement.

The Labour government of the 1970s was no better disposed towards the BBC, seeing it as 'establishment-minded' and innately conservative. Two incidents in particular underlined the willingness of ministers to confront this recalcitrant institution. In late 1976, at a dinner hosted by the Board of Governors in Belfast, the Secretary of State for Northern Ireland, Roy Mason, accused the BBC of assisting terrorists in its Northern Ireland coverage. He explicitly linked his accusation to threats about the licence fee which, in an era of high inflation, was a particularly potent weapon. This time the responsible Secretary of State, Merlyn Rees, was sympathetic to the BBC's position and alert to the dangers of political meddling – at least by other government departments. In his own words, 'I had to intervene on that. I wrote a letter to all my colleagues saying that the matter of the BBC was mine and nobody else's.'

Two years later, in 1978, the Labour Prime Minister James Callaghan had become sufficiently disenchanted with the BBC to support proposals for 'service management boards' which would have added another layer of political appointments below the governors. The effect would have been to weaken the BBC's independence from government, but the proposals were put on ice until after the 1979 general election.

It was therefore almost a relief to the upper echelons of the BBC when Margaret Thatcher's Conservative government came to power in 1979. She discarded the Callaghan plans. But it was already clear that the BBC would not be one of her favourite institutions, and that the growing tendency of government to use its various levers of influence was unlikely to diminish. Hers were libertarian, free-enterprise values, her radical creed favoured the free market, individual effort and self-help. Public institutions were at best to be tolerated as inevitable burdens, at worst held in contempt as superfluous. The BBC, in particular, was the antithesis of everything she believed in: subject to no marketplace disciplines, the recipient of a flat-rate tax, and – in her view – populated with critics who were intent on undermining her political revolution.

The first warning signs had appeared as early as 1971 when Thatcher was Secretary of State for Education in Edward Heath's government. The BBC was feeling the effects of the economic problems of the late 60s and badly needed an increase in the licence fee. It went to the government and asked for a rise from £6.10.0 (£6.50) to £7. Only two members of the cabinet opposed the request: Ted Heath and Margaret Thatcher. It was probably the last time they agreed on anything.

The Prime Minister's own distaste for the BBC was personal as well as political. Her speechwriter, Ronald Millar, recalls in his memoirs a discussion prior to the 1979 election, when Mrs Thatcher was still Leader of the Opposition. The BBC had suggested that Thatcher and Callaghan take part in a head-to-head debate, on the American model. One of her aides said that the BBC would be displeased if she turned the invitation down. 'How displeased?' Thatcher asked him; 'Very displeased', came the reply. 'In that case,' said Thatcher, 'the answer is definitely no.'

Thatcher's natural antagonism was fuelled by two incidents within a few months of her election victory. Shortly before the election, she had lost one of her closest friends, the architect of her Conservative leadership victory, when Airey Neave was blown up in his car coming out of the House of Commons car park. This brutal terrorist murder was carried out not by the IRA but by a splinter group, the unknown Irish National Liberation Army. A few weeks later, an INLA spokesman was interviewed (anonymously) on the last *Tonight* programme (the forerunner of *Newsnight*). The interview had been given the personal blessing of the Director General, Ian Trethowan, because, in his words, 'There was obviously a legitimate interest in trying to elicit the motivation of an organisation which had committed so foul a crime and of which up until then virtually nothing was known.'

About a million viewers had watched the interview, and there had been a few dozen telephone protests ('By no means an exceptional response to a controversial broadcast', according to Trethowan). A potential crisis seemed to have passed without incident. Five days later, a letter appeared in the *Daily Telegraph* from Airey Neave's widow recounting how, while watching television a few days earlier, she had suddenly been confronted by a man representing her husband's murderers.

Reactions were violent. Thatcher denounced the broadcast in the House of Commons, and there followed a fortnight of hostile press coverage and hundreds of letters of protest. Trethowan later regretted his decision, but it was only a few weeks later that Northern Ireland again raised the temperature between the BBC and the Prime Minister. This time the problem was created by a frenzied political reaction to some distorted press coverage. It was not the last time that the press was to play a crucial role in fuelling Thatcher's animosity towards the BBC.

A *Panorama* crew, filming in Dublin, were telephoned by the Provisional

IRA and told to go immediately to a small village in Northern Ireland called Carrickmore, a few miles over the border. There, they found masked and armed IRA members occupying the village, although by all accounts scarcely striking fear into the hearts of the local villagers. The occupation, however, was in blatant defiance of a recent army assurance that it controlled the border area. The incident was duly recorded and the film sent back to London to await whatever treatment *Panorama* decided to give it. It was never transmitted.

There matters might have rested, were it not for a report of the incident which appeared in an Irish republican newspaper and was then picked up by the British newspapers. Many of these portrayed the incident, in graphic terms, as a deliberate and premeditated collaboration between the BBC and the terrorists to demonstrate the continuing strength of the IRA. By a fateful coincidence, these exaggerated accounts appeared on a day, 8 November 1979, when both the cabinet and the Board of Governors were meeting. At the best of times, Thatcher was not disposed to trust the BBC; in the wake of the INLA interview, she was outraged. Home Secretary William Whitelaw telephoned BBC Chairman Michael Swann to convey the cabinet's fury and demand an explanation. In the House of Commons on the same day the leader of the Ulster Unionists spoke of treason, while Thatcher stated, bluntly, that 'It is time the BBC put its own house in order.'

Within a year, Margaret Thatcher was presented with a perfect opportunity to set her own stamp on the BBC by exploiting one of the tried and tested levers of government influence: the use of her power to appoint governors. Constitutionally, the charter makes it clear that the Board of Governors *is* the BBC, but has nothing to say beyond that. For that reason, on the insistence of John Reith, the governors' responsibilities were more formally set down by J.H. Whitley, BBC Chairman from 1930–5. The 'Whitley document' made it clear that the governors had no executive authority and that their responsibilities were, in Reith's words, 'general and not particular'. The day-to-day running of the BBC was to be left to the Board of Management. The division of labour was more bluntly described by *Truth* magazine in 1947: 'It is obvious that in practice the Board of Management will run the show and the governors amuse themselves at their fortnightly meetings with general matters.' A more detailed codification, in much the same vein, was added in 1982 by the former governor, Sir John Johnstone.

These attempted clarifications have still left plenty of room for interpretation and confusion. The governors, part-time outsiders, are expected to act both as trustees of the public interest and also to safeguard the interests of the broadcasting service. In effect, they have two roles – of leading the organisation as well as regulating it – which frequently conflict, especially in times of crisis. The governors are appointed, like the bishops of the Church of England, in one of those peculiarly British arrangements, by the Queen in Council acting on the advice of the Prime Minister. By tradition, as vacancies occurred, governments had tried to keep a reasonable political balance on BBC governing boards. Also by tradition, certain groups were guaranteed representation: there were representative governors for Scotland, Wales and Northern Ireland; a trade unionist; an academic; and someone from a minority ethnic group.

Sir Michael Swann had announced he would step down as Chairman in the middle of 1980. Swann had been an emollient and collaborative Chairman, who during his seven-year stint had sought always to achieve unanimity on the Board and smooth over divisions between governors and management. His attitude, following the abrasive approach of Hill, had come as something of a relief to the BBC's management. According to Leonard Miall, the distinguished BBC journalist turned research historian, Prime Minister Edward Heath told a group of American correspondents in 1973 that he had appointed Swann to re-establish the position of the Director General after the heavy-handed interventionism of Lord Hill.

There was an obvious successor. Mark Bonham-Carter had been appointed to the Board of Governors in 1975, had enormous political experience and was widely recognised as an erudite and astute man. He was also liked and admired by BBC staff. By 1980 he was Vice-Chairman and there was no other candidate with the same combination of experience and suitability.

But, to the newly elected Conservatives, Bonham-Carter had one major drawback: he was a distinguished Liberal. He had stood as a Liberal candidate at general elections, and in the 50s had briefly been a Liberal Member of Parliament. In the new political climate his background did not fit at all. According to journalist Michael Leapman, the Home Secretary William Whitelaw called Bonham-Carter to his office 'and told him regretfully that he and the Prime Minister, Mrs Thatcher, had decided that Conservative backbenchers would not approve the appointment to so vital a post of a man with his views'. Clearly, this was an opportunity Margaret Thatcher was not about to squander.

The man chosen instead was an altogether different character. George Howard had already been on the Board of Governors for eight years, and his other achievements in public life were confined to the chairmanship of the Country Landowners' Association. Howard was a big-eating, heavy-smoking widower, with a taste for brightly coloured kaftans and attractive women, who made frequent appearances in the gossip columns. His residence was the magnificent Castle Howard where he hosted the kind of hunting, shooting and fishing parties associated with the British landed gentry. He was also an old friend of Whitelaw's, who was no doubt aware that Howard had been one of the most outspoken critics of management conduct over the Carrickmore affair. Howard had no intention of being emollient, and on taking over in August 1980 announced that he intended to display a 'high profile'.

The following year, three more vacancies arose on the Board of Governors.

Each was filled by someone of a distinctly Conservative hue, and two were to have a profound influence on Milne's BBC. Stuart Young was a successful accountant whose brother, David, was a Conservative stalwart who was on the point of becoming a cabinet minister; Stuart Young was shortly himself to be thrust into the Chair. Jocelyn Barrow, a Trinidadian by birth, had in the 60s been General Secretary of the Campaign Against Racial Discrimination and was now seen as a 'safe' establishment figure. She was later to become Deputy Chairman of the Broadcasting Standards Council, set up by Margaret Thatcher in 1990 to monitor taste and decency standards.

The third newcomer, and the new Vice-Chairman, was William Rees-Mogg. Rees-Mogg had edited *The Times* for fourteen years. He had fought Chester-le-Street, in County Durham, for the Conservatives at a by-election in 1956, and again at the general election three years later. Under his editorship, *The Times* had enthusiastically embraced a number of Thatcherite causes, in particular the use of monetary policy to control inflation. He was clearly marked out as Howard's successor, a position denied him when he subsequently became Chairman of the Arts Council. Nonetheless, he remained Vice-Chairman of the BBC for the next five years.

Despite his faultless establishment credentials, Rees-Mogg exemplified the distrust and dislike of the BBC which had become common currency on the right. Like Thatcher, he saw it as complacent, arrogant and out of step with the times. He said later of his time as a governor:

> I was unpopular with pretty well everybody, including certainly many of the BBC broadcasters, because I was in conflict with the attitudes and atmosphere of the BBC – particularly during the period when Alasdair Milne was Director General. I thought the producer regime at the BBC at that time was moving away from the traditional standard of the BBC in respect of impartiality, was showing a kind of assertion of arrogance towards the rest of the community which in the end was not going to be acceptable.

One BBC insider, who had had dealings with him, put it rather more strongly: 'Rees-Mogg loathed the BBC and everyone in it; he couldn't disguise the malevolence.' The BBC had thus been saddled with a Vice-Chairman closely associated with Thatcherite thinking who was entirely out of sympathy with what the BBC stood for. His influence was to be profound.

These three new governors were shortly to be joined by three more of like mind. Malcolm McAlpine was a businessman and director of the family firm which had strong links with the Conservative Party (his brother was Party Treasurer). John Boyd had been General Secretary of the AUEW and Chairman of the Labour Party, but like many youthful Labour supporters, he had become progressively more right-wing with age and was described by Milne as 'a Salvationist Scot with a taste for Cromwellian discipline in the name of the Board of Governors'. And Daphne Park had moved from MI6 to become principal of Thatcher's old Oxford college, Somerville.

By the time Milne took over, therefore, the sheer scale of the politicisation of the BBC exceeded anything that had gone before. The Board of Governors had been transformed and a long-standing BBC tradition, that the Chairman and Vice-Chairman should have different political views, had been broken. In Milne's words, his predecessor Ian Trethowan had a 'mixed and moderate' Board; while 'I had an extremely right-wing Board. . . . Alwyn Roberts was the only one who could be said to be mildly left of centre. And he wasn't a wild radical.' (Roberts was, in fact, an academic who had been appointed as the Welsh Governor in 1979.)

When Milne made this point to the Home Office, the officials responsible agreed but were unmoved. 'They said that No. 10 was quite clear in its view that the Board should be as she wanted it. There is no doubt in my mind at all that she wanted to Thatcherise the Board.' Since it is the custom for the BBC itself to put up candidates, Milne had advanced the name of the ballerina Moira Shearer (once the star of Michael Powell's film *The Red Shoes*) who was married to the broadcaster Ludovic Kennedy:

> She was a great star of the ballet, a very intelligent woman. She was turned down flat, they told me, by Mrs Thatcher. She's a Liberal Democrat, not a violent leftie. They told me that Mrs Thatcher wouldn't have it, wouldn't hear of it.

Predictably, the barrister, playwright and long-standing Labour Party supporter John Mortimer received similar treatment.

If there were still any doubts remaining about the government's determination to exert pressure on the BBC, they were soon dispelled by the Falklands War in May 1982. Old hands who remembered Suez knew that broadcasters would be in the firing line. The difficulty this time was that, unlike 1956, there was no coherent political opposition. In 1982, the Labour Party was in disarray following its 1979 defeat and the leadership reluctantly supported military action to retake the occupied Falkland Islands.

For the BBC to present itself as neutral reporter, or to examine the case for and against a military solution, was therefore always going to create problems. Both *Newsnight* and *Panorama* tried to run objective, analytical programmes about the war's origins and the campaign, and were immediately set upon by drum-banging Thatcherite MPs and Fleet Street at its most jingoistic.

In response to *Newsnight*, a back-bench Tory MP asked at Prime Minister's questions on 7 May how Mrs Thatcher felt about the coverage. She responded that:

> Many people are very, very concerned indeed that the case for our British forces is not being put over fully and effectively. I understand

there are times when it would seem that we and the Argentines are almost being treated as equal and almost on a neutral basis.

On the same day, *The Sun* came close to accusing *Newsnight* presenter Peter Snow of treason.

The worst vitriol was reserved for the *Panorama* of 10 May. It had examined the views of the war's opponents, but had balanced these with extracts from a long earlier interview with Thatcher. The response was pandemonium. The next day in Parliament a former Conservative minister, Sally Oppenheim, denounced the programme as 'odious and subversive', a description which Thatcher endorsed: 'I know how strongly many people feel that the case for our country is not being put with sufficient vigour on certain programmes – I do not say all – of the BBC.' At the end of that week, *Panorama* conducted an opinion poll on viewers' opinions of the programme's Falklands coverage. The approval rate was 69%.

Two days later, Milne himself – as Director General designate – had to face the full force of the Conservative back-bench pack alongside Chairman George Howard. It was a nasty and acrimonious meeting, from which the MPs emerged boasting about 'blood on the walls' and 'roasting them alive'. Alan Clark, the eccentric but outspoken Conservative MP, almost certainly spoke for a great many in the room when he subsequently told two academic researchers:

> Although I don't think it had any particular effect, it is good for people in those sorts of positions to be roughed up. . . . It's quite funny, those sort of self-satisfied creeps on big salaries and fixed contracts, when they have a nasty time.

That was the climate in which, two months later, Alasdair Milne became Director General.

The press was important in establishing an atmosphere of fervent patriotism. Two of the biggest mass circulation papers, *The Sun* and *The News of the World*, were owned by Rupert Murdoch and were overtly populist with an editorial stance which was almost indistinguishable from the prevailing government philosophy. But Murdoch had no foothold in the more influential broadsheet press. In 1980 – in the teeth of bitter opposition – he acquired both *The Times* and *The Sunday Times* to add to his burgeoning worldwide press empire.

Murdoch's acquisition brought him influence as well as profits, for both *The Times* and *The Sunday Times* were read widely by Britain's opinion-formers and decision-makers. They were also valuable mouth-pieces for Murdoch's other business interests – despite the formal assurances Murdoch had been obliged to give about the papers' editorial independence. One of those developing business interests was broadcasting. In Australia he had acquired TV franchises in the two most lucrative markets, Sydney and Melbourne. In the UK, his first venture into broadcasting had brought him straight into a conflict with the British regulatory establishment when he tried to take over London Weekend Television in 1971. The then Independent Television Authority had blocked him, and he had come away with an unaccustomed bloody nose and an abiding hatred for the British regulatory system. Because of his newspaper holdings, the only way into British television was to by-pass regulatory controls via satellite. He already owned a satellite station which covered most of Europe, although the number of homes it reached was tiny and it lost money consistently. But satellite technology was still in its infancy, and he had his eye on the longer game.

As an aggressive entrepreneur who had set his sights on the broadcasting business, Murdoch viewed the BBC as a complacent institution sheltered from the rigours of the real world by guaranteed funding. More importantly, its size and share of the audience represented a real obstacle to his television ambitions. One obvious answer was to try to destabilise it.

Nevertheless, it still came as a shock when in January 1985 *The Times* ran three consecutive editorials condemning the BBC's request for a rise in the licence fee. It asked the government to question whether British television really was better than American, and concluded that the BBC should be broken up into a number of public service 'franchises', all of which should be allowed to take advertising. Although the editor, Charles Douglas-Home, angrily denied any proprietorial interference, it was scarcely credible that the correspondence with his boss's interests was pure accident. These editorials set the tone for *The Times*, and Murdoch's other British papers, for several years to come.

In 1983, Murdoch appointed as editor of *The Sunday Times* an even greater scourge of the establishment. Andrew Neil had been a member of the Conservative Research Department in the early 70s and, subsequently, editor of *The Economist*. He shared his proprietor's distaste for what he saw as cosy and uncompetitive collusion in the British establishment, epitomised *par excellence* by the comfortable duopoly which ran British broadcasting. Five years later, he was to be Executive Chairman of Murdoch's British satellite venture, Sky Television – while continuing to edit *The Sunday Times*.

Milne therefore faced a combination of political and commercial circumstances which did not augur well for the BBC's future. What he had on his side was the BBC's immense reputation and its uncanny ability to enchant even the most hardened critic. When George Howard was forced to retire as Chairman through ill health in 1983, the government appointed Stuart Young to succeed him. In appointing an accountant, and the brother of one of her cabinet loyalists, Thatcher no doubt hoped to turn the BBC into a more acceptably commercial organisation.

But Young was not a hardliner, and gradually concluded that the accusations of mindless extravagance, which were a commonplace of Tory folklore, were unjustified. As Milne himself was to write, following Young's death in 1986,

He did not come to the BBC as an unqualified admirer. Originally, he believed that the Corporation should accept advertising. But the more he delved, the more he became convinced that the licence fee continued to be essential to maintain the BBC.

Milne quotes Alwyn Roberts as saying that:

In Stuart Young, the BBC expected a critic and found a champion. His advocacy of public service broadcasting sprang from a deep conviction of the BBC's role, not only as a broadcasting body but as a force of unity and tolerance in British life.

In one important respect, however, Young did not disappoint. When he became Chairman, plans were well advanced for a BBC building in central London which would have been to the 80s what the original Broadcasting House building had been to the 1930s – a highly visible public monument to the role of the BBC as an historic and cultural institution. It was to be a building worthy of a leading British institution.

The Langham building stood opposite Broadcasting House in Portland Place and housed a number of BBC departments in a ramshackle maze of offices. Originally a Victorian hotel, the Langham had been bought by the BBC after the war and was badly in need of renovation. Under George Howard, a scheme had been developed to turn the Langham into a light, modern and bespoke building for the BBC's Radio Directorate. Norman Foster was given the prestigious commission. He inspired people with, in Milne's words, 'His vision of a building that was full of light and perspective, and one that would positively enhance Nash's processional way and his elegant church [All Souls] opposite.'

But the cost would be in excess of £100 million, and Young did not share Howard's taste for the grandiose. He was less flamboyant, more prosaic, more businesslike. Besides, by the beginning of 1985, a more pragmatic option was available: the White City greyhound track (originally built for the 1908 Olympics) was due to be flattened. It was not a pretty site, in the shadow of the A40M flyover, and a far cry from the Georgian elegance of Portland Place. But it was next door to Television Centre, it was suitable for purpose-built offices, and of course it was cost-effective for an organisation which was a custodian of public money. Foster's elaborate plans were discarded, and with Young himself in charge of negotiations the deal on the White City site was done by June. It was an important moment in the BBC's history, and as good a barometer of the prevailing mood as any row about a programme: a vital commercial decision, which might reasonably have been thought to be the responsibility of the Director General, had instead been taken by the Chairman.

Young's conversion to the BBC cause was, however, important when it came to resisting the government's efforts to exercise influence through the use of one of its other levers, the licence fee. To add to Milne's woes, the early 80s were a time of particular financial pressure on the licence fee. In the 50s and 60s, revenue had risen as more and more homes began to acquire TV sets and swapped their radio licences for the more expensive television licence. In the 1970s, although times were hard, the BBC was cushioned as viewers exchanged their black and white television sets for colour ones – and paid the more expensive colour television licence fee that went with them. It allowed the BBC to be a little more relaxed about the threats of financial sanctions which accompanied some of the political pressure. In contrast, by the mid-1980s, revenues were flat (and falling in real terms). The periodic reviews of the licence fee were therefore a potent threat and a useful government instrument for imposing what was – in its own view – some much-needed financial discipline.

The licence fee was due for renewal at the end of March 1985, and the BBC had calculated what it required to keep pace with inflation and finance the recent expansion into breakfast and daytime television. It needed a rise from £46 to £65. At a Downing Street lunch in autumn 1984, Thatcher had given her own response to this problem: 'Why don't you take a little advertising? A minute or two on the hour or whatever.' The proposal was not new. In May 1965 and again in February 1966, Tony Benn had put proposals before the Labour cabinet to make the BBC take advertising. It had been consistently opposed by a majority of the cabinet, and most importantly – even while he ranted against the BBC's inherent anti-Labour bias – by the Prime Minister Harold Wilson. In his diaries, Richard Crossman described the opposition as being based 'on the grounds that it's immoral to permit a virtuous organisation such as the BBC to be in any way related to commercial profit'.

Nearly twenty years on, an equally antagonistic Prime Minister had a very different attitude towards the profit motive. After a campaign of several months in support of the BBC's claim, spearheaded by Milne and Young, and after a thorough examination of the BBC's finances by accountants Peat Marwick on the instructions of the government, the Chairman and Director General went to the Home Office on 26 March 1985 to hear the verdict from Home Secretary Leon Brittan. The licence fee was to be raised to £58 for two years, not three. And there was a catch. The next day, Brittan was to announce a committee of inquiry into the BBC's finances to be headed by the free-market economist Professor Alan Peacock. The implication was clear: the Prime Minister was not about to impose advertising on the BBC, but she hoped to achieve her goals by the back door.

By this time Young had fallen ill. He had undergone surgery for cancer in 1984 and for much of his chairmanship, until his death in 1986, he was unwell. As a result, the Vice-Chairman, William Rees-Mogg, was in a better position to influence the Board of Governors than perhaps any Vice-Chairman before him.

It was at this point, as Milne attempted to cope with the mounting financial and political pressures, that a series of problems brought him into acrimonious conflict with the Board of Governors. They covered a whole range of broadcasting issues, from scheduling and programmes to editorial and legal questions, and taken together they led the governors to conclude that the BBC was out of touch and out of control. On the programming side, they had received no warning of the controversial decision by the Controller of BBC-1, Michael Grade, to axe the twenty-year-old series *Doctor Who*, and suddenly found themselves on the receiving end of the concerted wrath of the good Doctor's large and committed fan club. Meanwhile the popular consumer show *That's Life* was embroiled in an expensive libel action after making allegations about a real doctor who practised in Harley Street. With costs included, the settlement cost the Corporation close to £1 million.

Then the BBC had decided not to broadcast the Pope's Easter message on the grounds that it cost a lot and was watched by only a small audience. The Archbishop of Westminster complained directly to Stuart Young. The Board of Governors, in turn, made a public commitment that in future years the Easter message would be shown.

Finally, there was the case of the pirating of TV-AM's exclusive interview with Princess Michael of Kent, which exacerbated the governors' concern about lax editorial standards. The BBC's *Breakfast Time* programme had wanted access to the interview for news purposes, something which at the time was becoming a convention between broadcasters but had no legal or statutory force. Their commercial rivals had refused the request, and so the BBC had simply taped it off air and re-broadcast extracts. The offence was compounded by the fact that the BBC had concealed its chicanery by covering up TV-AM's very identifiable on-screen graphics with captions of its own.

This was too much for the governors who, following a private meeting on 1 May 1985, informed Milne that they had lost confidence in Alan Protheroe, the Assistant Director General and the man to whom Milne had entrusted the job of overseeing all BBC journalism. It was, therefore, Protheroe who was ultimately responsible for the *Breakfast Time* decision. He was shuffled sideways. And the governors insisted on another personnel change. They wanted the vacant post of Deputy Director General to be filled once again, and they had a candidate for the job: the Director of Resources for Television, Michael Checkland, an accountant who had been with the BBC for more than twenty years.

The Board's insistence on installing an accountant as second-in-command of Britain's largest cultural institution was scorned by those who had cut their teeth on programmes and learned their trade under some of the most revered names in British television. It was an overt recognition of the new political culture, fully reflected on the Board of Governors, in which accountancy was growing in status at about the same rate as creativity was being devalued.

But it was also a recognition of Checkland's achievements and his ability to look beyond the bean-counting. Though an accountant by training and career, he cared passionately about programmes and more specifically about the relationship between programmes and the resources needed to fund them. Having joined the Corporation as a cost accountant during the expansionist phase of 1964, he had risen rapidly through the ranks and by the mid-80s his star was in the ascendant. One programme maker remembered him in the late 70s mixing socially with programme makers in a way that was unusual for a man from his department and background. And amongst colleagues in Television Centre, while in charge of television resources, he had quickly acquired a reputation as a fixer and enabler.

Checkland had first made his name in 1980, when he delivered a paper entitled 'The Cost of Quality' to a Royal Television Society seminar. It was the first serious attempt to open a public discussion about the relationship between the cost of making programmes and what viewers saw on screen. Checkland's paper examined how costs per hour of television production – and in particular labour costs, which accounted for 60% of the total – would have to fall as more hours were broadcast and new technology was introduced. There was one immediate consequence of his speech: he suddenly found himself a very hot property on the job market and was offered the post of Managing Director of Central Television. For Checkland, born and raised in Birmingham, it would have been a return home.

But the BBC did not want to lose him. He was immediately asked to fly to Scotland to see Alasdair Milne, who was on a fishing holiday. He was persuaded to stay and given a place on the Board of Management as Director of Resources. Central, meanwhile, appointed one Bob Phillis who, some thirteen years later, was to follow in Checkland's footsteps as Deputy Director General.

Almost immediately, Milne gave Checkland and three other senior managers a task which was to become ever more familiar over the next few years: to find savings that would compensate for the revenue lost by the government's licence fee squeeze. The committee, chaired by Finance Director Geoff Buck, consisted of Checkland, David Hatch (then Controller, Radio 4) and Geraint Stanley Jones (then Controller, BBC Wales), and was given less than two months to report back. It was christened 'Black Spot' after the Whitehall nickname for the Treasury spending review committee, and it spent ten days touring BBC centres around the country followed by five weeks writing a report. It identified £32 million of savings to divert into programmes, and gave Checkland an insight into programme and financial operations across the Corporation which would soon prove invaluable.

Milne acknowledged the need for a deputy who had intimate knowledge of resources and expenditure at a time of financial hardship, but bitterly resented the governors' interference in selecting his management team. It was not the first time they had intervened. For his very first Management Board, Milne had wanted to appoint Bill Cotton as Managing Director of Television, but Chairman George Howard had insisted that this plum job go to the current Managing Director of Radio, Aubrey Singer. Howard, it transpired, had personally promised Singer that he would arrange it. Now, once again, the governors were tying Milne's hands with their own appointments.

It added to the sense of antagonism which was building between Milne and his governing board. Two weeks later, following another heated board meeting, Stuart Young wrote an uncompromising letter to his Director General which included the blunt warning that 'things cannot go on as they are'. Milne was not impressed. Returning to his office, he tore up the letter and recorded in his diary an equally uncompromising verdict on his meeting with Young: 'I thought he was crackers.'

But the problems which led to Young's warning were partly of Milne's own making, and his reaction epitomised the problem. The series of programming mistakes was seen as symptomatic of a regime which was becoming careless, wasteful and unresponsive to the new mood on the governing board and in the country at large. Milne did not help his own case by appearing aloof, even lazy, and unwilling to take time to explain his strategy. There were many around him, including his own supporters, who started to despair of his reticence and were fearful of his apparently dismissive attitude to a resurgent Board of Governors.

Milne himself was convinced about one of the main reasons behind that resurgence. Young's failing health meant that William Rees-Mogg was a powerful influence, particularly on editorial matters where Young felt less qualified to pass judgement. Milne describes Rees-Mogg as

... the evil genius behind the whole thing. William actually positioned Stuart the whole time. He denies it and says he wasn't interventionist. But sitting at endless board meetings with him, although he was very quiet and almost torpid at times, the rest of them tended to go with him.

Michael Leapman's theory about the source of Rees-Mogg's authority is persuasive.

He exerted a powerful influence on the Board because, amongst a group just below the first rank in British public life, he stood out as the best known, a man who moved easily in politics and journalism, who had cabinet ministers to dinner at his house in Westminster.

Certainly it was Rees-Mogg, a devout Catholic, who had been particularly angered by the decision not to cover the Pope's Easter message and who ensured that the Archbishop of Westminster received his assurance of future coverage. And it was Rees-Mogg who played a central role in what turned out to be a watershed – in the almost unanimous view of those involved – in the BBC's relationship with the Thatcher government.

CHAPTER THREE
FIRST BLOOD

If there was one subject which was guaranteed to rouse Margaret Thatcher to her most impassioned and intractable, it was Northern Ireland. For her, the IRA were irredeemably wicked, a message she expected all others to convey with equal passion. Five years after the murder of her close confidant Airey Neave, Thatcher herself had in October 1984 been the target of an IRA bomb at the Conservative Party conference in Brighton. Whatever notions she had of civil liberty and freedom of speech, they were never under any circumstances to be extended to terrorists.

In July 1985, following the hijacking of a TWA aircraft in Beirut and extensive coverage given by American networks to the Arab instigators, Thatcher railed against the media: 'We must try to find ways to starve the terrorists of the oxygen of publicity on which they depend', she told an American Bar Association Convention in London. A few days later, Thatcher was in Washington. At a news briefing a *Sunday Times* journalist asked her an apparently innocent question: what would be her reaction if a British television channel were to interview the IRA chief of staff? Naturally, she said that she would 'condemn them utterly'. This apparently anodyne exchange was to have a profound and lasting effect on the relationship between the BBC and the government.

Given the identity of the newspaper, the real motive for the question should have come as no surprise. It was prompted by a forthcoming BBC programme called *At the Edge of the Union*, one of a series of documentaries with the overall title *Real Lives* made by the Features Department (not Current Affairs, the usual thorn in the side of the government). The *Real Lives* series sought to get behind the public image of some well-known figures. Those profiled in *At the Edge of the Union*, made by the experienced producer Paul Hamann, were two of the leading protagonists in Northern Ireland: Gregory Campbell, leader of the Democratic Unionist group on Derry City Council, and Martin McGuinness of Provisional Sinn Fein. Both were elected members of the Northern Ireland assembly, and therefore paid a salary by the British government. The programme was to be broadcast on 7 August.

However, McGuinness was also rumoured to be chief of staff of the IRA. He denied it, but made no secret of his own endorsement of violence as a legitimate tool in the struggle for a united Ireland. That was enough for *The Sunday Times* which, as well as quizzing the Prime Minister in fairly general terms, sought more specific reactions from the Home Secretary, Leon Brittan, and the Northern Ireland Secretary, Douglas Hurd. Hurd was guarded in his response, confining himself to a general statement of concern about terrorists profiting from publicity. But the Home Secretary took the bait. On Monday 29 July, Leon Brittan released to the press a statement saying that the transmission of a programme featuring a prominent member of the IRA had security implications and would be contrary to the national interest. The implication of what he was saying was not lost on the London *Evening Standard* which led with the headline: BBC TOLD: BAN IRA FILM. In a letter delivered to the Chairman at Broadcasting House on Monday evening, Brittan elaborated on his statement and insisted that he was not trying to 'impose an act of censorship'. But his letter contained the ominous words 'terrorism thrives on the oxygen of publicity' and concluded, 'Even if the programme ... were, as a whole, to present terrorist organisations in a wholly unfavourable light, I would still ask you not to permit it to be broadcast.'

Suddenly, the stakes had been raised. It was one thing for a newspaper to provoke the Prime Minister into a robust reaction to a hypothetical question; it was quite another for the cabinet minister with responsibility for broadcasting to make a formal request directly to the BBC not to show a specific programme.

Young was immediately aware of the implications of Brittan's involvement. He had been informed of it just half an hour before the Home Office statement was released to the press and had called an emergency meeting of governors and management for the following day to discuss the request. The Board of Governors would have to make two separate decisions: first, whether to view the programme in advance; then, whether to ban it. It would be a fateful enough decision simply to have an advance viewing: this had not been done for fourteen years, since *Yesterday's Men* (on the lives of the members of Wilson's Labour government after they had lost office). It was a firmly established principle, underlying the division of responsibilities between the Board of Governors and the Board of Management, that editorial control remained firmly in the hands of the Board of Management. The governors' role, where necessary, was to make retrospective criticism without becoming embroiled in editorial decisions about forthcoming programmes. Alerted to a mounting crisis, the Board of Management watched the programme on Monday morning and decided unanimously that – with minor changes – it could go out.

Unfortunately, there was one significant absentee from both the Monday viewing and Tuesday's meeting of the two boards: the Director General. By a fateful coincidence, Alasdair Milne was on a short holiday in Scandinavia and unreachable as the critical events unfolded. By the time Michael Checkland contacted him, Milne was on a boat from Helsinki to Stockholm and could not make it back to London until Tuesday evening at the earliest. The problem was compounded by the fact that Milne himself did not know of the programme, in apparent contravention of strict procedures laid down for contentious programmes involving terrorists. News and current affairs guidelines stated unequivocally that 'Interviews with individuals who are deemed ... to be closely associated with a terrorist organisation may not be sought or transmitted – two separate stages – without the prior permission of the DG.' But these were two freely elected politicians representing official political parties, and the connection with terrorism was by rumour only. No-one involved had seen any reason to implement the procedure applying to terrorists.

Opinion amongst the governors was divided, but it was Rees-Mogg who argued most strenuously for seeing the programme. Young was marginally in favour, too, but for different reasons: he wanted the Board to be in the strongest possible position to make the case to Leon Brittan for rejecting his request, which they could not do if they had not seen the programme. But the accumulation of journalistic lapses over the last few months had by now raised serious questions of managerial competence, and Rees-Mogg's conviction was decisive. By a small majority, the Board of Governors took the historic decision to view *At the Edge of the Union*. Within a very short time of the screening starting, it was clear that reactions were unfavourable and criticisms gathered steam as one governor's hostility fuelled another's. By the time the Board regrouped and Rees-Mogg was invited to speak first, the die was cast. Stuart Young, aware of the enormous import of such blatant interference in response to a government request, warned in vain of the consequences. With Alwyn Roberts a lone dissenting voice, the governors decided to ban the broadcast.

Milne returned on Saturday 3 August, immediately watched a cassette of the programme and decided – like his colleagues the previous Monday – that it was transmittable. More than that, he decided that somehow the governors' decision had to be reversed. If the BBC's reputation were not to suffer severe and possibly irreparable damage, *At the Edge of the Union* had to be broadcast. After a series of telephone calls with individual governors, he succeeded in having an extraordinary meeting called for Tuesday 6 August to discuss a draft statement which envisaged *Real Lives* being transmitted in the autumn. By this time the issue had caused a national storm and BBC journalists – including, for the first time ever, World Service staff at Bush House – had called a one-day strike for the Wednesday. They were supported by journalists within ITN and independent radio.

The minutes of that hastily convened extraordinary meeting demonstrate the vast gulf that had opened between management and governors. They also reveal the resolute refusal of some governors to offer the slightest hint of compromise, an intransigence which itself had its roots in the political nature of their appointment. Sitting round the table along with Young and Rees-Mogg were Jocelyn Barrow, Daphne Park, Sir John Boyd, Malcolm McAlpine and

Alwyn Roberts, the last survivor from pre-Thatcherite days. In addition, there were three governors who had joined the previous year: the Scottish Governor Watson Peat, a landowner whom Milne himself had approved a year earlier but subsequently described as 'a man of unashamed right-wing views'; Lady Margaret Parkes, a JP and educationalist; and Lord Harewood, a cousin of the Queen and the man appointed *in lieu* of the management's choice, John Mortimer. Ironically, the newest recruit was Dr James Kincade, the Northern Ireland Governor who just a few days earlier had taken over from Lady Faulkner. Faulkner had declared herself 'utterly horrified' by the programme when the governors had viewed it, and Kincade (who had sat in on that meeting) had supported her. Critically, he was to take a softer line over the next few weeks.

Only one voice spoke up for staff concerns about censorship and in favour of the governors, having made their point, now taking a more emollient line: Alwyn Roberts. The BBC, said Young, was 'in turmoil'. Milne drew attention to the 'truly horrendous' reaction of staff to the Board's decision and to reactions abroad (glee in the communist world, dismay in the US), concluding that the BBC was currently 'out of control in many respects' because morale was so low. He read out his draft which most of them had heard over the phone the previous day and emphasised that a statement along the same lines should be released on that day.

Young's concerns, however, were different. He was angry at press coverage which had portrayed the governors as caving in to government pressure, and was concerned 'to get the record straight' by issuing a detailed statement from the governors. He was also particularly exercised by the way in which four interviews he had given to BBC journalists the previous Tuesday had been cut and therefore, in his view, distorted; as a result, he said, the constitutional responsibility of the Board to take major decisions had not been adequately conveyed. Jocelyn Barrow added that producers seemed to resent the Board exercising that responsibility.

When Milne tried to draw the meeting back to his own draft statement, it was McAlpine who returned to the theme of Young's interviews and the 'outrageous' distortion. For him a fundamental question for the BBC was how it controlled its journalists, and he urged that no decision be reached until after the strike. Rather curiously, for a BBC governor charged with acting as a trustee of the public interest, he added that, 'The listeners won't miss a day's news – they might even be pleased.' Having then dealt with changes to his own detailed statement, and with ten minutes to go to lunch, Young reopened the discussion on Milne's statement by inviting John Boyd to comment. Boyd banged the table and called for strong leadership and authority; if the Board agreed to show the film in the autumn, he said, 'We would deserve to be murdered.' On which note, the meeting adjourned for lunch.

The afternoon session began in similar vein. There had been some talk of buying space in the national press to publish the Chairman's detailed statement (thus by-passing any journalistic involvement), but the press office had advised that the unions might respond in similar fashion the following day. McAlpine said he was all for discovering whose side the unions were on. When Lord Harewood brought the meeting back to Milne's statement, the Director General repeated his opinion that this formula represented a way 'to get the Board back on course'. The implication that the Board had been misguided drew a sharp retort from Harewood, who said that it was 'not the Board which is off course, but the BBC which is shipping water'. This distinction between the BBC as an institution and the Board of Governors as a separate entity was a constitutional nonsense, but by now the gap was too wide for such niceties to be given any weight.

In what was becoming a losing battle for Milne, two governors revealed distinctly partisan views about the BBC staff's approach to terrorists. Part of Milne's suggested compromise involved mounting a major debate to discuss the problems faced by the media when dealing with terrorism. Daphne Park thought that the producers of such a debate would probably argue that it should include supporters of terrorist activity. Watson Peat went further, speculating that any agreement to show *Real Lives* might lead irresponsible producers to conclude that other 'flawed' programmes made without approval might eventually be transmitted.

Alwyn Roberts' argument, that the programme should be shown, in order to restore staff confidence and re-establish the perceived independence of the BBC, fell on deaf ears. Rees-Mogg added his voice to those opposed to any concessions, and Boyd ended with a stirring appeal for firmness: the situation was too dangerous to compromise the authority of the Board, and what was needed in the face of the 'manufactured indignation' of a number of people with too much time on their hands was strength of leadership. In case there was any ambiguity, Young spelt out the Board position for Milne: if the DG wanted to state publicly that *Real Lives* should be broadcast that would be 'a resignation statement or a firing statement'. Young himself, however, would not resign 'whatever hits the fan' and he hoped that neither Milne nor any of his colleagues would do so either. When asked what he planned to say on the matter, Milne responded, 'I will make up my own mind what I say, and when.' It was not a happy note on which to part.

The only chink of light in that unfortunate meeting was that the governors had stopped short of banning *Real Lives* for ever. They did not trust the management or the staff and were determined to give no ground; on the other hand, the furore which their decision had provoked caught many of them by surprise, and there was no need to go further than their short-term decision of the previous week. The programme stayed banned. The government had had its way. Moreover, though it could be maintained that the Board of Governors had acted independently of government, its approach to the issues and its prejudices about BBC programme makers were barely distinguishable from the convictions of the Prime Minister who had approved ten of the eleven members. It was not that the governors behaved as puppets of the government. It was that more liberal and independent voices, like John Mortimer or Moira Shearer, would almost certainly have argued in similar vein to Roberts and given greater weight to the importance of upholding the Director General's professional judgement in editorial matters. With but a single advocate, that case could not be given a fair hearing. The exclusion of such voices meant that the views of a significant proportion of British citizens were left unrepresented during that critical meeting. The governors may have been trustees of the public interest, but the 'public' they spoke for was a politically defined and deliberately restricted one.

Over the next few days the tension was almost unrelieved. Milne and his management colleagues released a public statement admitting to 'a failure to observe the guidelines at the highest levels' but leaving open the question of transmission after a few minor changes. Angry words were exchanged as Young and other governors complained about disloyalty in radio interviews, but by this stage every nuance and inflection was being scrutinised. It was another month before tempers had cooled sufficiently for the board meeting of 5 September to decide that the programme could, finally, be transmitted. Crucially, Rees-Mogg had in the intervening period changed his mind. On 16 October *Real Lives: At the Edge of the Union* was transmitted to nearly five million viewers with barely a murmur of complaint from its audience.

One of the concessions which Young had demanded in return for the Board's agreement was an investigation into the breakdown of governor–management relations by a newly retired governor, Sir John Johnston (who had recently been responsible for updating the Whitley document). Johnston was commissioned to prepare a paper which might serve as the basis for a reconciliation. He interviewed every member of each board individually, and his conclusions were an indictment of the mutual distrust which now existed between the two bodies. There was, he concluded,

> A widespread feeling among the Governors that the obligations and responsibilities of their office are viewed less seriously by senior management, sometimes to the point of implicit disregard or contempt, than either the Charter or their own understanding of their charge demands.

The governors often felt uninformed, and were not convinced that their views were passed on to BBC staff.

Johnston found feelings running equally high on the Board of Management:

> The Governors seem to them chiefly interested in criticism . . . dismissive of their professional knowledge and experience and mistrustful of

their capacity. . . . Board proceedings seem to them permeated with suspicion.

Milne subsequently confirmed the accuracy of that description of the management view, but was shocked at the depth of the governors' antagonism. He is,
in retrospect, prepared to accept partial responsibility:

> It was a terrible thing to read. It hadn't been like that three years ago, so
> I must carry some of the burden of blame for what went wrong. Equally
> so must they, because they should never have dismissed a programme
> which was perfectly reasonable in my judgement.

Milne is also convinced of the magnitude of the events surrounding that single programme: 'It was a major moment of truth for us because that decision
had to be reversed. We had to force it through and we never recovered from
that really, any of us.' It was also the defining, and possibly terminal, point of
his administration. 'When I engineered that it should go out, they clearly
decided that things should change.' Quite how they would change, and quite
how quickly, came as a shock to Alasdair Milne and those around him.

The months that followed were dominated in the upper echelons of the BBC
by the Peacock Committee. The outcome of its inquiries was assumed to be a
formality. The BBC's task was to persuade the committee otherwise, and
Brian Wenham had been appointed by Milne to spearhead the Corporation's
defence of its funding arrangements. The BBC's position was enormously
strengthened by the eloquent support of a Chairman who had come to believe
in both the BBC and the importance of its licence fee funding. At a meeting
with the committee in January 1986 he explained how, coming from a commercial background himself, he had initially favoured a commercial solution
to BBC funding; but that he had subsequently come to realise how destructive
it would be. In the end, the united stand of BBC Chairman and management,
combined with Wenham's battery of research reports and written evidence on
the damaging effects of advertising on the BBC, won the day. A vital factor in
the victory was the position of two key members of the committee – Peacock
himself and the financial journalist Sam Brittan – whose fervent belief in the
notion of consumer sovereignty led them to favour subscription rather than
advertising. When the Peacock Committee reported in July 1986, it failed to
do the Prime Minister's bidding and specifically recommended that BBC television should not take advertising. As for radio, the committee recommended
that the BBC should have 'the option' to privatise Radio 1 and Radio 2 if it so
wished. On this issue, the committee was divided: a majority arguing that
these stations should be privatised *and* carry advertising.

The narrow margin by which the Corporation had escaped from commercialisation became clearer a few days later when one committee member,

Alastair Hetherington (a former Controller of BBC Scotland), told the trade magazine *Broadcast* that Professor Peacock had announced at an early meeting of the committee, 'We are all agreed, aren't we, that we are going to have advertising on the BBC?' Indeed, even in December 1985, a draft of the report had still included the recommendation that the BBC take advertising. The more radical elements of the Conservative Party, while welcoming the committee's call for a revolutionary overhaul of the commercial sector, felt the BBC had been let off the hook. Of the committee's remaining recommendations, the ones which were given prominence at the time were about television's high-tech future, a world of scrambled signals, individual decoders, and pay-per-view services. It was three others, though, which were to dominate the debate on broadcasting policy over the next five years, and were to transform not just the commercial sector but the BBC as well. The first of these had its origins in a radical paper, called the Omega Report, which had emerged in 1984 from the Adam Smith Institute, a right-wing think-tank then beginning to make a serious impact on Conservative policy. It had proposed that the licences for ITV regions should be auctioned to the highest bidder rather than being allocated by a regulatory body on the grounds of quality and service. This idea was adopted by the Peacock Committee, along with much of the rhetoric (including, in parts, the actual words) of the Omega Report. Next, the committee also proposed that Channel 4 should sell its own airtime. Finally, and crucially for the BBC, it also recommended that 40% of BBC and ITV programming should be supplied by the independent producers who already made the bulk of Channel 4's programmes. The rejection of advertising was an important victory for the BBC; but that suggestion of an independent 'quota' had implications for the Corporation which were scarcely less revolutionary.

The announcement of Peacock's findings in July heralded six months of upheaval within the BBC which culminated in the toppling of the Milne regime and which set the framework for much that followed over the next eight years. On 1 August, a new Vice-Chairman joined the Board of Governors. Rees-Mogg had finally stepped down from an institution for which he never had much affection, and the government accepted that another overtly Conservative appointment would – even by its own standards – take the subversion of balance one step too far. The new Vice-Chairman would have to be drawn from Labour ranks. And the next best thing to a true-blue Tory was a candidate so far to the right of the Labour Party that he would not unduly upset the new ideological hegemony. Joel Barnett, a Labour member of the House of Lords, was approved by No. 10.

Barnett had been a Labour Member of Parliament from 1964 to 1983, when he had resigned his seat and gone to the Lords. For the duration of the 1974–9 Labour Government he had been Chief Secretary to the Treasury and had won a reputation as a tough negotiator when the time came for the Treasury to insist on major public spending cuts. On taking office, he joked to Milne that he was moving fast to the right and his daughter – who was on the BBC's General Advisory Council – told Milne that he was even further to the right than that. At Young's suggestion, and with Milne's agreement, a precedent was set for a BBC Vice-Chairman: Barnett was given his own office at Broadcasting House and his own chauffeur-driven car. Some had counselled Milne against this innovation, fearing that it was bound to encourage a shift in the balance of power even further towards the Board of Governors. They were prescient warnings, but Milne was in no position to alienate a powerful incoming governor.

Within four weeks, Barnett was to wield more influence than even he might have envisaged. Thatcherite Tories may have been disappointed by Peacock's failure to deliver, but a still more powerful lever now became available to those who felt the BBC should be brought to heel. Despite criticisms of his chairmanship, Stuart Young had commanded great affection from those he dealt with. Many felt he was not up to the job, and had simply been inserted as Thatcher's emissary at Broadcasting House, but he had a manifest respect for the institution he chaired. However, since his first operation for cancer in 1984, his health had deteriorated and as early as the *Real Lives* crisis he had sometimes seemed tired and in pain. By the summer of 1986 he was gravely ill and on 29 August he died. It falls to few Prime Ministers to appoint three successive chairmen of the BBC, but it now fell to Margaret Thatcher. Her political power was at its height, and there was to be an election within eighteen months. She needed someone she could trust.

In the excitable speculation that followed, several names entered and exited the frame. One, quickly ruled out on political grounds, was Joel Barnett. Labour was still Labour, however far to the right some of its supporters may have moved. Another, who ruled himself out, was Lord King, a favourite of Mrs Thatcher's who had transformed British Airways by taking on the unions and shedding staff. But one name that was never mentioned in the acres of speculative copy produced during September 1986 was that of Marmaduke James (Duke) Hussey.

Once again, William Rees-Mogg acted as a catalyst. Hussey was a friend of his; two men had worked together at Times Newspapers, they lived near each other in Somerset, and both were supporters of the Somerset county cricket team. Rees-Mogg believed that Hussey had the qualities to continue the job that he and Stuart Young had started, and while the search was on for a new Chairman he took the opportunity to promote Hussey's name to his friends in the government. Hussey also knew Milne's conservative predecessor as DG, Ian Trethowan, whose opinions on broadcasting were trusted in Downing Street.

Duke Hussey had served as a platoon commander in the Grenadier Guards during the war, until he was badly wounded at Anzio and his leg was amputated. After the war, he joined Associated Newspapers and in 1971 was hired by the Thomson Organisation as Chief Executive and Managing Director of Times Newspapers. His reputation as a tough manager was tested to destruction in 1978 when he attempted to force print unions at *The Times* and *Sunday Times* to accept new terms – and new technology – by locking them out (a decision supported by Rees-Mogg, among others).

Unfortunately, as Times Newspapers' Chairman and Editor-in-Chief Denis Hamilton recalled, 'Hussey had only a plan of attack, not of campaign.' He also made a fatal miscalculation, one surprising in a man who had spent almost thirty years in the newspaper industry. He had expected the print workers to settle quickly. Instead, in the casualised culture then prevailing in Fleet Street, the men who had been locked out simply signed on for shifts at other newspapers which were enthusiastically printing extra copies to take advantage of Times Newspapers' misfortunes. Hussey had been appointed by Hamilton in 1971, with a reputation as an able industrial relations negotiator. But when the print workers went back after the lock-out, even the few concessions made by unions on manning levels and redundancy were all but ignored. It was a personal defeat for the man who had established a high profile by leading from the front and taking on the unions. The consequences of that defeat were a bill for £39 million for Times Newspapers and the decision by its parent company to sell both titles to Rupert Murdoch.

When Murdoch acquired the two papers, he dispensed with most of the senior Thomson managers. Hussey, however, was retained on a consultancy basis, and then became a director of Times Newspapers. There was no obvious reason for his retention, but some unkind souls subsequently pointed to the Queen's much-publicised attendance at the bicentennial celebrations of *The Times* in 1986. A request for the sovereign's presence from the arch-republican Murdoch might have taken second place to other more pressing engagements. But Duke Hussey's wife, Lady Susan Hussey, had been a lady-in-waiting to the Queen since 1960; a request through her would be a different matter. Furthermore, Lady Susan had formerly been Susan Waldegrave, and her brother was the Conservative cabinet minister William Waldegrave. The Husseys moved in influential aristocratic and political circles, amongst people who were enormously important to Murdoch in the expansion of his business empire.

By 1986, despite the bicentennial celebrations, Marmaduke Hussey had faded somewhat from public life. He spent his days on a mixture of part-time public and private commitments: on the one hand, the chairmanship of the Royal Marsden Hospital, a place on the board of the British Council, and membership of a government working party on artificial limb and appliance centres; on the other a directorship of the publisher William Collins (another company in which Murdoch had an interest) and the co-chairmanship of Great

Western Radio, a commercial station based near his home in Somerset.

He was as surprised as the rest of the country by the invitation to chair the BBC. The story, as he tells it, is a revealing account of the establishment at work:

> I was quietly sitting at home one night, and the telephone rang. Someone said 'Is that you, Dukie?' and I said yes. 'It's Douglas Hurd here.' 'Oh,' I said, 'How nice', or words to that effect. I'd known Douglas for quite a long time, but we were acquaintances not close friends. He said 'Are you busy? Are you alone?' I said, 'I'm quite alone, my wife is out at the opera' and he said, 'Well, I've got rather an odd request to ask you: would you like to be Chairman of the Governors of the BBC?' I replied, 'You must be mad,' to which he responded 'I don't think you understand. I am the Home Secretary and I'm offering you this job on behalf of the Prime Minister.'

Hussey was given 24 hours to decide, and endured a sleepless night wondering about what he would be taking on. He was under no illusions: 'I was very doubtful about it, because it was an enormously big job. The BBC was patently into considerable difficulties.' But the approach was flattering and the allure too great to resist. The next day, he phoned Hurd and said 'Alright Douglas. I think we've made a ghastly mistake, but if it's really what you want me to do, I'll do it.' Hussey then asked for a brief, which seemed to take Hurd by surprise. 'A brief? A brief?' he replied, 'I don't want to worry about a brief, that's your problem. You will find out what the brief is when you get there.' Thus, in the appointee's own words, was settled the chairmanship of one of the largest cultural institutions in the world.

The political nature of the appointment was immediately apparent. The Conservative Party Chairman, Norman Tebbit, passionately convinced (at least in public) that the BBC was riddled with reds, announced in *The Sunday Times* that the appointment was designed to make it 'bloody clear' that change was demanded; Hussey, he said, was 'to get in there and sort the place out, and in days not months'. The Shadow Home Secretary, Gerald Kaufman, for his part, described Hussey's selection as 'outrageous', warning that if the Labour Party won the forthcoming election they would sack him. An anecdote recorded by the writer and ex-Channel 4 commissioning editor John Ranelagh reveals the kind of circles in which Hussey moved. Shortly after his appointment was announced, he bumped into Denis Thatcher and an acquaintance of Thatcher's at a London club. The acquaintance recalled:

> Denis Thatcher came in and started talking to [Hussey]. 'You've got to do something about that place.' Duke didn't open his mouth. 'You've got to do something about that place. It's a nest of vipers. A lot of bloody reds. You've got to get it back under control.' I said, 'Come on,

every government says that about the BBC, the Labour government said
the same thing. It must mean they've got it about right.' This infuriated
him. 'How can you talk such rubbish? It's well known they're a nest of
reds.' That was Denis Thatcher. He believes it. Hussey didn't say a
word.

Hussey would have been well aware, however, that Denis Thatcher's views
were not entirely unrepresentative of his wife's.

But there were still six weeks before Hussey was due to take over. Barnett was
therefore temporarily in charge and during the interregnum he became
embroiled in what was to appear as yet another journalistic disaster for the
BBC. *Maggie's Militant Tendency* was the title of a *Panorama* programme,
broadcast on 30 January 1984, which had its roots in the 1983 election. The
Conservative candidate for Stockton South, Tom Finnegan, had been dis-
owned by Central Office after he was discovered to be a former member of the
National Front. A Young Conservative report on links between the right wing
of the party and the extreme neo-fascist right was supported by senior party
members and amassed considerable evidence, including some which implicat-
ed serving MPs. The final report, which was published as an official
Conservative document, ran to 200 pages and led to the tightening of selection
procedures.

Phil Pedley, the chair of the Young Conservatives, approached James
Hogan, a *Panorama* producer, to offer him an exclusive based on the report.
The programme had extensive access to Conservative Party sources, and took
written statements from its interviewees – the research eventually filled two
four-drawer filing cabinets. Alasdair Milne was kept informed of develop-
ments and his Chief Assistant, Margaret Douglas, was closely involved. The
experienced author and journalist Michael Cockerill was the reporter.

Writs for libel were immediately issued by four of those named in the programme, including the MPs Gerald Howarth and Neil Hamilton. There were
also complaints from the Conservative Party: John Gummer, the Chairman,
and John Wakeham, the Chief Whip, met Milne on a number of occasions
over the course of the next six weeks. In response to their allegations of inaccuracy, the production team produced a 150-page document, and the Director
General was able to satisfy himself that the programme was, as reported in the
BBC house newspaper *Ariel*, 'rock solid'. He was not, however, willing to
show more than a fraction to Gummer or Wakeham, even privately, with the
threat of legal action pending. In the end, the two sides agreed to differ, and
Central Office fed their side of the story to the *Daily Mail*.

The libel case eventually came to court more than two years later, at the
very moment that Barnett was Acting Chairman. Two of the four libel actions
had been settled out of court, and Howarth and Hamilton went to court after

negotiations had failed to produce an agreement on the terms of a settlement. Some interviewees had declined to give evidence and by the first week of October – with the case due to start the following week – BBC lawyers had advised that the chances of success were no better than fifty-fifty; Protheroe was telling Milne to settle. On Monday 13th, counsel for the MPs started to put their case. By the Wednesday, Barnett had become extremely anxious about the costs involved and ordered Milne to settle.

His demand was backed by the full Board on the Thursday and the BBC settled before starting its defence, apologising to Howarth and Hamilton and paying them damages of £20,000 each and costs in excess of £500,000. The problem for the BBC's reputation was that the Corporation's case was never heard. As one editorial figure said, 'It was the worst of all possible worlds.'

It was a measure of how much had changed, even since 1984. Milne was no longer trusted by the governors; the press, whose anti-BBC tone was growing daily more strident, talked gleefully of another 'humiliating disaster'; one hundred MPs signed a motion calling for Milne's resignation. But for the BBC, it was more than a failure of nerve. It was also a failure of values. As one of those involved in the programme puts it now, 'The test of public service is to make programmes which go to the heart of the body politic and to defend them.' The BBC not only lost the will to fight but lost the will to publish, for even while settling the case it could have asked that the Conservatives publish the Young Conservatives' report. But it did not want to cause offence. The next round of licence fee negotiations was in progress, and there was an election looming.

On 30 October, within two weeks of the libel settlement, Norman Tebbit launched a ferocious attack on the BBC's news standards with a detailed critique of its main coverage of the American bombing of Libya six months earlier – in particular of the reporting of Kate Adie from the Libyan capital Tripoli. Tebbit – according to the Prime Minister's Press Secretary, Bernard Ingham – was speaking on behalf of the party, not the government, and Hussey confounded his critics inside and outside the BBC by leading a vigorous defence of the BBC's coverage. A letter to the Conservative Party Chairman, signed by both Hussey and Vice-Chairman Joel Barnett, affirmed that 'The Charter requires us to resist undue influence from any political party, and in no way be swayed by the imminence or otherwise of a general election.' Tebbit persevered, even to the point of irritating some of his own front-bench colleagues. But the tactics were in the same vein: not only tying up key BBC executives in time-consuming rebuttals but making reporters and editors acutely conscious of anything that might be construed by the Conservatives as biased. With hindsight, it is clear that Tebbit's attack almost certainly delayed the long-awaited 'sorting-out' of the BBC. But it did Hussey no harm to portray himself, very early on, as the champion of BBC integrity against such partisan attacks.

This was clearly the season for BBC witch-hunting. While Tebbit pursued his vendetta, three more politically inspired programming rows erupted to add to the sense of embattlement and disarray. The first concerned a four-part serial called *The Monocled Mutineer*, a First World War drama about the desertion of one Percy Toplis in the face of inhumane treatment from officers. It was a first-rate production with high ratings, but the BBC had made the mistake of billing it as 'a real life story'. Although it was based on fact, there was no certainty about the individuals involved or their behaviour. Once again, the right-wing popular press fell on this as an example of BBC left-wing propaganda, an attempt to glorify desertion and belittle patriotism. At any other time, it might have been worth a short diary item.

That row had broken during September. In early October, Daphne Park raised at a governors' meeting the question of a play by Ian Curteis about the Falklands war. Curteis was a distinguished screenwriter who wanted to portray the conflict from Thatcher's point of view – just as he had for Sir Anthony Eden in his BBC drama *Suez*. Alasdair Milne had encouraged him, and had reacted positively when he read the script in the summer of 1986. Milne, however, had a current affairs background and his drama department reacted differently. One of those who read it described it as

> . . . just awful – not because it was sympathetic to Thatcher or anything like that, it was just laughable, Toytown . . . the scenes with Thatcher looking at herself in the mirror, tears coming into her eyes, voice-overs of 'my boys', just really cringe-making.

This professional view did not accord with that of Curteis who became convinced that he was the victim of political censorship. The un-made Falklands Play became a political issue, fuelled by newspaper coverage in the *Evening Standard* and the *Daily Mail*, and compounded by the BBC's refusal to allow Anglia Television to acquire the rights to make it. The fact that the Director General had personally endorsed the play did not assist him in an atmosphere in which he was rapidly running out of friends.

The third problem, and the most serious, culminated in BBC offices in Scotland being raided by the Special Branch to impound programme material. Pictures of uniformed officers leaving BBC premises with armfuls of documents did little to heal the BBC's bruised confidence at home or its tarnished reputation abroad. By that time, however, Alasdair Milne had become the sacrificial victim.

A series of six programmes called *Secret Society*, made by the radical investigative reporter Duncan Campbell, had been commissioned by BBC Scotland for transmission on BBC-2. They were to cover various aspects of defence and security, a subject guaranteed to provoke the Prime Minister. One of the programmes concerned an alleged British spy satellite, code-named Zircon, and asked why the projected £500 million expenditure had not been approved (as it should have been) by the Public Accounts Committee. The governors, tetchy enough by this time anyway, had heard nothing about the programme; information started to reach them from two different sources. First, it was announced to the press in August as one of the BBC's forthcoming attractions. Second, Lord Barnett had, until his appointment to the BBC, been Chairman of the Public Accounts Committee. His successor, Bob Sheldon, was interviewed by Campbell, and complained to the BBC and Barnett that he had been 'set up'.

At successive board meetings the governors expressed dismay about the series, and their concern mounted as the publicity increased. Alan Protheroe, meanwhile, had visited the Pentagon in Washington and had been told by the Americans that the spy satellite programme would cause problems with their national security. On 5 December, he sent a private letter to Milne's home advising that the programme about Zircon should not go out. Milne viewed all the rough-cuts himself, and decided over Christmas that five of the programmes could go out, but not *Zircon*. On 15 January, he informed the Board of Governors. Three days later, *The Observer* broke the story with the headline BBC GAG ON £500 MILLION DEFENCE SECRET. The following day, Campbell announced that he would be showing the film to MPs in the House of Commons. From where the governors sat, it looked uncannily like yet another example of poor lines of communication and control. It was time to do something.

Duke Hussey had come to the BBC with a reputation for toughness. One of the first things he said to a senior executive, when he limped into Broadcasting House for the first time, was, 'Don't worry if I fall down, I'll get up again.' On 29 January, Alasdair Milne was summoned to the Chairman's office where both Hussey and Barnett were waiting. He was asked to leave the BBC immediately. The Board's decision, he was told, was unanimous.

Milne was incredulous. He realised he had opposition, not least because he had been effectively ignored by Thatcher when he approached her at Stuart Young's memorial service: 'I knew then that there were political problems of great proportions.' At the same time, Milne had spent almost all his adult life working for the BBC, and thought the continuing controversies were just an occupational hazard: 'Having lived through *That Was the Week, That Was* and a thousand other revolutions, these were the kind of problems the BBC lives with.' Throughout his career he had been highly effective in getting what he wanted inside the organisation, and was not averse to a touch of ruthlessness when necessary. But in the highly charged political atmosphere of the BBC in the mid-1980s the Director General needed other skills as well.

Even now, Milne seems stunned by the events of that day:

I didn't speak for a while. Joel Barnett said, 'It won't make any difference to your arrangements.' I hadn't thought about any arrangements, I was thinking about life. And I thought, Jesus Christ they're firing me. I thought I'd better do it with some dignity, so I said give me a pen. The piece of paper produced out of Barnett's pocket was already typed.

With the benefit of hindsight, says Milne,

What I should probably have said was – right, call a Board of Governors for this afternoon, I want to hear them all say it one after the other. But it was too dramatic, too overwhelming. I was caught. I never thought anyone would do that to me. Even now, long years afterwards, I can't credit it.

But the Board of Governors had made up its mind. Duke Hussey had started the way he meant to continue. Two days later, with an Acting Director General barely in place, the Special Branch invaded the BBC's Glasgow office.

CHAPTER FOUR
THE PEASANTS' REVOLT

Milne's sacking was traumatic, but not entirely unexpected. At least one senior television figure had predicted in December that Milne would be gone by February, and even his most fervent supporters had already accepted that his contract was unlikely to be extended beyond its 1988 renewal date.

Conspiracy theorists, especially on the left, have had no doubt that this was a predictable act of Tory malice undertaken at the earliest decent moment by the Prime Minister's torch-bearer in Portland Place. It was, they have said, no more than could be expected from an ideologically motivated government which was determined to impose its will on every facet of British social, political and cultural life. It was, perhaps, ironic that those who were most strident in defence of this thesis were also those who had, a decade earlier, proclaimed the BBC to be a tool of the establishment.

The truth was more complex. Certainly, Hussey would have been well aware of what would be deemed acceptable by those who appointed him. Norman Tebbit had said publicly that he should 'sort the BBC out'. But that is not the same as an explicit mandate to dismiss a chief executive, and senior politicians know better than to issue instructions. The most that can be said is that the new Chairman certainly knew that an immediate change at the top of the BBC would provoke few tears in Downing Street or the Carlton Club.

It also has to be said that there were some persuasive reasons for acting decisively. There had, over the last eighteen months, been too many managerial problems for anyone's comfort. Some, like *Real Lives* and the settlement of *Maggie's Militant Tendency*, could be attributed to the direct intervention of the governors themselves. Others, like *Secret Society*, stemmed more from poor lines of communication and control. There was a growing feeling that management was losing its grip. More importantly, there was a pervasive sense of a policy vacuum and a lack of any strategic direction at the top: the BBC was continuing to take the proceeds of a flat-rate licence fee and to involve itself in every aspect of broadcasting, oblivious to the new political and economic mantras of efficiency and privatisation. The words complacent and arrogant were frequently used, not only in the editorial columns of hostile, right-wing newspapers.

The problem had been aggravated by Alasdair Milne's style. As one of his senior colleagues put it:

He was an extraordinarily private, monosyllabic creature who had never done the thing which any DG has to do – he'd never shmoozed the governors. I'm prepared to take the view that at least half of them would have been reasonably content if they'd felt that things were being explained to them. [But] they felt they were treated in a dismissive or cursory way and that actually the guy wasn't running a decent shop. I don't think anyone can sensibly claim that Milne was a success.

In short, although Milne's dismissal was certainly welcome in government circles, Hussey and his Board could legitimately claim that their action was justified on practical grounds.

But if the fact of Milne's dismissal did not create shock waves, its manner most certainly did. As the internal telephones buzzed and huddled groups of BBC staff started to piece the day's events together, there emerged a tale of ruthless execution which left the most hardened observers feeling distinctly uneasy. It was not just the cursory ultimatum given in the Chairman's office during a meeting which took all of four minutes. It was the dissembling and meticulous preparation which had evidently gone before. There had been a retirement party the previous evening for the Welsh governor Alwyn Roberts, at which some participants detected knowing smiles but nothing was said. There had been a meeting of the governors in the morning, attended as usual by Board of Management members, at which Daphne Park and Watson Peat once again attacked Milne about *Secret Society*, arguing that the BBC should not have hired a left-wing, investigative journalist to make such a series. The only member of BBC staff who had any inkling of what was to follow was the BBC Secretary, Patricia Hodgson, who had been asked the previous Monday to investigate the constitutional propriety of dismissing the Director General. Her discretion had been total.

Traditionally, the governors' meeting is followed by lunch. Everyone duly adjourned to the sixth floor, where some members of the Board of Management were a little puzzled to find the usual place-names had been removed. But the meal started without any particular curiosity over the absence of the DG, Chairman and Deputy Chairman. It was only when Hussey returned twenty minutes later, tapped his glass for silence and asked the catering staff to leave, that there was any sense of something portentous in the air. Hussey was brief: 'I just have an announcement. The Director General has tendered his resignation, and that's all I've got to say. Thank you very much.' With little else to go on, the speculation over the lunch table was that Milne had decided to spend more time with his wife who had been suffering from cancer. As one participant put it: 'It was only when we all broke up after lunch, and people started ringing Alasdair, that the fact that he'd been knee-capped was established.'

One Board of Management member at the time – who believes that Hussey had always intended to target Milne – is convinced that the real significance of these events was in Hussey's realisation of the enormous power that had been vested in him: 'That's when I think Hussey realised [that] the only person who could sack him was the Queen. His firing of Alasdair, with that degree of ease, put him in a powerful position with the governors as much as with the executives.' His reputation was forged not only in the brutal, military-style manoeuvre which had paved the way for Milne's departure, but in the ease with which everyone was carried along. It was indeed a formidable exercise of power.

Checkland was asked if he would stand in as Acting Director General, though the Board believed that he might well support Milne and decline the invitation. Bill Cotton, the Managing Director of Television, had been asked to stand by, in case Checkland said no. In the event, he accepted.

Even as the tawdry tale began to unfold, and Milne's friends expressed their horror at such cynical treatment of a long-serving BBC stalwart, conversation turned inevitably to the succession. Two candidates initially emerged as favourites: Jeremy Isaacs, a distinguished television producer who had become the first Chief Executive of Channel 4; and Brian Wenham, whose equally distinguished career had seen him move up the hierarchy in classic BBC style.

Isaacs had become an imposing cultural figure. He had weathered the storms of bad publicity which had greeted Channel 4's arrival (CHANNEL SNORE and CHANNEL BORE were two of the more flattering tabloid head-lines), and had during his five years at the helm turned it into precisely the kind of mould-breaking minority TV channel which its creators had envisaged. He commanded enormous respect and affection from those who had worked for him. He was widely acknowledged as the kind of cultural figurehead who ought to be leading the world's most prestigious broadcaster. Wenham, mean-while, was the obvious inside choice, not regarded as inspirational but a programme maker with experience of both television and radio services, and imbued with the spirit and heritage of the BBC.

But there were objections to both which, with hindsight, were always going to disqualify them. They were part practical and part political, and it is impor-tant to disentangle the two.

The problem with Isaacs was, as one close observer put it, 'He's a terrible employee, he's a wonderful employer. He is very bad at the things that the people who [control] those jobs think are very important – namely pleasing them. He hates anyone with power over him at all.' In military terms, it is a familiar story: the brilliant general who commands unswerving loyalty from adoring lieutenants, but whose unorthodox tactics and lack of due deference to his own superiors creates consternation. Isaacs had, on occasion, reduced his Channel 4 Chairman, Edmund Dell, to near apoplexy.

Dell, like Joel Barnett, the BBC's Vice-Chairman, was a former Labour minister and a luminary of the party's right wing, whose former constituency, like Barnett's, was in the north-west of England. As erstwhile colleagues and political allies (though Dell, unlike Barnett, had abandoned Labour in favour of the newly formed SDP), they would not have been short of opportunities to compare notes. Certainly, the description given of Isaacs by one of his admirers virtually defined the kind of person that Hussey and Barnett wanted to avoid: 'He won't listen to people with knighthoods and peerages who come from the civil service or political parties and start ordering him about. He just can't stand them.' Three weeks before the final interviews Hussey was reported to have described Isaacs as 'Milne writ large'. There could have been no more succinct death sentence.

Wenham's problem was that he was an insider, part of the very *ancien régime* the governors were determined to overhaul. He was still on friendly terms with Ian Trethowan, Milne's predecessor, who in turn was close to Hussey. Trethowan suggested to Wenham that it might not be his turn this time round – which Wenham interpreted as meaning that he was effectively blackballed. It was not just that he was an insider – he was inextricably bound up in the Milne administration. As one senior executive put it, 'There was certainly a sense of something called the Old BBC and the direct line of succession would have been Milne to [Wenham], which would have been a continuation of whatever it was that he was getting wrong.' In the purgative atmosphere which Hussey was intent on creating, there was scarcely likely to be room for someone perceived (whatever the reality) as more of the same.

While politics with a small 'p' was effectively disqualifying the starting-line favourites, big 'P' Politics was reinforcing the message. One well-informed media correspondent believed that Isaacs 'causes Mrs Thatcher's temperature to rise', and was therefore out of the frame. His disdain for Mary Whitehouse and her moral crusade against some of Channel 4's more *risqué* programming also counted against him in Downing Street. One of the candidates was told by a senior back-bench Tory MP that a message had been sent via Denis Thatcher, along the lines of 'We don't mind who you have as long it's not Isaacs or Wenham.'

Disentangling the merits of individual personalities from the wider political context is difficult but essential to any discussion of political interference in the BBC. The problem is that politicians bent on interference are too canny to make their wishes known in any but the most oblique ways. Indeed, many would scarcely have seen it as interference, being so convinced of the institutional bias of the BBC that any 'nudging' of appointments decisions could be seen as a benign, almost charitable act. One ex-Home Secretary thought the

BBC was, in the absence of an effective official opposition in Parliament, attempting to play the part of unofficial opposition. But the most explicit and alarming description of the view from No. 10, and the way in which it was transmitted, came from Mrs Thatcher's speechwriter, Sir Ronald Millar.

In his recollections of the Thatcher years, Millar wrote:

> One had to watch and listen carefully, over a period, to understand the subtle techniques employed by some of the news and current affairs programmes of the BBC: the nuances, the delicate juxtapositions, the creative editing, the occasional making of news rather than the reporting of it that leaned left because that was the right way to think. These sinuous manoeuvres came from below, though above seemed to catch the infection and either refrained from intervening or went native.

Millar paints a picture of an organisation up to its neck in premeditated anti-government manipulation of news on a scale which would have done credit to a Soviet commissar. The main orchestrators were 'clever young high-flyers in current affairs who over the years powered the anti-Thatcher campaign into every home'. He complained of rigged studio audiences during political programmes, and a conspiracy which was so subtle that its protagonists would deliberately lie low for weeks or months – 'But after a suitable interval the piranhas would be back in business.'

Millar's vivid picture of political truths being distorted by the propagandists in Broadcasting House is significant, if only in revealing the extent to which paranoia was rampant in No. 10. For, as a Thatcher loyalist and intimate, he was privy to the thoughts and assumptions of the Thatcher inner circle. But no less significant is his claim that Thatcher herself 'turned a deaf ear and a blind eye' while her husband was vociferous and articulate on the evils of the BBC. Thatcher was far too experienced to whinge publicly about BBC bias and present herself as an open target to those seeking evidence of interference. Lofty disdain was a much more appropriate prime-ministerial stance. But she had her representatives on earth – in Norman Tebbit, in the massed ranks of baying delegates at Tory Party conferences, and in her husband. Any message conveyed by Denis would have been interpreted, not unreasonably, as having unofficial authorisation from the leader. It would not be lightly dismissed.

But it would be equally absurd to pretend that, had the two most obvious contenders for DG been card-carrying Conservative Party members, one of them would have been nodded into the job. The new broom had a mandate and a personal desire to sweep clean. Some believed that Hussey was simply finishing a job which Stuart Young was preparing to do before he died, and which he would have completed earlier had it not been for Norman Tebbit's full-frontal assault on the BBC's coverage of the Libyan bombing in the previous October. Hussey had won some friends in the BBC by his robust stand against Tebbit's ill-mannered outburst, and he could certainly not risk any link being made between a politically motivated attack and the sacking of the Director General. Now that he had done the job, in a way which effectively distanced Milne's removal from any political motive, he would not wish to be seen as a straightforward political lackey.

In truth, political expediency and the mood for real managerial change reinforced each other. The personality of the Chairman, as well as his political hue, was instrumental – he would want someone as DG who did not have a reputation for antagonism, with whom he could work and set about repairing the damage. In other words, the notion of explicit political conspiracy – of Tory grandees moving their pawns around the chess board in smoke-filled rooms – is misplaced. But it is perfectly true that, from this point on, the vital decisions that were being made about the BBC's key personnel and therefore its strategy and direction were inseparable from the prevailing political ethos. Hussey was a conduit for the new political and managerial orthodoxies which radiated from Downing Street to influence every facet of British industrial and cultural life. He was no government puppet, but there was little chance of him making any move which would seriously upset Downing Street's incumbent.

Given this political context, who would Hussey back as the first Director General under his chairmanship? As Broadcasting House speculation became feverish, and the odds lengthened on the joint favourites, attention turned to the less obvious candidates: to Michael Grade, the high-profile populist and currently Director of Programmes, who would almost certainly be judged too inexperienced; to John Tusa, highly regarded journalist and *Newsnight* presenter who had become Managing Director of the World Service operation at Bush House – but had been there only six months, and in the event did not apply; and to Paul Fox, who had left the BBC in 1973 to become Director of Programmes and then Managing Director at Yorkshire Television, but could make an ideal interim candidate until the next generation (Grade, Tusa) were ready to inherit. Michael Checkland, though acting as DG, was usually discounted because he was not a programme maker.

In the event, it was a rank outsider who – under Hussey's banner – suddenly started to make the running. Four days after Milne's dismissal, on Monday 2 February, *The Financial Times* named David Dimbleby as a serious contender. By the end of that week, with less than three weeks to go to the final interviews on 26 February, Dimbleby was regarded as a front-runner, although virtually every senior BBC executive found the idea absurd. Within the Corporation an elaborate lobbying process began in an effort to nobble the chances of this dark horse turned favourite.

Dimbleby was not an obvious choice. As a journalist and reporter, he had a high-profile on-screen reputation which was consolidated in the 70s with several spells as a *Panorama* presenter. He had anchored successive election programmes, in 1979, 1983 and 1987. But he had never been part of the BBC management team, and his managerial experience was confined to the chairmanship of a small, local newspaper company which owned, amongst other things, *The Richmond and Twickenham Times*. One BBC executive described him dismissively as 'a taker not a giver'. Another described his views of most people who work in BBC Television as offensive: 'Little people, ill-paid, living in houses in Twickenham.' Few believed he could give a wholehearted commitment to the organisation. Once the contest was over, it transpired that he himself believed he could have run the place in the same way a minister runs his department: providing the policy and strategic direction while civil servants put the dictates into practice.

It was not just the man himself that insiders objected to, but the BBC philosophy he represented. As DG he would, it was believed, place a neo-Reithian emphasis on serious journalism, drama and information-type programmes to the detriment of the lighter side of television life. As it turned out, under a different leader, that was precisely the battleground on which a ferocious internal debate would take place: to what extent should the BBC draw back from the soap operas, the comedy and the light entertainment which gives it its mass appeal and leave those programming areas to the increasingly competitive commercial sector? And to what extent must it continue to appeal to mass audiences in order to stay rooted in everyone's life and thereby justify the licence fee? There was no doubt in most people's minds where Dimbleby stood in the spectrum of opinion, and to populists like Cotton and Grade his vision was anathema.

Hostility to Dimbleby was aggravated by the political dimension: he was seen as a Central Office candidate, the favoured child of what one senior executive called 'small country-house Tories'. This was partly due to Hussey running him so strongly, and concerns about Hussey's political motives. But it was also fuelled by conversations and rumours, all of which suggested that a Dimbleby appointment would be welcomed by Downing Street. One high-profile BBC presenter reported on a dinner conversation with Professor Brian Griffiths, a close Downing Street confidant and policy adviser who was to be instrumental in promoting many of the fundamental changes inflicted on the BBC. Griffiths indicated that a Dimbleby appointment would please No. 10, but also that Dimbleby was assumed to be the broadcasters' choice. He was swiftly disabused. Suspicions seemed to be confirmed by another radical Conservative, Sam Brittan, the day after the winner had been announced: 'It was a pity that Dimbleby's candidature was overturned by a peasants' revolt', he said on the BBC's *Breakfast Time*.

That peasants' revolt dominated much of the internal politicking in the three weeks up to the Board interviews. Paul Fox made it clear that he was not prepared to go through the rigmarole of an appointments board, but would take the job if it was offered. Michael Grade, meanwhile, had set off for a holiday in France on the day Milne went, but swiftly arranged to return for a day to dine with Hussey. He made it clear to friends that he would not hang around if Dimbleby were appointed, but then had to resolve a difficult dilemma: whether and at what point to make it clear to the Chairman that Dimbleby's appointment would provoke his resignation. He also had to decide whether to go for the job himself.

In the event, persuaded by the need to state an alternative case to Dimbleby's rather than by any realistic chances of success, Grade decided to apply. His own determination to go if Dimbleby won was reinforced by reports that John Tusa was of much the same mind over at World Service. With two weeks still to go, it was clear that a head of steam was building up to thwart the Chairman's favoured candidate – but with no obvious alternative for those who opposed him. After a meeting with Joel Barnett, one BBC executive concluded that the only compromise solution would be Checkland coming through the middle with a strong editorial deputy.

Grade's own candidature provided at least one ironic twist when he decided that the best preparation would be a dry run of the interview, with colleagues firing governor-type questions at him. To play the governor roles, he chose his own deputy at BBC Television, Peter Ibbotson, and his ex-colleague and successor at LWT, John Birt. At this mock interview he stated his belief that BBC journalism needed an injection of fresh talent from ITV. No names were mentioned, but his mock inquisitor and former LWT colleague might have been forgiven for thinking he was in the frame, and could expect a favourable review when it came to canvassing opinion on a strong editorial appointment. If Grade had Birt in mind, it was a choice he would have personal cause to regret.

By the time of selection day on 26 February, there was no firm favourite. Some argued that Dimbleby's campaign had been too blatant, had peaked too soon and had given his opponents too much time to collect their ammunition; others that the governors were, in one executive's colourful words, 'starfuckers' who could not resist the lure of the famous face and famous name – especially given their craven deference to the Chairman, who was bound to force through his own candidate.

For the candidates, the interviews offered their own clues. Isaacs was told by John Boyd that: 'You do not seem to me like a man who takes kindly to discipline.' Wenham argued in favour of the *status quo* at news and current affairs, only to realise immediately that he had given the 'wrong' answer. Checkland was on before lunch. He had not, while Deputy Director General, thought seriously about succeeding Alasdair Milne, assuming that Wenham was the obvious candidate. It was only in the last few weeks, when, as acting Director General, he found himself able to deal calmly with *Secret Society* and the turmoil he had inherited, that he became convinced he could do the job. He knew he had performed well when he talked for twenty minutes without interruption, and showed that even an accountant could speak fluently on a range of issues. Afterwards he walked out of Broadcasting House through the *melée* of journalists camped on the pavement to have lunch with his secretary. None of them noticed him leave.

By 5.00 pm the interviews had been completed, and fifty minutes later the governors went into conclave. Television Centre began to buzz with rumour and nervous apprehension. One story had a commissionaire reporting a sighting of Paul Fox, given credence by another report that Fox had unexpectedly cancelled a longstanding lunch engagement in Leeds to get the 13.45 train to London. Another tale had a female governor overheard on her way to the toilet expressing unhappiness with Isaacs. Internal telephones burned with hearsay. Every titbit, every nuance, every movement was devoured, analysed and recycled as if this were election night – as, indeed, within the city-state of the BBC, it was. Only those who await the cardinals' puff of smoke from the Vatican could appreciate the sense of tension and nervous anxiety.

At Television Centre, the offices of Michael Grade and Robin Walsh (the Deputy Editor of Television News) became focal points for groups of wandering, pensive staff. One participant described the atmosphere in Walsh's office as 'a cross between the waiting room at a maternity hospital and a courtroom while the jury's out'. It was not just the direction of the BBC but, for many of those present, their own futures which rode on the result. Along with Walsh himself, the floating population included Jonathan Powell, Peter Pagnamenta, Peter Ibbotson, Jim Moir, Alan Yentob, and Sue Lawley. For all the mounting tension, a party spirit prevailed: Moir amused the crowds with jokes and mini-sketches, and Walsh started a *risqué* joke about a skunk but bottled out in the presence of Lawley.

Given the time taken over the decision, a certain light-heartedness was essential: as the deadline for the *Nine o'Clock News* came and went, it was clear that there was serious dissent in the boardroom at Broadcasting House. It was not until 10.20 that the tension was lifted when Ron Neil, Editor of Television News, came into Grade's office to announce an unconfirmed report he had just heard from Broadcasting House: it was to be a double-headed appointment, with Checkland and Dimbleby to be joint DGs. The party spirit evaporated. A 'horrible' decision said one, the worst possible outcome said another, a disaster for morale said a third. For twenty minutes, the shadow of David Dimbleby as Director General loomed large over television's senior managers, and the effect was one of abject misery.

Finally, at 10.42, the official word came from Richard Peel at the Broadcasting House press office. Never can a lowly press officer have received such a warm-hearted response from his senior colleagues: no, it was not Dimbleby, it was to be Checkland alone. The confusion had arisen for good reason. At 10.10, Hussey and Barnett had informed Checkland that he had got the job. But, they said, they were very anxious that he should have a deputy and they wanted it to be Dimbleby. Checkland made it clear that this would not be acceptable and offered to explain his reasons to the Board. Although aware of the high risk involved in refusing the Board's recommendation, he had seen at first hand the problems that Alasdair Milne had suffered with senior appointments that had been forced upon him. Checkland was well aware of the need for a senior editorial figure as a deputy, but wanted to choose his own. After deliberating for over four hours, the Board could hardly refuse. As the post-mortems started and the repercussions were analysed, one of the assembled coterie sat back and expressed the unanimous sense of relief on Television Centre's sixth floor: 'It's been a good day's work,' he said. 'We fucked Dimbleby.'

It is difficult to speculate on the outcome of a BBC under Dimbleby. What is certainly true is that, despite the universal sense of relief that Dimbleby had been thwarted, the appointment of Checkland was itself to trigger a number of events which Dimbleby's opponents neither anticipated nor welcomed. It seemed like a safe, if uninspiring, choice. In fact, the selection of Michael Checkland as the BBC's eleventh Director General had two important and immediate implications.

The first was a consequence of his professional background. For the first time in over forty years an institution devoted wholly to the making of radio and television programmes had as its leader a man who had never in his life made a radio or television programme. To much of the outside world, it was extraordinary that someone of the proven inspirational calibre of Jeremy Isaacs was sent packing while someone who could make the figures add up was given the job. It was also seen as a sign of Thatcherism tightening its grip on the cultural world. Good housekeeping was the contemporary political philosophy, and good housekeepers were well schooled in the art of matching income and expenditure. Never mind the quality of the programmes, seemed to be the message, we need a DG who can balance the books.

But, as Checkland himself recognised, the book balancer needed to be balanced – by a deputy of proven programme-making ability who had weight and credibility on editorial issues. Checkland would have to have a number two who, unlike previous number twos, would have real power by virtue of his (or her) production background.

The second, and the more ominous, point was that Hussey had been foiled. With the full support of the Board he had easily fulfilled the first leg of his mission, to get Milne out, and he believed he could achieve the second. Privately, he had all but guaranteed Dimbleby the job, and Dimbleby had assumed it was his. But several governors, led by Barnett, had been persuaded by the intense internal lobbying campaign that Dimbleby would be a disaster and were determined to resist. They ran Isaacs in opposition, aware that the most likely outcome would be an enforced compromise by both sides. Their case was strengthened by an impressive performance by Checkland, who offered them a reassuring prospect of efficiency, steady management and

a calming influence on the recent controversies and difficult Board–management relationship. He had also had the advantage of attending board meetings,
and was well aware of the governors' concerns and priorities.

But Hussey did not like losing. On Friday morning, he phoned Ian
Trethowan and complained that it had all gone wrong. Trethowan responded
that governors do sometimes feel they have a role of their own and cannot be
treated like the board of a commercial company. Hussey had appeared to be
playing the role of a cavalier newspaper proprietor – sack one editor, appoint
another more to one's taste. Even the BBC's governors were not prepared to
be manipulated in quite such a blatant fashion, but it meant the Chairman was
landed with a chief executive he would not have chosen. That would make him
all the more determined, when the succession to Checkland was being decided five years later, not to be denied again.

CHAPTER FIVE

AN UNHOLY ALLIANCE

There were obvious problems confronting the new Director General. The journalism, which had finally sunk Milne, needed to be sorted out if Checkland was to avoid continuing assaults from the government and Conservative backbenchers. Financial matters needed urgently to be addressed. But the issue which would ultimately have more impact on the BBC in the 1990s than any other was more obscure, a ticking bomb rather than a barrage. It was the question of what to do about the independent producers. During 1986 they had lobbied the government to persuade it that independent companies, working outside the BBC and ITV, should supply, as of right, a quarter of the programmes originated by the broadcasters.

The campaign for the independent production quota was one of the most audacious, and most successful, political lobbying campaigns of the post-war years. It was so audacious, in fact, that even the people who dreamed up the idea had initially half-dismissed it as a long shot. It was successful in that it achieved everything it set out to achieve in little over a year. (In contrast, the campaign for a fourth channel, Channel 4, took eighteen years to achieve its goal.)

It is a complicated story, and sometimes confusing. It is, though, revealing of the way in which the politics of the broadcasting industry were played out in the mid-1980s, causing divisions within government and also among the broadcasters themselves. The campaign and its consequences were a mass of contradictions.

Stripped to its essentials, the story goes like this: a group of small business people (the independent television producers) decided that the existing market for their product (television programmes) was too small. They therefore set out to persuade a government dedicated to free-market economics that, as a group, they should be given guaranteed access to two particular markets (BBC and ITV), a suggestion which in any other industry would have been ridiculed all the way down Whitehall. But in the mid-1980s, broadcasting was not like any other industry. In the battle for the BBC, this was an opportunity to outflank the Corporation that the BBC's political opponents seized, after their frontal assaults had failed.

The Prime Minister had been trying for some time to find ways of introducing more competition and more 'market discipline' into the BBC and ITV. Professor Alan Peacock's committee on the financing of the BBC was only the latest attempt, but while it had failed to find in favour of advertising it *had* waxed enthusiastic about the potential of independent production companies as a way of introducing competition. The result was one of the oddest political alliances of the decade, between a group of producers who were mostly liberal or left-wing, and a number of influential political figures who were evangelists for the free-market economics usually associated with the right. The two groups had different motives, but the same goal. Between them, these strange allies effectively ensured that the Home Office, not a natural supporter of the independent sector, had no choice but to endorse the idea, however reluctantly. The result was the biggest shake-up of the British television industry since the creation of ITV. Its effects are still reverberating around the industry, especially in the BBC, where the line which starts with the 25% quota leads eventually to Producer Choice.

Historically, the BBC and ITV had been organised as vertically integrated broadcasting organisations: they assumed responsibility for all stages of the production and broadcasting processes and expected to employ almost all the people involved at each stage. The independent production sector had developed in the UK as a direct result of the decision to create Channel 4 as a 'publisher-broadcaster' which would commission and transmit new programmes but not use its own staff or equipment to make them.

The idea of a publisher-broadcaster was nothing new; indeed it had been floating around since the first discussions about a fourth channel in the early 1970s, promoted by, among others, Anthony Smith (then Director of the British Film Institute) and later by the Annan Committee. Nor was the idea of an independent production company a novelty; Alasdair Milne had briefly run one in the mid 60s; and Jeremy Isaacs had spent some time doing much the same during a career break between leaving Thames Television and becoming the first Chief Executive of Channel 4. But the opportunities for such companies were few and far between.

What Channel 4 did, therefore, was to create for the first time guaranteed access to the market for independent producers. The principle was laid down by the first Home Secretary of Margaret Thatcher's government, William Whitelaw, in a speech to the Royal Television Society Convention in Cambridge in 1979 when he announced that independent producers should supply 'the largest practicable proportion of programmes on the fourth channel'. Even more important was the speed with which the new model took off. In his defining speech about the new channel, made at the Edinburgh Television Festival just a few weeks before Whitelaw spoke, Jeremy Isaacs had assumed that independent producers would be unable to supply much more than 15% of the fourth channel's requirements in the early years. In fact the response had been overwhelming. In 1982–3, the first year of Channel 4, independents had supplied it with more than half of its commissioned programmes, both by value (the cost of the productions) and volume (the number of hours broadcast).

Many of those who had lobbied for the creation of a fourth channel as a separate force in broadcasting (and not merely ITV-2) had immediately set themselves up as independents. They included people such as Michael Jackson, who had been coordinator of the Channel 4 Group, and John Wyver, previously the television editor of the London listings magazine *Time Out*. These were quickly joined by ITV or BBC producers who found the working atmosphere in the broadcasters stultifying and saw opportunities, both creative and entrepreneurial, in the new environment. Channel 4's headquarters in Charlotte Street, close to Soho, became the magnet for a burgeoning number of small independent companies. In the early days, as Channel 4's commissioning editors and cost controllers invented new systems for doing business more or less as they went along, there were good livings to be made, and creative fun to be had. The truth, though, was that for most producers, being an independent was more a lifestyle than a business. The bulk of Channel 4's commissions, then as now, were fully funded and removed most of the financial risk from the producer. In exchange, though, the production fee (which corresponded very approximately to net profits) was typically around 10–15% – a reasonable return if a company was constantly in work, but quickly dissipated if there were gaps between commissions. There usually were.

Seduced by the relative creative freedom – and undeterred by the risk of relative poverty – more and more producers abandoned their long-standing staff jobs with traditional broadcasting companies and took the plunge into the independent sector. The supply of programme makers rapidly outstripped the demand of Channel 4. By 1985, many of the same producers who had been centrally involved in the Channel 4 Campaign realised that they had to create new outlets for their work if they wanted their businesses to develop.

One of the driving forces behind this move was the drama producer Sophie Balhetchet, perhaps best known for her Channel 4 football series *The Manageress*. She had come into the television industry in 1977 as director of the newly formed Association of Independent Producers, set up by film makers such as David Puttnam and Simon Perry to promote British film production. The AIP had given its support to the Channel 4 Group – and with the establishment of Channel 4 Balhetchet had also established her own production company. Sophie Balhetchet had a reputation in the industry for being shrewd, intelligent, and well-connected, and her approach to the quest for new prospects for independent producers was characteristic.

Her first step was the creation of a small *ad hoc* group of producers which met at the Groucho Club in Dean Street, Soho. It became known simply as the

'Groucho's Group'. The core was half a dozen people who had been closely involved in the creation of Channel 4: they included Balhetchet herself; David Graham of Diverse Production (responsible for *The Friday Alternative* and *Diverse Reports* for Channel 4); the drama producer Lavinia Warner; and Michael Darlow, who had been one of the earliest campaigners for an independent sector. They met intermittently after hours to exchange ideas and learn from each other. Most of the later meetings took place in company production offices, although one was convened at a venue which would have been unfamiliar territory for most of the participants: at the suggestion of David Graham, it was held at the Institute of Directors, an avowedly pro-Conservative employers' organisation.

One meeting, in the Covent Garden offices of Warner Sisters, featured a brainstorming session on ways of increasing the market for independent productions. Someone proposed the startling idea of a production quota – actually forcing broadcasters to commission a minimum number of programmes from outside. Even as the suggestion was made there was laughter: determined as they were to think the unthinkable, this was one idea which stretched even this group's sense of the possible. According to one participant, 'I think some people in the room fully expected the idea to have been forgotten by the time we held our next meeting.'

Still, once on the table, the proposal prompted discussion about the level of such a quota. This was critical, for it needed to be high enough to have a real impact on the broadcasting organisations, and to survive the inevitable whittling down that would occur during negotiations. But it needed to be sufficiently low to be credible: for it was certain that both the BBC and ITV would ridicule the idea that the independent sector, whatever its successes at Channel 4, could supply a significant proportion of their programmes. One of the participants suggested a figure of 25%, and so 'The 25% Campaign' was born, starting life as an outlandish idea tossed out during a brainstorming session. It could, at any other time, have foundered on indifference or accusations of blatant commercial self-interest. But the 25% Campaign was blessed by the luck of good timing. The motives of these independent producers may have been commercial, but their agenda coincided exactly with that of another group whose motives were almost entirely political. The campaign found its first prominent ally in Professor Alan Peacock, whose committee was still hard at work collecting evidence.

David Graham knew Peacock personally, and shared his sympathies for liberal, free-market economics; Peacock was on the advisory council of a free-market think-tank, the Institute of Economic Affairs, of which Graham was a member. As well as taking evidence from independent producers, Peacock also took the trouble to visit what was then one of the largest independent production complexes, the Limehouse Studios in London's Docklands.

When it appeared in July 1986, the Peacock Committee's report argued that the independent sector would inject some much-needed competition into broadcasting. In addition, Peacock suggested that British television could not be truly competitive because of the existence of a 'cosy duopoly' in the form of the BBC and ITV. 'One way of introducing competition even while the duopoly remains', it said, 'is by enlarging the scope of independent programme makers to sell to existing authorities, as already occurs in the case of Channel 4.'

For Peacock, this was part of a broader analysis of the structure of the British television industry: 'The three functions of making programmes, packaging them into channels, and delivering them to the viewer or listener are distinct; and it is mainly historical accident that links them together.' In short, he linked the long history of vertical integration of production and transmission in the British television industry with what he perceived as its inefficiency, and proposed the emergent independent production sector as the solution. Hence his recommendation that 40% of BBC and ITV programmes should come from the independents within ten years.

The figure was greeted with derision by the broadcasters, but it gave enormous impetus to the fledgling 25% Campaign, which quickly raised a fund of £15,000 from a number of the larger independent production companies, borrowed an office from Michael Darlow, and hired a full-time worker. John Woodward was working for a company in Holland Park making corporate films and, in his own words, 'wanted to get into telly', when a friend showed him a brief news item in the trade weekly *Broadcast* headlined 'Independents to lobby for 25% of BBC and ITV'. He rang up to ask if they wanted help, expecting it to involve stuffing envelopes of an evening before repairing to the pub. It did not turn out quite like that.

The Peacock Report had failed on two counts: it had disappointed the Prime Minister by not delivering the expected verdict on the BBC, and its enthusiasm for the idea of pay-per-view programmes was dismissed by its many opponents as being too futuristic and based on a failure to understand the peculiar economics of broadcasting. Rumours emerged from the Home Office that it was being 'kicked into the long grass'.

However, some of Mrs Thatcher's advisers had been doing the same sort of thinking as Professor Peacock about the lack of market discipline in the broadcasting sector. Brian Griffiths, the head of the Prime Minister's Policy Unit, shared Peacock's background as an academic economist interested principally in monetarism and markets, as well as his interest in broadcasting matters. In the early 80s, from his position as Professor of Economics at City University in London, Griffiths had been an articulate defender of monetarism, and a staunch critic of inflation. He was also a frequent guest on radio and television current affairs programmes. Although he had joined the Policy Unit only the previous year, Peacock's arguments were not new to him, and he was sympathetic to the ideas about broadcasting and the marketplace.

David Graham, probably the only independent producer to be a member of the IEA, had written articles on broadcasting for the journal of the Institute of Economic Affairs. Griffiths had met Graham when the latter was a producer on *Panorama* and, after joining the Policy Unit, invited him to Downing Street on several occasions to discuss broadcasting. Griffiths was interested in the economic questions: how the industry was structured; who did what; how people were paid for what they did. Another way in which the IEA had influenced the debate was through a paper, 'The Choice of Cable', co-written by the consultant Cento Veljanovski in 1983. It had devoted a substantial proportion of its argument to the lack of competition in the broadcasting industry. Griffiths was now in a position to put some of the theory into practice.

The economists' case was strengthened by a healthy growth in independent companies. Channel 4 had weathered the early crises that attend almost all new broadcasting ventures, and the independent sector had proved itself more than capable of delivering a wide variety of programmes on time and on budget. Indeed, because of the idiosyncrasies of the internal accounting systems of both the BBC and most of the ITV companies, independent producers were alone in being able to reveal how much their programmes cost to make. This was music to the government's ears as was the producers' success in driving down staffing levels and other production costs by renegotiating or simply bypassing the industrial relations practices of the broadcasters.

In a political climate where the virtues of both competition and small businesses were being proclaimed from the rooftops, and both the BBC and ITV were regarded as being, in different ways, slothful and grossly inefficient monopolies, the independent producers' campaign found itself carried along on a following wind. Another member of the Thatcher coterie, along with Griffiths, was Lord Young, Stuart Young's brother and a longstanding political soul-mate of the Prime Minister. He had been Director of the Thatcherite Centre for Policy Studies from 1979–82, and had simultaneously been co-opted as Special Adviser to the Department of Industry. After a stint as Chairman of the Manpower Services Commission and Minister without Portfolio, Thatcher elevated him in 1985 to Secretary of State for Employment. Two years later, in 1987, he became Secretary of State for Trade and Industry. It was Young of whom the Prime Minister had once said, 'Other ministers bring me their problems. David brings me his achievements.' He, like Brian Griffiths, had the ear of the Prime Minister.

Young, whose instincts and background lay with the financial and business community, regarded broadcasting as an economic and industrial activity which should be subjected, like any other, to the rigorous discipline of the marketplace. Not for him the arguments of liberals who considered high-quality television to be central to the country's intellectual and spiritual welfare. Liberated from the regulatory and legislative red tape which prevented its expansion, he saw broadcasting as one area of successful private British enterprise which should be exploited – especially with the coming revolution in telecommunications, in which broadcasting would be heavily embroiled. At the DTI, he had responsibility for telecommunications. But at neither Employment nor the DTI could he control broadcasting which was jealously guarded by the Home Office.

Yet, in another important sense, broadcasting was more than just an industry. Commercial broadcasting – and the emphasis was quite definitely on the 'commercial' – was potentially a wealth creator which could drive a country's economy forward. For the economy depended on consumer demand: the more people wanted and bought, the more demand was created for goods and services, and the more jobs were created. And television advertising was the most powerful tool known to man for creating and fuelling demand. It therefore followed, from a strictly business perspective, that everything possible should be done to encourage the growth of commercial television. The problem, of course, was the BBC. It accounted for half of total viewing, time which could have been devoted to valuable commercial viewing. Those who watched its programmes were not being encouraged to buy or consume. The engine of wealth was being stalled. It was with this sort of outlook, both before and during his tenure at the DTI, that Young approached broadcasting and found a sympathetic audience from the Prime Minister.

Attitudes within the Home Office, however, were rooted in a very different history and ideology. Douglas Hurd and his senior civil servants were more sympathetic to arguments about the need to encourage domestic production, the enormous prestige and affection which the BBC commanded abroad, and the cultural role for broadcasting as a uniquely powerful platform for journalism, drama, comedy, children's and adult education, sport and so on. The Home Office was from the beginning less sympathetic to the Peacock Report and to the independent sector, and more sympathetic to the broadcasters. Hurd himself had little interest in the detailed workings of the television marketplace, and by the nature of his department's responsibilities he and his ministers and officials had rather more frequent contact with senior figures from the BBC and the Independent Broadcasting Authority – the so-called duopoly – than with the collection of mavericks who made up the independent production sector.

But in the mid-1980s, the DTI view was in the ascendant, and the independents, though small themselves, found themselves on the side of the big guns. By mid-1986, the Groucho's Group had reconstituted itself as the Steering Committee of the 25% Campaign. Others joined them, such as Phillip Whitehead, the former Labour MP who had been a member of the Annan Committee, John Wyver and John Ellis, who had both been closely involved in the Channel 4 Campaign, and Paul Madden, a former Channel 4 commissioning editor. All were at home in the world of broadcasting lobbying. They were clear that persuading the BBC and the ITV companies to accept a quota was going to take more than smooth talking, for both organisations were resolutely opposed to the idea. As Sophie Balhetchet recalls, 'We knew that this would never be implemented voluntarily by the broadcasters.' The 25% Campaign was designed from the outset as a single issue campaign about an independent production quota, with the specific intention of getting the idea backed by law.

The five months following the publication of the Peacock Report in July 1986 saw a whirlwind of activity. The battle was fought on three fronts, the first of which was the press. In the trade papers and nationals, members of the Steering Committee wrote carefully judged articles designed to assuage the fears of the broadcasters and the broadcasting unions about the effect of an independent production quota on the industry, without alienating the political figures who were crucial to their success. They focused on the complacency of the broadcasters in the face of rapidly changing technology and the threat from foreign television. As Phillip Whitehead put it in *Broadcast*:

> The competition to be feared is not that of the independents. The real threat is of multi-national competition, outside British ownership and control, wholly unconcerned with public service values and destructive of them. . . . This invasion, via the new technology, will make British television vulnerable in the 1990s. A sagging duopoly, with vastly lengthened lines of control and management, will not be competitive in this changed environment.

And in *The Guardian*, it was John Wyver, whose company, Illuminations, had a reputation for innovation, who set out the two sides of the independent equation.

> Independents have uncovered an enormous pool of new talent, have pioneered new forms of television, and have helped create a far more open and accessible system. . . . At the same time, it is clear that independents are more cost-effective, programme by programme, than either element of the comfortable duopoly. And this is important not because it attunes with any ethos of the present government but because of its implications for the future of programme making.

The second front was Whitehall. Members of the 25% Campaign assiduously cultivated civil servants in both the Home Office and the Department of Trade and Industry as part of a process of introducing them to the independent sector. They were, for example, invited to industry events like the London Screenings, where independent production companies sold their programmes to international buyers. And, like Professor Peacock, they were taken to the Limehouse Studios, where *Spitting Image* was produced for ITV. The visit exemplified the approach of the Campaign – attention to detail topped by a smile. For the civil servants, the highlight of the trip was meeting the *Spitting Image* puppets, who caricatured their political masters, in the studio workshops.

The final front was Downing Street and members of the ministerial committee on broadcasting which Margaret Thatcher had established and chaired herself. Other members included Douglas Hurd, Lord Young, William Whitelaw, and Nigel Lawson. Brian Griffiths sat in on the meetings; he was a key link for the 25% Campaign, because of his keen personal commitment to market-driven change. On one occasion, David Graham was in a meeting at his company, Diverse Production, when he was called to the phone to answer an urgent inquiry from Griffiths. 'I must know', he said, 'is IPPA [the independent producers' association] a trade association or a trade union?' Graham had the clear impression that Griffiths was in the middle of an argument at cabinet level about the independent quota. He explained that IPPA was an employers' association like any other, representing television production companies.

The Campaign's keenest supporter on the committee, Lord Young, took the opportunity to enumerate the shortcomings of the Home Office, referring to its sluggish response to the Peacock Report. In a political environment where the critical question about broadcasting had become the lack of competition within the industry, the Home Secretary was clearly out of step with his cabinet colleagues. Moreover, while the Home Office welcomed Peacock's conclusions that the BBC should not take advertising, it faced mounting political pressure from the Prime Minister. Her appetite for reform was only heightened by Peacock's failure to deliver the verdict she wanted. Douglas Hurd had to do something about the television industry (and be seen to do something) which appeased Mrs Thatcher but protected the Home Office's position.

And so in November 1986, within eighteen months of the idea first being mooted by a small and informal group of independent producers over a drink in an office in Covent Garden, the Home Secretary, Douglas Hurd, climbed to his feet in the House of Commons during the debate on the Peacock Report and announced that the independent producers would have 'their place in the sun'. Watched from the public gallery by the newly appointed Chairman of the BBC, Marmaduke Hussey, Hurd reminded the Commons that Professor Peacock's committee had proposed that 40% of BBC and ITV programmes should be made by independents within ten years. He continued, 'Some of the independent producers have campaigned for a figure of 25%, and a figure in that region seems to be a realistic goal at which to aim.' Then came the crunch: this 25% quota was to be achieved not within ten years, but four.

In fact, Hurd's speech to the House during the Peacock debate was a shrewd political performance and an eloquent demonstration of the art of the possible. While giving way on the independents, he closed off for the foreseeable future any discussion about alternatives to the licence fee, saying that

Peacock's arguments against advertising 'strike us as pretty forceful, and I believe the onus now rests on those who disagree with the committee's conclusions to disprove the arguments underpinning those conclusions'. At the same time, while announcing that the licence fee would be pegged (at £58) for eighteen months until April 1988, he also laid the ground for indexing it to the rate of inflation thereafter. This, he said, 'would ensure for the broadcasters a guaranteed income on an established basis and reinforce their independence from government.' The BBC had been spared exposure to the cold winds of the marketplace; but its protector, the Home Office, had been forced to concede ground to the right on other fronts.

The first concession was a promise that the government would expect a system of competitive tenders to play a part in the allocation of ITV licences in the next franchise round. This was a Peacock recommendation which had been presaged in the IEA's 1983 monograph on cable (the authors of that, in turn, had taken it from an American economist, Leo Herzel of the University of Chicago, who had in 1951 advocated the competitive auction of the broadcast spectrum). The second was the independent production quota, and even here the pill was slightly sweetened. There had been a division within the ministerial committee on broadcasting about how ITV and the BBC would respond to the quota proposal, with Young, Lawson and Thatcher all believing that it would be resisted. Douglas Hurd and William Whitelaw, however, had argued that the broadcasters could be persuaded. Accordingly, Hurd told the House, he had arranged to meet the chairmen and directors general of both the BBC and the IBA 'very soon' to discuss how they would achieve the quota target.

Producers involved in the 25% Campaign were surprised, as were some MPs. The broadcasters, though, were dumbfounded. Some senior figures (for example Lord Thomson, then Chairman of the Independent Broadcasting Authority) had been saying publicly for some months that they would have to learn to live with the independents, but none had expected such a fundamental shift so quickly. As Raymond Snoddy of *The Financial Times* noted the following week, 'The independent producers have won a spectacular victory in their battle for access to the commanding heights of British broadcasting.'

From the perspective of the 25% Campaign's highly placed political supporters this was just what they intended. For them, the creation of the 25% quota represented the coming of age of a new force in British broadcasting and at long last the imposition of some measure of market discipline on the apparently intractable broadcasting industry. Perhaps the oddest fact about the whole chain of events was that the question of an independent quota had not featured at all in Peacock's original terms of reference from the Home Office. The Thatcherites had won an opportunistic victory with the help of allies among the growing band of independent producers who conveniently gave the attack cultural credibility. One trade unionist described the independents' role as that of 'a Trojan pony'.

It was several weeks before the shell-shocked broadcasters were able to formulate their response. By now Sophie Balhetchet was the new Chairman of IPPA, the producers' association, and David Mellor was the new minister with responsibility for broadcasting at the Home Office. When the broadcasters did respond, the difference in style between the BBC and ITV was revealing. ITV, while protesting that they were being cautious rather than negative towards the proposals, adopted the classic confrontational position which characterised much of their approach to industrial relations. One meeting, held at the headquarters of the Independent Broadcasting Authority in Knightsbridge and chaired by the IBA's Director General John Whitney, was typical. 'The hostility was unbelievable', remembers one participant. One ITV executive tore up his papers and shouted at Brian Tesler of LWT (supposedly on his side of the negotiating table) that independent access to ITV would happen only over his dead body.

The BBC, on the other hand, was ostensibly more cooperative. Douglas Hurd had called in Alasdair Milne in December 1986, before the latter's departure, and told him he wanted some action. It was a difficult request to ignore, since at the time the BBC was commissioning about 80 hours a year of independent production, from a total of around 5,500 hours of new productions (around 1½%). Milne's view was hostile. He did not believe that the 25% figure was achievable, and said publicly that the BBC would resist attempts to push it into a position in which the Corporation would, in his words, unravel 'like a ball of string'.

Milne recognised that the independent production quota confronted the BBC with a problem which was fundamental to the way it worked. At one level it was a simple equation: if in future the independents were to make 25% of BBC programmes, when they currently made less than 2%, then the BBC would need fewer staff – on a very simplistic calculation, close to 25% fewer. Opponents therefore predicted mass redundancies. The independents had two answers to this. First, those no longer working for the BBC would not leave the industry, but would simply work outside the BBC; indeed, they might find – as the 25% campaigners most certainly had – that they enjoyed it more. Second, the BBC had recently expanded its broadcast hours, due mainly to the development of daytime television. But there was no commensurate rise in income, and considerable constraints on its equipment base. With the BBC's own figures predicting that hours would continue to grow, argued the independents, the BBC could not afford *not* to embrace them.

At a second level there was a fear that, if the independents did prove to be cheaper than the BBC, there was no reason why the quota should stop at 25%. The independents themselves had always argued that their production costs were, programme for programme, consistently lower than those of the BBC, by between 15% and 35%. Independents had to pay higher salaries, but hired in freelances on short contracts, and so were exempt from employment costs like pensions, national insurance, training, and so on. Furthermore, they could hire production facilities like cameras and editing time in a highly competitive open market, rather than continually carrying the costs of those resources, as the BBC did.

But at the time all such cost comparisons were little better than guesswork, because the BBC (like some ITV companies) separated out the direct cost of making its programmes from the 'resource cost' – the cost of using the plant and facilities. The latter was accounted for in a completely different way. Indeed during 1985 and 1986 BBC resource managers had attempted to compare their in-house costs with those of the independent sector, visiting leading independents such as Brook (of which Phillip Whitehead was a director), and David Graham's company, Diverse. The figures were never published because of the BBC's difficulty in putting a market value on the cost of its own resources.

This, then, was the third danger; that the impact of the independent producers would force the BBC to price its resources on a programme-by-programme basis, rather than valuing them for the overall benefit they gave to the Corporation. This was why Alasdair Milne believed that the advent of the independents would cause the Corporation to unravel. The distinction between 'cash' and 'resources' had already been criticised in a report on the BBC by the accountants Peat Marwick, who had argued that the system was a major cause of financial inefficiency and poor cost control. While they may seem both arcane and a long way away from issues relating to the diversity of programming, the independents had concentrated on these arguments about accounting policies, realising that once the duopoly had lost the political battle, this would be the next line of resistance. As Michael Darlow put it in one article,

> The institutional programme makers are playing an unreal game which makes them operate part with real money and part with unreal money. And when push comes to shove, what happens to the unreal money doesn't matter very much. ('Well, it's Monopoly money, isn't it?')

For this reason, wrote Darlow, 'Producers with experience of the BBC and ITV likened their experiences in the institutions to "being like a watchdog with his teeth pulled".'

BBC resistance did not rely entirely upon defending archaic accounting practices for their own sake. There were strengths in a vertically integrated structure which spread the cost of resources over many different programmes and departments. It meant that technical standards, studios, costumes, outside broadcast equipment and so on could all be maintained to the standards of excellence which historically the BBC had fostered and wished to preserve. Bill Cotton, the Managing Director, Television, was particularly opposed to independents. He believed that the BBC was the cornerstone of British production and that the keys to the BBC's strength lay in its access to talented staff and in its in-house production base – from cameramen to electricians to design to wardrobe to production.

But Cotton and Milne were part of the old guard, ill-suited to the new political landscape. Milne's dismissal meant he did not stay long enough to have to fight a battle he would certainly have lost. Michael Checkland's political instincts were better and he had already formed the view that the BBC would have to accommodate the independents.

Moreover, Checkland was aware of the emerging marketplace in facilities and production, and the opportunity for BBC Television to test its internal costs against those outside. In a deliberate break with his predecessor's policies, he had also made it clear, when he addressed his own staff after becoming Director General, that the BBC had to be seen to be more businesslike in its approach to its finances. Speaking to 300 of the Corporation's most senior managers in the BBC canteen, he had told them:

> We must be seen . . . as a modern thousand-million-pound company adapted to competition and change as many other organisations have had to do in this country, and do it with enthusiasm and not with regret at the passing of our imperial role.

Within a week of his appointment Checkland had met David Mellor at the Home Office to address the question of the quota, outlining an initiative under which the BBC would make funds approaching £20 million available to independent producers. Of this £13.5m – or 9% of the television production budget – would be in cash while the rest would be made up of BBC resources, including technical and publicity services. Maggie Brown, the media editor of *The Independent*, wrote 'No-one in television thinks this will be enough.' A fortnight later Checkland was briefing the press as part of a new strategy of openness, confirming that the BBC would move to 500 hours a year of independent production by the end of 1989. But, he added, the 25% target was 'absolutely impracticable' within four years. Mimicking the market vocabulary, while trying to steer clear of the worst excesses of market-driven practice, now seemed to be the emerging tactic.

Checkland's first formal public appearance as Director General was at BAFTA, the British Academy of Film and Television Arts in central London, in March 1987. By this time, the BBC had become firmly established as 'a billion pound company', to the continuing distaste of some of his colleagues. He announced a twelve-point plan for independents which, in terms of the Downing Street agenda, had some good news and some bad news. The good news was that in addition to the package already outlined, a further £4 million was to be made available immediately for independent production – representing a substantial increase on the minimal £1.5 million that had been spent in each of the previous two years. The bad news was that, once the 500-hour target had been reached, further progress would be subject to a review of independent productions and comparisons of cost and quality with BBC productions.

By coincidence, that same BAFTA conference was Sophie Balhetchet's first public appearance as Chairman of IPPA. She had been told beforehand that Checkland would be announcing the BBC's initiative on independent production, and had been promised sight of his speech the night before. In the event she was told the headlines virtually as Checkland was getting to his feet. This ambivalence characterised much of the BBC's dealings on the whole question of independent access.

Checkland's announcement was a recognition that – in principle at least – the BBC had conceded to the independents. But it also crystallised for many the real, practical issues raised by independent access. Who would own the international rights to independent programmes commissioned by BBC Television? Who would control publicity for independent productions? Who would sign the cheques for independent programme-related expenditure? If the BBC insisted on countersigning cheques, which some managers considered essential, it was bound to delay the production process and generate some sharp questioning from the BBC finance department.

In other words, the easy part for the 25% Campaign was over. It was one thing to get the government to give its blessing to the idea. The longer haul, though, was to negotiate the 'terms of trade' on which those independent programmes would eventually get made. If the events of 1986 had been a *blitzkrieg*, 1987 was the beginning of a war of attrition in which every line in every schedule of every contract became a new battle. As John Woodward recalls,

> The attrition was to set the deal terms and the business conditions under which independents worked, because the BBC's immediate reaction was, 'If we have to work with these people, we'll reduce them to the status of freelances and not recognise them as businesses and companies with shareholders who need to see a profit.' Turning a promise from the government into reality in terms of hours of programmes made by independents was an extremely long hard slog. As far as the BBC was concerned that was to do with a management that had set its face entirely against independent production, that was determined to do the absolute barest minimum that they thought they could get away with.

Checkland's proposal therefore seemed to serve two purposes: offer the barest minimum for the time being, and stall in the hope that the whole issue could be buried should the political climate change. It was a vain hope, and there were already signs that it was not going to work. The previous December, just three weeks after Hurd's Commons statement, David Mellor had been the guest at a BBC dinner where he had emphasised that he wanted a real increase in independent production. While he did not necessarily want to see a mandatory quota, it was clear that legislation would follow if progress was not made. This underlying threat underpinned all the Home Office's dealings with the broadcasters on this issue: they did not want to legislate but, on the other hand, would if they had to. Hurd knew that he could get away with nothing less.

Along with a delaying strategy, the BBC also attempted to deal with the independents' impact by looking for different ways of funding their productions, thereby leaving the BBC's own resource base intact. Michael Grade, then Controller of BBC-1, and Bill Cotton had announced to the Board of Management the previous December a plan (which had also involved Michael Checkland as Deputy DG) to allow independents a much freer hand in looking for sponsorship finance for BBC projects. The intention was to cushion the impact on the BBC's finances, which would otherwise involve redirecting licence fee income away from the Corporation's own production base and into outside companies.

This idea was resisted by the heads of departments, for a variety of reasons. Some took a philosophical line, that this type of funding was incompatible with public service broadcasting; others had practical concerns, ranging from editorial control to the impact of the scheme on other sources of external finance, to the types of programmes which were most likely to attract sponsorship revenue. One casualty of the row was an independent programme for *Arena*, made by the director Jeff Perks. *Night Moves* was about the road hauliers who drove the length of the country, and was conceived as an evocation of the classic 30s film *Night Mail*, about the postal train from King's Cross to Glasgow. The programme had been commissioned by the Head of Music and Arts, Alan Yentob, and Perks' company – Riverfront – had secured some funding from the Road Haulage Association. It was pulled because the source of outside funding was deemed inappropriate, and was not shown until other ways had been found to complete the budget. But the headlines in the trade press reflected the BBC's political difficulties rather than any change in practice; as the BBC executive producer responsible for the programme later reflected, 'I couldn't for the life of me see what was different between that and something we do a lot ... which is, say, a film about a rock band or music which we co-produce with a record company.'

Michael Grade also tried a different tack, with a publicity onslaught to emphasise the BBC's commitment to the independent sector. He asked BBC Television heads of departments for a list of programmes in the pipeline in which independents were involved – to include not only full-blown commissions (of which there were very few) but co-productions and development deals (such as a small advance to producers to enable them to do further research on a project with potential). In the end the list ran to about fifty programmes, of which a high proportion were development deals. Journalists from the nationals and the trade press were invited to the sixth floor of

Television Centre for a news conference.

Unfortunately, the press office sent a press release to the Independent Access Steering Committee (IASC), which, as the successor to the 25% Campaign, was negotiating terms. John Woodward knew that very few of the programmes on Grade's list were fully fledged independent commissions of the kind intended by the government. He got permission to attend, wrote a hurried press release, and jumped on the Tube to White City. At the end of the news conference, he made himself available to journalists and ensured that the independents' view of what Grade had been saying was properly represented. Despite Grade's undoubted skill with the media, the 'spin' on the stories the following day did the BBC no favours. Grade's reaction was to write to Woodward to say that he could not set foot on BBC property again without written permission. It was all further evidence of a calculated delaying strategy: to carry on looking as if the problem was being addressed until the political pressure was lifted.

It was as much a matter of practicality as principled disagreement or sheer obstinacy. Even if the BBC had wanted to comply with the wishes of the government, very few insiders had experience of the sort of companies they were dealing with, the world they worked in, or of the language they used. It was not until the autumn of 1987 that an Independent Planning Unit was set up to liaise with the production companies on contractual issues. Prior to that, the issue of responsibility for independent producers was lost in a series of interdepartmental turf wars between BBC Television, BBC Enterprises and BBC Co-productions.

At the same time the BBC continued to talk publicly of the cost and quality review which would follow once it reached its initial target for independent productions. One senior figure who reiterated the policy at a conference in Birmingham found himself firmly rebuked by a civil servant from the Department of Trade and Industry. He did not understand, said the mandarin, quite what the BBC chap meant: there was no question of a quality review. The BBC would take a 25% independent production quota. There was silence from the attendant BBC personnel.

A strategy which was slightly more successful, however, was to argue with the Home Office about the definition of the 25% – 25% of what? Originally, the Independent Access Steering Committee had specified 25% of all originated programmes, a formulation which excluded acquired programmes (such as films) and repeats. The BBC argued for news and news-related programming to be excluded, which reduced the size of the quota by a third, to around 17% of originated programmes. Skirmishes ensued about the definition of 'news-related' – at one time it included *Panorama* and a raft of current affairs programmes – but even when those had been resolved news remained outside the quota. It was a minor victory.

The delays could not go on for ever. In the end, appropriately, the decisive engagement took place inside No. 10, at an all-day seminar on broadcasting convened by the Prime Minister in September 1987. Nigel Lawson, Douglas Hurd, and Lord Young were all in attendance as a succession of senior industry figures made presentations. For the first time, representatives from the independent sector – David Graham and Michael Darlow – were there too, treated as equals. While some of the speeches were way off-target as far as Mrs Thatcher was concerned, Darlow scored a bull's-eye. The independents, he told her, introduced competition into the broadcasting industry – of supply, between companies competing for commissions, and of demand, as broadcasters sought the best programmes. It was music to the Prime Minister's ears. The independents' final victory was not long delayed.

In the end the BBC signed an agreement on terms of trade with the Independent Access Steering Committee before the year was out. It did not mean that the negotiations were complete – those would continue for several years. Nor did it mean that the BBC had become reconciled to independents. The truth was more shabby. The negotiations with the ITV companies were proceeding even more slowly than those with the BBC, and the IASC pointed out that the BBC could get itself some good press, and some goodwill from the government, if they beat ITV to the punch. Since the view inside No. 10 had now hardened on the need for legislation to enforce the independent production quota, there was nothing to lose. The deal was done. It created a formidable engine of change which, more than any other, was to transform the organisation and its internal workings along the lines favoured by the government and its theorists. Brian Griffiths and his friends had done a good job. Inside the BBC the reforms on which Checkland was embarking were now more urgent than ever.

CHAPTER SIX
A TALENT TO AMUSE OR A MISSION TO EXPLAIN?

Even before Checkland had been appointed, a conventional wisdom had been established amongst the governors that 'something must be done about the journalism'. That was, of course, partly the ticket on which Hussey arrived at his job, and his abiding interest in the 'difficult' political stories of the recent past confirmed a general view that BBC journalism was in a mess. The accumulated detritus of *Real Lives*, *Maggie's Militant Tendency*, *Zircon* – all of which had generated their own momentum of adverse publicity – demanded a 'resolution'.

The truth that lay behind these problem programmes – and the general impression of journalistic chaos – had less to do with bad journalism than with politics and management. *Zircon*, in particular, was the perfect example of a first-class piece of investigative journalism which was instantly devalued by the row it created. That programme, like the others, had been beset by three interlocking problems. There was the relentless battering of a hostile government, convinced of the BBC's inherent bias; and there was a governing board which, at best, was too politically compliant to resist these assaults and which, at worst, may have contained individuals with malevolent intent. But this combination of malicious government and compliant board had exposed a third problem: a fundamental organisational flaw, a structural weakness at the heart of BBC journalism.

The problem was that there was no early warning system. There was no shortage of inventive producers or departmental heads who were prepared to initiate difficult, challenging and politically uncomfortable programmes. In the lower echelons of the BBC, there was still a certain fearlessness despite the difficult environment. But further up the hierarchy the controllers and managing directors were having to deal with almost incessant flak, and it was diverting their attention.

The system meant that the man charged with overseeing journalistic standards, Alan Protheroe, was not sufficiently plugged into it to know where potential dangers lay. By the 1980s, this was probably more important that at any previous time in television's history. The medium had reached a point of maturity where, whatever the party of government, it was seen as a potentially decisive weapon in the battle for electoral hearts and minds. Programmes about difficult political issues were therefore bound to create a reaction, all the more so with a government that was so openly hostile. In these circumstances, it was more essential than ever to have a mechanism in place which would alert senior managers to potential problems before anyone started asking awkward questions.

As it was, Protheroe was constantly being brought in too late, fighting fires rather than preventing them. Too often he was not being told what he needed to know in order to prepare Milne and others for the inevitable barrages. As a result, senior managers were constantly pushed onto the defensive, appearing ignorant of a programme's origins or the justifications for its content. In the words of one senior editor, 'People saw an organisation from time to time out of control. The professionals were supposed to be holding the reins, and yet the horses were bolting. And the thing was just rattling along behind as best it could, trying to stay on its four wheels.' It was one thing to know exactly what you were doing and then to be seen to defend your decision robustly. It was quite another to stumble into problem areas without, apparently, any serious thought.

The reason was historical, and had its roots in one of Milne's earliest decisions. Under Milne's predecessor there *had* been a Director of News and Current Affairs (Dick Francis) with managerial responsibility for all news output and a broad remit to intervene in current affairs where necessary. But the remit had been ill-defined and therefore difficult to carry out. Milne abandoned this confused arrangement, but also rejected the creation of a separate News and Current Affairs Directorate because it 'removes at a stroke a large segment of Television and Radio's responsibilities and carries within it the seeds of dissension and disharmony over scheduling and expenditure'. That turned out to be a prophetic diagnosis, but Milne's solution carried its own seeds of disharmony. With all news and current affairs programmes delegated to their respective television and radio directorates, the man appointed to oversee journalistic standards was outside the programme making system. Protheroe was too far removed from the creative centre. As one public relations disaster followed another during 1985, three people came separately to the conclusion that the BBC urgently needed a fundamental organisational change.

The first, significantly, was Bill Cotton. Managing Directors of both Television and Radio were supposed to hate the prospect of a separate news directorate, because it meant ceding control of a substantial chunk of *their* airtime. TV news should belong to TV. Radio news should belong to radio. But Cotton had grown tired of the problems which current affairs, in particular, was creating. Shortly after Milne had been sacked, Checkland, as Acting Director General, had called a meeting to discuss whether to turn Broadcasting House into the centre of BBC news (radio and television), and move everything else to the White City site. Amongst others at the meeting were Cotton, Brian Wenham (Managing Director, Radio), Ron Neil (Editor of Television News) and John Wilson (Editor of Radio News and Current Affairs).

The idea got nowhere. But Bill Cotton suddenly launched into a passionate plea for a News and Current Affairs Directorate. Cotton was a showman, an entertainer for whom television was a medium made for fun. Suddenly, he had found himself saddled with this beast which was creating havoc in the press and political circles, which he was unable to control and which he wanted off his back. Once the Managing Director of Television was prepared to surrender a part of his schedule, it became a very serious prospect.

At the same time, Michael Checkland had been sitting next door to Milne, and standing in for him when he was away. Checkland's very first board meeting as Deputy DG was when he took Milne's place for the crucial battle over the screening of *Real Lives* and he, too, could see that Protheroe had an impossible job which gave him responsibility but no power. He concluded that a command structure with real power, rather than a mopping-up operation, was required.

Meanwhile, from radio, came another influential voice. John Wilson had been appointed Editor of Radio News and Current Affairs in 1981 and had favoured a separate news directorate even while it was unfashionable. In the eyes of some of his radio colleagues, this was to make him rather suspect: news and current affairs are such an integral part of BBC Radio, and particularly Radio 4, that to lose control of it would leave the Radio directorate with significantly less power. Wenham, in particular, and his deputy David Hatch were appalled by the idea.

Wilson's views had been born of his own experience during the Milne era, and the frustrations of dealing with people whose background was not in journalism. During the Falklands war, for example, he was involved in a number of rows with Monica Sims, then Controller of Radio 4, about clearing the airwaves for a statement from the House of Commons or an update from the Ministry of Defence. For him, it was a moment of national crisis which the BBC had a duty to cover live; for Sims, it meant abandoning listeners who preferred the afternoon play to the noise of the Commons.

Wilson wanted to operate news and current affairs in an atmosphere where people understood what it was about instead of arguing with people whose hearts were in drama, comedy or sport. There was a lot of sniping anyway at the resources going to news and current affairs – too much money, too many people, too much airtime. When you were continually having to fight your corner and watch your back, it interfered with the proper conduct of good journalism.

But those who argued against the merger of news and current affairs were not just concerned to safeguard their empires. For television, in particular, there were strong journalistic objections. Television Current Affairs had grown up as a separate entity in ramshackle offices in an old film studio in Lime Grove, a sufficiently distant walk from Television Centre to have developed its own culture and way of life. It had produced some of the most innovative and ground-breaking television journalism, as well as some real political scoops. To bring the two strands together would, said its critics, homogenise current affairs output and make it subservient to the news values prevalent in newsrooms: it would force current affairs into a daily news straitjacket which the BBC had so far avoided.

Nevertheless, the idea of a new and powerful News and Current Affairs Directorate had gathered sufficient momentum to make it inevitable. It was a major plank of Checkland's vision for the BBC during his interview, and was vigorously supported by Grade during his. Not surprisingly, it also seemed to the governors to offer an ideal solution to the problems which had so vexed them, as well as an opportunity to kill a second bird with the same stone and find an experienced programme maker to act as deputy to Michael Checkland.

As Checkland himself recognised, his own appointment meant that his deputy would have to come from an editorial background. Checkland had made his reputation as a superb organiser who cared about programmes, and he had impressed the governors at interview. But he lacked editorial experience. He did not have the credibility or authority to take on the task which he himself, the governors, and several of his colleagues were now convinced was essential after the public relations disasters of the last eighteen months: to sort out the journalism. It was a job that clearly required someone of considerable weight, experience and expertise; someone of sufficient status in the industry to command the confidence of the BBC's large and diverse journalistic staff; and someone who would be perceived by the governors as – in their terms – an impartial figure.

It would also require someone with the diplomatic skills of Solomon to reconcile the competing demands – and competing personalities – of three separate baronies: Radio News and Current Affairs; Television News; and Television Current Affairs. Each had been run separately and had developed its own philosophies, creating factions which were frequently at loggerheads with each other. Such reconciliation was not going to be easy, since BBC editorial personnel did not always have the highest regard for their journalistic colleagues in other buildings. As one ex-BBC journalist put it: 'News people were cynical about current affairs people as being flirtatious and not serious; current affairs people looked on news people as being thick. So there was institutional hostility, there wasn't a collaborative sense.' On top of which, all news and current affairs staff – particularly in television – were generally regarded as exuding a distasteful arrogance, with 'the superiority of head boys from a very well established public school confident that no-one could do the job better than they were doing it'.

The job description, then, made the labours of Hercules look positively attractive: renew confidence in the battered reputation of BBC journalism, introduce a unified management structure, conciliate between warring factions, and sit at the right hand of a DG with no practical experience of programme making in general or journalism programmes in particular. Which giant of the industry might be available to undertake such a thankless task?

One thing was for certain: such a character would not be found within the BBC. Any BBC senior manager with the status for the job would be tainted with the odour of incompetence and prejudice that the new broom was required to sweep away. And anyway, once Hussey had been forced to give the top job to an insider, he would be looking at fresh blood for a deputy. According to one observer at the time, that was certainly the advice he was getting from Lord Goodman, who then had his ear: '[Goodman's] advice to Dukie was be very careful about going outside for a director general because if you do the chances are the organisation will run him ragged. But if you appoint from inside, then you must go outside for a deputy.' So it had to be an external appointment. But who?

Once Checkland had refused Dimbleby, there was little time to canvass opinion on a replacement. It had to be someone whom the people around him, and especially the Chairman, would be prepared to accept at short notice, and that meant someone familiar to his immediate colleagues. As Checkland took soundings, one name arose from different sources as someone who was not only an established current affairs producer and latterly a senior manager, but also a man who had forged an unusual reputation: as a practitioner with a *theory* of current affairs programmes. It was not a very sophisticated theory. Indeed, some thought it shallow and fundamentally flawed. But it was a theory. And it marked out its author as a man who had devoted at least a little reflection to how news programmes on television should be constructed. To those who thought – and were constantly reminded by hostile newspapers – that they were running a Corporation which was flailing around in an editorial vacuum, this was very good news indeed. From the governors' lofty perspective, a man with a theory was just what was needed to construct some order out of chaos.

The man in question was John Birt, currently Director of Programmes at London Weekend Television and creator of *Weekend World* – the programme on which Brian Walden painstakingly attempted to lead politicians through the logic of their arguments to a point of self-destruction. *Weekend World* bore all the hallmarks of Birt's own methodical approach to television journalism. More importantly, it was the living embodiment of the ideas which, in tandem with Peter Jay, he had developed twelve years earlier and which even then had created a flurry amongst BBC governors. It had also met with contempt from BBC managers.

On 28 February 1975, while head of Current Affairs at LWT, Birt had written a lengthy feature for *The Times* (of which Peter Jay was then Economics Editor). It started portentously: 'There is a bias in television journalism, but it is not a bias against any particular party or point of view – it is a bias against *understanding*.' Birt's theme was straightforward. Television news demanded that stories be no longer than two minutes, in order to squeeze as many items as possible into the traditional twenty minute or half hour bulletin. But to do that inevitably meant divorcing serious news stories from their wider context, thereby depriving viewers of the opportunity to understand economic, social and political debates in any true depth. Traditional studio discussions were a poor journalistic tool which 'scarcely ever promote understanding of complicated problems and are little more than an entertaining way of feeding the viewer's already existing prejudices'.

This heartfelt cry was based not simply on a conviction about the inadequacy of television, but also on a belief about its importance to democracy itself. Seven months later, at the end of September, Peter Jay joined Birt to produce two more articles pursuing the same theme. Their approach was logical and methodical.

The first article was diagnosis. Since Birt had outlined the disease in February, where did the problem lie? Answer: in television journalism's schizophrenic roots, half newspaper newsroom and half Hollywood movie ('the misbegotten child of two ill-assorted parents'). Birt and Jay painted a picture of unmanaged journalists randomly pursuing their discrete stories, with no sense of how they fitted together ('journalism is organised to collect innumerable nuggets of self-contained fact, to report an atomised world of a million tiny tales'). The resultant news values produced stories of attention-grabbing immediacy without context: foreign stories about Vietnamese orphans rather than an explanation of the Indo-China conflict; budget stories about the price of beer going up rather than an analysis of the underlying economic strategy.

The two authors painted a picture of current affairs programmes rooted in the movie tradition, dominated by the need for 'exciting locations and lively situations with animated talkers in between'. Furthermore, they pointed out, there is pressure on the reporter to establish himself as a 'personality' by conducting difficult or confrontational interviews with transgressors. All of which runs counter to the notion of methodical and informed (if abstract) background to give the highlighted problem a proper context.

After diagnosis, came the cure. On 1 October 1975, Birt and Jay called for no less than a reformed television service which would provide viewers with 'the maximum feasible understanding of the important (and diverting) events which happen in the world about them'. They prescribed the programmes, the staffing arrangements, and even the broadcaster which should be undertaking this awesome task. It was an uncanny portent of the radical shake-up that was to be imposed on the BBC twelve years later.

First, they argued for brief daily bulletins which 'would simply carry the bald news-breaks' without analysis. There would then be an hour-long 'flag-ship' bulletin to replace the traditional 9 pm programme, scheduled at around 10 or 11 pm, covering in depth no more than five or six stories. There would be a weekly, hour-long programme covering up to three stories and a month-ly 90-minute programme devoted to 'continuing themes of our times'. There would also be a range of feature programmes. All of these would be conduct-ed under the auspices of a unified news and current affairs department, with journalists organised into teams under subject editor (politics, foreign, finan-cial and so on). And despite (or perhaps because of) Birt's own position in ITV, it was BBC-1 which was recommended as the proper guinea pig for this experiment, since all BBC programmes were subject to the same management at some point. But there was a further, and even more prophetic, reason for fin-gering the BBC: that because the decision could be taken centrally, it was 'on the face of things better able to undertake a radical change, which will offend many entrenched interests'.

This thesis had already found resonance at the very top of the BBC, with Chairman Sir Michael Swann. Following Birt's first article, Swann had endorsed the argument at a university seminar in March 1975 and added, 'The need for greater public understanding of the intractable problems which beset us is so pressing that no effort is too great.' Even then, without a background of perceived journalistic disasters, BBC governors were fascinated by the notion of a theory of news. Swann arranged for copies to be made and dis-tributed to all BBC journalists, a gesture which was not universally welcomed by the staff. At one point, a bundle of the offending articles was hurled out of a window at the back of Broadcasting House and finished up liberally scat-tered over cars in the Duchess Street car park below.

Two years later, in 1977, the Annan Committee on the future of broadcast-ing came out with a withering condemnation of the BBC's current affairs output, and Chairman Swann decided to call in the men with 'a mission to explain'. It came as something of a shock to the then Director General, Charles Curran, who was walking along the third floor of Broadcasting House and opened the door of the governors' dining room, to be confronted by the sight of Peter Jay and John Birt deep in conversation with his Chairman. According to one member of the management team, 'The governors came quite close to the proposition that maybe we should bring these lads in and have them do their number on news and current affairs.' But Curran was having none of it because 'he was an austere, catholic fellow and said that as a theory of how you run news it is poisonous'. The result was a paper distributed to all gover-nors explaining that the theory of a bias against understanding was, in fact, a theory about the sociology of management and was therefore nothing to do with news. It seemed to do the trick.

This critique was only partly true. It was certainly correct that the organisational 'cure' had prescribed specialist subject areas under one roof, with implications for how staff and resources were distributed. But also implicit in the Birt–Jay thesis was a different problem: whether it was possible, within the confines of the television medium itself, to achieve their journalistic objectives without boring viewers into submission. After all, a ten-minute news bulletin conveyed less information than two broadsheet newspaper columns. How far could television go without alienating those who came to it wanting no more than a 'quick fix' of news? And if large numbers deserted, what were the implications for the rest of the schedule? Furthermore, there were a number of experienced, practising journalists who remained deeply sceptical about the idea that news could follow any theoretical nostrums. In their view, good journalism was a combination of instinct, experience and commonsense, not a set of prescribed values.

At London Weekend, however, as Controller of Features and Current Affairs, Birt had developed a distinctive brand of analytical current affairs which had tried to implement the broad lines of his original thesis. It was not a precise art, but he attracted a loyal following. According to one early recruit, 'We were developing Birtian television journalism on the hoof, and there were people who understood it and people who didn't . . . it was like Trotskyists and Stalinists.'

The essence of the Birtian process was summed up by one of its practitioners as 'method': a thorough process of research and telephone calls to work out precisely what the story was, and a series of draft scripts before any filming started. For devotees, there were two benefits to this systematic approach. First, it was a more economical way of using what could be a very expensive medium: 'It seems only sensible that if you are going to rush out, at hundreds of pounds a day to the Presidential Suite of the Hyde Park Hotel [to interview people] you should know what they're going to say.' Second, it offered a rigorous and stimulating intellectual environment in which to work: 'If you hadn't got to draft J of your script, you weren't thinking. . . . It wasn't artistic, but the intellectual stuff was brilliant.'

But the methodical approach also had weaknesses. Taken to its extremes (which in some cases it was), interviewees were doing little more than playing walk-on roles in a predetermined script. This sometimes meant coaching them in what they were supposed to be saying, even if – as could happen – they had changed their minds, wanted to elaborate or wanted to express themselves differently. There were reliable punters who would be prepared to come on at short notice and deliver the agreed formula. Andrew Neil, then industrial editor of *The Economist*, was one: 'It was true that you could ring up Andrew and say would you mind coming on *Weekend World* to say that the rate of inflation was closely linked with the velocity of money supply, and he would.'

Even its fans agreed that the Birtian method was 'easily abusable'.

More seriously, such a prescriptive technique did not lend itself to the more unpredictable type of investigative journalism which is often necessary to expose political, financial, industrial or other kinds of improprieties. This is based on a different conception of the journalist's duty: to uncover corruption and wrongdoing, or to challenge received wisdoms and official versions of events. Given the resources of newspapers or television stations, the journalist is in a more privileged position to ask awkward questions than the private citizen. It is therefore part of the professional ethos of journalism that it fulfils an important democratic function – not just of explaining issues, but of uncovering uncomfortable facts. The investigative role of journalism did not fit easily within the Birtian analytical model.

But it was undoubtedly true that *Weekend World* was one of the most admired ITV current affairs programmes of the 70s. It had helped to accelerate Birt's career, and in 1981 he was promoted to Director of Programmes. He was widely seen as LWT's next Managing Director. Having established his theoretical credentials in 1975, he had by 1987 established his managerial credentials also. When Checkland was taking soundings to find a name that would fill the gap left by his rejection of Dimbleby as a candidate, the name of John Birt emerged from three different and equally influential sources.

The first was Sir Paul Fox, who as Managing Director of Yorkshire Television had had plenty of opportunities for dealing with Birt at first hand. The second, and even more crucial, endorsement came from Michael Grade. Grade had never expected to get the DG job, but had performed well at the Board and was told by Hussey that some of the governors had supported him. At London Weekend, Grade had been John Birt's boss. He knew him well enough to invite him to rehearsals for his own DG interview. More importantly, he had for a long time espoused Birt's cause at the BBC: 'I had suggested to Alasdair a long time before that he should think about bringing John in to support him on the journalism side but he didn't like the idea. I was very supportive of him coming in, very supportive.' His journalistic qualities aside, Birt's attraction to Grade was obvious. Here was someone he thought he knew and could work with who would take charge of that part of the Corporation which by general consent needed sorting out and in which Grade himself had little experience. A triumvirate of himself, Birt and Checkland was an exciting and powerful prospect. His former underling, as Deputy DG, would formally be above him in the pecking order, but titles do not necessarily reflect underlying power: separate fiefdoms would allow each to pursue their own courses and programme strategies. It was an excellent theory. In practice, it turned out, John Birt did not see things quite the same way.

Birt's third supporter ostensibly had little say in the matter but was still, as an active member of the establishment, wielding influence from a distance. William Rees-Mogg may have relinquished his formal role as Vice-Chairman, but he was still one of those backroom figures whose opinions tended to have influence. He was unlikely to have forgotten his very first acquaintance with John Birt, almost exactly twenty years earlier when Birt was a novice 22-year-old *World in Action* researcher. In 1967, at the height of the 60s youth revolution and the 'generation gap', two members of the Rolling Stones were given prison sentences for possession of drugs, an absurdly heavy sentence for a relatively minor crime. But support came from an unexpected quarter. In one of the most celebrated editorials in its history – 'Who breaks a butterfly on a wheel?'– the ultra-establishment *Times* questioned the need and motives for such a swingeing sentence. Rees-Mogg was editor of *The Times*.

Birt had orchestrated a discussion programme on the issue, involving representatives of Church, State, press and the 'villains' themselves. He had abandoned the traditional set-piece studio debate in favour of a free-flowing discussion in the grounds of a Georgian mansion. Both Mick Jagger and William Rees-Mogg took part. The programme was not a great success, and was described by Birt himself as 'rambling, inconclusive and incoherent. Jagger was stumbling. The establishment was hesitant.' But an aspiring television researcher had made his mark on the editor of *The Times*, and another important link in Birt's patronage was forged.

If any further encouragement was needed, it would have come from Peter Jay. Jay – who at one point was himself favoured for the journalism job by Michael Grade – was Chief of Staff to Robert Maxwell and not inclined to leave. But he would certainly have offered his own endorsement to his co-theorist of twelve years earlier. Given the positive feedback which Checkland was receiving from all around him, the absence of any obvious alternatives, and the need for a quick appointment to appease the Chairman's irritation at not getting his own man as DG, John Birt became the obvious choice.

By this time, under the pressures of higher LWT management responsibilities, Birt's reputation had changed somewhat amongst some of his acolytes. Those who had been used to a free-wheeling if cerebral spirit during the 70s saw a more austere, more introverted personality emerging. One friend observed that 'for some reason his character changes as he crosses the front door of his office' and attributed the transformation to a lack of internal confidence and the need to hide 'some real missing skills' – in particular an awkwardness in dealing with other people.

Also becoming more apparent was the meticulous attention to detail which underpinned the *Weekend World* approach to current affairs. In 1981, before his elevation to Director of Programmes, Birt had been one of the applicants for the newly advertised post of Chief Executive of Channel 4. His application was supported by a one-inch-thick document, the result of detailed analysis of existing research, in which he laid out a comprehensive schedule for the first year of the new channel. Whatever its merits as an intellectual statement of intent, according to one of those involved 'It didn't have the passion that

Jeremy Isaacs's Edinburgh speech had . . . it didn't have the feel of a new kind of television.'

Birt was, however, committed to the spirit of public service which still epitomised most of British broadcasting. It had not been the business of broadcasting which had attracted him to Granada and LWT, but the excitement of making quality programmes. He would have to surrender his valuable share options in LWT and the prospect of substantial wealth to come, but this was an offer of enormous influence in the world's most famous public service broadcaster. There was, also, the probability of following Checkland to become the next Director General. The combination of power and prestige proved irresistible.

Checkland had made his choice and had it ratified by Hussey within three weeks of his own appointment as DG. Not for the last time in his BBC career, John Birt was not asked to attend a formal board for interview. Following a meeting on Tuesday 17 March, Hussey phoned round the governors and received their approval: John Birt was the man who was going to repair the BBC's now firmly entrenched reputation for 'ailing journalism'.

That same week, when Checkland addressed the meeting of BBC managers in the canteen, he was quite clear where the programming priorities lay: 'We need to strengthen our news and current affairs programming. This is a central priority in the BBC over the next five years; it is a core activity which we must nourish.' Checkland was certain in his own mind that a public service broadcaster had to get its news and current affairs right, which meant airtime, investment and someone with real clout to oversee it.

With the news leaking out over the weekend of 21–22 March, Checkland was keen to impress on his senior staff quite how important Birt's role was going to be. On 24 March, he confirmed Birt's appointment and his brief to oversee a unified News and Current Affairs Directorate with real power: its own budget for all network news and current affairs, in television and radio; responsibility for all editorial policy in news and current affairs; and responsibility for the recruitment, training and promotion of journalists. He emphasised the importance of his relationship with the Deputy Director General: it must be 'next door' to him, he said, as crucial as the relationship between Director General and Chairman.

In other words, the price for the failures of the previous eighteen months was to be an unusual concentration of power in a single directorate, one that at some stage was almost bound to create dilemmas for other branches of the BBC's output. There were many programme makers who feared that the attention being lavished on this single area was becoming an obsession which could dangerously distort the BBC's balance. The Corporation did, after all, make some of the best comedy, drama, and sports programmes in the world – programmes which, moreover, sustained the BBC's ratings performance and thereby justified the continuation of the compulsory licence fee. And the

DG–DDG axis which Michael Checkland had underscored excluded by implication a whole raft of BBC entertainment programmes. It was an axis born of government pressure, of some incompetence, and of a governing board now determined that they must get journalism under control. But it created an imbalance in the power structure and priorities of the Corporation.

As Checkland had predicted, neither the merger nor the identity of its new supremo was well received. As rumours began to circulate around Broadcasting House, senior members of the existing regime started analysing the implications. It did not look good for those who had played an integral part in Alasdair Milne's BBC, some of whom had been horrified by the Birt–Jay thesis and Swann's serious thoughts about imposing it (and its authors) on the Corporation. As one member of the current affairs set-up put it, 'Birt–Jay was the anti-Christ.' Another said at the time, 'It'll cause a lot of pain: a sign that Hussey really does distrust the whole internal machine. Peter Pagnamenta [head of TV current affairs] and Ron Neil [head of TV news] will be distraught.'

The hostility had not diminished when Birt arrived two months later. A combination of his outsider status, the theoretical stance, his lack of any experience in hard news reporting, and the nervous anxiety of long established BBC producers who felt beleaguered, left Birt isolated from the beginning. In meetings, his new colleagues could barely disguise their antagonism. Birt did not help his own case by appearing ignorant of BBC output, admitting at the very first weekly news and current affairs meeting he attended that he had not listened to the radio for a long time. His confession was not well received.

But he had come with a brief to reorganise, and with firm direction from Michael Checkland that it needed to be done swiftly, even in the face of stern resistance:

> I said he'd got to get on with it. I said 'I don't want any working parties in the BBC, we've got to get on with it and force it through. You're going to have immense problems with some of the established reporters who aren't going to like some of the things that we're suggesting but you've got to have the courage to do it.' And I used the word courage deliberately because I think it was a very difficult job for anyone, to come in and create the fusion of radio and television news and current affairs.

Birt's 'mission to explain' had been a public manifesto, and he had already agreed with Checkland that there would be a number of specialist current affairs programmes along the lines of his original articles. It was only a matter of weeks before his new BBC colleagues realised that the Birt–Jay thesis was to become the blueprint for a wholesale upheaval in BBC journalism.

Just five weeks after getting his feet under the News and Current Affairs table, Birt decamped with thirty of its most senior members to the extravagant surroundings of the Woodlands Park Hotel, near Leatherhead. Woodlands marked the beginning of John Birt's unflinching campaign to implement his manifesto. For five days, from 1 July to 5 July, his new charges were subjected to a catalogue of criticisms which served as the basis for introducing his new structure and new philosophy. It was also the first opportunity for BBC executives to witness at first hand some of the qualities with which Birt's ex-LWT colleagues had become familiar: in particular a meticulous attention to structure and a timetable from which there was little deviation.

His opening statement on the first day was particularly harsh on television current affairs. Too many programmes seemed languid, he said, made by people with too much time on their hands. Some programmes lacked impartiality, there was too much rudeness to interviewees, not enough editorial supervision, and investigative programmes needed to seek legal advice early. His conclusion was characteristic: 'The systems are wrong and need to be changed.' There should be a new structure in place by the autumn. One participant reflected on the underlying psychology which seemed to motivate Birt in language that was to become more familiar over the years: there was 'a need to control, to make ordered patterns. He wants to arrange the programmes neatly in clear categories, and then control the content ... he can't live with untidiness, and current affairs has always been an untidy area.'

In the same vein, there was a critique of the 'soft, woolly journalism' of current affairs and of the tendency to send camera crews out without a carefully constructed plan of what was required from the filming. The motto was: 'You should know what you're doing before you go on location.' There were no concessions to the sometimes innately chaotic nature of programme making, particularly of investigative journalism, and also of another style which the BBC had pioneered on the *Tonight* programme – the documentary tradition which had its roots in film-making rather than in journalism. Observers noted the implicit confrontation in the approaches of Birt and Peter Pagnamenta, in charge of television current affairs, and the utter conviction with which Birt was propounding his philosophy of journalism.

The event left some participants with an uncomfortable feeling that a straitjacket was about to be imposed which would at best cramp and at worst stifle completely any innovation or creativity in BBC journalism – particularly journalism in awkward political areas. In a discussion on *Panorama*, Birt suggested there was too much concern about audiences and that too many programmes were prepared to make dramatic play of some contemporary social problem without any examination of the underlying policy issues. Was this, wondered some, more than a simple plea for Birtian 'contextualisation'? Would it not lead inevitably to bowdlerised journalism in which the ruling party was given a somewhat less hostile ride than previously? It raised the unpalatable prospect of a philosophy of current affairs which, however worthy it might be in intent, ultimately betrayed one of the most important canons of journalistic practice: to challenge authority.

The political implications made several people uncomfortable, particularly in view of the Chairman's known political sympathies. Not even the most determined conspiracy theorists put Birt and Hussey into some kind of unholy alliance. But, equally, the kind of philosophy which Birt preached and had implemented with *Weekend World* at LWT did, by general consent, tend to lose impact in its determination to 'explain'. A government that felt itself the constant victim of partial, ill-informed attacks would not be averse to the less direct, more analytical approach which was the hallmark of Birtist current affairs. Hussey himself, of course, would not as Chairman be involved in the day-to-day programming strategy. That was up to his DG and Deputy DG. It did, therefore, come as something of a surprise to discover the origin of a report in *The Independent* newspaper that BBC insiders thought the problems of current affairs would take two years to sort out. The report, it transpired, came directly from a briefing by Duke Hussey.

It was clear by now, barely six weeks after his arrival, that Birt would not be diverted from his mission. Here were the first stirrings of the single-minded determination for which Birt was to become famous over the next six years. As one insider put it: 'With John, you got John's baggage. . . . John might have been a flat-earth man, and if you hired him you'd have got the flat-earth philosophy with it.'

Moreover, he was determined to insulate himself from the hostility which had greeted his arrival and which was now being compounded by a didactic and mechanistic approach. He seemed determined, in the words of one news editor, to 'libel the past' more than was either deserved or necessary. And his manifest discomfort with large groups made matters worse. 'John's pretty graceless . . . with groups of people that he doesn't know very well', said one colleague who had sympathy for his predicament.

Another, who was sympathetic to Birt's critique of BBC journalism, questioned his chosen tactic of overt and seemingly unremitting criticism:

> It had become legend that John had written off everything that had hap-
> pened prior to him arriving which I think was, to the extent that he had
> said that, very foolish. On the other hand, John had decided in the kind
> of enormously rational way he decides things, that he was going to cause
> a cataclysm and he caused one.

Within four months, that cataclysm claimed a scalp which neither the governors not the Director General had bargained for.

Two senior departures had already been announced. Alan Protheroe decided to take early retirement in August. Less predictably, Brian Wenham, Managing Director of Radio, concluded that the top echelons of the BBC were becoming a little crowded. Michael Grade was clearly favourite to take over as Managing Director of Television on Bill Cotton's retirement, leaving no foreseeable space in television. And the creation of both a News and Current Affairs Directorate and a new Regional Directorate had stripped radio of much of its empire. It would be reduced to 'gramophone records and a bit of drama'. Wenham decided he would leave in August, allowing enough time to hand the baton to his deputy, David Hatch. Protheroe and Wenham represented a significant part of the BBC 'old guard' associated with Alasdair Milne. Duke Hussey would not have shed many tears at the news of their respective departures.

Immediately on returning from Woodlands, Birt announced his plans: Lime Grove to close as a matter of urgency; the recruitment of more specialist correspondents; and four specialist units to be established, covering politics, economics and industry, social affairs, and foreign affairs. Each would have at least one weekly programme devoted to its specialism.

Then, ten days after Woodlands, came the day of reckoning. A series of appointments on Wednesday 15 July saw Peter Pagnamenta sacked and Ron Neil promoted to be Birt's deputy. The 36-year-old editor of the *Nine o'Clock News*, Tony Hall, became Editor of News and Current Affairs, Television with a testimonial from Birt which sounded curiously uninspiring. According to *The Sunday Times*, he praised Hall as an 'extremely thoughtful young man who considered all the questions very thoroughly'. As Hall's number two, Birt brought in the editor of London Weekend Television's *London Programme*, Samir Shah, who was candid about where he stood in the 'mission to explain' debate: 'I know John's views on journalism and share them.' Jenny Abramsky, Editor of Radio 4's *Today* programme, became Editor of News and Current Affairs, Radio. The new regime was now in place, with barely a current affairs representative amongst them. The clear-out was complete. The ghosts of *Real Lives* and *Maggie's Militant Tendency* had been exorcised.

One further promotion was important in Birt's efforts to solve the structural problem in BBC journalism exposed during the latter part of the Milne era. John Wilson, who had for six years been Editor of News and Current Affairs in Radio, accepted a new position as Controller of Editorial Policy. He had a wide-ranging brief, concerned both with developing a set of guidelines for journalistic standards and with troubleshooting in areas of potential danger. Unlike Protheroe, Wilson's role was to try to involve himself at an early stage in the programme making process and to act as a source of expert help and even reassurance rather than as a restraint.

But the brief was to extend across all programme areas, including documentaries and drama, as well as current affairs. However well-intentioned Wilson's appointment, it was inevitably seen as an attempt by John Birt to extend his influence. It was little consolation to those who felt threatened that Wilson was not part of the News and Current Affairs Directorate. It was clearly part of the structural reorganisation to monitor difficult areas, a problem which Birt was explicitly charged with correcting. And anyway, Wilson was officially attached to the new Policy and Planning Unit, whose expanding influence was itself becoming a matter of concern amongst some programme makers. It took well over a year for Wilson to convert people to the idea that he was there to help them, rather than being a Birtist infiltrator. But the suspicions levelled at him were part of a wider anxiety about the emphasis on news and the power invested in John Birt.

In two crucial ways, Birt's position differed from his predecessor's: cash and airtime. Birt was a boss with £80 million a year to spend on his restructuring and invest in his new approach. And he had the right to airtime, to ensure that the programmes in which his directorate was investing would be aired at a time and on a channel which he felt was appropriate. Even the 'old guard' agreed with that. As one put it: 'That was the right way to do it – you've got to give the fellow the chance of actually getting onto the airwaves. If you don't have airtime, you are powerless to do anything.' But, he continued, that power should be 'much more regulated than it became. I wouldn't dream of going as far as they've gone'.

How far 'they' were going to go became clear to Michael Grade and Bill Cotton fairly soon after Birt's arrival. Just before Woodlands, it had been announced that Grade would take over from Bill Cotton as Managing Director of Network Television after Cotton's retirement in April the following year. Although the promotion had been all but a formality, Cotton was delighted that he would not be leaving a vacuum. On the contrary, he had persuaded the man whom he believed to be the most exciting television executive of his time to bring his exceptional talent for entertainment to the BBC.

Bill Cotton was the embodiment of a BBC entertainment tradition as old as Reith himself. Son of the famous band leader, he had been a light-entertainment producer in the late 50s when the department was headed by the showbusiness luminary Eric Maschwitz (who himself was made the BBC's first Director of Variety in 1933). For most of his career, as Head of Variety then Head of Light Entertainment, and then controller of BBC-1 and, now, as Managing Director of Television, Cotton had devoted himself to bringing the best of comedy and light entertainment to the country's television screens: and not just to any channel, but to the public service broadcaster. He had booked comedy acts like Morecambe and Wise and The Two Ronnies; it was down to him that the *Morecambe and Wise Christmas Show* was as much a part of Britain's heritage as the FA Cup Final and Richard Dimbleby's commentary on state occasions. Shows like *The Likely Lads, Porridge, Dad's Army, Steptoe and Son* and *The Good Life* had been essential viewing for millions. They had made the nation laugh.

But these programmes did more than provide amusement on festive occasions. Through its high-quality mass entertainment the BBC made everyone feel that it was part of their lives. It was not just a worthy if somewhat peripheral presence, providing an authoritative voice on all things political but little of everyday relevance. It was not like the public service broadcasters of Australia and America, unloved and irrelevant to the majority of tax or licence payers. The BBC's entertainment shows legitimised the licence fee by making the on-screen return visible, substantial and frequent.

Just as important, as Cotton well understood, were the political repercussions. By cementing its relationship with viewers, these programmes enhanced the BBC's reputation with politicians. In Cotton's own words: 'No politician dare touch you as long as your programmes are right and as long as the general public like what you produce.' For both populist and pragmatic reasons, Bill Cotton's belief in the BBC's duty to entertain was absolute: 'I actively think the licence fee is about producing programmes that include actors, musicians, dancers, commentators; people like [Kenneth] Clark, Bronowski, those type of shows, things that can't be done by a newspaper.'

It was to continue, and consolidate, that tradition of popular public service broadcasting that Cotton had recruited Grade – in fact, had gone to America to talk him into returning to the UK. For Cotton, Grade's skill lay in his ability to buy in entertainers, whether they be comics, musicians, scriptwriters, actors, directors or whoever. Others from Grade's hugely successful showbusiness family had been eminent sellers – agents for the top performers – but Grade was 'a man who buys talent and gives people opportunity'. He had been in his BBC job only three years, but was already respected by his colleagues. Not only was he easy and assured with the stars of the entertainment industry, but he even succeeded in getting a beleaguered BBC some rare positive publicity. Cotton knew that the Corporation badly needed a heavyweight popular entertainment figure in senior management. No wonder, then, that he was so excited about recruiting his successor: 'I was so pleased with myself, I thought I'd done the one thing at the end of a 33-year career. . . . I'd really found the right man for the job.' In advance of his own retirement, Cotton had effectively handed over to Grade.

Grade, of course, was delighted with the appointment of both Checkland and Birt. It was not just that, for his personal ambitions, the new team seemed to represent the best of all possible options. He also believed it was good news for the BBC. Birt, he had been told, would be responsible for news and current affairs and would deputise for Checkland in his absence – a role which was perfectly acceptable to Grade. John Birt had a different view, as the appointment of John Wilson confirmed: that his remit extended wider than news and current affairs, and that his editorial brief covered the whole Corporation. It would therefore, inevitably, impinge directly on the television service.

The problems began very soon after Birt's arrival, when he started to involve himself in documentaries and drama scripts. In Grade's own words: 'I first realised that something was wrong when I started getting memos from

John about the output on television, which I thought was slightly off.' Grade, after all, was Managing Director, Television. Whatever Birt's vision of BBC journalism, Grade was responsible for what was coming out of network television. Birt's encroachment in those affairs was, as far as Grade understood, not part of his job.

Grade went to see Checkland.

I said 'This is ridiculous. Because between you, John and myself we've actually got the best team in British television. Between the three of us, what we don't know about British television isn't worth knowing. You'll worry about the money, John'll worry about the journalism, and I'll worry about the ratings and the quality of television.' I was really looking forward to it.

Checkland accepted that, at the beginning, Birt had been straying into areas like *Everyman* and was employing a generous definition of current affairs. He agreed to put a stop to it. But it gradually emerged that the views which John Birt and Michael Grade held about their respective roles did not match. Worse, they were mutually incompatible.

This confusion was another legacy of the received wisdom that the BBC's journalistic output was sub-standard. Whatever Birt's personal aspirations within the BBC, this was not a unilateral attempt by an ambitious individual to subvert normal practice and expand his empire. It was part of the job description. In Grade's view:

Obviously having seen the journalism do for Alasdair, and with his own insecurity in not being a programme maker, [Checkland] felt doubly insecure about the journalism. In his anxiety to get John, he had obviously oversold the job to him or had had to give ground or something. He couldn't deliver without upsetting me, and that was the problem.

Here was the 'dissension and disharmony' which Alasdair Milne predicted as the result of a powerful News and Current Affairs Directorate. Grade wanted to safeguard his television empire. Birt was not about to concede any ground which might diminish his influence. There was a deep and irreconcilable fault-line between Michael Grade's vision of the BBC, run by a trio of complementary talents, and the vision offered to – or won by – Birt. The rumbling grew louder through the summer and autumn of 1987, and in November it finally erupted.

Things came to a head with the case of the Channel Controllers' selection board. BBC-1 and BBC-2 each had their own Controllers, responsible for commissioning and scheduling their respective channels and reporting to the Director of Programmes. Grade had continued to be Controller of BBC-1 while Director of Programmes, and in April 1987 the BBC-2 Controller, Graeme McDonald, had announced he would step down at the end of the year.

Thus, with Grade's elevation to Managing Director, Television, both posts would be vacant (the title Director of Programmes was to disappear). These appointments were crucial, not just to BBC Television but to the BBC itself. In tandem with Grade, the successful candidates would be shaping almost half the television viewing of the British population, at a time when the funding and structure of the BBC would be under sustained political scrutiny and its very survival at stake. At a decisive moment in BBC history they would be responsible for what was, in effect, the shop window.

Candidates were, as was the BBC custom, to be interviewed by a selection board whose make-up was defined by the nature of the job. In this case, the seniority and significance of the jobs called for the BBC top brass: the Chairman and a selection of governors, certainly. The Director General, of course. The Managing Director, Television, because the controllers reported to him. But what of the Deputy DG? Michael Checkland was clear in his own mind that some issues, like the need to overrun on news bulletins, would require collaboration between Birt and the two channel controllers. They had to be able to work with each other, and it was therefore reasonable that they should see each other at interview. Grade, however, was adamant that Birt's presence would send a signal throughout the Corporation – that Grade was not, after all, captain of his own ship.

Here was the defining moment of those two conflicting visions of Birt's role. Grade pleaded with Checkland and Birt that he be allowed to run the television service without hindrance, but to no avail: 'Clearly Michael [Checkland] had the support of the Chairman. It wasn't a battle I could win, and I realised that this was going to be the way of things for the next few years. It held no interest for me.' John Birt sat on the controller appointments board, and Michael Grade decided he would be gone by Christmas.

His decision might have been made a little easier by the knowledge that another plum job was about to become available: Chief Executive of Channel 4. On the face of it, this was not the right job for Michael Grade. Channel 4 had been set up in 1982 with a statutory duty to provide programmes for tastes and interests not catered for on other channels. It was unique, not just in Britain but throughout the world, for showing commercials and being funded by a levy on television advertising, while having a specific public service brief laid down by Parliament. The brief also ensured that it would remain a minority channel. Yet here was a populist entertainer, a showman with an enviable track record in popular television. Could he possibly be the right person to run a channel which commanded less than 10% of the country's viewing, and was restricted from taking much more?

As part of a deliberate policy to encourage permanent renewal and innovation, Channel 4's senior staff were given contracts rather than staff positions. This applied equally to Jeremy Isaacs. His second contract was due to end in 1988, and he had accepted the post of General Director of the Royal Opera

House at Covent Garden. His job was advertised and, in November 1987, the board of Channel 4 was interviewing candidates.

By Friday 13 November, it had interviewed all the main contenders and, in the words of one member of the panel, 'We'd come to the conclusion that there was no-one to appoint.' Eminent as the interviewees were in their fields, there were no household names; a bigger figure was needed. At this point the chairman Sir Richard Attenborough dropped his bombshell: 'Dickie suddenly said on the Friday, I have got one other candidate up my sleeve – Michael Grade.' Grade, it transpired, had made it clear to Attenborough that he would be available if approached and could be interviewed the following day. The board agreed to reconvene on the Saturday at Attenborough's house in Richmond 'and after half an hour's chat we knew Michael was the right chap'.

Grade's reputation stood in stark contrast to Isaacs's high culture, and his appointment created a furore amongst some of the *literati* – not least from Isaacs himself, who bitterly opposed it. But for some close observers of the Corporation, it was not a total surprise. Two months earlier, Grade had given a high-profile address to the Royal Television Society at its biennial jamboree in Cambridge, and had chosen Channel 4 as his theme. Intriguingly, he had argued for its privatisation. While this appalled those who clung to the public service vision of Channel 4's creators, it chimed well with those who embraced the current political fashion for free-market theories. For Margaret Thatcher and the leading proponents of a radical Conservative ideology, the notion of privatisation had become synonymous with efficiency, productivity and greater benefit to the nation. Any organisation given artificial protection, and therefore not subject to the discipline and rigour of the competitive marketplace, was to be distrusted.

Politically, the timing of Grade's speech was particularly delicate. Following publication of the Peacock Report the previous year, the government had embarked on a wide-ranging review of broadcasting policy which was to culminate in a new strategy certain to embody its attachment to the free market. Although the review was still in its earliest stages, ministers and civil servants were already thinking about the main planks of the government White Paper which would emerge the following year. At the centre of the White Paper would be the future of commercial broadcasting: ITV and Channel 4. The potential role of Michael Grade in all of this had been raised – coincidentally – in conversation with a BBC Board of Management member during the summer by Gordon Reece, a close adviser to Margaret Thatcher. In discussing the future direction of the BBC, Reece had volunteered the question: 'What happens if Grade goes to Channel 4?' It seemed, at the time, to be an absurd question. Four months later, to the astonishment of virtually everyone else, it had proved remarkably prescient.

Reece was a powerful man, whose advice on the placement of influential public figures was regularly sought by Downing Street. His question, and the bizarre sequence of events which followed, raises the spectre of political machination at the very highest level in an effort to ensure that politically acceptable figures would be running the country's major media outlets. After all, most of Fleet Street was loyal to Thatcher, and the BBC seemed at last to be in safe hands. ITV was about to be subjected to the bracing challenge of the free market. Which only left Channel 4 – whose present incumbent was known to be a political dissident and had already been all but blackballed by Downing Street for the BBC job. Michael Grade's bid, on the other hand, had attracted no such opposition.

The idea of such a wide-ranging conspiracy is entertaining but scarcely credible: political connivance is rarely so well organised, and almost never so successful. And anyway, on taking up his new job, Grade became convinced of the case against privatisation. In conversations with ministers, he was a passionate advocate of insulating Channel 4 from the free market and he persuaded Downing Street to retreat from full privatisation. While Channel 4 was eventually forced to compete with ITV, it remained an independent trust with a continuing mandate for minority, innovative programmes.

It would be wrong, nevertheless, to exclude any notion of influence from the wider political environment. Reece's question can be explained easily enough by the rumours circulating at the time about Grade's growing rift with Birt, which showed no sign of being resolved. And it was public knowledge that Jeremy Isaacs was off to the Royal Opera House at the end of the year. Michael Grade was committed to the BBC – and to Bill Cotton who had brought him in – but he had always had feet in different camps, always been the sort of person to stay in touch with other options. He was not a born and bred BBC man. As the summer wore on, and the BBC wore him down, those who knew him found that he was not discounting the possibility of a move. Channel 4 was the only obvious post with any attraction.

At the same time, Grade would have been perfectly aware of the prevailing political ethos and the fact that – however indirect and subtle the pressure might be – Downing Street's influence spread like tentacles. It was not a question of having to recite Thatcherite mantras in order to be eligible for high public office. But it was, certainly, a question of showing oneself to be open to different arguments and not to be automatically prejudiced against the current political nostrums. As Isaacs and Wenham had discovered, Downing Street did have the power to disqualify. Grade may have wanted to ensure that, should it finally come to the crunch, he would not be disqualified by association with a policy position which was unacceptable to a fervently ideological Prime Minister or her acolytes. In a more consensual or less driven political atmosphere, it is hard to see why Grade would have so publicly made the case for Channel 4's privatisation just as the search was beginning for a new Chief Executive. While we can discount the idea of Margaret Thatcher moving pieces around the broadcasting chessboard with calculated precision, the shadow of her hand certainly loomed large over the pieces in play during 1987. By the end of the year she would not have been unhappy with their new positions.

One last drama was to be played out before the year-end. The timing of *Newsnight*, BBC-2's daily late evening news analysis programme, had long been a bone of contention, because it broke all the traditional rules of scheduling: that regular programmes should have a fixed, recognisable place in the schedule. But *Newsnight* roamed, starting any time between 10.30 and 11.00 pm. The reason was simple. BBC-2 always started a programme at 9 pm to meet *The Nine o'Clock News* on BBC-1 to offer viewers a complementary non-news programme. Fixing a 45-minute programme at 10.30 meant confining BBC-2 to programmes of a fixed 90-minute duration or a permutation of 90 minutes – in other words, severely reducing its flexibility to offer films or drama of over 90 minutes or programmes of odd duration like 80 minutes.

Those who were keen advocates of the role of news programmes wanted *Newsnight* fixed, and John Birt now added his voice to the campaign. But those who championed drama, entertainment and other programme genres had always resisted the call. Bill Cotton felt particularly strongly about the need to consider non-news audiences who, after all, still comprised the majority:

> I said you are denying the main part of the audience a minority channel.
> I said as far as I'm concerned the public now had the news at 5.45, news
> at 6, news at 7, the news at 9 and the news at 10 and I don't think there
> is anything that could be happening that is that important that they need
> to alter anything.

But once the cause had been taken up by Birt, it was clearly going to have more legs. Cotton realised the battle was probably lost, but felt sufficiently strongly to ask to put his case to the Board of Governors.

For Checkland, however, this was strictly a management issue which did not require referral to the Board of Governors. But the manner of Checkland's announcement of his decision on the matter was unfortunate. At a press conference given by himself and Birt shortly afterwards, the Director General was caught unawares by a journalist's question about the programme's future. Rather than evade the question, he confirmed that, from the following April, *Newsnight* would have a fixed start time of 10.30. In retrospect, Checkland regretted this lapse of tact, but the row was fuelled by apologies which Cotton received not only from Checkland but from Duke Hussey. Was this not confirmation that it was the Chairman's hand at work, probably in league with the Deputy Director General? Checkland, however, saw it all rather differently. The Chairman had no say in the decision, but was simply backing his chief executive, whose announcement had been precipitate.

The fact was, however, that Cotton had been ignored and was being systematically marginalised. He was due to retire anyway on 22 April and had no intention of leaving before then. But he knew now that, whatever consultation he might be involved in and however loudly he might protest, crucial decisions about the future were being taken elsewhere. Grade had gone, Cotton was going, and there were few staff left with the stature to withstand the new shift of emphasis.

It was particularly ironic that the *Newsnight* row should come at the end of a year which, by conventional standards, was a great success for the BBC. Writing in the trade magazine *Broadcast* in April of that year, William Phillips reflected on the Milne era and the BBC's recent ratings. He wrote:

> The fact remains that BBC TV never competed harder than under the much maligned Alasdair Milne. Ten years ago, ITV captured 55% of home viewing, pitting one channel against the BBC's two. Last year both systems had two channels, but commercial TV's share was 54%. Last autumn BBC had half the top 20 series, and 22 of the 50 highest-rated series, including all 3 factual series. . . . This is the unresponsive, expensive, elitist BBC. Why doesn't it proclaim such statistics?

The answer, certainly by the end of 1987, was that journalism rather than ratings had become the major preoccupation for the BBC's ruling elite. It was the beginning of an era in which the BBC's duty to be in the vanguard of popular programming began to be questioned in both political and BBC circles. The entertainers who had fought hardest for the BBC's right to make popular programmes were on their way out, giving rise to a number of questions not just about the conduct of journalism but about the right approach to public service broadcasting. Was the talent to amuse making way for the mission to explain?

CHAPTER SEVEN

A QUESTION OF HOUSEKEEPING

Michael Grade's abrupt departure for Channel 4 left a huge and unexpected hole in the management of BBC Television. The man he had been about to replace as Managing Director, Bill Cotton, was resolved not to stay a day past his retirement date, and the problem was made worse by the fact that the two new channel controllers, Jonathan Powell on BBC-1 and Alan Yentob on BBC-2, were still learning their jobs. With continuing turmoil in News and Current Affairs as John Birt sought to merge the two departments, the last thing the BBC needed was a television service which was rudderless and drifting.

The solution, when it came, was as sudden and almost as surprising as had been the appointment of John Birt the previous year. Sir Paul Fox was one of the leading figures in the British broadcasting industry, regarded as a no-nonsense manager who had proved himself both at the BBC and in ITV. He had left the BBC fifteen years earlier to join Yorkshire TV as Director of Programmes, and had subsequently become Managing Director. Prior to that he had had a successful BBC career, starting in sport before becoming Head of Current Affairs and ending up in charge of BBC-1. He had steered Yorkshire through one round of ITV franchise renewals, in 1981, and was known not to be enthusiastic about the prospect of another.

Fox had been approached before about other jobs at the BBC. His name had been canvassed by Bill Cotton, in particular, for the post of Director General the previous year, just as his name had been circulating the last time the DG's job had been vacant, in 1977. Fox's response had been the same on both occasions: if the Board of Governors wished to offer him the position, he would accept, but not if his name was only to be added to the short-list to swell the numbers.

This time, though, it seemed that the nature of the approach was different, and when the phone call came he was, in any case, looking for a change. 'I was coasting along at Yorkshire,' he says, 'but I was miles away from programmes just being Managing Director.' The next phone conversation was with Michael Checkland one Saturday morning, and Fox suggested he might be interested in the job. Checkland, almost immediately, called Duke Hussey, who approved, and Checkland and Fox arranged to meet in a hotel in Surrey, half way between their respective houses. The deal was done in less than an hour.

Fox was 62, and already past the BBC's retirement age; indeed, he was older than the man he was replacing. He agreed to take the job of Managing Director, Television, for three years, even though it was clear to him that now there was a separate Directorate of News and Current Affairs the Managing Director of Television had less power than before – and less, it seemed, than he had enjoyed as Controller of BBC-1 in the early 1970s. Fox, however, could see that there was a job to be done. 'What I thought the BBC needed was a period of calmness, and I thought I was the right chap to bring that about, to stop it being so excitable, to stop the arguing and the feuding within the place.'

The next stop was to meet Hussey, who told him he must also meet the BBC's Board of Governors. Fox agreed, but insisted on the same conditions as previously; yes, he would meet them, but only to be introduced as the Managing Director-designate of the Television Service. He was not prepared to go to Broadcasting House for a formal interview, or put himself in a position where the governors might subsequently turn him down for the job. Hussey agreed, and so it was that Fox was invited to tea with the governors at Claridges Hotel in London's Mayfair, a favourite haunt of Hussey's, to spend a civilised forty minutes chatting over cucumber sandwiches. His appointment, which had been a closely guarded secret, was announced a week later.

There was an irony in all of this which did not escape Paul Fox. In his former role as Managing Director of Yorkshire Television, he had been one of the two ITV nominees on the Board of Channel 4, and had therefore played a part in the appointment of Grade as Channel 4's Chief Executive. Fox's role had been limited, since the negotiations with Grade had been carried out by Sir Richard Attenborough; nonetheless he was aware that in solving Channel 4's problem of securing a suitable successor to Jeremy Isaacs, he had helped create the vacancy at the BBC which he had been invited to fill.

Fox had been away from the BBC for so long that almost all the faces round the Board of Management table were unfamiliar; the two he did know he had met through his involvement in the Royal Television Society. The Board already had the appearance of being the creation of Michael Checkland, rather than the legacy of Alasdair Milne.

Among Checkland's early promotions were two men who had worked with him on the Black Spot spending review committee. David Hatch had joined the Board of Management after being promoted to Managing Director, Radio, succeeding Brian Wenham, who resigned in the middle of 1987. Hatch had started as a radio comedy producer, working with people such as John Cleese and Bill Oddie on shows like *I'm Sorry I'll Read That Again*, later becoming in turn head of Radio 2 and Radio 4. Geraint Stanley Jones had been moved by Checkland from Director of Public Affairs to run a newly created directorate in charge of the BBC's regional broadcasting – a tough and politically sensitive role when resources were being squeezed in the regions. (Regional MPs in all areas are accustomed to the coverage they get from regional television and local radio, and they keep a close watch on any changes to the stations.)

Checkland's financial experience stood him in good stead at a time when the BBC's income was no longer increasing while its commitments continued to expand. The government's perception of the BBC as an inefficient bureaucracy was critical, and it was clear that the Corporation would be squeezed through the simple mechanism of reducing the real value of the licence fee. Through Black Spot and his other work on resources, Checkland was intimately acquainted with the places where savings could be made without damaging programmes, and he was able to explain to the governors how he planned to do it.

Effectively, he had two strategies in mind, both designed to get the government off the back of the Corporation. The first was purely defensive; to cut costs and to ensure that the string of editorial misfortunes of the past few years were not repeated, making the BBC a harder target for a hostile media. The second was to initiate change, rather than simply responding to external pressures.

These strategies were made more necessary than ever by a stark change in the BBC's financial circumstances. The 70s and early 80s had seen a continuing rise in the licence fee income, as viewers upgraded their sets from black and white to colour, and paid for the more expensive licence as they did so. As a result, income had increased in real terms by 6% per year through the early 1980s, and the BBC had used the money to launch its breakfast television service, to start daytime programming, and to improve production values. Now the transmitters had been built and the colour television boom had come to an end. The timing could not have been worse; the government was looking for blood from the BBC just when the BBC needed once more to worry about increasing the licence fee, and the negotiations with the government that this would involve.

In the years since the issue had last been critical for the Corporation, there had been a revolution in management practices. In the private sector, the recession of the early 1980s had driven many companies out of business and had forced those that survived to concentrate hard on increasing productivity by cutting staff, modernising systems, and operating more efficiently. A corporate culture that owed a lot to the United States measured company success by profitability, and financial virility by the size of the takeover deal. It was an attitude encapsulated by a famous speech in Oliver Stone's film *Wall Street*, in which the villain, Gordon Gekko, tells a shareholders' meeting that 'Greed is good'. The speech was meant ironically, but in some cinemas it was cheered to the rafters.

The government's attitude towards the public sector in general was that it represented a cost, to be reduced wherever possible, rather than an asset to be cherished. Most public sector institutions were squeezed indirectly or directly by the Treasury, through cuts in their grants which required them to either cut their services or to save money by modernising. Some changes, such as efficient financial management, were long overdue. In the best institutions the pressure for change was translated into a new attitude towards effectiveness; a clear view of what services were being delivered to what users at what resource cost, and why. In many cases, however, all that happened was that a veneer of private sector management practice, intended to improve 'profitability', was superimposed upon a public service organisation to whom the concept of profit was entirely alien and almost impossible to define.

The BBC escaped much of this, partly because its income was not within the direct control of the Treasury, and partly because of its arm's-length relationship with the State. But if the wind of reform was sweeping through other parts of the public sector, the BBC had to be seen to be changing as well. As one insider recalls:

> Michael thought that with a Corporation with an income in the region of a thousand million pounds a year, as it then was, you needed to have financial systems capable of controlling expenditure, and there needed to be a carefully mapped-out plan of how to use the income over a fixed period. Michael decided it was no good muddling along in the way that people had muddled along in the past.

One of Checkland's first projects was to set up a working party (which became known as Priorities for the Future) to achieve some rapid savings. One of its recommendations was that some support services which had, historically, been performed by BBC staff should be contracted out to external organisations. The BBC had started down this route tentatively in the mid-1980s, but the programme now gathered pace. Throughout the BBC, cleaning, catering, and security services were put out to tender in a long and complex process which started in 1987 and took four years to complete.

The approach to finance has been one of the central arguments surrounding the BBC in recent years. In economic terms, broadcasting is a complex product, being both capital- and labour-intensive (a programme requires a lot of people, as any programme's credits reveal, using large amounts of expensive equipment), but also requiring constant innovation and development (new programmes are essential in refreshing the schedules, and even established ones change while on air). Even apparently formulaic programmes do not have the same production requirements from week to week. As Keith Anderson, of BBC Television's Programme Planning Department noted:

The Television Service deals with the two diametrically opposed requirements of a large capital-and-labour intensive operation which is efficiently planned on a continuous use basis, and the making of programmes that are individually created and produced. Even two programmes in the same series, such as *Tomorrow's World*, will not have the same requirements week in week out; the content will change and method of production will vary.

Critics sometimes appear to imagine that the systems which have been reformed by Producer Choice and the other initiatives of the early 90s had been in place since the days of Lord Reith and the launch of television in the 1930s. In fact the financial systems used to run the BBC in the 1980s had been invented in the late 1960s, when the BBC had also faced a financial crisis which, as in the 80s, threatened to tear the organisation apart.

Professor Tom Burns described these reforms, implemented by the then Director General Hugh Greene after a report from the management consultants McKinsey, as 'the industrialisation of the BBC'. It was these changes that had created the split between 'resource' costs and 'cash' costs, which is incomprehensible to outsiders and frequently misunderstood. The underlying assumption was that the BBC's huge investment in equipment and in people was an asset which could easily be wasted; to prevent this, resources were allocated to programmes by a central Resource Department relatively late in the BBC's annual programme planning cycle, with the aim of ensuring the fullest possible use. As Keith Anderson explained, there was one vital difference between resource planning and financial (or cash) planning. 'Resource planning has to take account of incidence as well as quantity. If £100 cash, available today, is not used, it can be spent tomorrow. If a studio available today [is not used] it may well be allocated to another show tomorrow.'

The McKinsey reforms introduced one other important change. The producer of an individual programme was given the managerial responsibility for keeping within the agreed budget of cash and resources, and delivering the programme to the accepted editorial standard at the right length and at the right time for the agreed transmission slot.

But this centralised system did not make the BBC entirely self-sufficient. It bought services from outside as and when they were needed. One former senior manager put it this way:

> You worked the thing on the basis that you were buying in bulk, you kept your resources in bulk, but you never kept them up to a hundred per cent of what was needed. So you were always going into the open market for additional studios, additional editing, additional everything else. And you knew there were certain peaks of the year, after Christmas, for example, when you would do that. Generally you kept your resource base as low as was reasonable to sustain the throughput.

The effect of these reforms on how BBC Television worked in the 70s and 80s was described by Stuart Hood, a former BBC Controller who, from a left-wing stance, became a stern critic of the Corporation.

> We have to return to the concept of television as an industry like any other. If a management group is concerned with productivity it will be best pleased if it can make long-range projections about the use of the labour force at its disposal and of its resources, which in the case of television are the studios, editing suites, camera crews, set designers carpenters, electricians, directors, and their immediate assistants. . . . Unfortunately such rationalised planning, which is highly effective when the end-product is uniform and identical as in a car factory, makes it difficult to accommodate a television programme which is exceptional either in the time it takes to produce, the amount of labour it involves, the number of film or electronic camera crews it requires, or the time it takes to edit the film or tape. Industrial planning pushes television towards programme series which require much the same effort at all level – hence the increasing trend towards series.

Despite Hood's pessimism, and despite the fact that this industrialised and centralised system sounds like a nightmare, it nonetheless managed to produce a significant number of exceptional programmes. A glance through any television yearbook reveals a succession of outstanding programmes during the 70s: from *Mastermind* to *The Brothers*, *The Ascent of Man* to *Porridge*, *Days of Hope* to *Sailor*, *Fawlty Towers* to *Grange Hill*, and from *Empire Road* to *Pennies from Heaven*.

There is now a small, if significant, body of literature about the management of innovation and creativity, almost all of it recent. As Geoff Mulgan has noted:

> Recent work has established that much of the best innovation comes from structures which link producers and users or from loose types of speculative open-ended structures which can encourage the unknown and the unpredictable. For excessively tight control can often prevent innovation because it demands that the value of any experiment has to be guessed in advance.

One successful recipe seems to be the development of groups of people who work closely together in a secure environment and who are given the opportunity to take risks. Anthony Smith, who started his career at the BBC in the 1960s, has written that:

> The great innovations in television have come about because of the existence of well-funded groups of producers, both in the BBC and the ITV companies. Among the most remarkable of these were the BBC's Lime

Grove studios and Kensington House, which initiated in the period between 1957 and 1980 most of the accepted genres of the medium: the magazine programme, the documentary series, the various styles of political interview, the filmed reporter-led feature, the dramatised documentary.

Thus, it is not too fanciful to suggest that the BBC stumbled upon a way of working which was conducive to creativity and innovation, without actually realising what it had managed to do.

Whatever the benefits of the system recommended by McKinsey (and by the mid-1980s it may well have been reaching the end of its organisational life) it had one serious drawback for the Corporation. In the political environment of the 1980s, dominated by a culture in which managers were expected to know the price of everything, it was impossible for the BBC to say how much any one programme cost; this enraged the BBC's critics, who made unfavourable comparisons between the Corporation and the companies in the independent production sector where programmes were costed in full, to the last pound.

How efficient the BBC was at this time is still a matter of debate amongst those who ran it. One executive says it is a mistake to confuse costings with efficiency.

You can work out the cost of things, it depends what degree of information you want. No-one apportioned the below-the-line costs [resources] to individual programmes. They assumed that if resources were used up to what appeared to be economic capacity, then that had to be efficient. And it didn't usually matter whether Studio 1 was being given over to Jonathan Miller who was making *Shakespeare*, or was doing 43 editions of *Top of the Pops*, as long as what you got coming out the other end was *Shakespeare* and *Top of the Pops*. Cash budgets were a different matter, and those were spent.

Paul Fox, similarly, is adamant that in the late 60s and early 70s, he knew where his money was going.

When I was the editor of *Sportsview* or *Panorama*, I knew what my budget was, I knew what my resources were, I knew when I was going over budget or when I still had money in hand. When I was controller of BBC-1, I knew what my budget was. There was a very simple way of saving money when the financial year came round; you ran a few more feature films, you ran some repeats, that was the way to save money.

Other contemporaries of Fox have a less favourable view of the BBC's financial systems. One executive remembers budgets being thrown together in the back of the taxi on the way to the relevant meeting.

Whatever the rights and wrongs of the system, other broadcasters apparently thought it worth learning from the BBC. As Michael Checkland observes,

> In those days we were on the tourist map. Every other broadcaster used to come to us to talk about cost control and about how you allocate resources, which is why I get agitated when I hear people say, 'Nobody at the BBC knew what anything cost.' We knew exactly what everything cost, but what we didn't do was allocate every cost.

Financial systems are not neutral. Their function is to help make an organisation work, and their design reflects the prevailing view of the organisation's priorities. The way in which the BBC traditionally costed its overheads reflected its conception of itself as a single, unified organisation. In financial terms it was a vertically-integrated radio and television company, controlling all the stages involved in broadcasting, from development through production to post-production and transmission. (In such organisations it is notoriously hard to assign accurate costs to each stage of production, as has been discovered in other vertically-integrated industries, such as the oil business.) In management terms it was a place where any of the Corporation's resources could be switched from area to area as required. So a cameraman might work on an arts programme one day, and a drama or a current affairs programme the next; and studios were deployed as required by the demands of the production schedule.

The merit of such a system was that it protected the skills and resource base of the organisation. But it had significant drawbacks. One was that it made adjustment to change slow, since it was difficult to assign a reliable pricing mechanism to any resource, and therefore to tell whether a piece of equipment, or a studio, was being used because it was necessary or just because it was available. A second problem was political, and this was at least as serious as the problem of financial management. For if the BBC did not have a financial system that was transparent, if it was not able to show where the money went, then it represented a soft target for any critic who wished to argue that it was cumbersome, inefficient and bureaucratic, spending money on overheads that ought to be spent on programmes. At the time there was no shortage of such critics. It was not surprising that, as Director General, Checkland decided that things had to change.

In March 1988, the BBC had the opportunity to appoint a new face to implement these changes when the Director of Finance, Frank Fitzpatrick, left the Corporation to join Guinness. His replacement, Ian Phillips, came to the BBC after a long career elsewhere in the public sector. He had spent fourteen years with London Transport (and had been on its board for the last five) and a further five years at British Rail, where he had been Director of Finance and Planning.

Phillips greatly admired the BBC, which he regarded as being extremely good at delivering television and radio programmes which viewers and listeners enjoyed. He also liked Michael Checkland and respected his abilities, perceiving in him someone who – like himself – knew that changes had to be made, but who valued the BBC as an institution. As Phillips observed,

> British Rail and London Transport and the BBC are all organisations where money is hugely important, but it's not what the organisation is about. The organisation of the BBC is about putting decent programmes on screen and on air, but it's not about profit maximisation, it's about the use of financial resources in a way that maximises value. In the case of the BBC the reason that the fight for resources is so difficult is that actually nobody knows whether drama costing ten times per hour as much as sport is actually ten times as valuable.

Phillips, however, did have serious concerns about the BBC's financial systems, which he thought were antiquated. And he soon got hints of other concerns. Hussey, for example, found it enormously irritating that no-one in the BBC could tell him how many people worked for the Corporation. Phillips agreed; although there were a number of different ways of doing the calculation, it was a matter only of deciding which of these was the best representation. In this, Checkland seemed to be more reluctant than he needed to be about responding to the Chairman's request.

Again, Phillips was astonished when he attended his first meeting of the BBC's Investment Committee, responsible for approving all significant investment decisions. Very few proposals were ever turned down, even though many were couched in language of such density that it was impossible to work out from the papers the benefits of spending the money. One of the problems was that many of the investment decisions were about engineering projects, and Phillips realised fairly early on that the BBC suffered from the same complaint as British Rail, that of 'over-engineering' – designing equipment to the best possible technical specification, which was significantly above that which was needed to do the job. Reform of this took longer than Phillips would have wished. As he recalls now,

> Mike's strength was that he had a very sound understanding of the pace at which the organisation could happily be pressed. I think from the outset I was always telling him that he could actually go faster than he thought he could, not as fast as John Birt would have done, but faster than he was himself prepared to go.

The sense of a lack of financial and managerial control was made worse by an attitude prevalent among staff towards spending the Corporation's money. One outsider, who joined at a senior level in the mid-80s, was shocked by this. In his mind it was exemplified by the BBC's attitude towards cars. Everyone on the Board of Management had at their disposal a chauffeur-driven Ford

Granada, and an equivalent car for their own personal use. Other cars could be, and were, borrowed from the car pool as necessary.

At producer level, it was characterised by an almost indiscriminate use of cars and taxis.

> When you said [to department heads] 'It's not acceptable that you're spending £150,000 on cars', they would agree, and we'd cut it . . . but you'd still see programme editors chauffeured into work in some silver Mercedes, and you'd haul them in, and they'd say, 'Oh, I was in a cutting room until two o'clock this morning.' There was no paperwork on any of this.

The systems were out of control, but new systems were difficult to implement because of an ingrained BBC culture.

Staff members might justify this, at least to themselves, by saying they were worse-paid than their counterparts elsewhere in broadcasting (which was true at the time), but spending money on hire cars and lavish hotels would be hard for them to justify to viewers and listeners, mostly less well-off, who paid their wages through the licence fee.

Despite the financial upheavals, Paul Fox found on his return that, as far as programmes went, the Corporation seemed to be more in control than it had been under Milne, even though difficult programmes were still being produced, for example in the Documentary Features Department at Kensington House. Paul Hamann, who had produced *Real Lives*, made more films about Northern Ireland, as did some of those who worked for him. What Fox instituted was an early warning system, so that producers working on sensitive subjects flagged them in advance.

In addition, there were some dramas coming through which were based on fact, which had been a difficult area for the BBC in the past. The first of these to land on Fox's desk was *Tumbledown*, which had been the subject of intense controversy ever since it was first commissioned two years previously, in 1986, by Michael Grade. Charles Wood's screenplay told the story of Robert Lawrence, a young Scots Guards officer who had been badly injured during the Falklands war, and of his treatment at the hands of the defence establishment during his recovery. It had been the subject of newspaper criticism from its first conception; as early as September 1986 the *Daily Mail* had branded the film as 'left-wing, subversive, anti-Establishment'.

There was political flak too, from members of the government, fuelled by the BBC's decision to press ahead with *Tumbledown* while continuing to refuse to produce the Ian Curteis script known as the Falklands Play, which Alasdair Milne had encouraged in its early stages. (Indeed, when the Prime Minister first met Checkland at Chequers after he had become Director General, the Falklands Play was the one issue which seemed to provoke her displeasure.) For his part Fox thought that *Tumbledown* was – in his own

words – 'a wonderful programme'. He told Checkland that it would be difficult, but that it was entirely defensible.

In the weeks ahead of transmission of *Tumbledown*, the political pressure
became enormous. The controversy prompted Lord Annan, the peer who had
chaired the Labour government's Royal Commission on Broadcasting in the
70s, to say during a debate on the BBC in the House of Lords (and before the
film had been shown) that he believed there was

> a tiny clique of producers and writers who produce programmes that
> consistently denigrate not just the policy of the government but the
> authority of the State and our country's foreign policy. Its objective is to
> cover these with slime.

Grade had taken the responsibility of shepherding *Tumbledown* through the
newspaper flak to the screen, and with his departure that task now fell to
Jonathan Powell as Controller, BBC-1. Planning the press campaign alone
took days. The Ministry of Defence hated the film, as they had done ever since
Lawrence had shown them an early draft of the screenplay. They were briefing sympathetic journalists, in particular on *The Daily Telegraph*, while the
BBC was busily counter-briefing journalists it knew to be supportive. Powell
remembers going away one weekend during this period to stay at the house of
a friend in Hampshire. He spent most of the weekend on the phone, talking to
the press office and to the programme makers, advising them on what to say,
rehearsing their conversations with journalists. The pressure from the newspapers was certainly intense. Looking back, Powell recalls, 'It was as if your
whole energies were focused ridiculously just on getting this thing to transmission. You had this very real sense that you might not be able to transmit
it.' It was transmitted in June 1988, to general critical approval, with a short
cut made at the last minute at the instigation of Paul Fox. Despite the good
reviews the media storm continued unabated for some weeks.

Two other dramas caused Fox problems. The first was *Slipper of The Yard*,
a comedy about Jack Slipper, the detective who pursued the Great Train
Robber Ronnie Biggs to Brazil. The film had been shelved because of legal
qualms. Fox advised that it should go out, not least because it represented
£200,000 worth of production, and Checkland agreed. Slipper sued, and the
governors settled out of court.

Another libel action was brought by the investigative journalist Duncan
Campbell, the presenter/reporter of the *Secret Society* series, who claimed that
the central character in a BBC film, *Here is the News*, a kinky investigative
journalist called David Dunhill, was based on him. This was the only non-
current-affairs programme referred up the BBC hierarchy during Fox's time as
Managing Director, Television, to John Birt (in Michael Checkland's
absence). Birt had a meeting with Fox, the BBC-2 Controller Alan Yentob,
and the BBC's legal department, and they thought the film broadcastable, an

opinion shared by counsel. When Campbell sued, however, the BBC settled before the case came to court. Fox would have fought both Slipper and Campbell, but 'The programmes went out, and that is the important thing. The fact that we then paid is one of the hazards of the job.'

Paul Fox's return to the BBC, combined with Ian Phillips' arrival as Director of Finance, sparked one of the few management initiatives of the 80s which came from inside the organisation rather than being driven by fear of what the government might do.

About a year after Phillips joined the Corporation, Fox took him out for dinner. Inevitably the conversation turned to the BBC and Fox commented that the thing he had noticed after coming back from Yorkshire Television was that there were far too many people around. It was a view with which Phillips agreed. Although his background in public transport did not allow him to make a professional judgement about the proper staffing levels for broadcast production, he had spent his time talking to people who could. Mark Shivas, in the Television Drama Department, was an old friend from school, and Tim Suter, then a manager in Radio Drama, was also a friend. Their opinions tallied with Phillips' experience in British Rail, which, put simply, was that organisations that had not experienced internal changes for a few years tended to have too many people working for them.

From that brief dinner-table conversation, events moved quickly – surprisingly quickly. Phillips mentioned it to Hussey during a conversation the following morning, who responded that it was a good idea, and that afternoon he discussed it with Michael Checkland. Checkland was concerned about a related issue, and realised that Phillips' project could provide a solution. During the summer of 1989 a series of strikes over pay had taken the BBC management completely by surprise, and it was now necessary to find cuts elsewhere so that they could increase pay. The following Monday a committee was set up, with a brief to recommend ways of releasing extra resources. It started work in July 1989, and was to report in six months.

In addition to Phillips, the committee's members were Will Wyatt, recently promoted by Paul Fox to the position of Assistant Managing Director, Television; Michael Green, the Controller of Radio 4; Mark Oliver, a consultant who had recently joined the BBC's staff in the Policy and Planning Unit; and Hugh Williams, then Controller of BBC North West, who was married to the presenter Sue Lawley. The BBC penchant for the obvious nickname meant that the committee itself was quickly dubbed 'The Phillips Screw'. In contrast to the leakiness of the typical internal BBC committee, few of their findings were public when they reported to the governors, which caused some trepidation among staff. In retrospect it is likely that this lack of rumours enabled the committee to persuade the Board of Management, and the governors, to back their most controversial proposals without giving opponents the chance to lobby against them.

The cuts they recommended in January 1990 went across the board, but the largest savings by far, representing nearly £400 million, would come from the axing of two prestigious projects – the new radio building and the new news and current affairs building, both to be constructed at White City. The argument they made was a simple one; that news and current affairs was performing perfectly well as it was, staff numbers were likely to fall in the future rather than increase, and that to construct new buildings was to repeat the classic BBC mistake of the past of investing in capital rather than putting the money into programmes. This last was a view with which Duke Hussey agreed; at a conference in December, he had said that the BBC spent 'too much money on bricks and mortar and not enough money actually on the product . . . we don't need large buildings'.

The all-day meeting which was convened to discuss the report – with the Boards of Governors and Management sitting jointly – was bound to be a tough one (Phillips later confided that it was the toughest day of his life). The news and current affairs building was to be the jewel in the crown of John Birt's merged News and Current Affairs Directorate, and it had already been announced; so any change might be read by staff as a dilution of the BBC's commitment to the area. Further, Michael Checkland had already told Phillips privately that while he was in favour of axing the radio building, he was opposed to scrapping the news and current affairs building.

The meeting of the two boards was held on 25 January 1990. To start with, the mood was conciliatory – with a general acceptance that everyone would have to take their share of the cuts. The discussion of the budget cuts proposed for the News and Current Affairs Directorate had been delayed until the afternoon, and negotiations over lunch had agreed savings of around £5m on a budget of comfortably more than £100m. Despite the apparent agreement at lunchtime, Birt's deputy at News and Current Affairs, Ian Hargreaves, remained implacably opposed to any cuts whatsoever when he spoke on the subject in the afternoon. Checkland was furious.

John Birt was also furious, but for different reasons. When the discussion turned to the news and current affairs building, the tone of Birt's speech surprised many who were present. 'He gave one of the most ludicrous speeches of all time. He was like a little boy with a paddy on', says one person who was present that afternoon.

> He was stamping his feet, not metaphorically, he was stamping his feet.
> His speech ran along the lines of, 'When I came to the BBC one of the
> reasons I came was that Mike [Checkland] wanted me to sort out news
> and current affairs, and he promised me a new building'.

Afterwards, the view of some who had witnessed the event was that Birt, in the space of the afternoon, had blown his chances of becoming Director General. One of the governors, Keith Oates, who was also Managing Director of Marks and Spencer, told a member of the Board of Management that Birt's performance under pressure had been revealing. Reportedly, Oates' view of the incident did not endear him to Hussey.

Nor was Birt's outburst successful. The longer Phillips had watched the performance, the more he resolved that the news and current affairs building would not be built. He got his way, eventually. The governors' report for the year notes only that: 'There was scope for economies in the original scheme and it has been modified accordingly.' The plan was finally killed off in the following year's budget. The site is still a car park.

CHAPTER EIGHT

KEEPING THE WOLVES AT BAY

From the sober, post-recessionary perspective of the 90s, it is sometimes difficult to recapture those heady, frothy days of the late 80s when business was booming, property prices were soaring and success was defined almost wholly in terms of profit. In ministers' speeches and in tabloid headlines, in company boardrooms and the crowded champagne bars of the City, there was a common language. The key to prosperity was low taxation, freedom from government intervention, deregulation, privatisation, consumer choice. This was the manifesto on which Margaret Thatcher and her Conservative government had been elected for a third consecutive term in 1987, and which seemed to be vindicated by an economic climate in which a spending boom was fuelled by the explosion of credit. Riding on the back of this 'economic miracle', perhaps more than at any time in their previous eight years in power, Conservative ministers in the late 1980s became evangelists for the free market and private enterprise. Their message was popularised by an almost slavishly supportive tabloid press, with the *Daily Mail*, *Daily Express*, *Today* and – most raucously of all – Rupert Murdoch's *Sun* carrying the torch for free enterprise policies.

The corollary to this celebration of market power was the vilification of anything which smacked vaguely of old-fashioned collectivism. For over thirty post-war years, until the financial crises of the mid-70s, a political consensus had supported the concept of public provision. In electoral terms, there had been alternating Conservative and Labour governments which had fought bitterly over policy issues like trade union reform, nationalisation and comprehensive education. But the notion that publicly funded institutions and the investment of public money could work to the greater public good had never been seriously challenged. Certainly, the BBC had been attacked before. During the 70s, many on the left were contemptuous of an organisation which they saw as steeped in Establishment values and disseminating a conservative view of the world. (This view was reinforced by a much-publicised programme of research by the Glasgow Media Group which analysed the vocabulary used in news and current affairs programmes to support its allegations of an entrenched right-wing bias.) This left-wing hostility was compounded by a funding system which took no account of income or means and was therefore disproportionately expensive for the poor.

Although part of the political folklore of the left, these anti-BBC sentiments were never absorbed into a deeper, more coherent political world view. They did not resonate with the political and economic concerns of the time. Partly this was because Labour under both Harold Wilson and Jim Callaghan had been an essentially pragmatic party, usually seeking a compromise between its own left and right wings. Partly it was because the left, which was comfortable with collectivist solutions, found itself emotionally schizophrenic about a publicly funded body which it nevertheless associated with the right. And partly it was because during much of the 60s and 70s there was little sense that economic well-being could be attributed to an over-arching political principle which the BBC somehow violated. For all these reasons, the profound concerns being voiced by a few left-wingers never got much of a hearing at the top table.

All this was in stark contrast to the ideological certainty of the Thatcherite era. Here was a government which had devoted time and energy to developing its philosophy, through well-funded, right-wing think-tanks like the Adam Smith Institute and the Institute for Economic Affairs. It had been in power long enough to implement many of the policies incubated in those think-tanks. It was a government with the confidence born not just of three consecutive election victories, but of big majorities which allowed the Prime Minister to ignore the doubters and pragmatists within her own party.

Moreover, for nearly three years following that third, crushing victory, the government's economic miracle appeared to prove that the ideology actually worked. In time, of course, the miracle was exposed as a temporary illusion, a political sleight of hand created by high borrowing and inflated house prices. At the time, it felt as if the elixir of Economic Truth had been found; and the philosophy that gave birth to it was hailed as a panacea that could profitably be extended across the whole realm of economic and cultural life.

In this atmosphere of triumphal free-marketeering, the BBC did not exactly stand out as a model institution. It transgressed every rule in the radicals' book. It did not earn its money through the normal mechanism of market operations, but was entitled as of right to a fixed revenue. That revenue was derived from a compulsory tax on households and its non-payment was a criminal offence. While businesses throughout the land were cutting jobs (or 'downsizing' as the consultancy jargon had it), the BBC appeared to be a lumbering bureaucracy. While businesses were being encouraged to compete vigorously to increase their share of home and foreign markets, the BBC was being handed an absolute monopoly. While lean, mean and efficient were the watchwords in public and private sectors alike, the BBC stood accused of being fat, complacent and incompetent. Given the spirit of the times, it would have been hard to invent a more offensive institution.

The BBC was accustomed to the hostility of governments which suspected it of political bias, and skilled at deflecting the assaults of outraged ministers. That was nothing new. One very experienced executive recalled Anthony Eden's premiership in the mid-50s, claiming that 'Eden would have taken over the BBC at the time of Suez because it stood up to him and said we are going to broadcast Gaitskell's response.' For him, the degree of intimidation or pressure being exercised by Margaret Thatcher and her colleagues on a day to day basis was no different to that brought to bear by their equally abrasive predecessors:

> I find it surprising that people think Norman Tebbit and Mrs Thatcher were so hard on the BBC. Harold Wilson was just as bad . . . his hatred of the BBC was appalling. So the Thatcher thing doesn't surprise me – I'm only surprised that people within the BBC were surprised by that.

In other words, the BBC had long been on the receiving end of governmental displeasure, and had accepted that it was the price paid for independence. Tebbit's sustained attacks over the Libya coverage were no different from previous allegations of anti-government bias.

But this time, something *had* changed: not the accusations of bias or the vehemence of the insults, but the wider political environment. Both Eden and Wilson may well have been driven apoplectic with rage over what they saw as unforgivable sins of omission or commission, but their governments were not intent on the wholesale dismantling of the public sector. By the late 1980s it was not just the output which caused offence but the very nature of the organisation which produced it.

Even that was not the whole story, because the BBC of the 1980s faced two further sources of deep-seated and influential hostility. The first was provoked by John Birt's unrepentant criticism of the Corporation's current affairs output. However justified those criticisms, it was simply not possible to bawl out some of the most eminent names in British broadcast journalism without provoking a backlash. As one observer put it:

> Who are all these people . . . who are their closest allies? Their closest allies are their contemporaries with whom they worked in Fleet Street or in regional papers when they learned their trade. So it was not surprising that aggravation about what John had done stirred up a frenzy that is hard to match. If you look through the Briggs history [of the BBC], I can't see anything approaching the hostility that there was to John at the time of his taking over and for several years after. . . . The bitterness didn't decline; the determination to get even with John continued.

Radical change always creates antagonism. In the case of a journalistic department, there are so many outlets for that antagonism that it can always find expression. There was no shortage of stories about Birt the cack-handed manager or Birt the government lackey, and those who told them were not always motivated by disinterested concern for the BBC's health and vitality. These stories, and others, were seized upon by those elements of the press which shared the Denis Thatcher view of the BBC as a nest of conspiring leftists – in particular the mid-market *Mail* and *Express* papers.

There was, however, yet another factor which ensured that a substantial and influential section of the British press lined up in opposition to the BBC. In the late 80s – as today – around one-third of national newspaper readers read a paper owned by Rupert Murdoch's News International: *The Sun, Today* and *The Times* during the week, *The News of the World* and *The Sunday Times* on Sundays. From the middle of 1988, Murdoch was launching himself on one of the most expensive and hazardous ventures of his career: a four-channel television service delivered direct to British homes via satellite, receivable with a wall-mounted dish. It was an enormous risk and a direct challenge to the long-established terrestrial system.

Murdoch had been running the Sky Channel in Europe for several years. It was transmitted from a low-power satellite, and only European cable companies could afford the huge dishes necessary to pick up the signal. It was then redistributed via those cable systems to any home which bought the cable package. Although some countries – like Belgium, Holland and to some extent Germany – had invested heavily in cable, it had barely started in Britain, where Sky's English language programming might stand the greatest chance of success. With more orthodox entry into the UK via an ITV company blocked by the IBA – and with his unceremonial dumping from LWT nearly twenty years earlier still rankling – Murdoch had to seek other means of exploiting what he believed to be a rich seam of British television gold.

The chance came with the privately owned Astra satellite, launched in 1987 and capable of carrying sixteen television channels. Because it transmitted at medium rather than low power, its signal could be received by a 60-centimetre dish – small enough both to be mass produced at affordable prices and to attach to residential flats or houses without collapsing the walls. Astra's area of coverage (its 'footprint') comprised most of Europe, including the whole of England and Scotland. This was Murdoch's route into what he perceived as the closed shop of British broadcasting. He decided to withdraw from the rest of Europe and launch a package of four channels from the new Astra satellite directly into the living rooms of Britain.

The announcement came on 8 June 1988. At the same BAFTA venue at which Michael Checkland had made his debut appearance as Director General one year earlier, Murdoch laid into traditional concepts of public service values: 'Broadcasting in this country has for too long been the preserve of the old establishment that has been elitist in its thinking and in its approach to programming.' His plan was astonishingly ambitious: to build, virtually from scratch, a greenfield television system of four channels which would be operational inside eight months. In October, work started on Sky's offices and studios at Osterley in west London.

It was not just the four long-established terrestrial channels that Murdoch was taking on. Further refinements to satellite technology meant that it was now possible to launch high-powered satellites capable of transmitting exceptionally clear television pictures to even smaller reception dishes in people's homes. By international agreement, each country was allocated a frequency on which it could launch and operate one of these high-powered satellites. In other words, these direct broadcast (DBS) operations were part of each country's broadcasting system and were subject to each country's domestic regulations. Astra, by contrast, was a free agent, subject to no regulatory body. The government had handed Britain's DBS operation to the IBA to administer, and after examining a number of bids the IBA had awarded the franchise to British Satellite Broadcasting (BSB). It had promised a quality, three-channel system, funded by a mixture of advertising and subscription, using the latest and most sophisticated technology. BSB was due to go on air in September 1989, and at the time of bidding for and winning their franchise they had the skies to themselves. Now, there was going to be a satellite television war. And Murdoch was launching first.

In order to make this enormous gamble work, Murdoch had to do two things. First, he had to persuade British viewers that the four existing channels did not satisfy their needs, and that £250 – the price of dish and receiver – was a small price to pay for doubling the range of television choice. Second, those who were persuaded of their craving for more channels had to be convinced that his four-channel Sky system was a better bet than the promised three-channel BSB. At his disposal were the perfect organs for disseminating the evangelical message necessary to bring off the coup – national newspapers reaching a third of the newspaper reading population.

There was no pretence in these papers. As William Shawcross has recalled, from the moment the announcement was made the 'plugging began at once. In the months to come, Murdoch's papers, in particular *The Sun, The News of the World* and *Today,* all became shameless cheerleaders for Sky.' But to complement the positive messages, there had to be negative messages which could drive home the boring, ineffectual and unadventurous nature of the programmes on traditional channels. The BBC was a priority target, accounting as it did for nearly half of all television viewing. If the BBC and its programmes could be systematically undermined and viewers persuaded that better fare lay elsewhere, Sky would be the beneficiary. For Murdoch, personal gain fitted neatly with his political philosophy. He was the archetypal Thatcherite, despising the notion of a public institution living off compulsory taxes. A little later, when the BBC was to become a useful ally in his bid for sporting rights, his aversion diminished. But for the moment he needed to push viewers in the direction of Sky, and the BBC therefore deserved as much scorn and contempt as his newspaper editors could heap upon it.

The Sunday Times, once a great campaigning paper, had a starring role in the game plan. When things at Osterley seemed to be slowing down, Murdoch co-opted *Sunday Times* Editor Andrew Neil to become Chairman of Sky Television. Neil needed a loyal henchman to take charge of corporate affairs, and turned to his paper's media correspondent, Jonathan Miller. For several months, therefore, *Sunday Times* readers were getting their news and information about the BBC through the somewhat subjective filter of Sky Television's corporate mouthpiece. It was an absurd anomaly, of which most *Sunday Times* readers were blissfully unaware.

The sheer scale of Murdoch's cross-promotion began to raise eyebrows, even within Conservative circles. BSB commissioned a study from the European Institute of the Media which demonstrated just how blatant it was, and then began to lobby for restrictions on cross-media ownership to be applied to all satellite TV channels. This activity persuaded the Murdoch papers to tone down their raucous support, but hostility to the BBC was never far from the surface in their broadcasting stories. In the middle of 1989, the Broadcasting Research Unit published research which compared the attitudes to the BBC of News International newspaper readers with those of readers of other papers. Even when demographic differences were eliminated, readers of *The Times*, *Today* and *The Sun* were considerably more hostile to the institution, its programmes and the licence fee. The relentless diet of anti-BBC stories and editorials seemed to be hitting its target.

Perhaps even more importantly, it added significantly to the sense of siege inside Broadcasting House. It was bad enough trying to survive in a deeply hostile political environment; when the enemy had the additional motive of commercial self-interest, the result was potentially lethal. The press cuttings circulated every day to senior personnel were not for the squeamish. As one head of department put it:

> My abiding memory over those years is the real sense of confrontation with the Tory government and with Thatcher . . . that was really palpable. Usually the relationship with government is something in the mists and miles away but people felt it very strongly because you had her and then you had the press: in particular *The Sunday Times* and *The Mail* who would just go for the place at any excuse. . . . You felt powerless, that was what got everybody in the end, you felt that there was simply no justice.

For broadcasters, press reaction has always been important – perhaps disproportionately so – because it represents a sort of public opinion. It is clearly a refracted opinion, but it is something to set against the incestuous peer-group discussions and the occasional angry outburst from the green-ink brigade of

Tunbridge Wells. By the late 80s, there was an almost paranoid sense of an anti-BBC conspiracy involving most Fleet Street editors in cahoots with Downing Street. Unfortunately, with very few exceptions, it was an excusable paranoia. The BBC had certainly faced hostile governments before, and it had faced press criticism before. But never in its history had it been subjected to the combined malevolence of political hostility, commercial self-interest, and a dominant political ideology which opposed its very existence. Under pressure from the combined forces of press and Prime Minister, it would have required an iron will for the BBC to stand up for what it believed in and to sustain its reputation for independence from government. In the event, there were compromises both in corporate strategy and programmes.

Corporate strategy, in particular, was a central concern during 1988 and 1989. With the BBC Charter expiring in 1996, it was clear that there would have to be a fundamental debate well before that time about the Corporation's role and funding. But before that, there was a more pressing problem. For the government was preparing a White Paper, based largely on the report of the Peacock Committee, which would formalise the proposals, already presaged by Douglas Hurd in 1986, for a wholesale reorganisation of broadcasting's commercial sector. The broadcasting equilibrium was about to be shattered, and while the BBC was not in the immediate firing line it would certainly be affected. It needed to have a position.

It was fortunate for the BBC that ITV franchises were due to expire at the end of 1992. If any changes were to be made to the system for allocating those franchises, they would have to be in place by the end of 1990 to allow eighteen months for the process of reallocation. And there was no doubt in government circles that change was essential. The franchises had last been awarded in 1980, according to a system that gave the Independent Broadcasting Authority complete discretion over which of the competing bids was successful. Although criteria were published, it was an essentially subjective process of decision-making which was not open to appeal. In a statement, subsequently much-quoted, the IBA's Chairman concluded, after the event, that 'There must be a better way.' The government agreed, and was determined to dress the new allocation process in some of its own ideological clothes.

Much of the ground-work had been done by the Peacock Committee, which had applied some free-market thinking to the knotty problem of ITV franchises. It was ironic that a committee which had been set up to reform the BBC's finances actually delivered a report which left the BBC more or less intact but paved the way for sweeping reforms of the commercial sector. Among their proposals was the suggestion that some kind of objective selection process should be introduced through an 'auction' of franchises, which would then secure for the Treasury a decent return – in effect a rent – for use of the country's airwaves. It would, moreover, be a source of financial discipline, something which the Prime Minister was quite determined to impose. It was bad enough that ITV companies enjoyed a monopoly of television advertising in their respective regions, but this sin against one of the basic principles of Thatcherism was compounded by the many extravagant deals concluded between ITV companies and their trade unions. It was no secret that technical staff in the private sector made a good living from their agreements with employers, and that this was not always related to the work being arduous or the hours long. The Prime Minister had herself sounded a note of warning when – at the broadcasting seminar at Downing Street at the end of 1987 – she had famously accused ITV of being 'the last bastion of Spanish practices'.

The Prime Minister had two valuable allies in her assault on ITV. She had elevated David Young to the Department of Trade and Industry, where he was intent on creating a new climate of 'drive and enterprise' (in a large-scale advertising campaign, the Department was actually branded as 'The Department for Enterprise'). It was an essential part of Thatcherite doctrine that successful economies were driven by small businesses, which needed the promotional power of television. But television's extortionate cost put it out of reach of all but the largest businesses. Young's DTI wanted the price of air-time brought down, and the most obvious means to do this was to break the ITV monopoly and introduce competition into commercial television.

But the most important driving force came from the Treasury, where Nigel Lawson was basking in his reputation as the architect of the great economic miracle. He was looking for ways to increase the Treasury's income, and was not sympathetic to arguments about the cultural role of broadcasting. Looking back at the White Paper debate, the BBC correspondent James Naughtie later wrote:

> Lawson is by nature an impatient, aggressive character and he finds the cosy world of broadcasting – for so he thinks it is – most unattractive. He was . . . the minister least convinced by the arguments about quality and public service. He argued consistently that the market could manage taste and that the government's business was to wipe out paternalism.

The triumvirate of Thatcher, Young and Lawson was a formidable alliance.

As with the battle over the independent production quota, Douglas Hurd, who was, as Home Secretary, responsible for broadcasting, found himself opposed to his cabinet colleagues. As a vastly experienced politician, he was used to defusing the more explosive products of right-wing think-tanks. But this time there were good reasons for accepting some fundamental reform of the ITV system. The companies were not presenting a united front in their lobbying of ministers. Their arguments were transparently self-interested, and insensitive to the prevalent political philosophy. And the ITV system as a whole was still suffering from the political fall-out from Thames Television's investigation into the SAS's killing of three IRA terrorists in Gibraltar.

The programme, *Death on the Rock*, was a first-rate example of investigative journalism, a tribute to British commercial television's public service commitment to expensive current affairs programmes in peak time. It questioned the official account of the shooting given by government sources, and asked a number of uncomfortable questions about why the suspects were not stopped earlier and whether proper warning was given before the shooting started. Implicitly, it was suggesting that the security forces might have pursued a shoot-to-kill policy which would – if true – have been a fundamental negation of the right to trial. It was the kind of policy more associated with authoritarian police states.

No lesser figure than the Foreign Secretary had tried to persuade the Independent Broadcasting Authority not to transmit the programme, to no avail. The IBA's Chairman, Lord Thomson, was a robust figure who understood precisely the relationship between regulator and government. Having taken all necessary legal advice, he found no difficulty in rejecting the Foreign Secretary's request. He later wrote: 'Sir Geoffrey Howe did his duty and I did mine, and if you do not like that sort of conflict of duty between government and broadcaster, then you should not be Chairman of an Independent Broadcasting Authority.' As broadcasters recognised by now, IRA terrorism was the one issue that was guaranteed to send Mrs Thatcher into orbit. The programme was broadcast on 28 April 1988, just as the government was shaping its plans for commercial television's future. When Thatcher was asked whether she was furious about the programme, she replied that her feelings went 'deeper than that'. ITV had been warned.

Six weeks later, on 10 June, there was another salvo in the battle between the DTI and the Home Office. On the DTI's initiative, the government had suddenly announced it would be 'holding exploratory discussions' about arranging for BBC-2 and Channel 4 to be transmitted from the new DBS satellite on the two spare channels which had not yet been allocated. This little wheeze would, from an economic perspective, have two advantages. First it would immediately boost prospects for the new BSB system, forcing consumers who still wanted to receive the minority channels to buy receiving dishes. Second, it would free the enormously valuable terrestrial frequencies for national commercial services, thereby trebling the volume of television advertising. From a cultural perspective, of course, it would deprive the vast majority of the population of free access to minority programmes. But culture was for the Home Office. Economic prosperity – and, as it happened, the allocation of frequencies – was for the DTI.

While this proposal sank almost as soon as it was launched, it remained a quirky illustration of the battle being fought in the corridors of Whitehall. And while that battle was essentially over the spoils of commercial television, the BBC was still being warned that it was under scrutiny. In a speech to the

Coningsby Club on 22 June, the Home Secretary twice told his audience that the decision had been taken to continue with existing funding arrangements 'for the time being'. But he served notice that there were other options under consideration, and that even he might not be the guardian angel that some had supposed:

> I do not myself think that the licence fee can be regarded as immortal. As choice multiplies and the average viewer has more and more channels to choose from, it will become less and less defensible that he should have to pay a compulsory licence fee to the BBC regardless of the extent to which he watches its programmes. . . . Subscription enables the viewer to pay precisely for what he wants, and I am sure that this is a direction in which the BBC should move.

The enthusiasm for subscription TV came almost entirely from the Tory think-tanks. Its attraction lay in the direct link between producer and consumer, which (the theory went) would make the BBC more responsive to audience demand. It was consistent with the notion of consumer sovereignty, one of the most dominant tenets of new Conservative thinking. But it was anathema to three of the most fundamental principles of public service broadcasting: that all programmes should be universally available; that it was part of the broadcaster's duty to innovate and surprise viewers; and that it should be independent of commercial pressures. A service available only to those who pay for it, and required to provide a diet of predictable and popular programmes to guarantee subscription renewals, would undermine the BBC's remit and would distort its schedules, narrowing its range of programmes.

Apart from the practical objections, there was a more fundamental philosophical objection: that in some areas of cultural and democratic life, people had rights as citizens as well as opportunities as consumers; and that one of those rights was free access to television's potential for information, enlightenment and inspiration. Although this argument held little attraction for those on the right of the Conservative Party, it was supported even by the Tory-led Home Affairs Select Committee. Their report, published on exactly the same date as Hurd's Coningsby Club speech, was decidedly lukewarm about the subscription option and concluded, 'It would be better to wait and see how BSB's subscription channel fares before risking the BBC's secure and proven means of funding for an untried, and possibly unreliable, source of finance.'

This argument did not impress the government. Its White Paper, published in November, announced its long-term plans for BBC funding: 'The government looks forward to the eventual replacement of the licence fee. . . . The government intends to encourage the progressive introduction of subscription on the BBC's television services.' Encouragement would take the form of licence fee agreements which, after April 1991, would grow by less than the rate of inflation in order to take account of 'the BBC's capacity to generate income from subscription'. It was a threat, but at least a long-term threat with time to marshall a defence. Meanwhile, the main focus of the White Paper was a total overhaul of the commercial sector precisely in line with the economic prescriptions of the Treasury and DTI: ITV franchises were to be auctioned to the highest bidder, without quality safeguards, and Channel 4 was to compete with ITV either as a private company or a free-standing charity. The BBC was on notice, but had for the moment escaped a full-frontal assault.

Partly, this was due to a recognition on all sides that, once the commercial sector had been sorted out, a wholesale examination of the BBC would follow. But that wholesale review could have been part of the 1988 White Paper, and it was certainly galling to some of the more radical proponents of change that yet again the BBC had eluded reform. Its escape was in part due to a perception that the apparently chaotic institution of 1986 was gradually being sorted out. As James Naughtie said:

> The BBC's success in fending off some of the nightmares . . . was partly due to Hurd's instinct that the new regime could be defended much more easily to his back-benchers than its predecessor. It was not that anyone in particular could be identified positively as 'one of us' but certainly it was possible for a Home Secretary . . . to argue that the corporation was facing up to the problem that the government had identified and was intent on moving forward.

Naughtie also suggested that the Select Committee's report may have had a significant calming influence on the Conservative back-benches, from which much of the original pressure had come and where 'mention of the BBC . . . can still produce infantile uproar'.

It was clear, then, that throughout the White Paper deliberations of 1988 and the consultation period that followed during 1989, the situation was volatile. Delicate discussions were being held. Raucous back-benchers were, for the time being, quelled. Influential cabinet ministers were restless and would need little encouragement to turn up the heat. The Prime Minister was not a friend. These were choppy waters which the BBC had to navigate with extra care. In particular, it had to make some awkward decisions about its response to the government's attack on the commercial broadcasting sector. For 35 years ITV – with its explicit duty to provide programmes of range and quality – had been an integral part of the British public service system. Channel 4, with its minority remit and complex funding structure, had continued the tradition. It was the system as a whole which had fostered Britain's reputation for the 'best broadcasting in the world', and that system was being fundamentally undermined. Could the BBC, seen as the standard bearer for public service broadcasting throughout the world, simply stand by and watch the edifice being dismantled?

For the most part, the answer was 'yes'. While ITV mounted a full-scale

1. Coming into his kingdom: Alasdair Milne on his appointment as the next Director General of the BBC.

2. Tension behind the smiles. Although BBC Chairman Stuart Young *(on right)* became a staunch defender of the Corporation, an accumulation of editorial mishaps led him to warn Milne *(on left)* in 1985 that 'things cannot go on as they are'.

3. Professor Alan Peacock, whose committee on the financing of the BBC disappointed Mrs Thatcher by failing to recommend that the Corporation take advertising.

4. 'The evil genius behind the whole thing'? William Rees-Mogg, Vice-Chairman from 1981 to 1986.

5. Maggie's triumphant tendency. Conservative MPs Neil Hamilton *(left)* and Gerald Howarth *(right)* celebrate their victory over the *Panorama* programme.

6, 7. Milne's nemesis. Chairman Marmaduke Hussey *(above)* poses with the cast of *Eastenders* just four months after he and his Vice-Chairman, Lord (Joel) Barnett *(left)*, had sacked the Director General.

8, 9, 10. The contenders for the crown. Candidates for the Director General's post in succession to Milne included Brian Wenham *(top)*, representing the BBC's 'old guard', Michael Grade *(above)*, who returned from America to be Controller, BBC-1, and Michael Checkland *(right)*, who came from behind to snatch the prize.

11, 12. John Birt as *(above left)* Controller of Features and Current Affairs at LWT and *(above right)* Deputy Director General of the BBC, on the staircase of Broadcasting House.

13. Sophie Balhetchet and IPPA Director Paul Styles, two of the moving spirits behind the 25% Campaign which won for independent producers a significant presence on BBC TV channels.

THE Sun

Friday, November 9, 1979   8p   TODAY'S TV: PAGES 14 and 15

FURY OVER TV STUNT

BLUNDERAMA!

BBC's astonishing deal with Provos

Daily Mail Investigation ... into the | **sensational TV series that's become a major talking point**

TISSUE OF LIES ON THE BBC

★★★   DAILY EXPRESS Tuesday September 30 1986   3

'Bias' storm as BBC axes Falklands play

By TONY DAWE   I was told to harden Maggie's image, says writer

A NEW STORM was raging around the rudderless BBC last night after an astonishing all-_____ about the Falklands War after he had refused to rewrite the script. latest example of Left-wing bias in the BBC.''

Daily Mail, Tuesday, September 30, 1986   PAGE 3

TISSUE OF LIES ON THE BBC   After row over Monocled Mutineer, a new storm

The BBC 'tried to distort Maggie role in war play'

14. From the Carrickmore incident in 1979, through the rows over *Tumbledown* and Ian Curteis's Falklands Play and the bombing of Libya, the tabloid press seldom missed an opportunity to belabour the BBC.

Daily Mail, Wednesday, October 1, 1986

Butterly **iased**
Bmorally **ankrupt**
Bpolitically **orrupt**

by Paul Johnson

'ALLO!
'ALLO!
'ALLO!
— See Page 3

DAILY EXPRESS

Friday October 31 1986   20p   ★★★   **THE VOICE OF BRITAIN**

DIRECTOR-GENERAL ACCUSES TORIES OF INTIMIDATION

BBC: TEBBIT GOES TO WAR

By ROBERT GIBSON Political Correspondent

Birt: 'Instructions'

New boss pledges to clean up BBC

Give us the facts—not BBC fiction

THE GROWING DISQUIET OVER THIS BIASED PUBLIC SERVICE

BASHING BRITAIN CORPORATION

Nigel Lawson . . . fuss is fading

15. Bill Cotton, whose hopes that Michael Grade would take over his role as the BBC's 'arch-entertainer' were dashed when Grade fell out with John Birt.

16. A safe pair of hands. Sir Paul Fox, the veteran who returned to the BBC to fill in the gap left by Grade's abrupt departure.

17. A still from *Tumbledown*, the Falklands war drama that fuelled accusations of left-wing bias at the BBC.

PR initiative and recruited some of the most eminent stars of stage and screen to their 'Campaign for Quality Television', the BBC was resolutely silent. There were those near the top of the Corporation's structure, programme makers who had spent a lifetime devoted to serving the public rather than the profit motive and committed to the principles of public service, who found the silence almost intolerable. But whenever the temptation arose to bang the table and denounce government proposals, dire warnings were passed down about the damage that outspoken criticism might inflict on the process of charter renewal. One senior programme maker vividly described the frustration:

> Ever since Peacock, the BBC's management line has been don't take things head on . . . because there was always a step a year away when, 'Oh, we'll get through that and then we can say what we think' – like their attitude to ITV when most people inside the place thought, 'Why aren't we speaking out, why aren't we supporting Granada and Denis Forman and people like that?' You could never answer back, you could never write to the newspapers, you could never get your own back, never get the bloody record straight.

The view from the top of the BBC was different. There, the opinion was that by getting drawn into an argument about ITV the Corporation would weaken its case in the arguments which lay ahead about its own long-term future; that it was more important, with the charter renewal debate just around the corner, to focus on the issues which would be decisive then. In 1989 satellite was still in its infancy, and cable virtually still-born, while the impact of the independent sector was too new to be assessed accurately. There may have also been a calculation that the old, highly regulated ITV system was reaching the end of its life, and that the commercial pressures of the multi-channel environment, exacerbated by the government's auction proposals, would see the end of much of ITV's public service commitments. Throughout the discussions of 1988–9, the BBC message to ITV was clear: 'We'd love to help but we've got our own battle to fight.'

The effect was to silence some potentially outspoken criticism of the damage that was about to be inflicted on commercial television. On the face of it, it seemed absurd: the world's most renowned public broadcaster had been reduced to the status of passive witness to a malicious and politically motivated attack on the fabric of British broadcasting. But it had to bear in mind the *realpolitik*. There was a potent alliance of enemies out there, waiting for an excuse to ambush the BBC. There was no chance of forcing the government to change tack in any significant way, and it was even arguable that – by weighing in on ITV's side – the BBC would simply provoke the hostile tabloid press to even greater rancour. In addition, the White Paper posed the BBC some specific problems; as well as the move towards subscription, it proposed removing from the BBC control of the night-time hours on BBC-1 and

BBC-2, and disposing of the BBC's transmitters. Each of these required some discreet lobbying to ensure they disappeared before the White Paper became the Broadcasting Bill. Better to save one half of the public service system than to risk all on some modest, and almost certainly futile, gesture of support.

Some inside the Corporation argued that this was a policy of appeasement which was doomed, because they were facing a government which did not deal in compromise. Every concession the BBC made would simply trigger the next demand, until the BBC was reduced, salami-style, to an insignificant rump. They preferred a more principled, if more dangerous, strategy: the BBC should fight while it was strong for the system as a whole. The cost of failure would have been enormous, but this approach was keenly supported by many BBC programme makers.

Under the new regime, it was almost inevitable that the less risky option should prevail. But it was not an unreasonable strategy. It may have been self-interested, and it was enormously frustrating for those who had spent many productive years in the commercial sector or who had friends there. It was also unfortunate that Hussey and Checkland were both using language that was uncomfortably close to the political language of the right. But there was a logic of sorts which dictated a corporate strategy of least resistance since the BBC was, after all, simply a means to an end – high quality, independently minded programmes. As long as its programming strategy did not suffer at the same time, a low profile might stand a better chance of keeping the institution and its integrity intact.

Unfortunately, such a neat conceptual distinction was impossible in practice. Although the BBC by now had established a Policy and Planning Unit with an explicit brief to deal with issues like this, a cautious approach in one part of the institution could not be hermetically sealed off from others – particularly when the man now in charge of the programmes most likely to cause offence had been brought in explicitly to sort out the 'problem' of BBC journalism. Programmes did suffer. And it was no coincidence that John Birt seemed to outsiders to be forging close links with Patricia Hodgson, who had become Head of the Policy and Planning Unit. Their common cause was caution, to the point where serious questions began to be raised about the BBC's long-standing reputation for independence from government.

This was compounded by the new systems and mechanisms which Birt had installed to ensure that current affairs programmes would abide by his rules. One current affairs manager, who shared Birt's view of some BBC journalism, suggested that his need to impose strict guidelines was more influential than any tendency to political kow-towing.

> From John one got a sense of, let's talk about what the rules should be, let's establish the rules; now we've established the rules, let's live by the

rules. That's John's view of life. Now I found that all a bit formal for my personal taste, but in an organisation like the BBC I think it is inescapable. . . . I certainly had a difference of view with John about some programme matters, but I never felt that he was pushing a view about a programme for any . . . political reason.

In early 1988, a *Panorama* investigation into the SAS was suddenly delayed for a week, provoking a number of renewed allegations about the BBC caving in to political pressure. One Birt supporter argued that, had it gone out as scheduled, 'It wouldn't be the greatest *Panorama* in history but it was the one that was in the *Radio Times* and it wouldn't be terrible. John took the view that it was not good enough and there was no chance of it being good enough by Monday night.' But this in itself was not proof of surrender to political forces: 'There was enough wrong with the programme for a credible journalistic case to be made for working more at it, but my view was that it wasn't that bad. . . . I knew what kind of impression would be created if we pulled it.' In other words, decisions about difficult political programmes were not being dictated by an insidious government-inspired agenda but by a revised journalistic code which laid greater stress on preparation and balance. It was nothing more than a logical end-point of trying to counteract the 'bias against understanding'.

But while Birt's vision of the new journalism was certainly no recipe for challenging current political nostrums, evidence began to accumulate that government pressure *was* taking its toll. Shortly after *Death on the Rock* was broadcast, with the row still reverberating, Birt himself confessed privately to an experienced broadcasting journalist that the BBC could not make a programme like that. It was a frank admission that the tactics of intimidation were paying dividends, and it was a philosophy which radiated down through the management echelons to the current affairs programme makers. It was not overt censorship, but that was unnecessary. It was clear from informal conversations and from the process of painstaking scrutiny that was being conducted at the highest level that anything which might risk direct confrontation with the government or the Prime Minister would be thoroughly vetted and – if necessary – pruned before transmission. *Panorama*, for 35 years in the frontline of disputes between governments and broadcasters, was particularly vulnerable. According to one recruit: 'There was an enormous sensitivity about what *Panorama* was up to: are we going to offend the government, are we going to cause a great deal of fuss? So that meant if you had a sensitive programme . . . you had people crawling all over it.' Throughout the BBC, the conviction grew that the News and Current Affairs Directorate was becoming safe, dull and narrow; that 'potential trouble was being sat on in no uncertain terms'.

While a compromise in corporate strategy might have been an acceptable short-term tactic, to adopt a craven programming policy as well was something else. It was one thing to preserve an important and valuable institution, but if the very basis of its importance and value is betrayed in the process, the strategy becomes self-defeating. Of course the BBC was doing other things than making challenging current affairs programmes. But its independence from government, and therefore its presence as a force for democracy and a bulwark against abuse or corruption or ill-considered policies, was one of the BBC's most abiding traditions. It was also one of the fundamental justifications for the licence fee system. By not appearing to stand up to government pressure, the Checkland–Birt regime sent a message to all subsequent governments of any political complexion: sit on us hard enough, and we will fold. To some extent other programme departments, frustrated by the apparent unwillingness of News and Current Affairs to do its duty, attempted to fill the gap. The Documentary and Features Department in Kensington House, a building some distance from the tentacles of Television Centre and therefore with a geographical advantage, used programmes like *Everyman* and *Inside Story* for what were effectively current affairs investigations.

Meanwhile, the Drama Department was doing its best to tackle difficult issues and resist the infectious caution that could be even more debilitating at the level of creative invention. A programme like *Casualty* was fiction, but it was fiction set in a contemporary hospital subject to the problems of the contemporary National Health Service, a very vulnerable area for the government. But for the most part, its writers did not feel they had to dodge the issues. The beginning of the series coincided with a bitter ambulance strike, which edged in to one of the early programmes. Arguments were featured about turning hospitals into self-governing trusts, one of the most contentious areas of Conservative policy. According to one of its script editors, 'We were aware . . . that we should reflect what was going on; it was about the NHS, it wasn't the NHS in fantasy land. It reflected what was going on at the moment, and that was one of its strengths.' And it did not shy away from some of the pressing difficulties which the Health Service was facing:

> It always showed that they were understaffed and under-resourced, that people had to wait for hours in the queue – because that was not only a fact of what was going on, it was also a dramatic source. [Not doing that] would have been like doing *M*A*S*H* without saying the Korean War was unpleasant.

Although individual producers may have had their personal prejudices, there were no guidelines and no sense of intimidation: 'I didn't feel there was an overriding political agenda [or] any kind of censorship.'

There had, in fact, been one instance of direct government interference which did have a material impact on the series. Edwina Currie, then Health Minister, had written to Bill Cotton complaining that all the staff smoked.

While this was probably a fair reflection of life in most hospitals, the Drama Department decided to exercise their judgement about the programme's responsibilities and smoking surreptitiously disappeared from the screen. But such was the neurosis in the BBC about accusations of succumbing to government whim that the relevant conversations 'all had to be managed in such a way that nobody knew we were responding to a perfectly fair request from someone within the government'.

Even in drama it was never possible to say for sure that programmes were untainted by political pressure. Anything from an episode of *Casualty* to a high-profile drama like *Tumbledown* – in fact, almost anything which sought to address contemporary Britain – could cause as much of an eruption as current affairs. There was always the possibility of a furious broadside at the smallest provocation, and therefore an ever-present temptation to avoid trouble at an early stage. One senior executive said, 'It really saps people's wills if it goes on for that amount of time. It has a debilitating effect. I don't think one could deny that ... things that were going to be trouble got scrutinised more heavily.' And that, in turn, can affect creative ideas:

> Inevitably that must find its way down. I don't think that people sit around and say no, we're not doing that, it's too much trouble. But people get debilitated all the way down, and where I suspect it has the most effect is in the writers and the producers who think: we'll never get this through so why bother to start it? It's what you don't know that's more important.

In other words, the steady stream of invective was producing dividends for the government throughout the Corporation.

There was no let-up throughout the White Paper discussions and passage of the Broadcasting Bill. Murdoch's papers, in particular, were building up to his launch of the four-channel Sky system which finally happened in a blaze of publicity on 5 February 1989. In viewing terms, it was a strictly symbolic launch: the day Murdoch himself pressed the button, fewer than 20,000 people could actually see what the fuss was about. But the symbolism was enormous, and chimed perfectly with the mood of the times: one man had invested his own money, or at least that of his bankers, in doubling the number of television channels overnight. It undermined at a stroke the case for broadcasting regulation, and provided, in the 24-hour Sky News channel, a service which would compete with both the BBC and ITN. No wonder that, when Margaret Thatcher celebrated her tenth anniversary in power three months later, just five people shared her top table: four eminent Conservative peers, and Rupert Murdoch.

In fact, it was not long before Murdoch had the opportunity to lay out his arguments and philosophy to the very people he was taking on. His arrival in

British television was acknowledged by an invitation to give the prestigious MacTaggart Lecture to launch that year's Edinburgh Television Festival. Some opposed the invitation on the grounds that five newspapers probably provided enough platforms for self-promotion without the offer of another. But Murdoch had now announced himself as a force in British broadcasting, and this was an opportunity for a first-hand explanation of the intellectual position which lay behind his distaste for the public service ethic. There was, without doubt, a case to be made which recognised the importance of television as a cultural force, but questioned the licence fee as the most appropriate method of funding; a case which recognised the real achievements of the BBC and ITV, but laid out a fresh vision in the emerging age of new technology. This was Murdoch's opportunity to present a coherent vision of the future.

On the day, that was not what the audience got. On 25 August, in front of the biggest crowd ever to attend a MacTaggart Lecture, Murdoch delivered a forty-minute harangue which was devoid of intellectual content. There was no pretence at a reasoned debate, no attempt to construct an argument. Instead, a string of gratuitous insults was interlaced with elementary inaccuracies and a political philosophy based on simplistic free-market populism. British television was reduced to a kind of antiquated paternalism while American television was elevated to the heights of cultural achievement.

Murdoch started by dismissing the placing of obligations – such as quality, diversity, minority and regional programmes – on commercial television as 'subordinating commerce to so-called public service'. It was described as a sort of British Establishment conspiracy, paternalistic and anti-democratic – even though the rationale of the system was a desire to ensure a plurality of voices. The implicit assumption was that the unfettered marketplace was the most important safeguard of democracy. Murdoch started from, in his own words, 'A simple principle: in every area of economic activity in which competition is attainable, it is much to be preferred to monopoly.'

This neatly side-stepped the intense competition for audiences which had existed in British television since the launch of ITV in 1955. It also ignored the growing power of enormous media conglomerates with a tendency to speak with a single voice. But behind it was a much more profound fallacy: that in every walk of life and in every field of human endeavour, any kind of intervention in the marketplace for the public good must somehow be bad for the human condition. In areas such as education, transport, training and health, governments invest public money, set standards of safety, or impose regulations to try to enhance the quality of the lives of their citizens. There was no room for such sophistication in Murdoch's political vision.

Next came the insults: 'Much of what is claimed to be quality television here is no more than the parading of the prejudices and interests of the like-minded people who currently control British television.' Britain's TV output was 'obsessed with class, dominated by anti-commercial attitudes and with a tendency to hark back to the past'. Then there were 'strangulated English accents' and dramas which were 'played out in rigid, class-structured settings'. Murdoch warmed to his role as self-appointed drama critic: 'Too much major drama, it seems to me, is set pre-World War One; indeed, anything post-World War Two is a major achievement these days.' Finally came the knock-out blow: 'British television has been an integral part of the British disease.' The jibes about drama seemed rather silly in the light of the fuss created by *Tumbledown*, so assailed by his own papers. More importantly, his litany of failure somehow managed to ignore every soap opera on British television, as well as several contemporary drama series and serials. Had these accusations not been made by a man of enormous influence on an important public occasion, they could have been dismissed as the ramblings of a saloon-bar bore.

Then, there was the glorification of American broadcasting and the factual errors. The Public Broadcasting Service in America, the audience was told, 'has helped enrich the American TV scene'. Murdoch had clearly missed the report of the government-funded Carnegie Commission, which had concluded in 1979 that, 'There is a sense in which Americans are denied what other societies consider vital: a flourishing public communications service uncensored by commercial imperatives.' A number of cable channels were reeled off as examples of the range of programming available to Americans, without any mention of their cost to the subscriber. Nor did he recognise that their viability depended on a population base big enough to generate large numbers of subscribers – 220 million in the US compared to 54 million in the UK.

Most bizarre of all was the charge of 'less than independent, neutered journalism'. Murdoch could not imagine, he told his astonished audience, 'A British Watergate, or a British Irangate, being pursued by the BBC or ITV with the vigour that the US networks did.' This argument was unsustainable on three counts. First, ITV programmes had been instrumental in exposing two miscarriages of justice following IRA bombings; the cases of the so-called 'Guildford Four' and 'Birmingham Six' had been reopened as a direct result of evidence of police malpractice gathered by television journalists. And Murdoch could hardly have been unaware of the investigative operation mounted by Thames for *Death on the Rock*: Andrew Neil, who was both the editor of *The Sunday Times* and Chairman of Sky, had been hounding Thames ever since in an attempt to prove their evidence bogus. Neil sat next to Murdoch throughout his speech.

Secondly, American networks had played no part in the explosive revelations about the Republican break-in at Watergate or about the 'arms for hostages' trade-off with Iran. As most people knew, the Watergate *exposé* was directly attributable to two journalists from *The Washington Post* backed by their editor and proprietor, while the Iran revelations were down to *The New York Times*. It was newspapers, not television, which were putting resources into digging out real stories in the USA.

Finally, and most hypocritical of all, was the notion that Murdoch himself was devoted to the cause of investigative journalism. Throughout his empire, his aversion to serious or challenging journalism had already been established. William Shawcross, in his exhaustive biography, concluded that Murdoch was contemptuous of those who sought to expose corruption or wrong-doing in high places and 'believed that Watergate-type investigations were not the purpose of journalism'. In other words, companies engaged in fraud, corrupt politicians, miscarriages of justice, or the origins of social discord were not the stuff of Rupert Murdoch's papers or TV stations. Coming from Murdoch, the charge that British television was failing in its journalistic duties was breathtaking in its audacity.

It would, in fact, have made a superb caricature: the scorned Australian entrepreneur, determined to wreak revenge for previous snubs, engaged in a rousing call for freedom of choice – and in the process revealing to the world his ignorance and shallow self-interest. The emperor's wardrobe was patently empty, but it was a sign of the times that the speech aroused little opposition, or even intelligent questioning, from the broadcasters present. Some days later, Paul Fox was allowed a column in *The Times* to counter some of Murdoch's more ridiculous assertions, but it took another Australian exile, the critic and presenter Clive James, writing in *The Observer*, to put Murdoch's speech in perspective.

> The moguls wanted a piece of the action. The moguls and the government were in cahoots. It wasn't fascism; nothing so intellectually challenging. It was just business . . . Filofax-minded Saatchi executives held the floor while people who had given their lives to public service broadcasting hung their heads. The discrepancy was already grotesque before Rupert Murdoch showed up in Edinburgh. We should thank him for demonstrating how grotesque it was. The wolf had come to lecture Red Riding Hood on how to find her way through the forest.

The 80s ended with a final twist in the country's media affairs which epitomised the battle in which the BBC was embroiled. With Murdoch's launch of his satellite television service, accompanied by the massed voices of his newspapers (including a front page headline in the *Today* newspaper), BSB had become even more incensed at what they saw as a blatant abuse of concentrated ownership. Their own launch was now due in the spring of 1990, and they had increased their lobbying for a government inquiry into cross-media ownership. The government, facing some uneasiness from its own backbenches, relented. On 14 December 1989, the Secretary of State for Trade and Industry announced that he was setting up an inquiry, to be run by John Sadler. But Sadler's brief was not cross-ownership; it was cross-promotion. His terms of reference were: 'To consider to what extent it is proper for media companies to promote their own, or any associate's, interests in the provision of media services or products.'

This would, of course, have an impact on News International. But it would go wider than that. For, encouraged by the government to seek commercial sources of revenue wherever possible, the BBC had been expanding its publishing ventures. Its listings magazine, the *Radio Times*, was an important source of revenue. So were the glossy magazines it published to link in with programmes. In line with the government's recommendation that it be more commercial, these publications were being assiduously promoted on screen. But this promotion was not well received by the major magazine publishers which had their own products to sell. The BBC was going to be a prime target of the Sadler Inquiry, and now had to prepare itself to fight another internal battle: how commercial could it afford to go without compromising its operating principles and creating yet another set of enemies? A few more wolves were preparing to join the pack outside Broadcasting House.

CHAPTER NINE
PIES IN THE SKY

There are a number of ways in which broadcasters can exploit their radio and television programmes in other countries or other media. Selling programmes to other broadcasters is just one of several ancilliary activities which can generate additional revenues; others include spin-offs, licences, and merchandising. One of the most visible spin-offs for the BBC is magazines, launched on the back of programmes and promoted with them. The *Radio Times* is the oldest and most profitable, but recent years have seen a whole range of new titles associated with popular consumer shows such as *Top Gear* and *Food and Drink*. Then there is the 'book of the programme', such as Michael Palin's *Pole to Pole*, videos of television programmes (*Blackadder, Fawlty Towers, Postman Pat*), and audio-cassettes of radio programmes (*Hitchhikers' Guide to the Galaxy*).

None of this is new. As long ago as 1932, *The Listener* published a table showing how the licence fee, then ten shillings (50p) a year, was spent. After deductions by the government (the Treasury routinely took a share of the BBC's licence fee income until the 1950s), and BBC overheads, the Corporation was only able to balance its books because of additional income it earned on top of the licence fee, 'mainly derived from the issue of publications ancillary to broadcasting' – principally the *Radio Times* and *The Listener*, which represented more than a tenth of its income.

As the licence fee was squeezed during the 1980s, and the BBC's broadcasting ambitions continued to range across the full spectrum, corporate eyes turned to these commercial activities – now grouped in the Enterprises Division – as a way of generating revenue. James Arnold-Baker joined from Fisher Price Toys in the summer of 1986 to run Enterprises. In November, Duke Hussey, newly arrived as Chairman, gave Enterprises' role his blessing by leading a sales drive to United States. And on becoming Director General in 1987, Michael Checkland announced that one of his objectives for the BBC was that Enterprises should develop as a commercial concern.

> I thought we had to be more entrepreneurial, I thought we had to really back Enterprises, and we had to be seen to be helping ourselves, because clearly one operates in a political situation, and in 1987 the Tory government was strong and vigorous. The BBC ... couldn't just sit there and ask for money from a licence fee.

The fruit of this new strategy was a five-year plan produced by Arnold-

Baker, which became known internally as 'the dash for growth'. Its objective was to increase sales by a third and pre-tax profit almost threefold in the five years from 1988–9 to '93–4, and to reinvest the proceeds in making programmes. Unfortunately, few of the existing businesses showed potential for significant growth, and Arnold-Baker therefore proposed 'to acquire substantial new businesses with sales of at least £70 million and profits of £10 million, over the five-year period'.

The principal problem with this strategy was that no-one had defined adequately the purpose of Enterprises, or its relationship with the rest of the BBC. Any broadcaster, public or private, wants to maximise the value of its assets, and most of its assets are in intellectual property such as programmes and programme concepts. For a public broadcaster, the revenue thus earned becomes a valuable source of additional funds. The BBC had recognised this as far back as the early 50s, when the Assistant Controller of Overseas Services – one Hugh Greene – proposed the creation of a central transcription service to coordinate the sale of BBC television programmes abroad. But during the dash for growth Enterprises was to expand rapidly into areas which had not even the most tenuous relationship with the BBC's core broadcasting concerns, thus fuelling a long-standing distrust of the division by those who were making the programmes which Enterprises exploited.

The case of the Magazines Division was a good example. The BBC had published the *Radio Times* since 1923, and it benefited enormously from having a monopoly on publishing the BBC's programme schedules. (The *TV Times*, launched in 1958, had a similar monopoly on commercial TV listings.) By the late 1980s, it was clear that this exclusivity was about to be ended, and that any publisher would be able to publish complete programme guides. The market was about to explode, and the *Radio Times* would suffer.

Having identified this risk, the Magazines Division of Enterprises launched a policy of aggressive expansion. It took majority stakes in Redwood Publishing in 1988 and Hyde Park Publications in 1989, and then took full control of Hartog Hutton in 1990. It also controlled a fourth company, World Publications. Between 1987 and 1990 these publishing companies launched twelve consumer magazines, including *Clothes Show, Educational Computing, Fast Forward* (a pop music magazine), *Good Food*, and a weekly children's title, *Playdays*. All were supported by considerable on-screen promotion.

This was precisely the issue which the Sadler Inquiry was charged with investigating, and John Sadler spent almost as much time taking evidence about the BBC's cross-promotional activities as about those of News International. The conclusion of his report, delivered in March 1991, was unequivocal: 'The BBC, in trailing its magazines and referring to them in programmes, has exceeded by quite a wide margin the extent to which it is proper for media companies to promote their own or their associates' other media interests.' He recommended that the BBC's practices be referred to the Monopolies and Mergers Commission as a matter of urgency, a suggestion taken up by the Office of Fair Trading. The following year the Commission, in turn, found that the BBC's use of free airtime to promote magazines had distorted competition in the magazine sector. 'We have', it wrote, 'identified actual or expected adverse effects on the public interest – increased risk of closure of magazines, discouragement of market entry, and a reduction in consumer choice.' It was a perfect illustration of the BBC's almost permanent dilemma in relation to its commercial strategy; in a hostile political environment it was damned if it did, and damned if it didn't.

But the BBC publishing companies went further than titles related (even distantly) to programme strands. They also published in-house magazines for BUPA, Marks and Spencer, British Rail, Unisys, W.H. Smith, Woolworths, and for a time both Virgin Atlantic and British Airways. At the same time, Enterprises took on a range of extraneous activities which had little connection to programme making: pub games, credit card authorisation, consumer exhibitions, even a BBC 'own brand' radio (an idea which was later abandoned).

By 1991, the division had taken on a life of its own. Even though James Arnold-Baker had joined the Board of Management (a Corporate decision intended to emphasise to his BBC colleagues the importance of the commercial arm, and to Enterprises that they had to act in a way which was consistent with the BBC as a whole), there was little evident link between Enterprises' activities and the public service ethos which underpinned the rest of the BBC. There were several issues which were causing concern: the political pressures on the BBC to be more commercial; the suspicion with which Enterprises was viewed by the rest of the organisation; even its separate location, in its own building down the road from Television Centre in west London. In 1991, as we shall see, Michael Checkland set up a series of internal 'Task Forces' to look at different aspects of the BBC's performance. The one devoted to 'The BBC, the Entrepreneur' criticised Enterprises' expansionist policy, concluding:

> The prescription to maximise turnover and profits at all costs – the dash for growth – should not be renewed. We believe this policy, understandably responding to the political culture of the late 1980s, has unearthed significant new profit streams for the BBC but has also taken us into ventures which stray some way from the Corporation's core activity or endanger its brand image.

There was even some question as to how good the super-commercial Enterprises was at maximising its own profits. Although separate figures for each Enterprises division are not published for reasons of commercial secrecy, those provided to the Monopolies and Mergers Commission showed that Magazines made a loss of £1.6 million on turnover of £76 million (comparable results for the other divisions were blanked out at the request of the BBC). Even the most profitable division, Television Sales, appeared to be under-performing. In 1990, for example, the BBC produced £600m-worth of programmes, but Enterprises generated only £42m in overseas sales, whereas Thames Television, with production expenditure of £171m in the same year, made £47m from sales. While the comparison is distorted because the Thames figures include co-production funding, the BBC's record was not impressive. The sense of a slow-moving bureaucratic organisation was illustrated by a joke told by one of its UK competitors: 'How do you stop the spread of AIDS? You give the worldwide distribution rights to BBC Enterprises.'

At the core, though, Enterprises' problem was not that it was especially badly run, or that its brief was unclear, or that the marriage of a commercial arm with a public service body was never going to be entirely comfortable. The central problem was that it was being used as a shield to protect the BBC from the political heat of the late 1980s. The dash for growth made good busi-ness and political sense. But when the political wind changed, so did the pressure on Enterprises. BBC Select was a prime example of a politically motivated initiative with dubious commercial prospects.

The idea was a relatively simple one. The BBC's night-time hours were almost entirely unused; the transmitters were idle because the available audi-ence was small. The 1988 Green Paper had included two proposals unwelcome to the BBC: taking away its night-hours; and a long-term move towards subscription to replace the licence fee. The BBC responded with a ser-vice that did both of these things. BBC Select, or night-time subscription television, was aimed at specialist audiences who would be willing to pay for programmes sent to their videos overnight, for viewing the following day. It required scrambled signals and special decoding equipment. It was both com-plex and expensive.

In September 1989 Enterprises set up a subsidiary to run the night-time ser-vice, and John Radcliffe, who had been running the BBC's Open University Production Centre, was appointed as head of BBC Subscription Television. It went badly from the start; the following February one service, British Medical Television, closed and despite other ventures in areas like accountancy and law, the service never prospered. Its losses (a few million pounds a year) were covered by profits elsewhere in Enterprises; by 1993 John Radcliffe had left, and the service was reduced to a few unscrambled services. But by then the threat to remove control of the night-time hours on BBC-1 and BBC-2 had long since vanished. With hindsight, this was clearly a project with only the smallest chance of commercial success, but it fulfilled the BBC's purpose admirably: convincing the government that it was serious about its business intentions, and defusing the political threat. Another heat shield had done its job.

While Enterprises was finding its dash for growth cut short, the rest of the BBC was confronting a commercial challenge on another front. On 2 November 1990 the satellite war, which had raged for two years as Sky attempted to corral as much of the market as possible before BSB launched its rival service, was resolved in spectacular fashion. After a period of intense and secret high-level negotiation, BSB and Sky announced they were to merge; but it was a merger in which Rupert Murdoch's Sky was the clear victor, with Murdoch himself in overall control. Instead of two factions embroiled in their own private battle, a single powerful enterprise had suddenly been created to take on the established channels – British Sky Broadcasting. Murdoch had achieved domination of the skies, and now had to set about repaying his huge debts. Where was the money going to come from?

BSkyB was never going to earn serious revenues from the sale of advertising, because audiences for satellite channels are too small (and too fragmented) for advertisers to pay substantial sums. The real money lay in selling subscriptions for individual channels or groups of channels. And the one service which attracts subscribers more than any other (even more than movies) is high-profile, big-name, domestic sporting events.

Sport is equally essential for a public broadcaster, but for a different reason. One of the functions of a public broadcaster, and certainly one of the justifications, is to make events of national significance available to every household in the country at no more than the cost of the licence fee. In doing so, it plays a cultural role in making the nation more cohesive. It creates shared experience. A trusted, high-profile news programme can do this, as can a sitcom or a successful drama. But the events which really unite the nation are Cup Finals, the classic horse races, or those rare Olympic triumphs in which victory really is for country rather than cash. It was in recognition of this fact that when ITV was set up in the 1950s Parliament had created the so-called 'listed events' provision, which ensured that no broadcaster could buy exclusive access to ten of the top sporting events (soccer's World Cup, the FA Cup Final and the Scottish Cup Final, Wimbledon, the Olympics, domestic test matches, the Grand National and the Derby, the Boat Race, and the Commonwealth Games, when held in Britain). The 1990 Broadcasting Act (which enacted the provisions of the 1989 White Paper) abolished the provision, allowing subscription-based satellite television to buy exclusive rights to any event. The only remaining proscription was that they could not be shown as 'pay-per-view' events.

When it comes to purchasing the right to broadcast major sporting events a company which charges viewers a monthly fee for a premium service will usually be able to outbid a network whose funding base is licence fees or advertising. From the very beginning, just three weeks after its launch in February 1989, Murdoch's Sky Television had made its intentions clear by scooping ITV for Frank Bruno's heavyweight title fight with Mike Tyson. A year later, Sky brought ball-by-ball coverage of the winter's test series between West Indies and England to the UK for first time. Two years after that, the merged BSkyB bought exclusive rights to the cricket World Cup in Australia, and refused until the very last match to allow the BBC even a highlights package. Then, in the same year, came the opportunity to demonstrate beyond doubt that satellite was going to be a formidable rival in British television sport. BSkyB's deal with soccer's Premier League illustrated perfectly the predicament of a public service broadcaster in the age of satellite television.

Until 1988 ITV and BBC had shared coverage of British soccer. Their cooperation had often frustrated the Football League, which had been convinced that it was the victim of a covert cartel, but there was little it could do. In 1988, however, there was a real contest. BSB (as it then still was) was beginning to plan its programme schedules, and was looking for a major coup to publicise its arrival on the broadcasting scene. It made what was then an extraordinary offer: £200 million to secure rights to First Division soccer for the next ten years. The BBC was unable to match that sort of money, but ITV was now worried enough to take immediate action. Its counter-bid of £44 million over four years was, because of the shorter time-span, worth more in real terms than BSB's offer. The scale of the deal astonished observers, but it was a strategic rather than a commercial decision. It had been orchestrated by Greg Dyke, John Birt's successor as Director of Programmes for London Weekend Television, in order to – in his words – 'strangle the satellite threat at birth'.

It had not quite succeeded in this, but it had embarrassed the BBC. For the first time in the history of televised soccer, the BBC was unable to transmit a single excerpt from the main domestic competition of Britain's national sport. There was no *Match of the Day*, the programme which had become a Saturday night institution. There was no *Football Focus*, the weekly programme which previewed the weekend's action with clips from previous matches. And the annual climax of the year's television sports calendar, *Sports Personality of the Year*, had to pass swiftly and embarrassingly over the year's soccer highlights because there were no pictures to match the stories. It left a gaping hole, at the very moment that the political threat to the BBC was reaching its peak. Just to rub salt in the wound, the 1988–9 Championship was the closest in the League's history. The two front-runners, Liverpool and Arsenal, met at Anfield in the last game of the season, and the championship was decided by an improbable Arsenal goal two minutes into injury time – live and exclusive on ITV, in front of twelve million viewers. For how much longer could the BBC claim to be the home of British sport?

When ITV's four-year contract expired in 1992 the stakes were even higher. BSkyB was financially stronger, but had not made the real breakthrough into British homes that had been widely predicted. What it needed was an exclusive deal to cover one of the country's most popular sports, in order to expand the sale of satellite dishes and turn an advertising-funded sports channel into a more lucrative subscription service. ITV had been averaging around eight million viewers for its live coverage. BSkyB could not hope to emulate that, but a soccer deal was sure to sell enough dishes and subscriptions to make a major investment worthwhile.

The stakes were just as high for ITV. Their apparently crazy £44 million investment had proved to be a bargain over the four years. Even unattractive matches between middling teams were attracting audiences of more than five million. Their lowest ratings in the final season had been 6.4 million, and a match featuring two of the big five (Arsenal, Manchester United, Liverpool, Everton, Spurs) could usually guarantee nine to ten million viewers. It was the perfect vehicle for a channel with a carefully planned and heavily promoted 'live and exclusive' sports policy, ITV's increasingly effective answer to fifty years of BBC sporting dominance. In a period of massive upheaval for commercial television, soccer had enormous strategic importance; and ITV had an ace in its hand. Its coverage was available to 22 million households, which guaranteed universal exposure for the sport and for the clubs' sponsorship deals. An exclusive deal with BSkyB, in contrast, would minimise television exposure and prejudice sponsorship revenue. In April 1992, the executive director of ITV football, Trevor East, bid £187 million to continue exclusive coverage for four more years. BSkyB countered with an offer worth around £200m a year.

Despite the limited number of homes with satellite receivers, a number of factors were now working in favour of BSkyB. First, the structure of football had changed and the top clubs (the former First Division of the Football League) had set up a new Premier League under the auspices of the Football Association; the new 'Super League' could do its own deals without having to include smaller, less glamorous clubs from lower divisions in the negotiations. Second, a number of the Premier clubs who were just below the top flight had become disillusioned by ITV's undue emphasis on the Liverpools, Arsenals, and Manchester Uniteds. These were the big draws, and earned the lion's share of TV revenue. But clubs like Wimbledon and Coventry felt increasingly marginalised, and were hoping for a fairer share of the television pay-out. By definition these clubs, rather than the top five, formed a majority in the new League. Third, one of the big five was Tottenham Hotspur, whose Chairman was Alan Sugar. Sugar was also Chairman and Chief Executive of Amstrad, the principal supplier of satellite dishes for BSkyB's service. A boost for satellite dish sales would be good news for Amstrad. Finally, BSkyB had a further advantage which had not been available to BSB in 1988. Its largest shareholder, Rupert Murdoch, could (and did) guarantee the wholesale support of his five national newspapers in promoting the new Premier League and its satellite television coverage. It would have been hard to think of a more blatantly anti-competitive use of cross-promotion, but the threat posed to such practices by the Sadler Inquiry was long gone.

This was the game in which the BBC suddenly became a key player. In an auction of this ferocity, it could not even consider competing, but it had the one commodity which BSkyB craved: universal coverage. While ITV considered its offer, BBC's Managing Director of Television, Will Wyatt was in discussions with Sky's Chief Executive, Sam Chisholm. A week before the Premier League chairmen were due to make the decision (on 18 May 1992) the Corporation concluded a deal with BSkyB to put £4.5m a year into the pot in exchange for match highlights. For less than £25 million over five years, it could not only relaunch the much-mourned *Match of the Day* on Saturday nights, but could over the course of a season bring to its viewers every single goal scored in the new Premier League.

The decision day was one of high drama. On the basis of the BBC deal, BSkyB was offering a package of £270 million over five years for sixty live games a year, with weekly highlights on the BBC. At 8.15 in the morning, ITV's Trevor East met the FA's Chief Executive, Rick Parry, to hand him ITV's revised offer: £262 million for just thirty live games per season, on the grounds that the big clubs did not want to risk over-exposure. Ninety minutes later, in the lobby of the Royal Lancaster Hotel where the club chairmen were about to meet, East spotted an agitated Alan Sugar on the phone to Sam Chisholm of BSkyB. According to East, Sugar ended the conversation with the angry words, 'Blow them out of the water.' Minutes later, Chisholm was on the phone to Parry with a revised offer of £304 million. Sugar's real moment of influence came two hours later, when Sir John Quinton, Chairman of the Premier League, called for a vote from the 22 club chairmen. It required a two-thirds majority to award the contract. With two clubs abstaining, fourteen had to vote in favour. Exactly fourteen did so, including, alone among the big clubs, Alan Sugar of Spurs. BSkyB had won, Amstrad shares rose, and as a result Sugar was – briefly – £7 million richer.

After the deal was concluded Parry was reported as saying, 'The BBC's position was critical because there is no way I would have recommended a satellite-only bid.' In the immediate aftermath, the BBC faced intense criticism for having made a 'pact with the devil'. Some accused it of, in effect, paying Danegeld by helping BSkyB to achieve a deal which would eventually erode the BBC's audience and with it any rationale for a licence fee. Dyke said publicly that it would have been possible to work out a joint deal between ITV and the BBC, although many in the Corporation were suspicious of him – hypothetical deals were easy with hindsight. Michael Grade, a lifelong football fan, was scathing about both the BBC and the Premier League. The League, he argued, had not understood the importance of keeping the national game in front of the whole nation, while the BBC had failed to realise the strength of its negotiating position. It should have demanded payment from Sky rather than vice-versa.

The BBC's position was not helped by speculation about conversations at the highest level – between Rupert Murdoch and his former sidekick Marmaduke Hussey. Rumours circulated about Hussey calling Murdoch on his car-phone, pledging the BBC's support for the satellite deal. A phone call *was* made from Hussey's car, after a lunch at the Savoy at which Hussey and Checkland had reassured Andrew Knight of News International that the BBC was not pulling out of the deal (contrary to rumours being put around by ITV). On the way back to the BBC afterwards, Checkland used Hussey's car-phone to call John Quinton and tell him the same thing.

It was a landmark decision for the BBC. On the one hand, it could rightly claim to be fulfilling its public service duties by bringing the best of British soccer – albeit recorded – to the screens of licence payers at a fraction of the going rate. In its own defence, it added another public service argument: that by doing this deal on League coverage it had also secured for itself continued live coverage of the tournament whose value and excitement was even more integral to the game than the League Championship – the FA Cup.

On the other hand, the BBC had deliberately colluded in a strategy which would deprive non-satellite viewers of any live League soccer for the first time in nearly ten years. Moreover, it gave succour to a competitive enterprise which was the antithesis of public service broadcasting, and was owned by the man who just two and half years earlier had condemned the very existence of the BBC. The argument went to the heart of a public service broadcaster's role in a programming area now exposed to the full force of the free-market gale. Checkland remains convinced that it was the right thing to do.

> You have to decide how the BBC, with finite resources and ever esca-
> lating costs, can keep in major sport if, as I do, you believe that major
> sport is one of the crucial things in public service broadcasting, and
> therefore we had to say, 'How can we best achieve that?' The way to
> achieve it was to come to some sensible arrangement with the new tech-
> nologies whereby they would take part of the exposure, leaving us the
> major events.

It was, in other words, a compromise in the same spirit as BBC compromises from its earliest days. As with the introduction of commercial television in 1955, when the BBC shifted its programme strategy to compete and hold on to audiences, so with the introduction of satellite television the BBC had to adapt to the times. There was an early recognition that sport was too expensive a commodity for an organisation on fixed public funding to be able to match its rivals' bids with rights fees. It could offer benefits to tempt sports bodies: covert sponsorship on a non-commercial channel; genuine concern for the integrity and development of the sport; promotion and coverage across two channels; association with the BBC's name and reputation. But it could no longer afford to offer cash. Its history and its pride in a long-standing sporting heritage determined which way the strategy would go.

New satellite channels were also causing problems for the BBC in other parts of the world. Its radio World Service was run by a separate directorate from its own building in the centre of London, and funded by a direct grant from the Foreign and Commonwealth Office rather than from the licence fee. It was internationally acknowledged as the best of its kind. Indeed, much of the BBC's international reputation rested (and still rests) on the quality of the news and features which the World Service transmits to almost every corner of the globe, a reputation initially earned during the Second World War and reinforced many times since. But although the number of radio sets in the world continues to grow, the number of television sets is growing faster, especially among opinion-formers in the poorer parts of the world. The BBC saw them turning away from World Service radio to Ted Turner's Atlanta-based Cable News Network TV station. It began to explore ways of launching a World Service Television service.

Initial inquiries to the Foreign Office about an additional grant to launch the service were rebuffed. Michael Checkland announced at the 1990 *Financial Times* Cable and Satellite conference that the television service would go ahead with or without the backing of the government, telling delegates, 'It is inconceivable that the World Service will not be on television.' In July that year the Board of Governors authorised the merchant bankers J. Henry Schroeder Wagg to raise £10 million through private investors to fund the venture. The following year, during MIPCOM-TV, the international television fair in Cannes, World Service Television was launched.

It was based in Television Centre (although some World Service radio staff were attached to the project) and consisted mostly of news material which was being filed for domestic bulletins, and additional programmes for which the BBC held the necessary international rights. Although the BBC was responsible for editorial and production matters, distribution was a more expensive business which it wanted to contract out. Accordingly, agreements were signed with Star Television, a satellite service in Hong Kong which broadcast to much of Asia, as well as with distributors in Africa and in Canada. But while the concept of World Service Television made sense as a means of capitalising on the BBC's international reputation, the practice raised a number of operational and ethical difficulties.

One problem was cost. Whereas World Service radio costs less than £3,000 per hour to produce, the BBC's domestic television news and news-related programmes cost upwards of £50,000 per hour. At those prices, World Service Television would be a non-starter, and a helping hand was needed. It came in the form of a funding convention borrowed from the Treasury approach to World Service radio, under which WSTV was charged only for those costs which would not be incurred if it did not exist. At a time when the BBC was heading towards the 'total costing' system of Producer Choice, this seemed inconsistent, but it was a measure of the Corporation's desperation to get World Service Television off the ground. The result was a hidden subsidy from the licence fees of domestic viewers (which was paying for most of the coverage) to the overseas viewers of WSTV.

A second hidden subsidy from the licence payers came by way of an internal reorganisation that, on the face of it, was purely administrative. World Service Television took over from Enterprises the responsibility of running BBC Relay, which marketed BBC-1 and 2 to cable television systems in Europe. As a result it inherited an income stream worth a couple of million pounds a year, which was now reinvested in World Service Television. As the Task Force on the BBC's International Role observed, this sum had previously gone to Enterprises which had ploughed it back into domestic programme production.

Apart from this financial sleight of hand, there was cause for more fundamental fears about this new hybrid. Historically, the World Service has been one of those unusual British compromises, funded by the Foreign Office, and taking direction from the Foreign Office in the matter of how many hours it broadcasts to which countries in what languages, yet still retaining its reputation for impartiality and the quality of its content. It was (and remains) an outstanding example of an institution whose ethos and internal culture are so strong that issues of funding and control become secondary. Not surprisingly, some producers who had spent their working lives in World Service radio were aghast at the prospect of World Service Television living off the reputation they had fostered. An internal World Service discussion note put it tersely:

> World Service TV is aggressively commercial – it has to be: it has no public funds. It will sell where and how it can. It must adapt itself to the marketplace. It can't be compatible with publicly funded World Service radio. It has to be almost completely market-led whereas radio has the luxury of being *value-led* [their emphasis].

They feared that, rather than the BBC's latest service benefiting from the BBC's worldwide reputation, it might devalue it instead.

The pessimists did not have long to wait. During late 1992 and early 1993, World Service Television ran an on-screen promotion for the channel which depicted world leaders and world events, including footage of the Gulf War, Bosnia, and the shootings in Tiananmen Square. On a visit to Hong Kong, Marmaduke Hussey dined with the Li family, who owned Star TV (which broadcast World Service TV to Asia) and also had massive business interests in mainland China as well as in Hong Kong. They impressed on Hussey that Star TV's Tiananmen footage was irritating the Chinese government, and that it would be helpful if World Service Television stopped showing it. On

Hussey's return, word went down to pull the promo. Despite increasing pressure from management, an outraged staff reacted strongly against such blatant self-censorship. The promo stayed.

World Service Television was the most risky of the BBC's satellite television ventures, but it was not the only one. At home, for the first time, BBC Enterprises took a stake in a commercial service, UK Gold, which was beamed from the Astra satellite into UK homes. It was a joint venture with Thames Television and the American cable companies TCI and Cox Cable. The BBC's contribution was access to those parts of its programming library which it thought had no further value for BBC-1 and 2: re-runs of *EastEnders* and *The Brothers*, *The Onedin Line*, *Are You Being Served?*, *Shoestring*, *The Goodies*, and *Dr Who*. When the other three parties later combined to launch a second satellite channel, UK Living, the BBC did a deal which brought in money for programmes which previously had no shelf-life. For the first time, it could sell recut versions of topical programmes such as *Kilroy*, whose value to the Corporation vanished with the closing credits, but which still had some interest for specialist satellite channels.

But it was the deals with Sky which continued to illustrate the dilemma of cooperation versus competition. At the end of 1992, as the ITV breakfast station TV-AM went off the air after losing its licence, their star interviewer David Frost announced that he was taking his prestigious weekend slot *Frost on Sunday* to – jointly – both the BBC and Sky News. BBC-1 would show it first, and BSkyB would re-transmit it immediately afterwards. The announcement confused those who had taken at face value statements in the BBC's annual report that the Corporation would not provide programmes which were available elsewhere; the Frost deal, predicated on just such availability, hardly seemed consistent.

And the BBC's relationship with BSkyB took an even more intimate turn when David Elstein, Sky's Director of Programmes, announced that the satellite broadcaster was giving the BBC a window to show episodes of an American comedy, *Seinfeld*, after a disappointing first run on Sky One. Even multi-channel viewers spend most of their time watching the terrestrial networks, where they are more likely to happen on programmes they had not intended to watch. A run for the series on BBC-2 would create the profile and visibility the programme needed in order to build an audience for subsequent showing on Sky One.

Just as in its sports deal, therefore, BSkyB needed access to the BBC's 22 million viewing households. And the BBC needed all the help it could muster to compensate for its increasingly vulnerable position in the new competitive broadcasting world. But for the BBC, working with Sky – especially on the football deal – brought an immeasurable bonus. As one highly placed broadcasting executive put it, 'A cynic would say that they'd bought off the Murdoch press.' After a decade of constant and virulent attacks, one of the

BBC's most aggressive opponents retired from the fray almost as soon as the cooperative deals were announced. The constant barrage of hostile stories, with their highly destabilising effect on the Corporation, gradually faded. At least for the time being, the Murdoch tanks were rolling off BBC lawns. And all it had cost the Corporation was a relatively small amount of money for some programming it wanted anyway but could not otherwise afford. From inside the corral it must have looked the perfect bargain.

CHAPTER TEN
THE ODD COUPLE

In covering the BBC's relations with BSkyB through to the apparent truce in 1992, we have leaped ahead of our main story. In 1990, the antagonism of the Murdoch papers was still as strong as ever, and the satellite TV front was just one of several on which skirmishing was active. In legislative terms, as the 1990 Broadcasting Act made its way onto the statute book, it was ITV, rather than the BBC, which was in the frontline. But the BBC were given frequent reminders that they were still on the government's agenda. By the beginning of 1990, the government was nearly three years into its term of office, the point at which Westminster and Fleet Street speculation turns to the next election. No government chooses to run the full five-year term, and both Thatcher's previous administrations had run only four before she felt confident enough of re-election to go to the country. It was possible, then, that an election was only a year away and any 'unfriendly' media would need reminding of their obligations.

There was a widespread perception that, by now, the BBC had become less unfriendly and that anything which might seriously trouble the Conservative Party was being checked, rechecked and edited to the point of banality. At least, that was the prevalent view about television, where the restructuring had had the greatest impact. But radio was different. Although radio was quite definitely an area in which the News and Current Affairs Directorate's writ ran, it was a more immediate and more fluid medium. It had therefore escaped the deadening consequences of painstaking scrutiny and a rigidly applied mission-to-explain philosophy. John Birt's background was exclusively in television, and it was television which was the root of the 'flawed' journalism he had come to remedy. Radio simply got on with its job and was delighted to escape the Deputy Director General's attentions.

But radio was influential. The four national radio networks, soon to be increased to five, commanded a third of all BBC expenditure. Additional money was available for the 39 local and regional radio stations. More importantly, over half of all radio listening in the UK went to the BBC, with the pop music station Radio 1 easily the dominant station in Britain. This was a bone of contention for the local commercial stations, which since 1973 had been struggling to make a living, and the popularity of Radio 1 was often cited by those who wanted parts of the BBC privatised. But Radio 4, home of most of the serious news and current affairs, had a guaranteed place in the sun. Even the most fervent privatisers accepted that a station wholly devoted to speech, including original drama and comedy, could never survive in the marketplace. Radio 4 was the touchstone of public service broadcasting.

Even more significantly, it was Radio 4 – much more than current affairs television – which was the main point of contact between the BBC and so-called 'opinion formers' – the people whose busy and influential lives left little time for the couch-potato life, but who relied on radio more than anything else to keep them informed of unfolding national and international stories. Virtually every Member of Parliament would at some point during the day tune in to Radio 4. And for most of them – including the Prime Minister – that point was invariably the breakfast-time *Today* programme.

A maximum of six million listeners tuned in to the programme at some point between 6.30 and 9.00 a.m. Because of the people it reached, and because it always dealt with the immediate political issues of the day, it carried enormous weight. If a Secretary of State or a member of the shadow cabinet wanted to explain, or launch, or attack a new policy, the *Today* programme was the ideal forum. Requests to appear were rarely turned down, and it staged some of the most enthralling political debates. The presenters were experienced BBC journalists who did not shrink from robust and persistent interrogations of evasive politicians. As the techniques for evasion and resistance became more sophisticated, so political interviewers in general were becoming even more insistent. This was particularly true on *Today*.

This did not always go down well with Conservative politicians. A daily news and analysis programme cannot accommodate the subtle arguments about contextualisation which had swept through television; it responds to events. *Today*'s *raison d'être* as a daily political programme is the face-to-face interview which pits questioning reporter against accountable politician on matters of immediate public interest. At its best, it is precisely the kind of public forum which helps listeners make up their own minds about current political issues, and thereby contributes to the democratic process. Since initiatives which are going to have real economic and social consequences are, by definition, taken by the party in government it is that party which (if journalists are doing their job properly) is challenged for explanations. But the longer the Conservatives were in power, the more it seemed to them that they, and they alone, were on the receiving end of daily, hostile interrogation.

By January 1990, there was even more reason for the government to feel embattled. The boom years had subsided into the beginnings of an economic downturn which few had anticipated. There was universal hostility to the new poll tax, which Margaret Thatcher had insisted on implementing against the advice of most of her cabinet. She herself was beginning to appear more obdurate and manic than ever, and was facing growing disquiet in her own party over Europe. The net effect was an unpopularity which the Conservatives had not experienced since the worst pre-Falkland days, and increasing sensitivity about how and by whom ministers were questioned. On the right of the party, there was a growing clamour against the insidious anti-Conservative bias which MPs were convinced ran through the *Today* programme.

But help was at hand. On 3 February 1990, the *Daily Express* headlined the results of an inquiry it had commissioned from the 'Media Monitoring Unit' on political impartiality in the *Today* programme. This authoritative-sounding body had recorded the output of *Today* for two weeks from 8 to 20 January, and delivered a withering indictment of the programme's 'serious failure to meet acceptable standards of impartiality'. Of the twelve reports examined in detail, it concluded that eleven had 'attacked government policy without the pro-government arguments being adequately aired' and that 'political pressure groups and organisations critical of government policy found a ready platform'. These 'subversive' pressure groups included the homeless charity Shelter, the government-funded Family Policy Studies Centre, the Salvation Army and the right-wing Institute of Economic Affairs.

It was clear to any serious reader that this was a bogus piece of research, comprising one page of 'definitions of balance and bias' followed by 28 pages of transcript and highly subjective analysis. But the impact was enormous; the findings were widely reported and provoked several articles and letters on the theme of the BBC's anti-government stance. In *The Times* the right-wing Conservative peer Woodrow Wyatt expounded his long-held view that 'the *Today* programme provides a steady drip-drip diet of anti-government propaganda'. He called in particular for the removal of *Today*'s long-standing presenter Brian Redhead, whom the right always suspected of harbouring socialist leanings and whose political standing, said Wyatt, was 'easily deduced'. (In fact, Redhead had voted during his career for all three political parties and once described himself as 'economically conservative and socially liberal'.) The *Express* itself used this as the occasion for another scathing editorial which reached the menacing conclusion that 'The Government should take appropriate action.'

Shortly afterwards, the Media Monitoring Unit was exposed by *The Independent on Sunday* as a shady one-man, one-machine operation administered from a rented desk in west London. Its source of funding was unclear, but its links to the right-wing were transparent. The director, Simon Clark, had been recruited in 1985 by Julian Lewis, who had made a name for himself through his relentless pursuit of CND and who had connections with a number of right-wing groups. Clark himself had made no secret of the fact that his operation was itself no more than a pressure group, and his first report in 1986 had left readers in no doubt about its aims: 'To help relieve the pressure which is being applied to the BBC and IBA by left-wing groups whose aim is to push broadcasting further into line with their political perspectives.' Like the Unit's first report (which used equally spurious 'research' to attack television current affairs), this latest offering was presented as evidence of systematic bias.

Again, it was no more than propaganda masquerading as research.

It was, however, a masterly stroke of propaganda. No-one was going to listen to the unknown Simon Clark's opinions about bias on the *Today*
programme, but when they were dressed up as 'findings' they found a responsive audience. The report provided the perfect pretext for the likes of Norman
Tebbit to blame broadcasters rather than government policies for his party's
unpopularity. Speaking at an Oxford college debate two weeks later, Tebbit let
his hair down: 'The word "Conservative" is now used by the BBC as a port-
manteau word of abuse for anyone whose political views differ from the
insufferable, smug, sanctimonious, naive, guilt-ridden, wet, pink orthodoxy of
that sunset home of third-rate minds of that third-rate decade the 60s.' Tebbit,
too, was becoming a little manic in his old age.

Two days before Tebbit's tirade, another right-wing organisation fixed its
attention on the BBC. This time it was the turn of the Centre for Policy
Studies, a Thatcherite think-tank with genuine credibility whose ideas had
been enormously influential throughout the 80s. The CPS announced that it
would be preparing a report to 'explore the relationship of the BBC to the rest
of television' and to examine ideas for privatisation and possible funding alternatives to the licence fee. Although it had not been commissioned by the
government, the Centre stressed that its decision to conduct an inquiry into the
BBC's future followed a meeting with the new Home Secretary, David
Waddington. The following day, the *Evening Standard* used this as yet another opportunity to call for the licence fee to be scrapped. The BBC, it said, had
given up its serious purpose and through sales of books, magazines and videos
was already adopting a commercial role: 'It is time to bring to an end the
nationalised capitalism of the BBC by abolishing the licence fee altogether.'
Election fever was mounting; and, the Broadcasting Bill notwithstanding, the
heat was again being turned onto the BBC.

The last three months of 1990 were an extraordinary period for British politics and British broadcasting. The atmosphere was febrile, with the
Conservative government facing sustained hostility as the economy weak-
ened, and rumours emerging of furious rows within the cabinet. Buoyed by
what he saw as mounting evidence of attempted subversion by broadcasters,
Lord Wyatt had taken the opportunity of the Broadcasting Bill's passage
through the House of Lords to insert a new statutory requirement for balance
and impartiality. It was a draconian amendment which would have obliged all
programmes to follow an 'on the one hand, on the other hand' formula and
would have eradicated the kind of investigative journalism at which British
broadcasting (and particularly ITV current affairs) had excelled. It had
prompted the unanimous opposition of journalists, regulators and opposition;
even some back-bench Conservatives were quietly uneasy. But it was also
known to have the personal backing of the Prime Minister.

This was the background against which *Panorama* had embarked upon a programme on the funding of the Conservative Party to coincide with the Conservative conference. Given the political and legislative context, it was a courageous – some might even say foolhardy – decision in the best traditions of *Panorama*'s independence, and demonstrated that its producers were still prepared to tackle potentially explosive issues. The programme traced the way in which secret donations were channelled to the Tory Party via small private companies and was trying to find evidence of personal rewards being promised in return for large donations. There was one problem: the only person it could find to make public allegations on those lines was Ernest Saunders – who had just been convicted of theft, false accounting and conspiracy in connection with the takeover of the Distiller's Company by his own firm, Guinness. At the best of times, it would not be good journalistic practice to feature unsubstantiated claims from a man who had been sent to jail for – in the words of the trial judge – 'dishonesty on a massive scale'. Given the delicacy of the moment, there were those who thought it positively reckless. Once again, John Birt stepped in to ban the interview from being shown and other cuts and qualifications were ordered during the course of a lengthy editorial meeting. The programme was broadcast on the appointed date, but appeared insubstantial.

Birt's intervention provoked a by-now-familiar response in Television Centre, where the incident was seen as another capitulation to government pressure, another abject surrender by the BBC to the forces of Thatcherism. But this case was more complex, and a perfect example of the dilemmas facing political television in a Thatcherite world. No-one doubted that persistent government pressure had made the upper echelons of the BBC more sensitive to programmes which attacked the government. But one of the reforms introduced by the Birt regime in order to remedy the perceived problems of the Milne era was a more rigorous checking process intended to ensure that particularly sensitive programmes abided by the strictest standards of accuracy. In other words, part of what Birt's changes were about was raising the threshold for what constituted acceptable evidence in investigative journalism. The corollary, in theory, was that any programme which jumped the new journalistic hurdles could be transmitted without fear. In practice, two questions remained unresolved: to what extent were the new criteria so detailed and unrealistic as to impair good journalism? And to what extent were they selectively applied according to an agenda laid down by Downing Street? There was growing concern that the BBC was subjecting itself to a form of self-censorship which was being applied – almost exclusively – to damaging revelations about the Conservative government.

In this case, Birt was not alone in seeing flaws to *Who Pays for the Party?* Two recent recruits to *Panorama*, both of whom would, in the future, be highly critical of more obviously craven decisions, thought the programme weak. According to one, 'It was rightly emasculated by the referral process because in my view it didn't stand up to having proved what they were trying to prove.' Birt's cause was not helped when the Conservative Party's Director of Communications, Brendan Bruce, boasted over a subsequent lunch that he had nobbled that particular *Panorama*. But Bruce had his own detractors at Conservative headquarters, and party spin-doctors are not averse to exaggerating their prowess – particularly when they are already facing internal criticism. Bruce was almost certainly pushing at an open door: circumstantial evidence from a single tainted source is not the basis on which to make serious allegations against a government which is still debating an important statutory constraint on broadcast journalism. It was not a stupid decision. But Birt was already a prisoner of his own reputation and future events would add grist to his accusers' mill.

A month later, on 1 November, the Broadcasting Act, which was finally to unravel the carefully structured fabric of British commercial television, received the royal assent. Even the Prime Minister herself was later – uniquely – to apologise for one of its consequences when the breakfast TV company TV-AM lost its franchise. It was a supreme irony that on that very day, at 6.30 pm, the Foreign Secretary Sir Geoffrey Howe initiated the events that led directly to Thatcher's overthrow 21 days later. Howe told Thatcher he was resigning because he could no longer support her isolationist stand on Europe. Twelve days later he delivered one of the most devastating resignation speeches ever heard in the Commons. It provoked a leadership contest from which Margaret Thatcher was eventually forced to withdraw. On 28 November, after eleven and a half years in power, she left Downing Street for good. Britain – and the Conservative Party – welcomed the more consensual tones of the new Prime Minister, John Major.

The first indication of a more emollient attitude in Downing Street came early in 1991. Major was facing a baptism of fire, having inherited the consequences of Iraq's invasion of Kuwait in August 1990. As the deadline passed for Saddam Hussein to withdraw, the allied forces launched an offensive to remove him and Britain was once again involved in a war which was certain to cost lives. Technology had advanced far enough since the Falklands war of 1982 for portable satellites to provide a constant barrage of pictures and reports direct from the Gulf, and the pressure, yet again, was on the broadcasters to support 'our boys'. On 17 January, with the war being played out in vivid detail on television screens throughout Britain, ex-minister Patrick Nicholls asked the Prime Minister to condemn the BBC for instructing reporters to say 'British troops' rather than 'our troops'. 'It is depressing', he thundered, 'that – even in a conflict of this sort – the BBC should be unable to distinguish between good and evil.' It was precisely the sort of question that would, in earlier years, have evoked an equally thunderous denunciation from Margaret Thatcher. But Major's reply confirmed that things were changing:

I believe that what the BBC is doing, in what has already been some remarkable reporting, is trying to keep proper balance ... precisely because so much of the world listens to the BBC, and because it is important to this country that they continue to do so.

It was almost possible to hear the sigh of relief from Broadcasting House.

In retrospect, it might appear that, after more than a decade in power, Mrs Thatcher had left the BBC relatively unscathed. There was no question that her aggressive style allowed plenty of latitude for sustained BBC-bashing from her political colleagues and media friends, and that this in turn made its mark on BBC current affairs. She was proud of her reputation as a 'conviction politician' who would not shrink from the consequences of the radical ideas dreamed up by her favourite think-tanks; and the familiar refrain, when some of those policies created waves of unpopularity, was that the media were to blame for their distortion and lack of clear explanation. Her period in office coincided with a growing sense that the broadcast media were particularly powerful instruments of propaganda, and therefore required subtle techniques of manipulation – photo-opportunities, sound-bites and spin-doctors became part of the political vocabulary. Added leverage could be gained by behind-the-scenes influence. Hugo Young, in his asssessment of the Thatcher years, records how in the run-up to the 1987 election her top television strategist gave him the rundown on the three main TV news providers: ITN was considered 'sound'; Channel 4 was unsound, but attracted too few viewers to matter; but the BBC was still a problem. By the time she went, a combination of her own Rottweiler approach and the constant battering of her supporters had ensured that the BBC was less of a problem.

But politics and current affairs are only a part of the BBC's activities, and much of its output remained essentially untouched. Sport, situation comedy, children's programmes, wildlife, costume drama, arts programmes, chat shows, were all featured with varying degrees of success or failure which had nothing to do with politics or the Prime Minister. Above all, when its chief antagonist was felled, the BBC was still there with its archetypally non-Thatcherite licence fee intact. True, some journalistic credibility had been sacrificed and some exceptionally talented people had been lost; but by the end of 1990 it was possible to say that the BBC had survived the worst and that the Checkland strategy had worked. John Major, it seemed, was a more congenial figure whose election signalled a return to a more consensual form of politics. He even liked the BBC.

But the truth was that Thatcher had left a powerful long-term legacy whose impact upon the BBC would go much further than television current affairs. First, there was a new management led by a full-time Chairman whom Thatcher had personally approved. Second, she had bequeathed a language and ethos which was gradually seeping into every crevice of the new BBC. The talk of markets, efficiency, cuts, product, niches, and enterprise was all more consonant with a Thatcherite view of the world than the old-style public service language of the early 80s and before. Many felt uncomfortable with the new vocabulary and what it represented, but justified it on the grounds that it amounted to no more than rhetoric, a superficial gloss designed for public consumption. In time, however, that rhetoric would insidiously work upon the institution, transforming its internal working practices and culture. This was to be the real influence of Thatcher on the BBC: as the political threat diminished, the new threat to the Corporation's survival turned out to come from within.

The crux of the matter was that Broadcasting House itself had become captive to government emissaries. In the course of nearly twelve years in office, Margaret Thatcher and her successive Home Secretaries had ensured that the governing board was packed with sympathisers. Some were old-style paternalists, others embraced that radical brand of Conservatism which had dominated Britain in the 80s and applauded the vocabulary of free markets, deregulation, consumer sovereignty, and 'downsizing'. Alasdair Milne had complained of an unswervingly right-wing board, but even in the mid-80s there were governors who would not automatically embrace every new mantra of organisational change. By the beginning of the 90s, the Board, like other public bodies throughout the land, was dominated not just by Conservative sympathisers but by those who spoke the language of the new right. There were some debates and dissension around the boardroom table, but they all took place within a forum virtually untouched by left-of-centre thinking.

Moreover, an election was imminent. The Gulf War's successful and highly visible conclusion had boosted the popularity of almost every Western leader involved, but the two main Western protagonists were also the main beneficiaries: President George Bush's poll ratings were so high in America that his re-election in 1992 was seen as almost a formality and John Major, too, was basking in reflected glory and under pressure from some quarters to cut and run to the electorate before the impact of a worsening economy began to erode his appeal. He declined, and by the spring of 1991 Britain was clearly heading for a recession every bit as damaging as that ten years earlier. The difference this time was that the party responsible had to call an election before June 1992. No Prime Minister likes to go to the wire, and an autumn election was on the cards – an election the government now looked likely to lose.

In April 1991, the Conservative Party had the perfect opportunity to ensure that, within the BBC, its influence would endure, whatever its electoral fate: Marmaduke Hussey's period as Chairman and Joel Barnett's period as Vice-Chairman were coming to an end. John Major may have renounced Thatcher's hounding tactics, but he was not about to surrender such easy political advantage. Hussey and Barnett had lunched both Home Secretary Kenneth Baker and his Permanent Secretary, Clive Whitmore, no doubt offering some assurances about their plans for continued reforms. Advertising, Baker's pet solution for the BBC, was mentioned. A few weeks later, on 16 April 1991, Baker announced that Hussey had been appointed for a further five years and Barnett for a further two. It was the first time in the BBC's history that a Chairman was given a second term of office.

Ten years earlier, this would not have been quite so significant. Although the Chairman and his board, constitutionally speaking, *were* the BBC, they had not, by tradition, involved themselves in the day-to-day resource and programme planning operations. Even those chairmen, like Charles Hill, whose appointments were explicitly 'political' had continued to see their role as essentially non-executive.

All that had changed dramatically with Hussey's appointment in 1986. As a result of the string of confrontations with government which culminated in *Real Lives*, Hussey had inherited a virtual breakdown in communication between the two boards, and a profound sense of a vacuum at the top. Governors were convinced that any half-way decent manager would have prevented some of the bungling, while managers were convinced that a conspiratorial right-wing board was constantly trying to encroach on management territory. Hussey was determined to demonstrate not just leadership but conciliation, and one of his very first moves was enormously symbolic. Traditionally, when both boards met together, the members of each would sit facing each other on either side of the long boardroom table in Broadcasting House. This epitomised to Hussey the confrontational relationship which had preceded him and which he wanted to change. At his first meeting as Chairman, he insisted that there should be no such divisions around the table and that the members of both boards should be intermingled. It was a small sign to signal a new spirit of mutual trust and cooperation.

But it also had a deeper symbolism. The practice of keeping the two boards separate may have come to represent hostility and suspicion, but its origins were in a very clear distinction between their functions. They sat separately because they were separate bodies: one whose duty was to run the Corporation on a daily basis, including making and implementing strategic decisions on programming; the other whose duty, historically, was to act as 'trustees' of the people, to ensure that the BBC was being run in the public interest and to maintain a broad oversight. The Board of Governors, by tradition, took no part in 'hands-on' management decisions. Whether Hussey realised it or not, there was therefore a greater significance to the rearrangement of places than simply healing old wounds; it signified a subtle blurring of the constitutional difference between governors and management. The new *glasnost*, in which everyone would participate as equals around the table, featured a much more active and prominent role for the Chairman and his deputy.

From that moment on, Hussey and Barnett became virtually permanent fixtures at Broadcasting House. Barnett had retained his office and chauffeur-driven car, and neither man had an onerous full-time job outside the BBC. For the next five years both became immersed in its daily running.

To insiders, it was an unlikely but fascinating combination. As one put it, 'This tall, six-foot-four-inch former guards officer married to the Queen's favourite lady in waiting, and this little Jewish accountant from Manchester, make a very odd pair.' While social opposites, they formed an alliance based on mutual support and mutual convenience:

> They need each other. Joel needs Dukie because Joel gets an office and driver and can use the BBC. Dukie needs him because Joel provides a political sophistication which Dukie doesn't have. For all the criticism of him, he is liked by both sides at Westminster. Tories find him acceptable.

Most important of all, it was an alliance which enabled them to dominate their fellow governors: 'Somehow they get on and manoeuvre the Board of Governors terribly well.' Slowly, they began to manoeuvre them into a greater involvement in decision-making.

The governors' new, more active, role was evident on several fronts. There were the libel cases – 'Every single serious action brought against the BBC was brought up at the governors' meeting . . . there was a list at each meeting of the Board of Governors.' Many Board of Management members were conscious of a new timidity on the part of the governors when they were asked to back the editorial decisions of their executive. According to one manager, 'They were terrified, terrified of the legal cost.' The new caution almost certainly had its roots in the settlement made over *Maggie's Militant Tendency* and the fact that the case itself seemed to have emerged out of the blue with no prior warning from Milne – another throwback to the perceived incompetence of the *ancien régime*. The result was earlier and more frequent decisions to capitulate, even when programme makers felt they had a strong case.

The governors also discussed programming decisions, although intervention in this area was rarer than some reports suggested; throughout the BBC's history, there had been instances of whimsical interventions by governors on individual programmes, and in this area Checkland's board seemed to be relatively hands-off. Most of the strategic programming decisions – on *Newsnight*, or *Casualty*, for example – were left to management. This was certainly not the attitude, however, when it came to issues of resources and staff numbers, the very area in which the Director General had most expertise. Fairly detailed matters relating to pensions and programme resources were subjected to close scrutiny by the governors. After more than three years, during which he had enjoyed a mostly cooperative relationship with his board, Michael Checkland gradually found them becoming restless about the need for

cuts and redundancies. Led by the Chairman and Vice-Chairman, they started
to flex their muscles on issues which should have been matters of day-to-day
management.

At the heart of the problem was the lack of any properly codified guidelines
for the precise conduct of the Board of Governors. Exactly what their duties
were, where the boundaries lay between management and governorship, and
at what point governors were expected to intervene, was entirely a matter of
convention and the personal inclination of the board at any one time. One governor who joined during Hussey's chairmanship tried to draw a clear
distinction between 'detailed management' (left to Board of Management) and
'strategic planning' (for the Board of Governors), but was happy to include
programming policy in his definition of strategy:

> Some of us would say that a really big investment in a programme is like
> a policy, if you're in a situation where every penny counts. A pro-
> gramme which casts a new light . . . on the general attitude of the BBC
> is an important cultural area.

It was therefore acceptable, in this view, for governors to involve themselves
in the commissioning of a new soap opera or an expensive drama series.

The same governor acknowledged a shift of power which had its roots in
the perceived failure of Milne's regime:

> The balance did shift in favour of the governors demonstrating that they
> had more of an interest in policy and a lot of people saw that as day-to-
> day involvement. [But] the governors were having to put their foot down
> over policy because nobody else would. There was a vacuum. . . . The
> governors had for many many years done very little that could be called
> giving any sort of lead at all in policy.

Others, of course, interpreted history rather differently: they argued that governors of old well understood their function and had generally been prepared
to allow the Board of Management to get on with its job. But there was an
inherent ambiguity waiting to be exploited by someone with enough time and
energy and a pretext. Duke Hussey had all three and, in concert with Barnett,
led the rest of his board into redefining the notion of strategy.

One of the major problems created by increased involvement was that it
revealed a lack of coherence amongst governors about some fairly crucial
strategic issues. At one meeting discussion turned to whether more money
should be devoted to drama and the probable impact on BBC-1's ratings. It
developed into a debate on the role of BBC-1, in which one governor insisted
that the BBC-1 Controller should be satisfied with 20% of the audience as long
as the programmes were high quality. Nonsense, responded a fellow governor.
If a sizeable chunk of additional money was to be invested in BBC-1, there
must be a ratings target attached to it. In his view, the Controller should be

asked to deliver 70% of the audience. The problem for Board of Management members present at that meeting was not just the massive discrepancy on a fundamental plank of network television strategy; it was the sheer idiocy of both extremes. Not even James Bond movies manage a 70% audience share in a four-channel system, while a 20% share for the BBC's flagship channel would provoke an instant challenge to the survival of a compulsory licence fee.

In fact, it was this ignorance and sheer mediocrity that BBC executives found most exasperating about the new model, hands-on Board of Governors. It might have been acceptable if power was being exercised by men and women of great intellect or vision, but for the most part the politicisation of the board had meant that many candidates of genuine ability were disqualified. There was only a limited supply of able figures who were also unobjectionable to torch-bearing Thatcherites, and those had long been exhausted. What remained was an unfortunate combination of low calibre and high prejudice. When the rumpus blew up over *Tumbledown*, branded as unpatriotic by right-wing Conservatives, one governor was oblivious to any editorial judgement about quality and compared it to the Ian Curteis play in starkly political terms: 'Why don't you do both plays,' he asked Bill Cotton, 'and let the public decide?' Cotton had to remind him that the BBC was not running a political beauty contest but making an editorial judgement about whether a play was any good or not. It had decided that the Curteis play was manifestly not.

By the middle of 1991, many of the BBC's senior executives had lost patience with a bunch of people whom they saw as eccentric, capricious and increasingly interventionist. With one or two exceptions, the great and the good had been replaced by the second-rate and the pedestrian who – in the absence of any clear set of criteria by which to make judgements – were guided by their own prejudices and an agenda set by a largely right-wing and often self-interested press. One senior manager delivered a verdict which reflected the contempt felt by many of his colleagues: 'A completely ineffectual bunch of tosspots. They were utterly hopeless.' Honourable exceptions were two governors who had joined the board in 1988: the crime novelist P.D. James, who in the words of one executive 'at least watches television'; and Keith Oates, Managing Director of Marks and Spencer, whose commonsense approach to management issues was widely praised. But for the most part, Marmaduke Hussey and Joel Barnett had little difficulty in dominating a collection of individuals who, in management's judgement, were irredeemably second-rate.

Hussey's reappointment was exactly the endorsement he was looking for, and an implicit mandate for him to continue in his dominant role. In the longer term, it meant he would have the freedom to lead the BBC through its critical charter renewal phase, and mould it as he wished. In the short term, it conferred on him yet again the most important task which the Board of Governors undertakes: the appointment of the Director General. Michael Checkland's term was to end officially in March 1992, but – unlike chairmen – it was not unprecedented for directors general to be reappointed. Checkland had decided that the bulk of his job was done and that he did not want to stay another five years. After his success in dealing with the Price Waterhouse audit of 1990, he wanted to see the BBC through the next government-appointed audit, which would be going through in 1992–3. He would then be happy to hand over to someone else who would see the BBC through charter renewal. Accordingly, he told the Chairman, he would only be seeking a two-year extension to March 1994. Unfortunately, Checkland had a rival. John Birt had made it known that he now wished to succeed Checkland.

Most observers thought Michael Checkland a success. He had picked up the baton at a time when the BBC was in crisis and its political foes were queuing up for the kill. He had negotiated it safely through the worst excesses of Thatcherite power, and could look forward to a period of consolidation and relative calm. The BBC had been overstaffed and bureaucratic, and he had presided over job cuts, redundancies, and efficiencies – mindful that this was the vogue vocabulary of the day and certainly what the Board of Governors had been demanding.

Moreover he had set out a sort of manifesto, his vision of what the BBC was about and where it should be going. The occasion was the annual *Financial Times* cable and satellite conference on 27 February 1991. In a carefully balanced speech, no doubt conscious that within six months the governors would be deciding his fate, Checkland reviewed his successes in the sort of language that would have gladdened Thatcherite hearts. He described his cost savings and reductions in resource levels, and emphasised the commercial success of BBC Enterprises. He looked forward to the internal 'market approach' which would allow producers to decide whether to use BBC or external facilities. He acknowledged the need to be 'leaner and fitter' to meet the coming competitive challenge. There was no question of abandoning the marketplace rhetoric at the very moment that government attention was about to switch to the BBC.

But, having paid his political dues, Checkland then committed himself wholeheartedly to two key features of the BBC's public service role. First, he said, it must make programmes across the board, and not just those which the free market could not support. The BBC was unique because it offered a mixed service 'built on a strong popular base. For the BBC, this base must be preserved.'

Second, he drew attention to the quality and innovation that could be sustained 'when you have a strong and confident production base'. But elsewhere in the system, that base was under threat. The auction system being imposed on ITV, its separation from Channel 4, and the new competition from satellite channels were all liable to create enormous instability in the commercial sector. There would be much greater dependence on independent producers, but there would be none of the infrastructure for training and long-term career development that any industry requires to thrive. And that, said Checkland, could threaten one of Britain's greatest strengths in the international arena: 'There has to be a critical and creative production mass at the centre of British broadcasting if it is to keep its identity in the face of growing competition from multinational companies with no obligations to the British audience.' The BBC, therefore, would remain central to a healthy domestic production base.

Checkland ended with a stirring and personal affirmation of the continuing need for public service broadcasting. There are no votes in it, he said, and it does not get much of a press.

> But as the world of broadcasting changes and the traditional values are increasingly threatened by the market pressure for ratings and revenue, we must stand and defend them. We should not have to apologise for a public service of quality delivered efficiently. It has an illustrious past and it can have an honoured place in the future. As a public service provider, the BBC is at the heart of the nation's broadcasting. We should take pride in it. I do.

It was a powerful statement of personal conviction at a pivotal moment in the BBC's evolution. With the BBC's current charter expiring at the end of 1996, the next eighteen months would see the emergence of a Green Paper to set the agenda for the BBC's future. In anticipation of that process, Checkland announced that fifteen charter review Task Forces were being set up to examine every aspect of the BBC's role and to 'set an informed agenda for the public debate'. Each Task Force 'team' would consist of seven or eight people whose brief would be to 'produce fresh ideas'. The emphasis was to be on younger staff who would be prepared, if necessary, to think radically, and the whole process was to be overseen by a steering committee of Checkland himself, John Birt, the Director of Corporate Affairs, Howell James, and the head of Policy and Planning, Patricia Hodgson. It was an initiative which would, eventually, play a significant role in the internal debates about the BBC future, not always to positive effect.

Checkland's manifesto was important politically. The BBC was entering the most critical period in its history, surrounded by a burgeoning number of commercial competitors, all struggling to make ends meet, and its Director General was staking the claim of this quintessentially public body to keep its place at the very centre of British broadcasting. His address at the *Financial Times* conference was a skilfully woven speech, which seemed to resonate with the more conciliatory, collegiate tone in public life being set by the new Prime Minister. Neutral observers could have been forgiven for thinking that this was precisely the approach that was now required to negotiate the BBC through the delicate period that lay ahead.

But the person who mattered now was the Chairman. And while Checkland had articulated his vision of the BBC's future in public, privately Hussey had decided that he must go. In the middle of June, two weeks before any decision was taken, Hussey told the Chairman of the Australian Broadcasting Corporation that the DG's contract would not be renewed. Partly, this was a consequence of his failure to have his own man installed as DG last time around. As one senior Board of Management figure put it, 'When Hussey was then thwarted by the board because Mike Checkland did such an excellent interview, he made it absolutely clear that second time around he wasn't going to be thwarted again.' Not only had the second time now come around, but Hussey's enormous influence had been explicitly endorsed by the government: 'Having been given another five years, he thought he could walk on water. Once ... you get that vote of confidence from the government, you say "Listen – I'm going to pick my DG my way".' Another factor was that Hussey's relationship with Checkland, which had been mostly amicable and productive, was starting to turn sour as the perception grew that Checkland was not delivering what the Chairman and Vice-Chairman really wanted – cuts.

Checkland had arrived four years earlier with a pledge – that a BBC under his leadership would shrink. As he had said in February, cuts and efficiencies had been implemented and jobs lost. But it was still common currency that the BBC was a bloated, unwieldy and overstaffed bureaucracy which required further, deeper surgery. Stories abounded, fuelled by reports and editorials in the press, about unnecessary waste and duplication. It was an issue which greatly exercised the governors, who shortly after Hussey's arrival had asked for quarterly figures of how reductions were going, where they were falling, and how targets within each department were being met. According to one governor 'The issue of shrinkage ... was continually discussed [and] was continuously before us.' Six thousand staff had gone since Checkland took over but the board was demanding more, and faster. Checkland was convinced that cuts had to be an evolutionary process to avoid damaging the fabric of the organisation, and by December 1990 had begun to get visibly annoyed at the board's obsession with staff numbers.

The problem was that no-one really knew the basis on which 'shrinkage' was being demanded. The concept had become so deeply embedded in the prevailing political culture that cutting costs and staff from public organisations was becoming an end in itself – taking precedence over serious consideration of what staffing and resource levels might be required in order to carry out an organisation's task effectively. In this respect the BBC was particularly vulnerable because the only obvious comparisons were with other broadcasters from the commercial sector – who were going through a massive rationalisation process in the run-up to the new auction system. For the BBC there was

no bottom line to act as a barometer for its success or failure, only its programmes and its reputation. There was no yardstick for measuring what was
required to sustain quantity and quality across two television stations, five
national radio stations and a string of local radio stations. There was only a
deep-seated and abiding conviction that there were too many people.
Marmaduke Hussey wanted them out, quickly.

Observers distrusted his motives on two counts. First, there were his
undoubted political loyalties. By ensuring the Chairman and his board were of
a broadly like-minded political complexion, the government had guaranteed
their uncritical adoption of its own approach to life in general and corporate
management in particular. As one industry figure said, '[Hussey] doesn't like
to offend his friends, and his friends by and large are Establishment figures.'
The governors required no prompting to demand the same sacrifices of the
organisation they were running as ministers were demanding of government
departments and other public bodies. The question at board meetings would
always be, 'Why are we still employing more than 20,000 people?' It would
never be, 'Do the unique functions and performance of this cultural institution
require that we preserve the personnel and skills in which we have invested?'
The second question might have yielded the same answer, in terms of staff
numbers, as the first. But it was never likely to be considered with an open
mind.

Hussey attracted suspicion for a second reason, closely linked to the first,
but which his detractors regarded as altogether more insidious: an apparent
absence of any real affection for the BBC itself. Even the most sceptical chairmen in the past had 'gone native' – had been captivated by the creative
environment, by the peculiar atmosphere of Broadcasting House and
Television Centre, and by the glamour of broadcasting. Hussey had managed
to do more than stay aloof: according to many of those who worked with him
and listened to him, the BBC's Chairman exuded a disdain for his charge
which sometimes bordered on contempt. According to one close observer

> ... he appeared to have a considerable dislike for a good many people
> in the Corporation and what the Corporation was when he joined it. He
> still speaks of the Corporation as if he is not part of it. People do not
> believe that he has a genuine identity of interest or a paternal regard for
> an institution which is arguably one of the best in Britain.

So it was not simply that Hussey reflected the accepted political and economic
wisdoms of his establishment friends; he also appeared to have a deep-seated
sense of alienation from the institution they had appointed him to command.

Michael Checkland's unmistakable sense of pride in the BBC thus contrasted sharply with his Chairman's attitude, and Hussey wanted someone at
the helm who would implement his wishes at a speed he found more acceptable. Since his arrival as Deputy DG, John Birt had been assiduously courting

the governors as well as politicians. He had made it clear that his view on cut-backs was precisely in line with the Chairman's. In fact, he had gone further. He had persuaded Checkland that he should head a committee which the DG himself had set up to review Network Television Resources, and his confidential conclusion was to recommend a radical strategy, with swingeing staff and resource cuts – including the closure of regional production centres. It was precisely what Hussey wanted. And for John Birt's critics, that was precisely the problem.

One of the criticisms of Birt most frequently voiced since his arrival was that his main interest was the furtherance of his own ambitions. In the existing context of BBC power relations, that meant pleasing the Chairman, and Birt already had the reputation of someone who liked to please his superiors. In December 1988 Birt had been interviewed by ex-colleague Brian Walden on LWT. Walden ended the programme with a rather nasty googly:

> I think the nastiest thing I ever heard said about you . . . is that you are
> a submissive authoritarian, that's to say submissive to your bosses and
> authoritarian to all the people underneath you. Is that a fair characteri-
> sation of John Birt?

Birt replied that this was a myth 'put about by my now good friend [Professor] Laurie Taylor'. Myth or not, it was a characterisation which was endorsed by many of those who had had dealings with Birt over the years.

More importantly, it was a characterisation which prompted questions about motives. Was he recommending massive resource cuts and closures because he was convinced that these were in the BBC's best interests? Or was he recommending them because they were in John Birt's career interests? His critics pointed to four years of manoeuvring ('He must sleep with Machiavelli under his pillow', said one), and were in no doubt about the conclusion: here was a ferociously ambitious man who charmed all those he met by seeming to agree with them. On the very day the governors were due to decide between Checkland and Birt, *The Times* reported an anecdote from Tory MP Peter Bottomley which summarised Birt's reputation: 'I remember him at a Cup Final with friends on either side cheering for different teams. Birt seemed equally pleased whichever side scored a goal.'

As with Hussey, there was a widespread feeling that Birt was ultimately indifferent to the reputation and heritage of the Corporation he desperately wanted to direct. Previous directors general had come up through the ranks, and in doing so had become imbued with the BBC's traditions. Birt had so far shown little sense of pride in what the BBC had achieved and little sign of cherishing its history. Even his former supporters were uncertain about whether he felt any real affection for the institution:

> I really am not sure. I think in many ways he feels he will do his ten

years in the BBC, five years as deputy DG, five years as DG and go off
somewhere else. At the end, you've got to love the BBC and really
believe in it. . . . It is not a business, not an institution, it is something
much, much bigger than that.

It was because of the magnitude and significance of the organisation that
the Director General's job was expected to be advertised: when £1.5 billion of
public money was at stake, it was not unreasonable to expect the appointment
of chief executive to be open to all suitably qualified candidates. There would
have been no shortage of capable applicants. But in an extraordinary display
of personal power, Hussey persuaded his fellow governors that a competition
was unnecessary: Birt and Checkland were the only credible candidates, and
the governors could decide between them at a specially convened meeting.
Thus, one of the most important and coveted cultural appointments in the
country was to be decided in a closed meeting room, without interviews and
without any knowledge of the credentials of other potential candidates. Even
the two protagonists were not required to produce personal statements of aims
or strategy, nor to submit to collective questioning by the board. In the words
of one outraged senior executive, 'It was a carve-up – there's no other word
for it.' It was certainly an astonishing dereliction of the board's duty, which
many governors later came to regret. But by then it was too late; Duke Hussey
had had his way.

The crucial meeting took place over dinner on 1 July 1991, and found the
governors split down the middle. A decision had to be taken by 11.40pm to
allow Sir Graham Hills, the Scottish governor who had been appointed in
1989, to catch his train home. By that time, Hussey had persuaded one
Checkland supporter to change his mind, and the Chairman had his man – but
at a price. He had to agree to extend Checkland's contract by one year until
March 1993, after which Birt would take over. At 9.20 the next morning, the
offer was put to Checkland who had no idea whether his proposition for a two-
year extension had even been put to the board. It was clearly an absurd
situation in which there would effectively be dual leadership for 21 months,
and some were convinced that Hussey fully expected Checkland to refuse. For
three hours, Checkland canvassed his colleagues who were unanimous in
wanting him to stay to see through some of the changes that were already in
train. At 12.30 he accepted the offer of a one-year extension.

Thus, the Chairman, who was widely viewed as deferential to his political
masters and remote from the BBC, had secured the appointment of a Director
General perceived as a man in his own image. In finally achieving his ambi-
tion, Hussey had done the BBC two major disservices. By flouting the normal
procedure for filling the top job, he had dented the BBC's reputation further
and reinforced the beliefs of those who saw a politically motivated conspiracy. And he saddled it with a 21-month period in which neither the Director

General nor the Director General-elect could command with complete authority. This was precisely the time at which the BBC needed effective leadership to do battle on three fronts simultaneously: the government's proposals for its future; its own definition of strategy and direction in a more commercial environment; and its internal management structure. It was always going to be a tough campaign. Now, the Chairman had handicapped his own army.

CHAPTER ELEVEN
LAME DUCKS AND TRAPPIST MONKS

Over the next eighteen months, two fundamental issues about the BBC's future – the way the Corporation was to be run, and the definition of its public service mission for the 90s and beyond – became inextricably bound up with a third: the negotiations with government about renewing the charter. An extraordinary period of intense negotiation, second-guessing and critical internal debate was punctuated by the uncertainties of a general election. Although the relationship with the government of the day had never been absent from the BBC agenda, this agenda was now dominated by the preparation of a government blueprint for the BBC's future. Even when the process was complete, there remained a number of crucial questions. What was the cost to the BBC of securing its survival? Had the threat of wholesale change been deliberately exaggerated to justify radical management changes? And how much had the cost-cutting and organisational upheaval to do with Hussey's prejudices and Birt's self-advancement?

It had become increasingly clear that there *was* a cost to journalistic integrity. Several months before the decisive governors' meeting which appointed Birt, yet another *Panorama* row had erupted along now familiar lines: that the BBC was intent on giving the government a soft ride. This occasion was more serious for Birt, and for the BBC, because his decision appeared to have little editorial credibility.

Two *Panorama* producers had uncovered a story which was sensational: that British machine-tool manufacturers had been exporting to Iraq – against official government guidelines – equipment which was destined to form part of a massive piece of offensive weaponry, the so-called 'supergun', capable of inflicting serious damage on neighbouring countries. After several months of investigation the researchers had put together a detailed description of the supergun's specifications, how components had been smuggled out, and how key British officials were turning a blind eye. The programme, in the words of one insider, was,

An absolutely outstanding piece of journalism. If you look at what's emerged after that programme and the House of Commons select committee reports . . . that programme is literally not a millimetre out – down to the size of the thing, the size of the barrel, the size of the parts that were moved, the direction it was pointing in, where it was located, the grid reference on the map. It was . . . an extraordinarily accurate programme.

The timing was even more sensational. The programme was scheduled for transmission Monday 14 January, just as the offensive against Iraq was being launched. With British forces involved in a major war, *Panorama* was about to reveal that a potentially lethal part of Iraq's armoury had actually been exported from Britain. No-one doubted that this was going to be a difficult programme whose revelations would almost certainly provoke opprobrium from the usual collection of back-bench Tory jingoists. Equally, no-one questioned its accuracy. It was precisely the sort of scoop on which journalists establish their professional reputations and which would usually win a hatful of industry awards.

John Birt blocked the programme. At a furious meeting involving the programme's makers and senior news and current affairs managers, his was the only voice arguing that public opinion would not tolerate a programme about Britain arming Iraq at the very moment that British servicemen were going to war with Iraq. In the words of one participant, 'John appeared to think that there was something comparable between Britain going to war with Iraq under the guise of the United Nations and Britain going to war with Germany at the time of the Second World War.' Others tried to persuade him that this was different: that Britain was not fighting for its own survival and that British livelihoods were not being threatened. In the Second World War, with the country fighting for its life, it would have been deeply demoralising to show that Britain had armed its own enemies. But this was a war on foreign soil with mostly Americans in the firing line. It was not analogous.

Despite the anger and frustration of those around him, Birt insisted that the programme must be postponed. But the story was far too good to keep under wraps. The journalist Paul Foot revealed some of the details in his *Daily Mirror* column, and Dr Chris Cowley – *Panorama*'s main source – became disillusioned enough to talk to one of ITV's rival current affairs programmes, *This Week*, which rushed out its own version. It was inferior, but it was first. There was no outcry, and six weeks later *Panorama* finally limped in with the original. By then, it was history.

Even those who had been brought up at LWT under the Birtist umbrella now began to question his motives. Was it really just a matter of trying to second-guess public opinion (itself a dubious exercise with investigative journalism which might prove discomfiting)? Or was there something altogether more alarming – that Birt remembered the enormous ructions between the BBC and the Thatcher government over coverage of the Falklands war and was determined to avoid any repetition? Then, Thatcher had condemned the BBC's insistence on neutrality, and *Newsnight* and *Panorama* had run objective, analytical programmes about the war's origins and the campaign; and the Chairman and Director General had, for their pains, been personally vilified by Conservative back-benchers.

There was no suggestion that a heavy government hand was being placed on John Birt's shoulder, reminding him of the BBC's 'responsibilities' in times of national turmoil. But there was a growing feeling that Birt was trying to pre-empt pressure through the exercise of extreme and journalistically damaging caution. This self-censorship was all the more insidious because the government could properly plead innocence. Other decisions might have been attributed to the 'mission to explain' philosophy or the tighter controls or referral procedures. This time, while some mention had been made of 'gaps' requiring more detailed exploration, the overriding motive seemed to be the fear of provoking a row while the BBC's future and possible survival was under scrutiny.

For the government was already preparing a Green Paper which would determine the ground on which the battle for the BBC would be fought. Despite Thatcher's departure, the Home Secretary, Kenneth Baker, remained a committed Thatcherite and for him and many of his colleagues the BBC still represented an offensive reminder of how some public sector institutions had survived his mentor's revolution intact. If John Birt saw his mission as saving the BBC Charter, the prognosis at the beginning of 1991 was not optimistic – a view unlikely to be discouraged by ministers aware of what sustained uncertainty might achieve. Even those who were not prone to conspiracy theories started to worry about the ground that was, apparently, already being conceded to government influence, and the debilitating effect on BBC journalism of a long-drawn-out charter renewal debate.

That debate started in earnest two months later, on 11 March, when the Centre for Policy Studies published its own report. With John Major now in office the CPS had lost some of its power base; but it was still an influential force in pushing radical policy ideas onto the government's agenda, and therefore in ensuring that any debate was conducted on terms initiated by the right. Given that the report had been commissioned under Thatcher and that an election was looming, most observers anticipated a scathing attack on the BBC as an institution, and on its structure and funding.

They were only half right. In its tone, the CPS pamphlet, *A Better BBC*, written by former BBC journalist Damian Green, acknowledged the traditional strengths of the BBC and supported its survival to provide some form of public service broadcasting. Its tone was not one of implacable opposition, and its author was keen to recognise that the institution embodied some virtues which Conservatives should admire: it was generally well regarded, was internationally successful, and promoted respect and admiration for Britain overseas. At the outset, the report announced its retreat from a dogmatic adherence to the free market and declared that 'Value judgements are to be made about individual programmes, or about television channels, beyond those made by audience ratings and market forces.' It also talked about the importance of 'culture', although it could not quite bring itself to remove the inverted commas from a word which tended to evoke a dismissive sneer in Thatcherite circles. In its recommendations, however, the CPS was true to its radical roots.

The report argued that with cable and satellite channels emerging, 'The *status quo* of a compulsory licence fee with all proceeds paid to the BBC is bound to become indefensible.' But it did not go for complete abolition of the licence fee or for turning the BBC over to the private sector. Instead, it resuscitated the idea, first mooted by the Peacock Committee, of a Public Service Broadcasting Council which would distribute the proceeds of the licence fee to any programme maker or broadcaster whose idea seemed worthy of the 'public service' tag. The BBC, then, would become just one suitor amongst many trying to persuade the good people of the PSBC that its programmes were deserving causes. It was soon dubbed the 'Arts Council of the Airwaves'.

For the CPS – and for the Conservative Party – this was a very promising line of thought. It offered a radical solution within a framework that was not governed by knee-jerk hostility to public service broadcasting. It accepted that some cultural goods would not be provided by the marketplace, and that these should be purchased by the licence fee payer. The question then remained as to whether this public service operation should be provided monolithically by a single organisation or whether it should be opened up to competition. Given that competition was one of the central tenets of Conservative thinking, the PSBC offered the perfect bridge between public service and Conservative radicalism.

At the same time, by not immediately threatening the BBC, it did not alienate the Tory grass roots who were strangely fond of this uniquely British institution. Damian Green did the rounds of the party circuit to argue his case and was struck by an almost schizophrenic attitude amongst party members. There were many Conservatives who were convinced that the BBC's journalism was biased against them, and that it was a bloated, bureaucratic, arrogant institution. But these tended, ironically, to be the core BBC audience: devoted listeners to Radio 4 and disproportionately high viewers of BBC-2. They would not appreciate a Conservative Party which destroyed an institution they relied on and (journalism aside) admired.

From the BBC's point of view, the PSBC option was doubly lethal. In the longer term, as more and more competitors made inroads into the funding which had traditionally been ear-marked for the BBC alone, it would be reduced to a fraction of its former size. It would therefore lose the critical mass of creative talent which had been responsible for much of its quality and originality. Concerns about size were, of course, partly institutional self-interest. But they were also based on a view that the BBC fostered a unique ethos for programme making which could not be sustained if it was scaled down significantly.

More importantly, the PSBC concept reflected the philosophy of the right, which held that the role of public service broadcasting was simply to fill gaps left by the commercial sector. It was a view which had already been forcefully advanced by Cento Veljanovski from the Institute of Economic Affairs, and was part of the right's conviction that the market should prevail wherever possible. There was no question about the outcome of such a strategy: it would eventually remove from the BBC *any* programme sufficiently popular to sustain itself on a commercial channel. Soap operas, situation comedy, mainstream sports coverage and light entertainment would all eventually fade from the BBC, since no Public Service Broadcasting Council could justify spending money on a sitcom while commercial channels were making fewer and fewer current affairs or arts programmes. As critics of the PSBC were quick to point out, the end result would be a BBC reduced to the same parlous state as its marginalised sister institutions such as ABC in Australia or PBS in America – making low-rating, worthy programmes, losing popular affection and becoming a progressively easier target for financial cutbacks and political assault.

The irony, as John Birt gradually took the reins in anticipation of his accession in 1993, was that reports began to seep out of high-level management discussions about the need for the BBC to take the 'high ground'. There was more talk about an 'increasingly competitive marketplace' and about the BBC's role in quality programming. And it was never altogether clear in what sense the word 'quality' was being used. Was this becoming the new code for certain types of programmes absent from commercial television, perhaps a more acceptable way of saying 'upmarket'? Or was it a more general term to describe aspirations across all programmes, whether popular or minority? Suspicion began to grow that it was the former: that Hussey and Birt were intent on taking the BBC down a road which was not a million miles removed from that proposed by its political enemies, and previously resisted at all costs. Fears could have been allayed by an unequivocal statement that committed the BBC to making programmes across the board. None was forthcoming.

This was partly because the dual leadership made it difficult to speak with a single, unambiguous voice. And it was partly because a debate on the issue was still being resolved amongst the upper echelons of the BBC in a way which was inextricably entwined with the political debate about the BBC's future. In public, attempts by journalists to establish exactly what type of programme was now being defined as acceptable were rebuffed. In private, there seemed to be a widening rift between those who saw the entertainment role as fundamental to the BBC's survival and those who wished to move closer towards the 'market gap' model.

A classic example of the consequences of such indecision surfaced in 1991. In the middle of the year, the BBC had suffered its worst ratings since the mid-80s. Bill Cotton, now the head of an independent production company, condemned the BBC for being 'obsessed by journalism' – a barb aimed squarely at John Birt – but in fact Jonathan Powell had recognised that a problem was brewing and had been planning a new BBC-1 schedule for nearly two years. The problem, as Powell saw it, was that *Wogan* had reached the end of its natural life and was becoming a liability, while ITV had introduced a third episode of *Coronation Street*. The result was an audience which disappeared at 7.30 or 8.00pm, and was impossible to retrieve with the *Nine o'Clock News*. He needed some strong, popular, early evening programming. Checkland, conscious that BBC-1 was the litmus test of BBC popularity, had agreed to make new money available for popular drama.

Powell's plan was twofold: first, to replace *Wogan* with a new thrice-weekly soap opera, and, second, to turn the highly successful hospital drama *Casualty* into a twice-weekly serial. Preparation was crucial, first to commission a new soap opera from scratch and second to prepare Terry Wogan for his imminent disappearance, while asking him to continue until the new soap was ready to launch. Powell had done his research and was convinced it would be a successful strategy. He was on the point of commissioning the extra *Casualty* programme and the new (albeit ill-fated) soap, *Eldorado*, and a few days from announcing the new initiative at a press conference, when Michael Checkland advised him to run his plan by the governors out of courtesy.

The governors had been persuaded of the need to take action and offered no objections. But, across the table, Powell could see that John Birt was fuming. Since he was the man who would be in charge when the new schedule was implemented, Powell went to see him immediately after the meeting. Birt was angry because he regarded it (rightly) as a major structural change to the schedule on which he had not been consulted. More importantly, it was a strategy with which he profoundly disagreed. He thought it would produce an anti-creative, copycat schedule, giving the BBC three peak-time soap operas (the highly successful *EastEnders* was the third) when ITV also had three (*The Bill*, *Coronation Street* and *Emmerdale Farm*). And all this at a time when BBC-1 was aiming to be a distinctive channel and the debate about charter renewal was about to take off. He told Powell that he, Birt, was the only person in the building who knew how to talk to politicians. In his own mind, it seemed, Birt was making an explicit connection between where the BBC should be going and what sort of BBC would be most likely to receive government blessing, and therefore secure charter renewal. After a series of discussions, Birt effectively gave Powell a choice: he could have one soap opera but not both. Powell had already squared Wogan and the work on *Eldorado* was by now well advanced because it was an independent production. It was no choice at all, and the plans for *Casualty* were dumped, leaving a hole in the BBC-1 schedule at a crucial time of the day for audience building.

This kind of debate was of much greater significance to the BBC's future than questions about whether current affairs programmes were too 'soft' on the government. Powell was happy to accept a schedule which avoided formulaic game shows like *Blankety Blank* or *Wheel of Fortune* which – because they were both popular and cheap – could be found in abundance elsewhere. But there seemed to be no coherent view about what place other types of light entertainment should have in a BBC of the future. What about *Noel Edmunds' House Party*, the anarchic Saturday night show which featured guest celebrities, slapstick humour, viewer participation, and regularly attracted over ten million viewers? That appeared to be acceptable because it was 'a BBC show', but *House Party* would have been equally at ease in an ITV schedule (and ITV would have snapped Edmonds up in 1993 had the BBC not met his financial demands). In drama, there was also confusion. Long-running drama series and sitcoms are the fundamental building blocks of a popular channel around which the more serious and experimental programmes can be scheduled. Shows like *House of Eliot*, *Lovejoy* and *Miss Marple* were, Powell believed, precisely what the BBC needed to keep the hearts and minds of licence payers. But while for him *Miss Marple* represented 'an absolute touchstone of BBC popular entertainment at its very best', his DG appeared to find it at the limits of acceptability.

Powell's concern was shared by others who recognised that a BBC which defined itself in terms of what other channels were not doing would be more, rather than less, vulnerable to government intervention. There were rumours that Radio 1, having survived the government's privatising clutches, was finally to be chopped by the BBC's own axe-wielders. Popular music was available 'in the marketplace', went the argument, so what was the channel's public service function? The problem was that it was all shadow boxing. Checkland's *Financial Times* speech had committed the BBC to covering the waterfront, but he was on his way out. Birt was widely quoted as favouring a move 'upmarket', but could say nothing until he formally took over. A year later, the duo were satirised by Michael Grade as 'The lame duck and the trappist monk'. Without a firm hand on the tiller and with no-one prepared to talk about actual programmes, the debate centred around petty semantics. Words like 'distinctive', 'high ground', 'upmarket', 'non-commercial', 'quality' and 'elitist' were traded without anyone being prepared to define what they meant for actual programmes and real viewers or listeners. But there was no doubt of the desire, in some quarters, to move the BBC to more of a PSBC model.

That was particularly ironic given the political thinking on the BBC at the time. For although the Centre for Policy Studies had become used to its reports influencing government thinking, its impact on the current Home Secretary was minimal. Kenneth Baker had not abandoned his hostility to the Corporation, or his belief in a neat solution which would make the BBC both competitive and accountable: advertising. Despite the findings of the Peacock Committee, and the consensus shared by virtually every broadcasting analyst in the country that there was simply not enough advertising cash to sustain four half-way decent terrestrial channels, Baker was still wedded to Thatcher's favourite panacea. Green Papers, by tradition, explore all the policy options. But they explore some options more seriously than others, and in doing so indicate the direction of government thinking. The draft Green Paper which the Home Office drew up prior to the 1992 election was very serious indeed about advertising.

It remained a draft Green Paper, because – with the election looming – the government was not going to make a manifesto commitment to wholesale changes on which the Conservative Party was not in broad internal agreement. There was no point in courting controversy on an area of little electoral interest, and anyway, it might smack of overt intimidation. On the other hand, the Conservatives were not averse to firing a few shots across the BBC bows as all thoughts of an autumn election were abandoned and the stage set instead for a grand political showdown in the spring of 1992. At the Tory Party conference in October 1991, Party Chairman Chris Patten called on supporters to 'jam the BBC switchboards' at any sign of anti-government bias. And in January 1992, Kenneth Baker felt himself compelled to remind the BBC of their duty to remain impartial and of the impending government review. Not for him any careful demarcation between government responsibility and party political advantage.

With the outcome of this election more uncertain than either of the previous two, television attained a greater significance in the communications mythology of the two parties than ever before. The Conservative Party knew it could be confident of support from every large circulation newspaper except one. It therefore wanted to minimise any negative coverage from television. The Labour Party, meanwhile, was relying on television to counteract the press imbalance and had perfected its own photo-opportunity and sound-bite interviewing techniques. As the campaign approached, both sides regularly made their views known in robust terms to news and current affairs editors. Such thinly disguised attempts at intimidation were now regarded as a routine part of the political process, and the recipients were well versed in the art of rebuffing them. On the other hand, the programme makers were acutely aware that every news bulletin, interview and political item was being dissected in all three party headquarters for the slightest hint of anything that might be interpreted as bias.

In such a highly charged atmosphere *Panorama*, again, deserved all credit for tackling what was widely regarded as the most important electoral issue: the economy. In a programme due for transmission on the eve of the campaign, *Panorama*'s subject was the economic mess in which Britain was now deeply mired. The aim of the programme was to examine, in an analytical but accessible form, where the blame lay for Britain's economic problems and whether – as the government maintained – a faltering world economy was the main culprit. *Sliding into Slump* was written and presented by the BBC's Economics Editor Peter Jay, the co-author of the Birt–Jay thesis, a man who was not renowned for his ability to simplify complex economic arguments for mass audiences. To the surprise of many of his colleagues, however, this was by common consent an impressive programme – clear and comprehensible – which placed much of the blame on the former Conservative Chancellor Nigel Lawson.

This conclusion was not entirely unpalatable to the Major government, which had been discreetly distancing itself from the more outrageous policies of its predecessor (the poll tax had already been dumped), and which to some extent might therefore benefit. In terms of the BBC's role, this was exactly the kind of democratic, journalistic function a public broadcaster should be performing for its licence payers at a moment of great political significance. It was particularly relevant to an election where the economy featured heavily, where there were more undecided voters than ever before, and where a partisan popular press were more concerned with propaganda than accuracy. The programme's clear, analytical style meant it should have been one of the crowning glories of John Birt's journalistic reforms.

On the Wednesday before transmission the editor of weekly programmes, Samir Shah, pronounced the programme 'a little backward looking'. The makers added material about the different economic policies on offer and what the electoral choices were. On the Friday Shah announced that it was still too backward looking and that he was pulling it. The programme was not referred, and at least one senior editorial figure remains convinced that, if it had been, it would have been broadcast. Others, though, found it unlikely that Birt did not know, and inconceivable that Tony Hall was not in some way involved in the decision. The consequences were swift and predictable. Those who had long been convinced that Birt was leading the BBC down a path of closet connivance with the government saw this as the final confirmation. Even his supporters from LWT were shaken and started to wonder, in the words of one, 'where he was coming from'.

The decision made no journalistic sense because there was no suggestion of editorial bias; and it was always certain that the programme's script and conclusions would find its way into the public domain (it was published in full in *The Guardian*). As with *Supergun*, instead of getting credit for fulfilling its public service remit to provide authoritative, independent information, the BBC was vilified as a gutless creature living in the government's pocket. Yet more damage was done to the reputations both of the BBC itself and of the man who would be running it within a year. The irony was that, shortly after the Conservatives won the election, it became an accepted orthodoxy even within the Party that Britain's economic problems had their roots in the Lawson–Thatcher boom. Once again the BBC had got there first; once again it had censored itself.

The Conservative victory meant that John Major could now mould his own cabinet and had a mandate for his own manifesto, rather than having to adopt the personnel and ideas inherited from Margaret Thatcher. One manifesto commitment had particular implications for the BBC: the setting up of a new Department of National Heritage (DNH) which would take over the Home Office's responsibility for the BBC, and therefore the Green Paper on charter renewal. It had always been an anomaly that the department with responsibility for crime and law enforcement, immigration, drugs and censorship should also be responsible for broadcasting, although the great strength of the Home Office was the seniority of the incumbent minister. The DNH by comparison was a junior cabinet post, with a ragbag of responsibilities including sport, the arts and the creation of a new national lottery. It was the British answer to the European model of a Ministry of Culture, but its establishment was not greeted with enormous gravity. It was soon dubbed the 'Ministry of Fun'.

Previous experience suggested that the responsible Secretary of State would be influential in deciding the BBC's future, and there was some relief at Broadcasting House when the name of David Mellor was announced by Downing Street. Mellor had been Chief Secretary to the Treasury, the lowest rung on the cabinet ladder, and as a friend of John Major had played a major role in his leadership campaign. The appointment was half-expected by Mellor himself, who thought he would get his own department and believed the new Heritage brief fitted him like a glove. He was keenly interested in music and the arts; he enjoyed sport and shared Major's penchant for Chelsea football club. He was a high-profile operator who knew how to generate publicity, and, as minister with responsibility for broadcasting at the Home Office, he had been instrumental in mitigating the worst excesses of Thatcherite thinking during the passage of the Broadcasting Bill through Parliament. Politically, he was precisely in tune with the thinking which was now emerging from the post-Thatcher Conservative Party: less ideological and more pragmatic, but still steeped in the language of markets and privatisation. Most important of all, he clearly leaned towards the culture side in the 'culture or industry' debate about broadcasting. He enjoyed the company of broadcasters, and regarded himself as a supporter of the creative community. He was friendly with the Managing Director, Radio, David Hatch, and, in particular, a friend and a fan of John Birt.

It was immediately clear that the Baker Green Paper was not appropriate for the Major–Mellor regime and would have to be redrafted. To assist him, Mellor brought in the civil servant who had been with him at the Home Office, Paul Wright. Because of their background at the Home Office, Wright and his colleagues at the DNH were imbued with the values which had informed that department's thinking on the BBC over the years. As professional civil servants they had, of course, worked to the political brief provided by Baker to produce the first Green Paper. But they had also worked closely with Mellor during the battles over the Broadcasting Bill, and understood Mellor's view of the world. They set about producing a new draft of the Green Paper. Meanwhile Mellor's newly-appointed special adviser, Chris Hopson, started acquainting himself with some of the more radical options proposed for the BBC from within the Conservative Party. In the post-election atmosphere, he soon concluded that the real political threat came not from advertising but from renewed interest in the Public Service Broadcasting Council.

This was partly because of the intellectually coherent case set out by the PSBC's original begetters, the Peacock Committee. This case had been reinforced by, most recently, the Institute of Economic Affairs, whose book *Freedom in Broadcasting* (edited by Cento Veljanovski) had set the intellectual agenda within the Conservative Party, and by Damian Green's paper for the Centre for Policy Studies. Moreover, Green himself, in the wake of the election, had joined John Major's Policy Unit at No. 10, where he now had responsibility for broadcasting policy.

Mellor had a difficult balancing act to perform. He wanted, in the words of one government adviser, 'to keep the BBC show on the road'. His instinct was for the *status quo*. But at the same time he fully supported the reforms which Checkland had started and Birt now seemed to be stepping up, and was aware of the mounting hostility towards Birt. A fundamental plank of the Birt argument had always been the need for change in the face of a hostile government, if the charter was to be renewed. It was essential that those promoting reform inside the BBC could continue to use the threat of government action in justifying continual changes to their internal opponents. If that threat was removed, if the Green Paper produced nothing but glowing tributes to the BBC's achievements, there would be no pressure to continue the reform programme.

But when the rewritten Green Paper emerged it was so effusive in its praise for the BBC that it could have been drafted by the Corporation's traditionalists. No group was more alarmed by this than the BBC's management, who suddenly perceived a real danger that the government's position could appear less radical than its own. There followed the strange spectacle of the BBC lobbying the government privately to make sure that the final version of the Green Paper would take a tougher line. The draft was dispatched for a re-write.

At the same time, Mellor could not afford to lean too far the other way and to favour the really radical options, which would also undermine Birt's position. His critics inside the Corporation would then argue that there was no point in going through the pain of change if the BBC was going to be broken up anyway. Mellor's tightrope performance was based on one central premise: that Birt's approach was right. The implementation of reforms which acknowledged a changing market outside, which seemed to be cutting waste and instituting reforms through an internal market, was not only in tune with Mellor's thinking but was also in line with the continuing government programme of changes in health and education. It also mirrored the processes which had been imposed, through privatisation, on former public sector businesses like British Gas, British Telecom, and British Airways. The BBC, because of the way it was funded, was a more complex proposition. But if the BBC's management itself was prepared to drive through market-based reforms, Mellor was committed to giving it the political support it needed. His attitude differed markedly from that of Kenneth Baker and the Thatcherite mainstream in that it was not rooted in assumptions about the BBC's political complexion. The spotlight had moved from political prejudice to working practices, and the motivation was neither spite nor revenge. It was still, however, rooted firmly in the political philosophy of the moment: the philosophy of a Major government rather than a Thatcher government.

In walking that tightrope, the crucial moment for Mellor came when he addressed a high-level strategy meeting of BBC management and governors at a hotel in Lucknam Park. There was no prepared speech, there were no notes. In the car on the way down to the hotel, Mellor rehearsed a few of the main points with his adviser but when he stood up to address the BBC hierarchy he spoke unprompted for thirty minutes.

It was a speech which set the tone for the debate, and delivered precisely the message which BBC reformers would have wanted: you are on the right road and we see no need to interfere at the moment – but the journey's not over yet. Mellor was also quite clear about the order in which the government and the BBC should announce their respective visions: he strongly advised that the BBC should remain silent until the government had published. This would pre-empt those critics (mostly from the right) who wanted major reforms, who would not be satisfied with the BBC's proposals, and who would then lobby the government to take decisive action. BBC management took the hint. But the price was over six months of silence while industry observers clamoured for some indication of where the BBC was going. The sense of confusion already created by a dual leadership imposed by the Chairman was now aggravated by the gagging advice given by the government.

Having laid out the terms of this implicit deal for the BBC, Mellor had to deliver his side of the bargain and square the right of the Conservative Party. The political climate had changed, and radical reform of the BBC was now a position confined to a fairly small group of hardliners within the party. To ensure the idea did not regain momentum, Mellor sought to neutralise the argument about the Public Service Broadcasting Council by excluding it from the Green Paper, or at worst reducing it to a walk-on role. The view inside No. 10 was that the Green Paper should include all policy options, and a series of drafts and revisions shuttled between the DNH and Downing Street.

These delicate manoeuvres were still proceeding when Mellor became the first victim of what turned out to be a whole string of tabloid newspaper *exposés* featuring prominent Conservatives. Facing a barrage of increasingly graphic revelations about his affair with an actress, Mellor was finally forced to resign. It signified not just one man's exit from ministerial office, but the end of a cosy relationship between most of Fleet Street's popular newspapers and the Conservative Party. No longer could the government expect free, uncritical publicity for its policy initiatives. The ride was going to be rougher than it had been during the previous ten years.

The appointment at this stage of an ambitious card-carrying Thatcherite to the DNH would almost certainly have disrupted the finely honed balance that was being struck. In the event, John Major appointed Peter Brooke, an affable old-timer from the paternalist school who had earlier resigned from his post at the Northern Ireland Office after indulging in an ill-advised sing-song on an Irish chat show the day after an IRA bombing. He was (despite that indiscretion) a safe pair of hands, and someone with neither a reputation for radical thinking nor any visceral aversion to the BBC. When the Green Paper was finally published on 24 November, the notion of a Public Service Broadcasting Council was given as much – and as little – space as the options of advertising, subscription and direct taxation. Although critics observed that it was 'too Green', in that it appeared to be filleted of preferences, the tone was unmistakable. Essentially, the government indicated its support for the one option which even two years ago had seemed remote – the *status quo* and the licence fee. The Checkland–Birt reform programme had won the political battle that would set the context for the debates to come.

It had been a long period of self-enforced silence for the BBC, during which any clues to the battles being fought within its corridors were seized upon with glee. In the manner of seasoned Kremlinologists, experienced observers of Broadcasting House would scrutinise official publications or dissect public statements for any indication as to the BBC's vision for itself. A classic example was the Chairman's foreword in the BBC's annual report, published in July. It emphasised how, with charter renewal approaching, efficiency and accountability were the two key aims, and set out 'the promise we lay before the licence paying public'. There then followed a virtual blueprint for the 'market gap' solution:

> The BBC's service must be thoroughly distinctive. We accept that in due course the market will come to provide a fully adequate supply of certain kinds of programming. . . . As the marketplace fills with new traders, the BBC must ensure its wares are quality wares and are not being sold at the next stall.

The next paragraph added a vague and confusing promise to reflect public taste and meet 'a clear public need', but even this was defined in terms of what the 'commercial market' might not provide. Just as old Soviet heroes were airbrushed out of photos by succeeding, revisionist regimes, the word 'popular' had been excised from BBC vocabulary.

A rather more dramatic incident punctured the silence on 21 October, when Michael Checkland appeared on the platform for a 'future of the BBC' debate staged by the Royal Television Society. Asked a relatively innocuous question about the governors, he launched into an impromptu attack on his Chairman: the BBC should not have the same Chairman for ten years, he said, still less someone who would be 73 in the year of charter renewal. The governors as a whole were out of touch, and it was ludicrous to have, effectively, created a dual leadership for nearly two years. His outburst had not been planned, but was a measure of the frustration that Checkland had felt at his treatment the previous year. He left a stunned seminar to catch a plane for a Commonwealth broadcasting conference in Botswana. After such outspoken criticism, it was unlikely that Checkland would see out his term as Director General. In the event, he announced on 10 November that he would be leaving at Christmas, two months early. After nearly six years in charge, Michael Checkland officially gave way to John Birt on 31 December 1992.

The reform programme, it seemed, had done its job. It was even possible for the Chairman and Board of Governors to look back over the previous two years and claim that their impatience with Checkland's progress, the appointment of Birt and implementation of an even more radical reform programme had secured the ultimate prize: the *status quo* had, after all, become not just an option but the favoured option. It was a seductive argument, and one the governors themselves were keen to advance. But it was not justified by the facts.

First, Mellor had made it clear that he was concerned about inefficiency and that expenditure cuts were essential to sustain his own and the government's support. This was by now familiar territory in any debate about the public sector: health, education, the civil service and local government had all been subjected to frequent, ritualised denunciations of bureaucracy, red tape, waste and the squandering of taxpayers' money which the government was determined to eradicate. Such outbursts laid the groundwork for the subsequent cuts and redundancies, which in turn were followed, typically, by a short respite and then another flurry of scandalous stories about waste, bureaucracy, and so on – and more cutbacks. It had become part of the Conservative creed that the only antidote to waste was a bottom line. As senior managers of most large companies were well aware, a bottom line tended to conceal rather than eradicate inefficiency and the problem was as much one of size as profit motive. But, politically, allegations of inefficiency were common currency.

Even the most dutiful of BBC loyalists did not pretend that every one of the 25,000 staff jobs in BBC television and radio when Checkland took over was absolutely essential to the Corporation's duties. Checkland had made it clear that he would cut, and the anguished cries that accompanied some of his decisions were testimony to the number of cost-cutting measures he imposed. But the cuts which Birt's Television Resources Review had recommended, and which were subsequently announced in September 1991, went well beyond what Checkland had proposed or deemed necessary. They were in danger of inflicting real damage, not just on staff morale but on the skills base and corporate infrastructure which were vital to the BBC's standing. For that reason, the swingeing cuts and closures proposed under the Birt–Hussey plan were made against Checkland's better judgement, but – from the end of 1990 – were being demanded by a Chairman and Vice-Chairman who took it as axiomatic that waste was endemic in the public sector. Had the Chairman and governors been prepared to back Checkland and his record against the government, calling in evidence the job losses, closures and efficiency measures which had been the dominant feature of the previous five years, the political effect might have been just as fruitful. Even under Checkland, the BBC had been taking drastic and very public action. That was what reassured Mellor, and he did not require the same measures in spades to convince him that the BBC was serious.

Second, the engine of change which the government most favoured in its quest for efficiency in the public sector was precisely that which the BBC had decided to adopt – the internal market. This was originally a Checkland initiative, although it was not destined to start until April 1993. But the commitment had been made and the whole organisation was preparing for the massive upheaval it entailed. Checkland's BBC had shown itself perfectly willing to adopt the government's clothes.

Third, there was no evidence that Hussey's strategy made the slightest impression on ministers who were implacably opposed to the BBC anyway. The 1991 cuts were announced at the very time that Kenneth Baker was overseeing a Green Paper which committed the BBC to advertising. Given his hostility – shared by a few cabinet colleagues and large numbers of backbenchers – even the summary dismissal of three-quarters of the staff and the flogging off of Broadcasting House was unlikely to have dissuaded him from the view that the only acceptable BBC was a commercial one. Baker's antagonism was deep-rooted. So Hussey could not claim that he forced through the appointment of Birt in the interests of saving the BBC from government action because, at the time, the option of saving the BBC was not available.

The final, and most significant, factor was the government's new and unaccustomed electoral fragility. Thatcher's power had been founded as much on the enormous margins of her election victories as on her approach to politics. Major's majority had fallen from over 100 to 21. It was certainly enough to govern; but it was not enough to feel confident about taking on controversial causes which might test that majority. Although the BBC was not the most popular cause in the world, it commanded enough affection to mount a vigorous and potentially troublesome defence of its corner. Far better for the government to make threatening noises and thereby ensure that the wished-for revolution was imposed voluntarily from within rather than imposing it from without. A Checkland regime committed to Producer Choice and further cuts on a longer and less damaging time-scale should have been sufficient for an embattled Conservative government. In fact, Checkland's 1991 *Financial Times* speech would have been both ideologically and politically acceptable to Mellor, to Brooke and to John Major. It was Duke Hussey's ego which lay behind the appointment of John Birt and the pain that was subsequently inflicted. Charter renewal was a convenient excuse.

Two days after the Green Paper was published came the BBC's own document, *Extending Choice*. In 88 pages, it set out the blueprint for 'The BBC's role in the new broadcasting age' and contained some carefully worded clues to the debate on strategic direction that had been raging in Broadcasting House. *Extending Choice* contained the distilled wisdom of the fifteen charter review groups. In setting out a 'clear public purpose', it emphasised how the broadcasting marketplace was being transformed, and how the BBC had to adapt to the new world order. Its future role was then contrasted starkly with its past:

> In the past, as a dominant provider, the BBC had an obligation to cover all audiences and broadcasting needs; in the future it will have an obligation to focus on performing a set of clearly defined roles that best complement the enlarged commercial sector.

It then outlined the four roles which would form the framework for the BBC of the future: news and information; British culture and entertainment; education; and communication between Britain and abroad. These were almost infinitely flexible roles which required finer definition to be meaningful (they could easily have served as a blueprint for the combined ITV/Channel 4 service), but the next paragraph seemed to make it clear that *Extending Choice* was moving the BBC towards a market gap position: 'Over time, it should withdraw from programme areas or types in which it is no longer able or needed to make an original contribution.'

Further on, however, the document explicitly precluded the notion of focusing 'only on providing services that meet the minority needs of smaller audiences – needs that clearly will not be met in the commercial market'. It acknowledged that this would force the BBC into the 'cultural ghetto' which had so damaged ABC in Australia and PBS in the US, and that, therefore, 'the BBC should . . . maintain regular contact with all viewers and listeners, and deliver programming which appeals to them'. The *but* came one sentence later, and looked suspiciously like something which had been inserted either by a different hand or by someone conscious of the need to balance two conflicting aims: '. . . but it should do so in a way which places the greatest importance on developing services of distinction and quality, rather than on attracting a large audience for its own sake'. It was difficult to interpret such delphic language, but it seemed categorically to rule out imported Australian soap operas like *Neighbours*, which fulfilled no obvious cultural role but were demonstrably good at combining low cost with high ratings.

At the press conference which accompanied the launch of *Extending Choice*, however, Birt and Checkland would not be drawn on the implications for individual programmes. The reasoning was obvious: to be drawn on one programme would open the door to a flood of questions on whole schedules, and BBC programming policy would then run the risk of evolving via question and answer sessions with journalists looking for a story. But the stonewalling on even simple questions, like the future of *Neighbours*, did suggest that the polished generalities of *Extending Choice* concealed many unresolved disagreements.

In fact, the biggest specific programming hint in *Extending Choice* was in the section on radio. Again, it emphasised that priority would go to networks 'which are truly distinctive and unlikely ever to be matched in the commercial marketplace'. This time there was no 'but', only a tribute to Radios 3 and 4 which 'currently come closest to being unique'. Radio 1 had, coincidentally, just celebrated its 25th birthday. During that quarter century it had introduced a whole generation of young people not just to pop music but to the BBC. It was a perfect example of a BBC service which was plugged into the mainstream, was an integral part of the lives of millions of young people, and through its universal availability and demonstrable popularity helped to legitimise the licence fee. Politically, it was radio's equivalent of BBC-1 entertainment: a useful defence mechanism against unwarranted attempts by governments to downgrade or demolish the Corporation. But *Extending Choice* did not mention Radio 1 by name, nor its contribution to the BBC's stature. It was the most significant, and potentially the most dangerous, indication that the 'higher ground' philosophy was still in the ascendant.

The press conference threw up one piece of additional information. Again anticipating the changing context in which the BBC would be operating, Birt forecast a viewing share of no more than 30% for BBC television – down from the current level of just under 50%. This was unnecessary, given that any forecast in a fast changing world was notoriously unreliable. It was a figure which was difficult to justify because there was no consensus, and there was an equally strong argument that a weak and fragmenting commercial television sector might struggle to keep up with the strength and stability of a resurgent BBC. Even if the BBC was convinced of its own pessimistic analysis, there was certainly no need to announce it to the world unless to do so offered some obvious tactical advantage. In his first serious public pronouncement since his appointment, the Director General-designate effectively conceded the competitive advantage.

It seemed especially unnecessary at a time of low morale, when Birt might have wanted to boost the confidence of his staff and silence those critics who still questioned his commitment to the institution. Conspiracy theorists referred back to a *Sunday Times* editorial two months earlier, in which Andrew Neil had announced his admiration and support for a strategy which concentrated on 'doing what the market does not do, or does inadequately or badly'. Neil had outlined the sort of programmes which such a strategy might entail, concluding that they 'should be able to command about a 30% share of the audience and ensure that the BBC made a distinctive contribution to the diversity of British broadcasting in an age of channel choice'. The antipathy of the Murdoch empire to the BBC in general and the licence fee in particular had evaporated, and the reason was clear. A BBC financed by subscription would compete for the very revenue on which BSkyB was beginning to thrive. It had to be avoided at all costs. A BBC funded by advertising would make it almost impregnably strong, as well as eating into another revenue stream for BSkyB. The PSBC option was certainly acceptable (and had been run by the *Sunday Times*'s irrepressible Jonathan Miller, masquerading as an objective commentator), but BSkyB at that time needed a moderately strong and secure BBC to help it in its crucial sporting contracts. Suddenly, there was a coincidence of aims between the Murdoch empire and the BBC; and suddenly, the newspaper which had been the BBC's most strident critic had offered its support, subject to the Corporation accepting certain limits. Two months later, those were precisely the limits to which John Birt's BBC was aspiring.

While questions about what sort of programmes should be made were still cloaked in ambiguity, there was no doubt about how programme making should be managed. Efficiency had become a vital part of the management rhetoric, and Producer Choice – the internal market – was going to be the engine for its achievement. As *Extending Choice* said:

> At the heart of the process of change is the Producer Choice initiative, which is currently being implemented throughout the BBC. . . . [It] has profound implications for the organisational, financial and operational characteristics of the BBC.

The theory had already evolved, the testing process had begun, and some of the problems it was creating had already been publicly aired. While many saw it as a perfect example of how a public organisation could harness new desktop technology to make its cost and accounting procedures more transparent, others saw it as another nail in the coffin of true creativity. There was to be no gradualism. As one senior executive said privately, 'This is a real revolution. We have no idea whether it's going to work.' One thing was for certain: it was going to cost jobs. This prospect, added to the upheaval he had already created in News and Current Affairs, cast a distinct shadow over the Corporation as John Birt took over the reins from Michael Checkland.

CHAPTER TWELVE

LEVELLING THE PLAYING FIELD

Producer Choice, more than any other single phrase, encapsulates the combination of change, modernisation, and disruption which has engulfed the BBC over the past seven years. The internal market system which now defines the relationship between the BBC's own departments, and also between the BBC and the outside world, represents the biggest change to the way the Corporation works since the McKinsey-inspired reforms of the late 60s and early 70s.

The first mention of Producer Choice was in an internal paper on the BBC's Drama Department. The idea developed during the course of 1990, and was first announced late that year by Checkland's successor as Director of Resources, Cliff Taylor. He needed to make savings of 5% a year over the two years from April 1991, and explained to the unions that to achieve these additional cuts he would need to give television producers more choice in spending their production budgets. Individual producers would have to be able to buy services outside the BBC, rather than go through the Resource and Planning Department.

The concept was not new, for Michael Checkland had considered something similar in the early 1980s, when he was still Director of Resources. What had changed was the broadcasting environment. A number of different pressures conspired to make it necessary for the BBC to introduce some financial mechanism which would enable it to measure its costs against the market outside. The first was that by 1990, such a market existed. In 1980, most television production work was done inside the BBC and the ITV companies; the facilities companies which existed to supply studios, editing and equipment, tended to service expensive productions such as feature films and television commercials. With the advent of Channel 4 there emerged a cottage industry of small companies supplying the facilities to make the programmes the new channel required. For the first time, it was possible for the BBC to ask itself what it might cost to make a given programme outside the Corporation.

Second, because of the legal requirement enshrined in the 1990 Broadcasting Act that the BBC commission a quarter of its non-news programmes from these same independent producers, it was certain that cost comparisons would be made between the independent productions commissioned by the BBC, and those made in-house. It also meant that in-house staff would be making fewer programmes than they had previously; with or without Producer Choice, significant redundancies were inevitable.

A third factor was the renewal of the BBC's charter. It was clear that the issue of the Corporation's efficiency, or lack of it, might dominate the whole debate about its future. David Filkin, whose Science Features department was to be one of the testbeds, later told the trade magazine *Broadcast*, 'The BBC's objective with Producer Choice is to identify the true cost of what we are doing before renewal of the charter becomes a major issue. We want to be able to knock the myth that the BBC is not efficient.' Roger Thompson, the series manager of *Bookmark*, was even more candid: 'This will enable the BBC charter debate to be fought on programmes and the rationale for having a BBC, rather than on its efficiency.'

But there was a fourth pressure which was perhaps decisive in ensuring that Producer Choice as a system emerged in the way that it did. This, like much of the BBC's policy-making, was the result of political conflicts within the Corporation. When he had become Director General, Michael Checkland had forecast a steady decline in staff numbers, by about 1,000 per year, from the 25,000 he inherited. This was driven both by the need to improve efficiency and by the need to reduce staff to allow for the programmes which would be made outside by independent producers. For the BBC, used to expansion, or at worst stasis, this represented a rapid contraction. For the Chairman and Vice-Chairman though, it was not fast enough.

John Birt, having sided with the Board of Governors, got his chance to promote his view when he was assigned to lead the Resources Review. Unlike the Phillips Committee, which had looked at ways of finding money across the entire organisation, this review was to look specifically at the Television Service, which accounted for some two-thirds of the BBC's spending. It became a battleground between the incomers who had joined the Corporation since Hussey became Chairman, and long-standing BBC staff. The latter group included Will Wyatt, about to become Managing Director of BBC Television, Keith Anderson, the Controller of Planning, and the Controller of Regional Broadcasting, Keith Clement; in the former group were John Smith, the BBC's Chief Accountant, who had followed Ian Phillips from British Rail, and Mark Oliver, a former consultant with Coopers and Lybrand now with the Policy and Planning Unit.

It took all of Checkland's authority to prevent the implementation of the swingeing cuts recommended by the review, which included the closure of the studios in Birmingham and Manchester (this was fortunate, given the BBC's subsequent emphasis on regional broadcasting). More seriously, it became a testing ground for the notion that the BBC could divorce its editorial function from its production work – and that it might not need its own studios or facilities. In arguing for this proposal, Birt was doing no more than reflecting the prevailing trend in the television industry. Subsequently, in applying this approach to the BBC – with his accustomed stress on minutiae and systems – Birt translated Producer Choice from a system intended by Checkland to make the BBC more efficient to the more far-reaching one which emerged. Birt's enthusiasm for cuts deepened a suspicion in the minds of many staff, however unjustified, that he had a hidden agenda – to break up the BBC and possibly even to sell parts of it off.

During the late 1980s, ITV companies had been quick to learn the lesson from Channel 4 that the different functions of a broadcaster could be separated, or even dispensed with, without going out of business. Their agenda was rather different; what Channel 4 had done to foster its own programme diversity, the ITV companies now did to release funds for the licence auction introduced in the 1990 Broadcasting Act. Rather than be outbid by new competitors, companies like Central, Granada, and LWT had stripped apart their production, facilities, and broadcasting divisions to reduce overheads and make themselves more efficient. It was a rapid and sometimes brutal process, involving significant redundancies and extensive closures. Indeed, at the height of this process Greg Dyke – now running London Weekend Television – was invited to speak at the annual BBC 'away weekend' for the governors and the Board of Management. His advice was not to cut staff numbers, but to hack at them – as if the problems confronting a small commercial television company facing a singular piece of government legislation were any guide to best practice in a public broadcasting organisation which was far bigger and more complex than LWT. For John Birt, however, the timing was perfect; Dyke's recommendations chimed exactly with the message he had been giving to the governors.

In designing Producer Choice the BBC created a similar split between the resource departments, which supply services to production departments, and the production departments, which make the programmes. The idea was similar to the concept of 'market testing', as developed by local authorities and the civil service: to make the costs of the BBC's internal transactions visible, and to make sure that those costs were comparable with charges outside. The Producer Choice Project Director, Michael Starks, spelled it out when Producer Choice started.

> BBC programme makers have to earn their income, by selling their programme ideas to channel controllers, in competition with one another and to some degree with independent producers. Overhead support services – libraries, computer services – have to earn their income from their users. In launching this initiative, the BBC is not turning commercial, or losing sight of its public service qualities and values.

Equally, though, the system was designed to do for the BBC what the ITV companies had already done by management *fiat* – it was a mechanism to strip the BBC down. As Starks explained to *Televisual* magazine:

> Producer Choice is designed to reduce tiers of administration, shed property, cut back expenditure on overheads, utilise capacity more fully, and increase investment in programmes. That is consistent with modern, efficient, clear-sighted public service broadcasting.

Prior to Cliff Taylor's 1990 announcement to the unions about the introduction of Producer Choice, there had been some isolated examples of programme departments running on a 'total cost' basis (rather than using the resource/cash system in place elsewhere in the Corporation). James Hogan, who ran Television News Events (responsible for conference and election coverage, among other things), had got permission in 1988 from the News and Current Affairs Directorate to use a total costing system, and returned a profit of more than £500,000, spent on staff increases. David Nissan ran a similar system as editor of *The Money Programme* between 1988 and 1992. 'Producer Choice gave me an opportunity to keep making my programme better without my costs getting higher', he told *The Independent on Sunday*.

> The staggering thing was how easy this was to do. The old allocation of resources was so inefficient that I had room to cut costs and recruit an extra reporter and an extra researcher, and assign more foreign travel at the same time.

The BBC's financial systems at that stage were both complicated to use and difficult to make sense of. As one manager put it, 'One was charged for things one hadn't used, undercharged for some things one had used, and double-charged for other things. I understood my way around it, but it wasn't valuable information.'

Under the new system, not only programme departments but also the resource departments would be subject to the same disciplines. Perhaps appropriately, Ealing Studios in west London, once the home of classic British film comedies such as *The Lavender Hill Mob* and *The Man in the White Coat*, were chosen as the Producer Choice guinea pig. The BBC had bought Ealing Studios in 1955, and it now housed the Television Film Services Department, which serviced BBC departments, such as drama, which still shot on film rather than videotape. Predictably, there were some redundancies almost immediately, both voluntary and compulsory. Among those who accepted voluntary redundancy were the best technicians in the department, who went freelance and took their work with them. Overheads, too, became an issue – one which was to recur throughout arguments about Producer Choice. During the first year of the pilot, in 1991–2, Television Film Services was not required to pay its overheads, but in the second year, when it did, it became clear that the department would make a loss if it had to pay for the costs of the maintenance of the Ealing Studios buildings.

In April 1992, the pilot was extended to the Design and Scenic Servicing Department, which employed around 600 people including costume, make-up, set design, and scenery assembly and construction. The department was required to pay its overheads (a contribution to the BBC's Corporate departments, like Personnel and the Policy and Planning Unit) but not its rent, and there was a tacit agreement that in year one it would not have to break even – as long as it did in year two. As with Television Film Services the previous year, the problems started to emerge only in the autumn, when the department was preparing its budget for the following financial year on the basis of the first six months trading under Producer Choice.

This time it was clear that the only way the department could break even the following year was by sacking people. There were further redundancies, this time compulsory, across all areas, depending on the business needs of the department. In addition, the BBC's make-up school was closed. Previously, places in the school had been advertised and applications had been competitive, based on talent and potential. Now it was replaced by a fee-paying make-up school which only the better-off could afford.

Redundancies were not confined to production staff. Some managers realised that they would be able to balance their books only by further extensive redundancies, and simply refused to write the budgets. The Head of Visual Effects, for example, prepared an optimistic first-year business plan on the basis that he could if it was necessary bring work in from outside to cover the BBC work he lost. But Producer Choice did not allow BBC resource departments to compete for work outside. Despite winning some outside work in the first few months, he was told to desist. Six months on it was clear that his department was not going to break even; he was summoned to see his manager, and left the BBC the same day. It was not necessarily that he was bad at business; just that – as was reported afterwards – he was not happy about taking responsibility for the redundancies wished upon him. Much the same happened in Television Film Services, where the manager declined to make additional cuts in his budget for the following year. He left shortly afterwards.

As Glynne Price, the former Head of Personnel for BBC TV, wrote in an article in *Television Week* in June 1992:

> The obsession with the market makes one wonder whether anyone at the very top believes broadcasting is the primary purpose any more. It appears to have been supplanted by 'management' – a pity, since the BBC was very good at one and is plainly abysmal at the other.

Indirectly, the introduction of Producer Choice claimed a far more senior scalp. In the summer of 1992, the Chief Accountant, Corporate Finance, John Smith, who was then preparing the accounts for the previous year, told Ian Phillips, the Finance Director, that there had been a £25m overspend in

18. Aiming at the stars. Rupert Murdoch with a model of the rocket that was to put Sky TV's Astra satellite into orbit.

19. 'The Mike and Dukie Show'. Chairman Marmaduke Hussey *(left)* and Director General Michael Checkland field questions from BBC viewers; in the chair, Sue Lawley.

20. On the one side...
The MacTaggart Lecture
at the 1989 Edinburgh
International Television
Festival; Rupert Murdoch
launches a tirade against
the concept of 'so-called
public service' in broad-
casting.

21. ...and on the other
The MacTaggart Lecture,
1992. Michael Grade at
Edinburgh – 'I have always
said that it is the BBC that
keeps us all honest.'

22. Will Wyatt, the Managing Director, Television, who in 1993 publicly reclaimed the BBC's public service role.

23. Alan Yentob, who ran BBC-2 for nearly six years before taking control of the Corporation's 'shop window' as Controller, BBC-1.

24. Jonathan Powell, Controller, BBC-1, until his resignation in December 1992.

25, 26. New brooms. John Birt *(on left)* outside Broadcasting House with his newly-appointed deputy, Bob Phillis, and *(right)* Liz Forgan, brought in by Birt from Channel 4, at the same time as Phillis, to run BBC Radio.

27. 'Fool's gold'. The set for *Eldorado* under construction.

28. The 'freelance' Director General. John Birt gives a lacklustre performance when confronted by the Director General-who-never-was, Jeremy Isaacs, on stage at the National Film Theatre.

29. The best of friends? John Birt and Michael Grade during a break at the Royal Television Society's Convention in September 1993.

30. Mark Tully, the veteran BBC foreign correspondent, whose outspoken attack on 'Birtism' summed up the feelings of many of his BBC colleagues. He resigned in July 1994.

31. The Bad News, June 1994...
Chairman Duke Hussey crosses a picket line in Portland Place during a strike by disaffected staff.

...and the Good News, July 1994
The headlines proclaimed John Birt's victory, with charter renewal in the bag.

THE INDEPENDENT

No 2,407   THURSDAY 7 JULY 1994   Published in London 50p

White Paper praises public service role but also backs wide range of money-making ventures

Birt's BBC is given its reward

London WESTWAY HO! STOP ME AND BUY ONE

THE BBC, with John Birt as its di- the BBC's valuable transmitter

Birt celebrates victory as BBC escapes intact

By Jane Thynne and George Jones

MAIN POINTS

● The BBC should remain a public services broadcaster, maintaining

and abroad should be expanded.
● A new Royal Charter should

the satellite station UK Gold and the expansion of World Service Television, will be able to operate services licensed by the Independent

THE BBC management received an

45p
Thursday
July 7
1994
Published in London
and Manchester

The Guardian

NEWSPAPER OF THE YEAR

Corporation safe for 12 years ● Dramatic rise in commercial activity

Victory for Birt's BBC revolution

Andrew Culf
Media Correspondent

THE TIMES

No. 65,000   THURSDAY JULY 7 1994

Charter to be renewed for 10 years

Birt triumphs in battle of the BBC

By Alexandra Frean and Jonathan Prynn

MAIN POINTS

television. Phillips's first reaction was disbelief, for the nine months figure had been virtually on budget, but he briefed Checkland (who was equally disbelieving) before going on holiday. Immediately he came back, he rang John Smith, who told him that the problem had got worse. Phillips called in the auditors and briefed the governors before they broke for the summer.

At this stage, Phillips believed the problem was difficult but manageable, but he calculated without the political nature of the BBC. The Corporation had set up an Audit Committee, chaired by the Vice-Chairman of the governors, Joel Barnett. Hussey had recently had a bad fall, and was in poor health. The overspend, which eventually totalled more than £50m, gave Barnett (who, some believed, still harboured hopes of the Chairman's post) the perfect opening to demonstrate leadership qualities. A series of meetings became a witch-hunt as the Audit Committee sought to apportion blame. Phillips' view was that, given the problem, he had taken the right steps to deal with it; the auditors had come in, and the accountant responsible for the muddle had been moved from his job. The cause had also been identified: a combination of 'double spending' (money being spent on buying services outside while paying for the same resources inside); a shortfall from the contribution that BBC Enterprises was budgeted to make to BBC Television productions; and some straightforward overspending. Although the missing money had been spent on programmes, budgets for the following year had to be trimmed rapidly to make good the error.

This was of little consequence to Barnett. As with the row over *Maggie's Militant Tendency* almost exactly six years previously, he decided that a tough line was required. Phillips was in the firing line, and for him the timing could not have been worse. The crisis finally broke in October 1992, just after Checkland had publicly attacked Hussey at a Royal Television Society seminar. As a result Checkland was about to step down as DG, and was in no position to support Phillips; and Birt had made it known privately that he would not back the Finance Director against Barnett or the other governors. Phillips agreed terms and left the following February.

Phillips had been a member of the committee responsible for implementing Producer Choice. It was chaired by John Birt, now Director General designate, and other members included Cliff Taylor, in charge of television resources, and his radio counterpart, Duncan Thomas; Michael Starks; John Smith; and a consultant from Coopers and Lybrand Deloitte, Alan Hammill. No fewer than four firms of consultants were hired to assist in the process; as well as Coopers, they were Deloitte, Price Waterhouse, Ernst and Young, and the change specialists Kinsley Lord. The number of outside advisers was perhaps justified by the scale of the task on which they were embarking: nothing less than the wholesale reconstruction of the way the BBC operated. What evolved was a complex system which is still developing. The explanation of Producer

Choice given to staff who have to implement the system runs to some sixty pages plus six appendices. In outline, this is how it affects the programme-making process.

Programme departments (which make programmes), the programme resource departments (which provide facilities), and 'overhead' units (which provide support services, such as library information) are defined as 'Business Units', and are each required to break even over the financial year. Their revenues come from selling programmes or services; their expenditures include charges for property (BBC buildings), capital (the equipment and cash they need to do business) and overheads (a contribution to the BBC's central services). These business units are to trade freely with one another; as the BBC's own Producer Choice 'Ground Rules for Trading' puts it, 'The intention is to identify resource costs and expose them to competition from outside suppliers which will enhance efficiency and push down prices.' Any department which does not achieve a break-even figure will be reviewed, but it requires a decision by the Board of Management to keep it open. The Director General holds a reserve fund which can be used to fund such deficits if necessary, or fund other unbudgeted projects (which can include programmes).

Producer Choice came into operation across the entire Corporation from the beginning of the 1993–4 financial year, which happened to fall on April Fool's Day. Prior to that, there had been a series of workshops, seminars, and other training exercises designed to prepare the BBC for the new regime. One of the most interesting of these was held at a south London hotel in late 1992, under the auspices of The Office for Public Management, a firm of public sector consultants. They ran a full-scale model of the Producer Choice system in which senior management compressed three years of production into a day and a half, trading with each other to get programmes made and transmitted. (The same group had run a similar exercise for East Anglia Health Authority during preparations for the NHS internal market.) The exercise was called 'Fast Forward', and different groups within the process wore differently coloured T-shirts to make it possible to follow the flows during the game. (The head of youth programming, Janet Street-Porter, who played the role of independent producers, was heard to summarise the process as 'You've got 70 prima donnas, you've got no script, you've got no story-board, it's live and it's important.') The point was to try and create an environment in which people could experience for themselves what might happen for real.

During this simulation, the channel controllers emerged as bottlenecks in the system – with the result that a *Harry Enfield Christmas Special* went out at Easter, and a production department which had a cash problem fixed it by making a programme on the quiet for ITV. Generally, though, those who implemented the system learned that it did offer them scope – but that it might also be volatile. One of those involved recalled:

You saw things happening which you hadn't expected, because the behaviour of people when the incentives change isn't necessarily what the architects might think it will be. If you have an institution which has worked in a fairly institutionalised way for a long time, and you suddenly change the incentives for everybody, a bit like Russia when you remove the Communist Party, then you shouldn't be surprised if the thing is difficult to manage.

The criticisms of the way in which Producer Choice was designed were manifold, and some problems emerged immediately. One was that the new system created more than four hundred different business units which then generated thousands of transactions as each unit acquired services from the others, adding a rich layer of bureaucracy to an already bureaucratic organisation. Another arose out of the ruling that resource departments should not be allowed to attract business from outside the BBC, except in fairly unusual circumstances, but still had to contribute to the BBC's overhead costs. The effect of this was that resource departments would shrink (because some producers would go outside) but would still have to carry the same centrally assigned overhead costs, creating a vicious circle in which it became progressively harder for them to compete against facilities organisations outside the BBC. The problem was compounded by the rules of trading: in bidding for work, businesses inside the BBC were required to include their share of overhead costs, while businesses outside could, of course, bid on the basis that they need only to cover the marginal cost of the work. The rules included in the Producer Choice guidelines, which were designed to ensure a level playing field between inside and outside, actually ensured that the pitch tilted towards external competitors. One example appeared even before Producer Choice was fully launched. The Drama Department found it could not afford to hire BBC make-up assistants because the cost of doing so was three times as much as hiring freelances. The wages of the BBC assistants were lower than their freelance counterparts, but their overhead costs were far greater.

Stories about the excesses of Producer Choice began appearing almost immediately. There was no shortage of disaffected staff willing to pass on some of the more outrageous tales, and no shortage of newspapers willing to print them. One Sunday newspaper even offered a bottle of champagne for the most ludicrous example. A scenery workshop in west London saved itself rent by cutting off half of the warehouse with a length of rope; the back half remained unpaid for under the new guidelines, but also unusable. There were the World Service staff at Bush House who had to stay overnight, and who were now being charged so much by the BBC for bed and breakfast that it was cheaper to check into the very plush Waldorf Hotel across the road. Costumes owned by the BBC wardrobe department were sold off – only for some to be bought back (at a fraction of their value) by the department which was selling them. Others were predictable. Studio engineers, faced with an £8 charge to use some music from the record library, started to tape everything they took out before returning it (exactly the sort of practice which access to the BBC record library was supposed to eliminate). Sometimes record library staff would suggest to producers that it was cheaper for them to buy a CD rather than borrow it, even though that was damaging to the library's trading position. Current affairs producers would ring friends on newspapers for information rather than call the BBC's own News Information Department and be charged £10.30 for the privilege.

Another object of ridicule were the flow charts which accompanied every Producer Choice document, no doubt intended to simplify the process. One, showing the procedure for paying bills, was reproduced in *Today* newspaper under the banner headline THIS IS RIDICULOUS. 'You have to hand it to John Birt', the story ran,

> His plan to streamline the BBC is making a real difference. The NHS people who showed us the 17 steps to change a light bulb could learn a lesson or two from him. Paying, for instance. At the BBC, it's got really sophisticated. . . . If you go with the flow chart you might get away with a mere seven stages. But it's more likely to take nine or ten – and could take 14.

Not surprisingly, parodies started to turn up on staff notice boards. One such parody, a 'Troubleshooting Flowchart', produced by a disgruntled engineer, was emblematic. It began with the question 'Does the Damn Thing Work?' – and if the answer was 'Yes' went on to the instruction 'Don't Bugger about with It'. Those who did 'bugger about with it' and were unable to conceal their meddling, found themselves ending up on a box reading 'You're Fired'.

John Birt was blamed for many of these flaws. One member of the Producer Choice Implementation Committee recalled, 'A lot of the systems problems with Producer Choice arose directly from John. Whenever he was given an opportunity for simplification or more detail, he would always go for more detail, and that is always the case with John on everything.' Throughout the Producer Choice development period Birt insisted that there was only one way to calculate costs, whereas most consultants agree that costing is a matter of what one is trying to measure. For example, working out the relative cost of a journey by car or by train depends on whether you own a car already, or if you have to go out and hire one. But the Producer Choice approach seemed to be to pretend that the BBC did not own the car even when it did, and then to add the cost of road tax, insurance and AA membership for good measure. As the distinguished drama producer Kenith Trodd put it,

> There is a frightening obsession with 'the level playing field' – an absurd idea anyway because trade is surely about maximising your

unlevel advantages against your opponents. Producer Choice is using the concept to penalise the BBC by taking away its natural and peculiar historic strengths.

Ian Phillips' view was that things could have been done more simply:

The changes you needed were those that were just enough to ensure the behavioural changes that you wanted to achieve. What you don't need is accountants gone mad producing figures that nobody's interested in, in a detail that you don't need to influence the decision. You need to be right enough, you don't need to be right to the tenth decimal place.

Producer Choice raised wider questions too. The BBC's business units were, quite properly for a public organisation, required to follow ethical business practices in areas such as training, equal opportunities, prompt payment, and so on, while competing with small businesses not renowned for such concerns. At the same time, staff incentives – in particular, individual performance related pay – were introduced from the private sector at exactly the time when they were becoming discredited elsewhere, on the grounds that they damage the teamwork which is essential in creative organisations. Finally, the whole system was unstable in one important respect. Although in theory there were planned targets against which performance could be measured, the devolution of decision making to the individual business units meant that the Corporation seemed to be abandoning any attempt to manage its overall size. As Professor David Vines argued to the Producer Choice Project Director, Michael Starks, during the BFI's Commission on the BBC,

I do not know of many organisations which leave the fundamental question of how big they are to an independent accumulation of individual decisions quite low down in the organisation. It is an odd way to make the fundamental decision about what you are.

This was one of the most pernicious aspects of Producer Choice: that it forced individuals to make a decision, under budget pressure, between the good of their programme and the good of the BBC as a whole. Kenith Trodd argued that, 'The new system gives you impossible choices; if you go outside because you can get a better price for a service, you are jeopardising jobs inside the BBC.' The same pressures produced effects at grass-roots level within the Corporation which contrasted sharply with the rhetoric of its leaders. One of the most alarming features of life for BBC employees in the early 1990s was that contracts grew shorter and shorter, to the point where they might be just weeks long (and some departments deliberately left gaps between contract periods to ensure that individuals did not accrue employment rights). The damaging effect this has on any organisation is clear; someone on a three-month contract will spend a month learning the job, a month doing it, and a month looking for the next one. And they are unlikely to share their best ideas with their temporary colleagues. Such practices are typical in the independent production sector, dominated by small companies and one-off projects, but did not help the BBC get the best from its staff. Although senior management tried to discourage this 'contract culture', department heads were unable to guarantee the volume of work beyond the end of the current financial year. Despite the fine rhetoric of senior management, Producer Choice made it impossible to justify longer contracts in practice.

In this environment of redundancies and closures, darker fears about the intentions of Producer Choice began to surface, fuelled by a continuing perception that Birt, the outsider, did not value the organisation. Nor did the armies of private sector consultants inspire confidence, not least because the language they spoke was abstract and alienating. Nick McCarthy, a representative of the trade union BECTU, recalls that one could always tell which departments had been through Producer Choice training programmes because of the change in the language used by managers. John Tydeman, the former head of radio drama, responsible for both discovering Joe Orton and encouraging Sue Townsend to write *The Secret Diary of Adrian Mole*, noticed that when he resigned the resulting vacancy was advertised as 'Business Unit Manager', a post he would not have applied for and would certainly not have been appointed to. Perhaps it is not surprising that a *Guardian* cartoon satirising the new Beeb-speak updated the BBC's famous motto, 'Nation shall speak peace unto nation', as 'Macro-political entities may exploit the market in talk-based product relevant to conflict resolution.'

The real fear was that the whole process was actually part of a hidden agenda which involved breaking up the BBC and turning it into a publisher-broadcaster – the same issue which had surfaced during the Resources Review. One of the questions which dominated discussions of Producer Choice before it came into existence was whether there was a point at which the senior management would decide that too much work had gone outside, and that the Corporation was in danger of collapsing. Would 40% be too much? Or 50%? For BECTU, alarm bells started to ring when, in a meeting with John Birt shortly after he became Director General, they were told that he would only be concerned if less than half of the BBC's work was still being done inside.

The blueprint for contriving a collapse of this kind was laid out by the Open University's Professor Stuart Hall, in an article in *Marxism Today* on the Thatcherite approach to public institutions. The first step – 'the Model' – involved capping the institution's income; then detaching or floating off as many operations as possible; then using market mechanisms to squeeze people and resources into the private sector. The second phase – 'the Strategy' – required three waves of managers: the first, to break the power of the professionals, restore managerial prerogative, and restructure the institution along market lines; the second, 'to tutor and educate public institutions in the mystery of market calculation'; and the third, to advise on implementing 'efficiency' measures. 'They have the advantage', Hall notes, 'of giving "cuts" a spuriously impersonal air.' It is impossible to read the description of the Model without thinking of the way in which the BBC's licence fee was frozen, then an independent production quota imposed, then services contracted outside the BBC; or of the Strategy without thinking of the way in which successive waves of consultants were used to implement Producer Choice. The effect inside the public institutions was described by Hall:

> Most people spend their working hours learning the new language of incentives, cost effectiveness, quality audits, performance indicators, and the rest of the managerial newspeak, in which the crude calculus of market forces is covered over by the thin fig leaf of systems analysis mumbo-jumbo and quack psychology.

Those staff who were not familiar with *Marxism Today* could see at first hand the effect of Producer Choice on the BBC. The case of Ealing Studios almost encapsulates it. It was clear very early on that Television Film Services (TFS), the Producer Choice guinea pig, would never break even if it had to pay the full rent on Ealing, and so a buyer was sought. BBRK, a small theatrical and film company, offered to buy it, and the haggling began. TFS planned to rent back from BBRK some, but not all, of the office space at Ealing, and the argument about how much (which would clearly affect the price of the deal) dragged on for months. A figure of 18,000 square feet was eventually agreed. The second condition was more controversial. The BBC also guaranteed to book the studios for a minimum period of time each year, even though – under Producer Choice – no resource departments had any such guarantees (and with them the studios might not have needed to be sold). Without the guarantees, it is unlikely the deal would have been done at all. It was hardly a level playing field.

Geoff Mulgan of the think-tank Demos has observed that one of the questions to ask of management systems is whether they value the ethos of the organisation as much as financial incentives. It is hard to examine Producer Choice closely and believe that it is the best way of preserving the ethos of the BBC. Addressing a conference on the arts and broadcasting in 1992, the director Richard Eyre recalled one experience:

> A few years ago I was filming *Tumbledown* on a cold hill in Wales, at night, in the pouring rain, and talking to a prop man. 'I like working here,' he said, 'you get to make good programmes.' 'Here?' I said. 'Here? In Wales? In the Black Hills?' 'No, no,' he said. 'I mean at the BBC.' 'Here' was a territory of the mind – a heartland if you like – and it's one that has been systematically eroded over the past few years by

the reductive logic of market economics.

The production of television and radio programmes is about teamwork, and on a successful programme everyone in the team – writer, director, producer, designer, cameraman, sound engineer, lighting engineer, editor, production assistant and others – makes their contribution to the success through the open exchange of ideas, from the large to the trivial. But as Geoff Mulgan has noted of other areas where cultural commodities are being produced, based on ideas and inventiveness:

> Excessive marketisation (sic) prevents peer appraisal and criticism, since it removes the incentives to reveal information to other potential competitors; it limits the collective innovation that comes from a free flow of information; it tends to make people short-term, against the long-term interests of the institution.

As so often, the size of the BBC, and the slowness of its rate of internal change, had meant that by the time it came to implementing change, the methods which it was intent on introducing had already been discredited elsewhere. The result has been the slow erosion of the skills, people and infrastructure that have enabled the BBC to earn the reputation it has among its viewers and listeners. The effect on internal morale was inexorable. Dennis Potter, for example, recalled being on the set of his film *Midnight Movie* and watching 'a middle-aged man on the far edge of the set start to cry after a phone call from some manager at the [Television] Centre'.

Some producers have already started to worry that the quality which the BBC used to take for granted is slipping away. As one explained, 'I always used to assume that if it wasn't perfect, it wasn't good enough. Now you don't. And it will show in programmes. It certainly showed in my last series.' Another observed wryly that although quality would fall, it would happen too slowly for viewers and listeners to notice.

The impact of Producer Choice made itself felt at all stages of the production process (though the impact was different in different areas and different regions). 'The way the BBC makes good programmes', wrote an anonymous radio producer in *The Times*,

> . . . is by lots of producers and researchers sitting around tossing ideas back and forth. If an idea – for a programme, or an item for a programme, or a particular pundit to pontificate on an item on a programme – sounds as if it might bear fruit, they'll take it further by making a telephone call or getting News Information to send some cuttings. Some ideas turn out to be good ones, some bad: the new system seems to be founded on the belief that a higher ratio of good ideas can be squeezed out by charging penalties for non-runners.

At the pre-production stage, television producers found they were now apparently expected to know information (about camera crews, studios, and edit suites) that previously had been held centrally, and the quality of shooting suffered as programmes found themselves using smaller, less experienced crews to stay within budget. At the editing stage, the internal market has changed the relationship between producers and video and film editors, who are now conscious that the producer represents business for them. The change does not necessarily produce the best programmes. As Anne Laking, who made the series *The Adventurers* for Science Features explains:

> Before, you would have stand-up rows with the VT [videotape] editor who would say, 'That's a terrible idea, it'll never work.' 'You'd say, 'There's no other way, it'll look fine, try it.' He'd try it, and it would look awful. There was some creative tension. You could ultimately overrule them because you were the director or the producer, but a lot of the time he would be right. Now what happens is that each of the VT editors know that if they're not asked for individually, their productivity is looked at, so they're loath to do anything that might irritate you. I would much prefer someone who says to me 'That idea's never going to work'. But if my liking you decides whether you keep your job, you're not going to say that.

The effects of Producer Choice reach far beyond the programme making process. For example, Gordon Croton, in charge of television training, condemned the impact of the system in *The Observer*. 'Many of the craft skills of editing, camerawork, directing and writing are being lost because of the rundown of training', he said in September 1993. His department's budget had fallen by a third over two years, as other departments said they could not afford to send their staff on courses. With more people on contracts, and with department heads unable to predict the demand for staff beyond the end of the current financial year, it was unsurprising. At the BBC's main training centre, at Wood Norton in Evesham, there were cuts in training and support staff. The management's argument was that since the BBC was not currently recruiting there was no need to retain staff for basic training, and advanced training (in lighting or editing, for example) could be bought in. The BBC's Research and Development department at Kingswood Warren in Surrey, responsible for such inventions as Ceefax and NICAM digital stereo, also suffered redundancies as staff levels were cut almost by half.

Despite its name, Producer Choice is not only about the way the Corporation produces programmes. It is also about control of the organisation from the top down, although this is usually obscured by the market rhetoric. Birt's view of the BBC was spelt out in the Fleming Lecture he gave in March 1993, just before the launch of Producer Choice.

Auntie – like so many other large organisations in the public and private sectors in the post-war years – became a vast command economy; a series of entangled, integrated baronies, each providing internally most of its needs. . . . Territorialism often stifled initiative. Nothing was transparent, everything opaque. It was Byzantine in many of its structures. . . . Creative freedom was frustrated.

It might have looked from the top as though creative freedom was frustrated, but that was not how it was experienced by the people who worked there. Instead those baronies – although difficult to manage – provided an environment where people were often able to do good work. As the former BBC Television Controller Stuart Hood wrote in 1970, 'The size of the BBC. . . means that not all activity can be controlled; that there are corners in which producers can work quietly at tasks which might be officially frowned on but which may, when completed, be welcomed by the authorities as signs of initiative.' The 'corridor culture', the network of informal discussions and contacts which is often the glue that holds large organisations together, may be one of the most valuable assets the BBC has.

Producer Choice is designed to use the BBC's financial systems to give the Director General tighter control over the programme making system than ever before. Under the new system, the DG agrees budgets with the channel controllers, using a complex system of typical or 'tariff' prices for the different types of programmes in the planned schedules. The funds to pay for the programmes are not released, however, until the programmes have appeared on screen, so that the Director General can ensure that what is being transmitted is in line with the BBC's stated aims and objectives.

In doing this, it is superimposing a new and complex layer of bureaucracy over what is, historically, already a highly developed bureaucracy. One former editor described the BBC as being 'structured like a government-in-exile in broadcasting, with many vestiges of Whitehall still left'. This is the BBC which, until it was exposed in the 1980s, used to provide an office to a retired member of MI5 who would routinely vet journalists and other staff; which, until the late 80s, used secretly to flag with a Xmas-tree-shaped stamp the personnel records of staff deemed to be politically suspect, thereby preventing their promotion above certain levels; and which, until recently, would, as a matter of course, have someone from the 'Establishment' Department sit alongside Personnel on interview boards to represent the Corporation's interests. (The word 'board' is taken straight from civil service use.) What Producer Choice has done is not to remove this bureaucracy but to add to it. While the intention is to reduce staffing, and many staff have gone – particularly in the craft areas – hundreds of staff have arrived to run the new financial systems.

Overall, there have probably been savings through redundancies and cost-cutting, but they are impossible to quantify. The position is confused because some who have left the staff have returned to work as freelances. John Birt claimed at the Royal Television Society Convention in September 1993 that the savings from Producer Choice were £100m in the first year, rising to £175m in year three and continuing at that level (£100m is an eighth of the Television Service's annual budget). What savings there have been seem to have been achieved principally by cutting budgets. And while BBC managers insist that money has been transferred from overheads into programmes, part of this is simply an accounting trick; where programmes use support services such as libraries, the cost of this now appears in programme budgets instead of being charged to overheads.

The defence of Producer Choice is simple enough; that a public organisation has to be clear that it is delivering its service for the lowest possible cost which is compatible with other objectives (such as equal opportunities and ethical business practice, both of which are specifically mentioned in the BBC's internal Producer Choice documents). As the current Finance Director, Rodney Baker-Bates, told the trade magazine *Broadcast*, 'I think in the 1990s any organisation taking public money has to show it is being as efficient as possible – otherwise you'd be in here writing about profligacy and waste.'

But whatever the public rationale for Producer Choice, the political subtext shouts far louder; that without it, the BBC could not have been confident about winning the battle with the government over the terms on which its charter was to be renewed in 1996. In this, *Extending Choice* and Producer Choice have to be seen as two sides of the same coin. On the one hand, in the absence of a clear sense from the government of what the BBC's purpose is, the BBC tried in *Extending Choice* to write its own version of what it was for; and on the other hand it then, via Producer Choice, tried to reassure the government that this purpose would be delivered to viewers and listeners as efficiently as possible.

From the outside, though, this seems like a double bind; that the only way to save the licence fee which underpins the BBC's status as a pre-eminent public broadcasting organisation has been to introduce a management system which is endangering the BBC's purpose as a broadcaster and which runs the risk of destroying the very infrastructure which has made it so effective. It is much easier to kill an innovative environment, and much harder to create one, than anyone imagines. To outsiders, it seemed as if the Corporation was prepared to settle for survival no matter what the cost. It is not surprising that so many of the BBC's friends have despaired of the changes.

Richard Eyre, perhaps, spoke for them all when he talked about Producer Choice at the Edinburgh Television Festival in August 1993, five months after its introduction:

When I worked in the Drama Department I was as ready as my colleagues to moan about the intractability of many departments, and their lack of imagination and the blackmail that they sometimes exercised. But was it *really* impossible to introduce a management that nurtured talent, encouraged innovation, believed in training, and was prepared to understand the priorities of programme makers, without resorting to the ideology of the firing squad in the shape of Producer Choice? And was it really necessary to sell off the Film Studios at Ealing in order to 'reorganise priorities'? To an onlooker, as I've been for some years, it seemed like the Americans in Vietnam, trying to win a war by exterminating a culture.

CHAPTER THIRTEEN
THE TIDE TURNS

The counter-attack against Producer Choice, and the management philosophy it represented, started in earnest with Michael Grade's MacTaggart Lecture in August 1992, although even before that, the salvos of criticism had been growing louder and more frequent. A year earlier Peter Goodchild, the BBC's Head of Plays until 1990, had defended the old order in *Broadcast* magazine, pointing out the creative benefits of what had seemed to outsiders to be an elaborate hierarchical maze:

> Paradoxically this bureaucratic structure has served much more to protect the producers within it than to bind or stifle them.... These standing armies of talent all under one roof have provided unique opportunities for day-to-day interactions crucial for the flow of ideas.

It was this critical mass of talent, he argued, which made the BBC special and needed to be preserved.

Since Goodchild had recently departed, his arguments could have been dismissed as misguided nostalgia. That was certainly not true of Paul Jackson, Director of Programmes at Carlton Television and emerging as one of the most important players in commercial broadcasting. Addressing the Royal Television Society in December 1991, Jackson had echoed the misgivings of Goodchild and reiterated the importance of a 'critical mass'. He warned that: 'As an outsider, I am beginning to get a creeping sense that the BBC may be seeking a commercial resolution to a non-commercial proposition.' He explicitly linked the recent fall in BBC television's share of viewing to staff and budget reductions:

> Might it not just be that, after three years of continuing revision of budgets and cutbacks in the major programming departments, programme makers themselves are so grossly under-budgeted and so totally demoralised and bewildered that they are producing less than their best work.

But it was Grade who launched the debate into the public arena. As one of nature's populists, he knew the value of the Edinburgh Television Festival as a publicity platform. At the end of August's silly season, and over a bank holiday, editors are grateful for copy of any kind. When the Chief Executive of one public channel launches a ferocious attack on the top management of another, it falls on newsrooms like a gift from heaven. The MacTaggart

Lecture is effectively the Television Festival's keynote speech, and Grade
used it as an opportunity for articulating all the fears about internal BBC
changes that had been circulating for months.

Part of Grade's effectiveness was his ability to speak eloquently about the
importance of the BBC in setting standards for all other channels:

> Where you have strong, benchmark public service television channels
> driven to produce excellent, home-grown programming . . . then all tele-
> vision has to aspire to the same quality in order to compete and gain a
> share of the viewing.

He himself was in a unique position, having seen at first hand the relentless
commercialism of American film and television, where he had worked immediately before joining the BBC. It was, he said, 'a thrill to know that the scripts
were once again more important than the deals, that the people who made the
programmes cared more about the finished product than almost anything else
in the world.'

There was no doubting his passion, or the chord which he struck with many
of the BBC producers and directors in the audience. When he turned his attention to what was going wrong, his scathing comments about centralised
management style ('sort of pseudo-Leninist') and the effect on staff morale of
internal reorganisation and staff cuts received loud ovations. Again, he linked
these changes to the quality of the creative process: 'Apprehension and insecurity do not create an atmosphere in which the imagination can flower. And
if that elusive flower withers, then the BBC will become just one more publisher of other people's ideas.'

The significance of Grade's speech lay not just in its rousing indictment of
current practices in the BBC, but in its passionate appreciation of what the
BBC allows creative people to do. While it was always easy to make fun of
some of the rigid, mechanistic language in which new management systems
(and Producer Choice in particular) were being defined, no-one had really
spelt out the way in which some inefficiency might be essential to a cultural
organisation run for quality rather than profit.

There will always, said Grade, be 'false starts, dud ideas, and needless
extravagances' because the process is 'governed by the canons of art rather
than the laws of industrial mass production. There are economical ways of
doing it just as painting by numbers is a more economical method of producing a picture than trying it Rembrandt's way.' Grade also denounced the
'enervating' caution in current affairs and in dealing generally with the new
post-Thatcher government. But this had been done before, and Grade was no
politician. His real credibility and his real impact – as an ex-BBC person
whose creative credentials were unimpeachable – came from articulating the
growing sense of despair of those within the BBC who fervently believed in
what they were doing but took the view that top management did not share

their aspirations. As a result of his speech in Edinburgh, Michael Grade made them feel he was one of them.

After Grade's speech, and during the countdown to Birt's formal accession, the rancour seemed to swell almost daily. One former BBC producer, the much-respected Roger Bolton, again singled out staff morale as the central problem and described the sense of 'frustrated affection' felt by those within. 'The BBC has a deep and abiding hold on those who have worked for the corporation', he wrote in *The Guardian*, and contrasted this with the apparent indifference of those at the top. 'The overwhelming impression given by those who now run the BBC is that they have no affection for it and for its past achievements and no real respect for its programme makers.' One month later, Richard Eyre attacked the BBC's 'loss of nerve and loss of vision'. An anonymous producer, quoted by Raymond Snoddy in *The Financial Times*, talked about the consequences of the new 'contract culture' in which short-term employment, often no more than three or six months at a time, was replacing permanent staff: 'I think there is a crisis of morale. All these changes are taking place and [there is] no real sense of where we're going.'

All this meant John Birt became the BBC's twelfth Director General in an atmosphere of unprecedented turmoil and apprehension within the organisation. Given the background and history of his appointment, it was certain that in his first few months every decision taken and every statement made would be placed under the media microscope. It was not just the eighteen months of enforced corporate silence that was over, but the personal silence of the man who had already been demonised. While the political heat now seemed to be off, the sacrifices which had been imposed in order to reduce it had created a groundswell of internal resistance which did not augur well.

Birt's first move on taking over was to confound his critics by making two new appointments which attracted universal praise. Would-be dictators tend to surround themselves with people less competent and charismatic than themselves. Birt appointed two people with long and distinguished careers in broadcasting, both of whom were admired, in particular, for their effectiveness and their open manner with staff. Bob Phillis was a career manager in the Checkland mould, who had run Central TV and Carlton before being recruited as Chief Executive of Independent Television News. ITN faced financial crisis, and – by general agreement – was in need of substantial cuts and restructuring. He had kept the respect of the staff despite widespread redundancies, and was regarded as a likeable and approachable character who could achieve financial discipline with a human face – exactly the combination of personal qualities which seemed to elude Birt. He was brought in as Birt's deputy to take charge of the BBC's commercial affairs, with a parallel brief to look after the World Service following John Tusa's retirement. Over the next eighteen months, it was to become a pivotal appointment.

Along with Phillis came Liz Forgan, a passionate devotee of the public service philosophy in broadcasting. She had made her reputation in print
journalism as one of a succession of highly successful editors of *The
Guardian*'s women's page, and had been recruited as a Commissioning Editor
to Channel 4 by Jeremy Isaacs. In 1988, she became Director of Programmes
from which position she had vigorously defended the absolute right of journalists to challenge the voices of authority. She had argued forcefully for the
BBC to withdraw from commercial activities on the grounds that the commercial tail would end up wagging the public service dog; and because –
ultimately – those activities might jeopardise the BBC's right to the licence
fee. But she had always defended the right and duty of the BBC to be popular
as well as high quality, and at Edinburgh in 1991 had enthusiastically endorsed
the BBC's need to keep Radios 1 and 2. It was nevertheless surprising that
Forgan was made Managing Director of Radio, a medium in which her
experience was limited to guest appearances. There was also some consternation at the removal of Forgan's predecessor, David Hatch, who had lived and
breathed radio since his days as the highly successful producer of *I'm Sorry
I'll Read That Again*. Hatch became Special Assistant to the Director General,
an indeterminate job of some influence but no power. Later in the year, for the
second time in his career, he gave the traditional after-dinner address to the
annual Radio Festival. 'I am told', he said 'that you get two chances to give
this speech – once on the way up and once on the way down.' He paused.
'Welcome to my second speech.'

Taken together, the appointments of Phillis and Forgan were reassuring.
They showed, first, that the BBC could still attract the very best managerial
and creative talent available; and, second, that John Birt was not the dedicated control freak portrayed by his detractors. He wanted to surround himself
with capable people. Reassurance was important, given the statement of policy which accompanied the announcement of these appointments. In a 35-page
document called *Turning Promises into Realities*, Birt outlined a massive
agenda of managerial and organisational change designed to turn the theory of
Extending Choice into practice.

First, there was to be a year-long Programme Strategy Review whose objective was to provide 'detailed programme and channel strategies against which
our future achievements can be measured'. It was to be an explicitly creative
exercise headed by Liz Forgan and Alan Yentob, now temporarily in charge of
both BBC channels after Jonathan Powell's departure in December. And
although 'distinctive and original' were again important keywords, the market-
gap language of the Chairman's annual report statement was notably absent.

Second, there would be a continued drive for efficiency, through the implementation of Producer Choice, and for accountability, through a new Annual
Performance Review which would measure achievement against aims. This
would culminate in a 'fuller, more open annual report, containing more mean-

ingful information'. Third, the traditional hallmarks of a bureaucracy – 'terri-torialism, red tape, confusion of purpose' and unclear lines of responsibility – would be cleared away. This would involve a number of changes: a smaller, streamlined corporate centre; a new Resource, Engineering and Services Directorate with responsibility for the resource business units created under Producer Choice; separation of programme commissioning and scheduling from programme departments; programme rights to be held by programme departments which could then choose what deals to make with BBC Enterprises or other commercial outlets; and the unification of World Service Radio and World Service Television into a single directorate. Finally, in a clear attempt to persuade staff that he was sensitive to their concerns, Birt emphasised the importance of a workplace 'which is involving and which enthuses each member of staff to play their full part'. He announced that every member of staff would be invited to attend a day-long workshop and – to some wry amusement – that a new Masters Degree would be inaugurated tailored to the BBC. He also foreshadowed an eventual move to bi-medialism, with radio and television production merging into single programme-making direc-torates.

It was a comprehensive plan whose central aim was, according to BBC publicists, 'modernisation'. Its core thesis – that a labyrinthine bureaucracy required urgent and extensive overhaul – gelled with the experience of most BBC executives as well as current political wisdom. Its publicity value in terms of the charter review debate was vital and David Mellor (from his new platform as over-exposed media pundit) did his bit to support his friend, say-ing, 'Nothing on this scale has ever been attempted before in the many decades since the BBC was created.' This was patent hyperbole, but the overwhelming 'new broom' impression could not have failed to impress the sceptical politi-cians who held the BBC's future in their hands. The problem was that, despite attempts to allay staff fears, Birt had still not overcome his fatal flaw: an inability to convince the troops of the ultimate good of what he was doing. The ideas, some of which had been brewing for many years, were mostly sound and uncontroversial. But the overall impression of a wholesale transformation expressed in textbook management-speak served only to reinforce the fears of many staff who feared either for their jobs or for the thriving creative atmos-phere of the BBC or – in many cases – for both. To some, the new structures and systems – 'The restructured, streamlined BBC, full of clusters of people measuring each other's performance against annual committee-established norms', in the words of the *Telegraph*'s Brenda Maddox – sounded even more Orwellian than what had gone before. Seven weeks later, the simmering resentment of John Birt which lay just below the surface in many parts of the Corporation erupted in dramatic fashion. It very nearly cost him his job.

On 28 February, *The Independent on Sunday* carried the front-page headline

BBC HELPS ITS CHIEF TO AVOID TAX. The reporter, Chris Blackhurst, had received information that the Director General was not a member of staff but was paid on a freelance basis through his own company, John Birt Productions. Through a simple check at Companies House Blackhurst had discovered the accounts of John Birt's company, complete with income from Birt's salary as Deputy Director General and full details of his 'administration expenses'. Inquiries to the BBC press office had elicited the admission that, even as DG, Birt was being paid in the same way. In the days that followed, there was particular merriment at the item described as 'wardrobe' costs, £3,666, most of which, it was assumed, reflected Birt's penchant for Armani suits. 'Armanigate' was born.

The headline contained a strong implication of financial impropriety, and a hint of scandal. In that sense, it was a complete non-story. There was nothing illegal in Birt's arrangements, the amount of tax saved was small, and his accounts contained far more detail than company directors were required to provide by law. Throughout the television industry it was common practice for salaries to be paid through a company, a move which reflected the fluidity of employment and the rise of the 'contract culture'. It was certainly common practice in the private sector, from which Birt had come, and not unheard of in the BBC. The tax-saving aspect was a red herring which obscured a less tangible but more profound issue.

It came down to a question of belonging. Birt's reputation, whether justified or not, was of someone for whom the BBC was no more than a career staging-post. He had spent much of his first six months in news and current affairs disparaging the work of people who were widely respected, and had never expressed real pride in the BBC's past or present achievements. This may have been partly political. In his bid for the top job, and to preserve the BBC from severe political intervention, he may have felt it appropriate to distance himself from any grandiloquent celebration of what the BBC stood for. But it left the widespread impression of a man who was not, at heart, a passionate loyalist. In the words of *The Daily Telegraph*, his financial arrangements 'evoked images of the type of financial planning appropriate to a part-time worker offering a part-time commitment'. For a chief executive who already had a severe problem in the low level of staff morale, this was not good psychology.

Much fun was had by the nation's columnists in applying the semi-detached principle of employment to other public institutions. Among the new companies suggested were Archbishop of Canterbury Ltd, Metropolitan Police Commissioners and Associates, and Cabinet Secretarial Services plc. Ian Aitken, in *The Guardian*, proposed a freelance queen, who could solve her financial difficulties by taking advantage of 'tax-free provision for polishing the Crown Jewels, feeding the corgis, getting Philip's uniforms cleaned and other similar functions inseparable from conducting a well-ordered monarchy'. But the point was a serious one. Even after the privations and traumas of the 80s, the BBC was still more than a cog in the wheel of the British television industry. It had a status and a role in British society which set it alongside other quintessentially British institutions. It should have been unthinkable that a Director General would be anything other than a fully paid-up public servant.

In some ways, such criticism was unfair to Birt, who had given up enormous executive share options when leaving LWT and who had been offered seven-figure sums while Deputy DG to put his name to ITV licence applications. This was hardly the mark of someone only in it for the money, and one former colleague described him as 'genuinely interested in public service'. He had told another that, although it had been a difficult decision to make, in the end, 'There is no better job than being Director General of the BBC.' There was no question, then, that he saw it as the pinnacle of his career rather than a stepping stone. But having achieved the pinnacle, neither Birt nor Hussey could appreciate the symbolic nature of his freelance status at the very time that staff desperately needed reassurance. They had always felt that he was not 'one of us', and this seemed to be the final confirmation.

By an unfortunate accident of timing, Birt had agreed to be interviewed by former Channel 4 Chief Executive Jeremy Isaacs on 9 March on stage at the National Film Theatre. The occasion was a curtain-raiser to a two-day 'Commission' organised by the British Film Institute in which an independent panel was to take evidence and compile a report on the BBC's future. As BFI director Wilf Stevenson pointed out in his opening remarks, the BBC's Royal Charter had only once in its 66-year history been renewed without a Royal Commission – and that was in 1946 when a post-war government of reconstruction had more pressing matters on its plate. Even then, former Director General Sir Frederick Ogilvie had complained, in a letter to *The Times*, 'Is the future of this great public service to be settled without public enquiry . . . into the many technical and other changes which have taken place in the last ten years?' Nearly fifty years later, there was even greater cause to put the same question, and the BFI Commission was a brave attempt to do what was manifestly the government's duty.

Although it had nothing like the same gravitas as a Royal Commission, it was a significant public occasion in which the Director General of the BBC could be expected to map out a coherent and invigorating vision for the Corporation's future. The problem was that the event now coincided with a debate, not just about Birt's tax and employment status, but about his very survival. Isaacs, in no mood for delicacy, started with a series of questions about the tax revelations and about a mysterious 'secretary' who was paid by Birt's company and whose identity was exercising large sections of the press (as everyone suspected, it turned out to be his wife). The result was a wooden and defensive performance instead of a passionate *credo*. Towards the end of an altogether uncomfortable interview, Birt himself seemed to sense the irony implicit in his lacklustre performance when faced with an interviewer who was widely seen as the best DG the BBC never had. 'Do you think', asked Isaacs, 'that the language you use is always direct and earthy enough ... to motivate, to lead and to inspire the programme makers of the BBC?' It was an awkward question with a revealing answer:

> I hope so, Jeremy, but you seem to be pointing at a difference that others have noted between us. You are such a person yourself. . . . You are a brilliant leader from the front, a great orator and an eloquent man.

It was a generous appraisal of Isaacs, but the implicit contrast highlighted a point that did not escape Birt's critics: that someone of real presence and charisma, an Isaacs or a Grade, would never have looked so vulnerable in trying to defend themselves and their institution. On the other hand, said Birt's defenders, had they been in Birt's place there might have been no institution left to defend.

Behind the scenes at the BBC, most senior managers had decided that losing the Director General after such a long period of uncertainty and instability was simply not worth the pain. Not all agreed with him or even liked him, but all became convinced that, for the good of the Corporation, he should not be forced into an ignominious resignation. With some careful orchestration by Margaret Thatcher's favourite PR guru, Tim Bell, two letters appeared simultaneously in *The Times* of 15 March. One, signed by all ten members of the Board of Management, proclaimed John Birt as 'The best person to lead the BBC'. The other, signed by six of the Corporation's most senior (and high-profile) journalists, went much further than a simple statement of support.

In a style which was scarcely a model of objective reporting they attributed 'the attacks on the Director General' wholly to malice on the part of the disaffected: 'John Birt's real offence is to be the architect of the plan which is effecting radical change at the BBC. . . . What we are seeing here is a last minute and underhand attempt to destroy it by destroying him.' Such a blatantly one-sided assessment of the issues behind the row was as inaccurate as the claim that it was nothing but a principled and altruistic response to an issue of abstract ethics. Everyone knew that this had become an enormously complex issue, in which real questions about the nature of public service and Birt's ability to lead were inextricably bound up with real anger (and some fear) about the changes he had imposed. For BBC journalists, one of whom was ultimately responsible for BBC news reporting of this matter, to deliver their own subjective verdict breached every canon of that impartiality which Birt himself had been so keen to inculcate. It was an intemperate letter, and one passage in particular, which attacked the hostile voices 'too cowardly to give their names in public', was to have serious consequences later.

Given such clear messages of support from senior management and staff within the Corporation, it became impossible for the governors to do anything other than back their Director General. In fact, as several Board of Management members pointed out privately – followed by newspaper columnists and editorials in unusually broad agreement – it was the governors themselves who had placed the BBC in such an invidious position. More precisely, it was the Chairman and Vice-Chairman who, alone on the governing board, had known about and authorised Birt's freelance arrangements. However insensitive Birt had been in failing to understand the implications of his status, he was simply continuing a long-standing industry practice. It was Hussey and Barnett who represented the BBC and its traditions and who were ultimately responsible for the Director General's appointment and the terms of his contract. Birt was not helped, as Hugo Young wrote in *The Guardian*, 'by Hussey–Barnett stitching up his job without the opportunity to prove he was better than any other candidate. He's been dealt a devastating blow by their contempt for the culture they were supposed to be defending.'

Once again, the spotlight had returned to a Chairman and his deputy whose single-minded determination to run the BBC on their terms had inflicted real damage on the Corporation's standing. Many of their fellow governors were furious at discovering that the terms of Birt's contract had been concealed from them, and at the impossible position in which they had thus been placed. They made their feelings known, but were persuaded in the end that resignations would be counter-productive. A bland statement issued on 18 March simply noted that, 'The question of whether resignations would be in the interest of the BBC was discussed ... it was agreed that they would not.' But Hussey was chastened. After six and a half years of wielding unprecedented power as Chairman, he had only survived one of the greatest internal crises in BBC history by the grace of the governors he had dominated for so long. He was in their debt, and from that point on his chairmanship began to revert to the more orthodox and less influential style of his predecessors. Three weeks of public ignominy had gone to the roots of institutional morality, and left a nasty taste about contemporary standards of probity within the BBC. Hussey had survived, just, but the saga had yet again raised some fundamental questions about the appointment, accountability, and power of the BBC's governors and Chairman.

For John Birt, the problem of confidence in his leadership and management skills continued. In his Fleming Memorial Lecture, delivered on 30 March, he was contrite about the damage caused by the whole tax affair, and delivered a powerful eulogy of the BBC as an institution – including tributes to a host of BBC programmes, presenters and characters from the past, and special mentions for both Radio 3 and Radio 1. But, however eloquent his praise and however profound his regret, the massive uncertainties of Producer Choice were still to be implemented two days later. For BBC staff, increasing numbers of whom were being placed on short-term contracts, fear and insecurity were the real issue. And their hostility was not diminished by the news at the beginning of April that Birt was to receive a pay rise of £50,000 while staff had to be satisfied with the agreed public sector norm of 1.5%. The increase was designed to compensate him for his loss of earnings after moving from self-employed to employed status, and was justified by comparisons with the vastly inflated salaries now being offered to experienced executives in ITV. But inevitably it added to the sense of alienation amongst staff already feeling unloved.

The sense of embattlement was not helped by a tendency amongst Birt's supporters to attribute disaffection to a Luddite or 'old guard' resistance to change at all costs. Grievances were, certainly, magnified by the availability of several former BBC executives to pass judgement on Birt's reforms in opinion columns and letters. Not all of the judgements were models of objective criticism. The trade union BECTU, which represented large numbers of BBC staff, was not always considered in its resistance to almost every reform. But it remained absolutely true that a great many dedicated BBC professionals were becoming profoundly unhappy with their working conditions and with a management style which they saw as deeply unsympathetic to their own notions of public broadcasting.

Moreover, they resented the 'propaganda' message that this was simply an obstinate reaction by a small, hardcore clique to much-needed reorganisation. The antagonism was plainly more widespread and included many long-standing BBC people with personal experience of the BBC's legendary waste and creaking bureaucracy, people who were sympathetic to the call for change. As one producer put it,

> He thinks it's just the staff whingeing because there's been this painful period. He has no sense of the alienation that exists between the staff and the top level of management. I feel I'm a BBC person, I don't feel John Birt is. . . . Lots and lots of us feel like that.

In the BBC, as in other large organisations, complaints about management incompetence were nothing new, going back to the days of Reith himself. The difference, in 1993, was that such criticism did not take place within a framework of a shared sense of purpose. It was becoming a difficult and debilitating atmosphere in which to do good creative work. Various tales of 'fear and loathing' aimed squarely at John Birt leaked out of Broadcasting House, but in the middle of July they became the focus for another explosive public speech – this time from someone within the BBC itself.

Mark Tully was one of those BBC radio correspondents to whose name the epithet 'veteran' was invariably attached. For nearly thirty years he had been living in and reporting on India, and was admired for his enormous knowledge of the sub-continent and his ability to convey it to listeners. He had been asked in January to deliver the keynote speech to the Radio Academy's annual Festival in Birmingham, and had planned a colourful ramble round his career in India. But Tully had been dismayed by the letter to *The Times* signed by BBC journalists, and by the tales of misery he had been hearing about the internal reforms. He had been surprised, then disturbed, by the widespread feeling of anger and decided that his Radio Academy address would provide an ideal platform from which to speak for the disaffected. In his own words, 'Only the voices of those members of staff who approve of the changes have been heard so far.' He decided to give the other side of the argument. The impact of a trenchant attack by such a high-profile name was magnified when *The Independent on Sunday* ran it as their lead story two days before the conference.

Tully was angry about two things. First, that the BBC of old was being denigrated as a fossilised institution incapable of change; and second that the 'revolution' which was sweeping through Broadcasting House was being imposed with a ruthless and autocratic determination which allowed for no dissent. He was particularly concerned about the 'personality cult' which he believed centred on Birt himself, arguing that, 'So many managers parrot his name that many of the staff feel there is some sort of Big Brother watching them.' He spoke of the fear which prevented staff from speaking their minds, and worried about the dangers of a mechanistic approach:

> Surely a broadcasting organisation which depends so much on individual human talent needs to have some flexibility, perhaps even an element of chaos, to allow for experimenters and eccentrics. Great programmes often emerge from apparent chaos. Social engineering, which is now being attempted within the BBC, does not have a very happy history.

Fear, rather than bureaucracy, was the enemy of creativity and ideas. And fear was now rampant.

It was an enormously powerful speech, whose impact was intensified by the consummate delivery of a seasoned broadcaster and public speaker. It won Tully a prolonged standing ovation, and posed some very difficult and very public questions for the Director General's reply the following day. In what was widely regarded as his most effective performance to date, Birt responded by outlining some of the exceptional material available from BBC radio – delivering in particular a rousing defence (again) of Radio 1 and the BBC's determination to resist its privatisation. But he was not prepared to compromise on 'the myth that the BBC was already efficient' and laid into the 'unwieldy, command-style economy' which had characterised programme funding before Producer Choice. He acknowledged the radical nature of the changes and for the first time tackled the potentially harmful effects of short-term contracts.

The one area in which Birt had no effective response, however, was the question of staff morale. His cause was not helped by leaks from within the BBC two days earlier about his planned response. According to BBC sources, he was to portray his critics as 'old soldiers polishing their campaign medals'. The phrase was never used, but it conveyed the very attitude that Tully had attacked. Tully himself had been taken aback by the overwhelming reaction to his speech and the warm reception he had received from BBC insiders. Of 100 supportive letters, 40 were from BBC staff. When he entered the club at the World Service building, Bush House, a week later, staff burst into spontaneous applause. In lifts and offices elsewhere in the BBC, people congratulated him and thanked him. He also found that the impact extended well beyond the confines of the BBC: that he would bump into people from other areas of public service that were undergoing 'reform' – doctors and academics – who were also fearful of speaking out and who wished someone would represent their fears in the same way. 'One of the strange things about my speech', he said several weeks later, 'is that it seems to have struck a much wider chord.'

That chord was to do with the nature of organisational change, a process which – through direct government intervention rather than by proxy – had been imposed upon schools, hospitals, universities, the police and many other areas of British public life. In all these cases, the government, as the main agent of change, bore the brunt of popular hostility. In the BBC's case, the hate-figure was the chief executive. Furthermore, as many private companies had learned, there were certain ways in which chief executives could effect real transformations in cooperation with, rather than in opposition to, their workforces. In one of the most penetrating articles about the nature of the BBC's problems following the Tully–Birt double act, Christopher Lorenz in *The Financial Times* analysed John Birt's dilemma. He compared the vilification heaped on Birt by his own staff with the case of Jack Welch, the chief executive of General Electric in the US, who had implemented a similar programme of transformational change. The difference was that Welch had been successful in winning his staff round. Birt had not because he was 'a less effective leader and his problems are partly self-made'.

Lorenz highlighted a number of those problems, but two in particular were decisive. The first was personality, or what Lorenz called 'his uncommunicative and uninspiring public persona'. It was not just Birt's critics who sometimes despaired of his pedestrian, unspontaneous style. Good friends knew him to be a man of natural wit and humour who, in private, could be genuinely entertaining, but somehow the BBC had emasculated his image. One of his ex-LWT colleagues once asked at a meeting: 'If there's anybody in the room from the BBC, I'd like to know what you've done with him, because I think the man that I see now is actually a *doppelgänger* for the real John Birt who's in a cupboard somewhere.' Birt's problem in this respect was not an isolated phenomenon. Both the ex-leader of the Labour Party Neil Kinnock and even the grey Prime Minister John Major were frequently said to be sharper, funnier and more interesting in private. The glare of attention focused on those in high public office in modern societies can tame even the most ebullient personalities. In Birt's case, there was a particularly unfortunate contrast with his erstwhile rivals for the DG's job like Michael Grade and John Tusa, both effective and charismatic performers who were liked by their staff – Grade at Channel 4, Tusa at the World Service. But whatever his private persona, the public face of John Birt lacked both inspiration and gravitas.

The second problem almost certainly stemmed from the first. According to Lorenz, 'Other errors flow from the advice he has been given by some of the accountancy-based management consultancies on which he has relied to an excessive extent.' Caution, and the need to have difficult decisions supported by external and 'objective' advice, had led to the introduction of numerous and expensive consultancy studies into virtually every aspect of the Corporation's activities. Management consultancies were not new to the BBC. McKinseys had been called in by perhaps the most charismatic Director General of all, Hugh Greene, in 1968 and had completely overhauled the BBC's corporate structure. What was new was the sheer scale of the external interference. It was rumoured that Coopers and Lybrand had a permanent office next to John Birt's, and that he was more inclined to seek their advice than that of his own colleagues. In July 1994, Birt revealed that £6 million had been spent on consultants in the previous eight months, and that the Corporation could not estimate how much had been spent in the last few years – a strange dereliction, given the repeated emphasis on transparency and meticulous accounting.

The trouble with management consultancies is that their approaches are usually formulaic. They work on the basis that there are certain immutable principles – of management or structure or employer–employee relations – from which a broad set of solutions can be derived. Some of them have more experience than others, and the best can boast a wide-ranging practice which straddles private and public sectors. But within any organisation, particularly one as eccentric and organic as the BBC, there are always unique factors which defy universal principles. The shrewd consultancies know that the best guide to the problems – and potential – of an organisation comes from the people who work for it. But Birt's insecurity meant he was prepared to trust few inside the organisation, and even those who believed in the need for change found themselves treated with suspicion.

Perhaps the most public example of the consultants' advice back-firing on the Corporation was the series of workshops designed to explain to staff the principles of *Extending Choice* and the new strategic vision for the BBC. It was an attempt to achieve, in classic consultancy terms, precisely the consensus and unity that leaders of transformational change had managed elsewhere by helping staff – in their own dreadful language – to 'buy into' or 'own' management-led changes. This is done, in Lorenz's words again, 'by co-opting change agents among existing employees at all levels, and inspiring them rather than ordering them to enthuse their own colleagues'. For most BBC staff, the process of enthusement in the workshops bore more resemblance to a PR exercise. There were corporate videos on BBC history, on finance issues, on quality and on the independents. And there was a series of small group exercises which involved identifying BBC 'values' which should be treasured and carried into the future. Finally, there was a session on preparing questions for the Director General when he arrived at the end of the day.

At one of these events, he faced some persistent questioning from a senior producer who said bluntly,

> If you want us to change, we ought to feel we are part of the vision and that this is our vision – we don't feel that. All this kerfuffle over the recent months has done nothing to inspire staff with trust or to make them feel that you are one of us again. What are you going to do about it?

Birt's response revealed a dangerous ambiguity about where his priorities lay. He acknowledged that staff disillusionment was a problem, then added: 'I was only this afternoon with the Heritage Secretary trying to fight for our licence fee as part of charter renewal.' It was not the kind of management message which was required to bring staff on-side, and fuelled suspicion that staff morale was secondary in Birt's mind to the wheeling and dealing in Whitehall. But the real error made by those who set up the workshops was to suppose that the kind of formula successfully applied elsewhere would work amongst people who were sceptics by nature and communicators by profession. Most of those on the receiving end of the *Extending Choice* workshops found them at best spurious and at worst deliberately propagandist.

Inevitably, Tully's speech at the Radio Festival dominated the headlines. It was therefore ironic that, in terms of the BBC's future, it was not the most significant event of the conference. On the same day, Alan Yentob and Liz Forgan gave a press briefing on the progress of their Programme Review which had started at the beginning of the year. It was, essentially, a half-time report and it marked what appeared to be a public renunciation of the 'elitist' market-gap position for BBC programming. Taking this briefing – rather than the Tully critique – as its front-page lead, *The Independent* quoted Yentob as saying,

> The BBC clearly looks after the ABC1 audience but there is a sense from our research that we perhaps look after them too well . . . we need to talk to the whole audience and address them all in different parts of the schedule. That other audience is not so well served.

Although portrayed as a dramatic U-turn, there had been no sudden switch to what was being described as a 'downmarket' strategy. Technically, in fact, there was nothing inconsistent between the Yentob–Forgan position and any of the more recent pronouncements by John Birt, in which he rejected outright the 'Himalayan option'. It was one of those subtle shifts of emphasis which are often translated by journalists into black-and-white confrontations between competing factions; nevertheless, however much Broadcasting House might object to simplistic reporting, it was irrefutable that such language would not have been heard twelve months earlier.

Confirmation that there had indeed been a rethink came from the new annual report which was published two weeks later. Banished from the Chairman's foreword this time was any talk of 'wares' and 'market stalls'. In fact, the word 'market' had been eradicated completely, in favour of a ringing endorsement of the need 'to ensure that the BBC continues its proud tradition of service both to the United Kingdom and the world'. Even the name of John Reith was invoked. More importantly, the word 'popular' made a dramatic reappearance – like a disgraced leader suddenly reinstated in the Soviet pantheon. The BBC had, said Hussey, 'a responsibility to serve all licence-payers with programmes that are popular as well as distinctive'. Again, there was no explicit contradiction of all that had gone before. But the change of tone was manifest, especially when it was emphasised by the clearest possible signals that those who believed passionately in the BBC's needs to keep its popular roots were now having their way.

The need to reassert a belief in populism had never been so urgent. Just eight days before the Radio Academy conference, industry ratings were published which created exactly the public furore that those who argued for popular programmes had always warned about. Official BARB figures showed that for the week ending 27 June BBC-1's share of viewing had slipped to 28.9%, its lowest point for eight years. As BBC executives were keen to point out, some of the shortfall was due to a larger than average share for BBC-2 because of its extensive coverage of the first week of Wimbledon. But it was the reaction to the ratings rather than the cause which made these figures significant. Moved, perhaps, by a perception of permanent crisis at the BBC (and by the lack of any major news stories elsewhere), commentators seized upon this apparent slide in the fortunes of the mainstream BBC channel to speculate about the future of the licence fee. It was back to the age-old question: why should people be asked to pay a compulsory fee of over £80 a year for a service which seemed to be providing less and less of what they wanted? A BBC which is losing viewers and listeners sees support for a universal licence fee ebbing away.

Publication of the BBC-1 ratings switched the spotlight to entertainment programming. Was this the legacy of the undue emphasis on news and current affairs, of the news bureaux and jobs for journalists which had been created since 1987 at the expense of investment in the lighter side of life? Powell had warned of an impending drop in BBC-1's fortunes, and additional weight was added by the arch-entertainer Bill Cotton. 'The BBC is forgetting', he said, 'that it has always been the entertainer of the nation, that its core activity is to make programmes that people enjoy. America has Hollywood and Britain has the BBC.' Although a somewhat exaggerated view of the BBC as prime protector of the nation's entertainment heritage, it was an accurate enough statement of the BBC's duty to make the nation laugh as well as to keep it informed. Cotton was an instinctive entertainer, and no-one of his calibre had emerged to take his place. Partly, this was due to several years of comparative indifference to – or at least lack of encouragement for – unashamed populists. But it was also because initiatives which had been aimed squarely at generating mass audiences had failed to work. The most spectacular failure was the soap opera *Eldorado*. It had been launched amid enormous hype and expectations in July 1992 after internal research had shown that it would improve BBC-1's share by between one and two percentage points, and was promoted as the answer to the BBC's early-evening ratings problem. It never recovered from a disastrous start (one early episode plumbed the depths, with just 2.8 million viewers), and one of Alan Yentob's first actions after becoming BBC-1 Controller was to announce its demise. The decision was taken in March, the final episode shown in July. This was not just a matter of the BBC losing its instinct for a hit show, because even the most seasoned entertainers were deceived. Michael Grade wrote in *The Guardian*: '*Eldorado* is a hit. I predict it will run and run.' Even the 60s BBC had seen failures. The difference in those days was that they were overshadowed by the successes.

As it happened, Cotton's warnings were by now unnecessary, since the BBC was already moving to bring in new blood in two crucial areas. In April, it had announced that Charles Denton would be joining as Head of Drama. Denton had been Director of Programmes at Central, then head of one of the biggest independents, Zenith Productions, the maker of *Inspector Morse*. He was widely regarded as a heavyweight with a real ability to create mass-appeal drama. Then, in August, the BBC announced that for the new post of Head of Entertainment it had poached from Granada TV David Liddiment, a man whose television repertoire included the very light entertainment show *You've Been Framed*. He replaced Jim Moir, a jovial figure who had been around for a long time and whose departure initially prompted Cotton's public outburst. In fact, it was part of the BBC's desire to invigorate rather than run down its entertainment programming.

The same spirit of populism was also starting to infuse current affairs. When Glenwyn Benson had been appointed as the new editor of *Panorama*, she was immediately identified as one of John Birt's LWT cronies who was liable to knock severe holes in the Monday night schedule with dry, analytical programmes on difficult issues. Initially, as her critics delighted in pointing out, a succession of worthy but dull programmes did indeed produce a steady ratings decline. During the summer, however, the agenda had been changing perceptibly. There had been a number of high-profile investigative programmes devoted to issues like police corruption, the unravelling of Terry Venables' financial affairs, rape sentencing and vigilantes. From a low point of under 2.5 million, *Panorama* raised its average audience to over 4.5 million and had, by general consent, started to achieve a new self-confidence. Whatever the strategic direction, journalists do not like playing to empty houses, and it was Benson herself who had pushed for a change in *Panorama*'s direction. But, as one current affairs editor said, 'She was pushing at an open door.'

But while outsiders were detecting a tangible movement away from the 'upmarket' model, internally, producers were still receiving mixed messages. It was one thing for *Extending Choice* to make sweeping statements about 'distinctiveness' while still reaching all audiences, but the BBC's programme makers had to interpret exactly what this meant in their everyday professional lives. One documentaries producer came back from her workshop more confused than ever:

> I can't visualise what kind of programmes I'm being expected to come up with as ideas. If people say to you, I want a popular idea, you go away and think along a certain framework, you think 'popular idea'. If people say to you, 'I want an elitist idea that is a marquee event which no-one else would do', then you think in a completely different way. I have no sense of what it is we're supposed to be getting because we're being told both things. I think we're supposed to come up with populist marquee events which are elitist but which appeal to a wide audience. It is really confused.

A good example of the mixed message in action was a new programme called *999* featuring the emergency services in acts of heroic rescue. It was patently derived – and even took its name – from a voyeuristic American show called *911* and involved the reconstruction of terrible accidents. There was no question that its main purpose was to deliver audiences in the drive to improve BBC-1's ratings performance, but it was not enough to stop there. According to one of the producers, 'Because it's the BBC you have to address the question of what you do with potentially voyeuristic material, and the answer was to put some public service interest into the programme, the "what to do if" sections.' Research showed that these segments, far from being a turn-off, held viewers' attention as much as the reconstructions themselves. But this was sheer good luck rather than careful planning: 'They were put on as a kind of public service sticking plaster, and it came as a surprise that the stuff put in as a BBC gloss to make it palatable was liked just as much.' In the quest for populism, then, there were times when distinctiveness was more of an afterthought than a driving force. It was not surprising that it left several producers feeling rather hazy about their creative responsibilities. The sense of conflicting messages was reinforced by press reporting which often seemed inconsistent. The BBC, inevitably, blamed the press, but even the most respected journalists felt hampered by Broadcasting House. According to *The Guardian*'s Media Editor, Georgina Henry:

> One of the things that really irritated me about reporting the BBC then was all the mixed signals that got thrown out. Are we Himalayan peaks or are we upmarket or downmarket or middle market? Are we low-brow or are we high-brow? We all filed different things. . . . They blamed the press for it. I think it's because they weren't speaking with one voice.

Confusion about the BBC's direction was compounded by the very public resignation at the beginning of August of one of Britain's most long-standing and popular disc jockeys. On his Sunday morning show on Radio 1, broadcasting to five million listeners, Dave Lee Travis announced that he was leaving the BBC because of 'changes being made here which go against my principles'. Yet another instance, it seemed, of the popular being sacrificed in the drive for more distinctiveness. But the reasons were complex, and centred on some difficult strategic decisions for the BBC about its popular music station which was supposed to be aimed at a young audience. The problem was that the station, which throughout the 70s had been pioneering and popular amongst the young, had grown old with its audience. For the new generation, it was as 'hip' as their parents. Dave Lee Travis, at 48, was precisely the sort of DJ beloved of the 60s generation which was making Radio 1 a laughing stock to the under 25s. To restore the balance, changes had to be made – even at the price of some top DJs and the *angst* of many thousands of forty-something Rolling Stones fans. It was easy to see the resignation of 'DLT' (and that of his fellow DJ Simon Bates, which followed shortly after) as part of the same 'elitist' pattern as other unpopular changes, but to do so would have been wrong. The speed of change may have been unfortunate but the motives were still consistent with populism.

At the same time, there were signs of reversal – or at least correction – in other areas. Modifications to Producer Choice were announced which would reduce the number of business units, and make the whole process less clumsy and less mechanistic. Birt's commitment in his Birmingham speech to longer contracts began to be implemented, and some contract staff even found themselves being offered staff jobs. Observers noted an unaccustomed silence from the Chairman, and there was some speculation that he would be gone by the autumn of 1994.

At the Edinburgh Television Festival, playwright Dennis Potter delivered a spectacularly withering indictment of the Birt–Hussey regime which – like Grade's speech the previous year – made the following day's front pages. As an example of beautifully scripted and memorable theatre, it could not be equalled. But as an intelligent critique of life at Broadcasting House, it was over the top and a year out of date. The following day, a motion condemning the BBC was overwhelmingly defeated after a highly effective speech from the Deputy Director General, Bob Phillis. His easy, open and persuasive manner contrasted sharply with Birt's awkwardness, and increasingly over the next few months it was Phillis who represented the BBC on public platforms. A combination of the tax affair, the continuing staff malaise, the miserable ratings performance and the very public attacks from a number of public figures seemed, towards the end of 1993, to have forced the new management team into a significant change of emphasis. What had become disparagingly known as 'Birtism' was in retreat.

CHAPTER FOURTEEN

THE NEW WORLD ORDER

Within the BBC there was now a consensus that the rigid application of Producer Choice principles was resulting in too many absurdities and that there were now enough silly stories of paper-clip requisitions being completed in triplicate to cause real problems – not just in PR terms but for the BBC's own stated objective of achieving the best business practice. Three weeks after Edinburgh came the biennial Royal Television Society convention at Cambridge, attended *en masse* by all the industry's key figures. When Liz Forgan – who had lost none of her forthright honesty since joining the BBC – called Producer Choice 'a shambles', it was clear that another reorganisation was on the way. Six weeks later, John Birt announced that the original 480 business units would be cut to less than 200 by the following April and that 'There will be longer-term relationships and fewer sources of supply.'

Much the more significant event of the Cambridge convention was the keynote address by Heritage Secretary Peter Brooke. At this point, the BBC might have expected some generous acknowledgement of the enormous upheavals it had undergone in the name of efficiency and transparency – the very objectives which the government had constantly been telling it to embrace. They had been embraced with vigour, and had caused much soul-searching and a great deal of pain. But politically, this was not the time to concede the upper hand. Instead of praise, Brooke issued barely concealed warnings about the fragility of the licence fee and the possible death of the organisation. He made it clear that the BBC was expected to continue with its reforms because, without them, 'The future of the licence fee in the short term, and of the BBC itself in the longer term, might need to be reconsidered from a very different perspective.' The emphasis throughout was on the need for change and the dire consequences of stasis: 'We might . . . find ourselves contemplating, rather sadly, the demise of a dinosaur. Organisations which cannot adapt to changing circumstances will not survive.' This was, of course, precisely the message which the management team had been impressing on staff since Checkland's appointment, and which had underscored virtually every strategic move of the last seven years. There had been a constant swirl of changes, all aimed at delivering the kind of organisation in the kind of condition which would receive the government's blessing. Yet still, after all that turmoil and all that rhetoric, here was the minister responsible – in the words of Brenda Maddox in the *Telegraph* – 'smiling while he waves the cane behind his back'.

As it happened, the cane had been applied three months earlier, in the shape of the accountants Touche Ross. They had been asked in the middle of June – as Checkland had anticipated – to conduct an inquiry into whether the BBC gave value for money, and whether recommendations made by rival accountants Price Waterhouse three years earlier had been implemented. By the time of the Cambridge Convention, there were already rumours that the BBC itself had been so successful at improving efficiency that the Touche Ross report was recommending a licence fee *reduction*. This would not have surprised those with long experience of dealing with accountants working to a government department brief, frequently overseen by Treasury officials intent on squeezing out savings wherever possible. One observer with long experience of negotiating for public money was convinced of the cynicism with which such accountancy reviews were carried out, and the further demands that inevitably followed every concession:

> My understanding of the Treasury has always been that whatever it is that you offer up they take it and they ask for more. So if you can demonstrate that you've got £200m of savings to make they'll take £200m and ask for another £200m; if you can demonstrate £100m, they'll take another £100m. They're absolute bastards.

Had the government taken the opportunity of cutting the licence fee, it would have fulfilled all the warnings issued by the opponents of reform – who had forecast that, once the BBC had completed its root and branch reforms in the hope of avoiding cuts (or worse) the government would impose exactly the penalty which it had been threatening if change had not occurred. The absurdity of such an outcome did not escape Peter Brooke. Had the Touche Ross option for a real cut in the licence fee been accepted, any further exhortation from government to make efficiency savings would have lost credibility. This time, the Treasury philosophy did not prevail and at the beginning of November Brooke duly announced that the licence fee would rise with inflation, up £1.50 to £84.50. John Birt was delighted, and a circular was immediately issued to all staff from the Director General's office to underscore the news:

> The significance of today's news is that such [efficiency] savings will *not* go to reduce the licence fee, but rather can continue to be invested in programme developments. Thus, the BBC can and will remain a creative, thriving, and dynamic organisation in the critical period during

which we negotiate a new Charter.

Ostensibly, both sides were happy. The BBC had been rewarded for its efficiency drive, and the government still had a much bigger stick to wield – charter renewal. But even the licence fee settlement was not the unalloyed BBC success portrayed by the Director General. Commenting on how fair and sensible the government's decision was, Brooke's predecessor, David Mellor, wrote in *The Guardian*: 'This settlement will also allow the BBC to reduce its debt, a little-commented upon problem which has been causing both Whitehall and Broadcasting House some concern.' In fact, the terms agreed had been rather more stringent than the BBC being 'allowed' to reduce its debt. The BBC had pledged that by 1996 – the end of the current charter – borrowings would be reduced to zero from their existing level of close to £200m. In effect, the consequences of this unstated (or understated) arrangement was to take £200m out of the BBC over a three-year period, the equivalent of an annual budget cut of around 5% a year over the three years, rather tougher than the previous licence fee settlement negotiated by Michael Checkland and Ian Phillips. It was a compromise which left the BBC with more of a PR success than a financial victory. As one insider commented: 'It was in everybody's interests not to make a big deal about this. The government were happy for the BBC to be seen to have done well, and the government were quite happy to have done well themselves.'

In tandem with these private licence fee negotiations, the BBC was the subject of a rather more public process of political consultation. The National Heritage Select Committee had decided at the beginning of the year to conduct an inquiry into the future of the Corporation. Select committees had become an important part of the British parliamentary process since their inception in 1979, acting as Parliament's check on the executive. Each government department was 'shadowed' by a committee of about a dozen back-bench MPs. Although all committees had a built-in majority for the party in power, they did not always slavishly follow the government line and had on several occasions been prepared to inflict embarrassment and real political damage on ministers and their departments. They could call witnesses, and with the advent of television cameras their proceedings had taken on a new significance. Their reports – while certainly not binding on government – were not usually ignored. After the Home Office had published its radical Green Paper on the future of broadcasting, which preceded the Broadcasting Bill, the Home Affairs Select Committee had won widespread praise for its comprehensive and knowledgeable inquiry and the balanced report which followed.

With the Department of National Heritage now taking responsibility for broadcasting, the conduct of the select committee inquiry revealed one of the side-effects of moving broadcasting from a major to a minor government department. Unlike its Home Affairs predecessor, the Heritage Select

Committee did not consist of MPs who were knowledgeable about the main broadcasting issues. Indeed, they had a chairman – Labour's former shadow Foreign Secretary Gerald Kaufman – whose black-and-white view of the BBC's future essentially condemned it to imminent extinction in the face of new technology and the melange of emerging cable and satellite channels. His sense of technological determinism was so overwhelming that he would not acknowledge even a role for politicians. In one of the most illuminating exchanges, Simon Albury, Director of Public Affairs for the ITV company Meridian, expressed his hope that the committee would 'seek to sustain those four [terrestrial] general services until they are not needed'. Kaufman interjected: 'It is not a question of whether they can be sustained while we need them, it is a question of whether they can survive whether we need them or not. . . .' In his closing remarks on that penultimate day of the hearings, Kaufman went even further: 'We may be approaching not only the last round of licensing but also the last charter for the BBC.'

Throughout the hearings, those called to give evidence were struck – and occasionally struck dumb – by the constant references to 'dramatic change', 'revolution' and the 'enormous impact' of cable and satellite. At one point, Kaufman intervened again to hypothesise on the death of the American networks: 'Is it not very likely that with that kind of explosion taking place in the United States the conventional networks . . . are going to become irrelevant?' Committee members, it seemed, had become so blinded by science that they were in danger of losing all perspective. Precisely the same revolutionary predictions had been made about new technology twelve years earlier by the then Minister of Information Technology, Kenneth Baker. In the intervening period there had been some technological advances in cable and satellite, but on both sides of the Atlantic these had made far less impact than had been predicted. In the United States, where around two-thirds of all homes were hooked up to cable television, the three terrestrial networks still took 60% of the viewing. In the UK, cable and satellite channels were commanding just 6% of total viewing and a smaller proportion of advertising revenue. While no-one doubted that a new technology-led consumer environment would emerge, there was no consensus on either the speed or the precise applications which might eventually succeed.

Scientific blindness was compounded by a generous helping of ignorance. Labour MP Joe Ashton – a long-standing critic of the injustice of a flat-rate licence fee with no concessions for those on low incomes – became very exercised about the 'persistent clashing' of television schedules and asked Yorkshire Television's Managing Director, John Fairley, 'Might it not be better if you did a deal with the BBC and they showed a minority programme while ITV showed something hugely popular . . . and they could then have their turn the night after?' Fairley responded, with commendable restraint, that he would 'not mind doing a deal with the BBC'; but the whole questioning process revealed an enormous gulf between the established practices of the broadcasting industry and the MPs' grasp of the real world. Ashton surpassed himself the following day when he wondered why those who could not afford to pay their licence fee were not simply disconnected from the BBC, just like those who defaulted on their water or electricity bills.

But beneath the almost embarrassingly uninformed approach, the thrust of the questioning revealed a preoccupation which spelt real danger for the BBC's prospects. Ashton correctly identified something close to ten million households without a wage-earner; with the consequence that, in his words, 'Almost fifty per cent of people who ought to have television licences find it very difficult to put their hands on £83 in a lump sum.' It was precisely these people who, according to even the most partisan research, were prepared to see the BBC take advertising or to confine themselves to watching Channel 4 and ITV to save themselves the cash. Once again the debate was returning to the conundrum of a regressive tax compulsorily imposed, a solution which still offended both wings of the political spectrum: the redistributors who sought to protect the poor and the economic libertarians who sought to protect absolute freedom of action. The sub-text was unmistakeable: as the annual licence fee started to bump up against the magic £100 figure, political opposition might become irresistible – regardless of the party in power.

The Select Committee's final report, published on 2 December 1993, contained the same mixture of heady enthusiasm for the new technological dawn and barely concealed aversion to the licence fee. It did, in fact, endorse the licence fee – but in language which conveyed the painful soul-searching which accompanied the members' deliberations: 'After considering the various funding options the Committee has, with great reluctance, come to the conclusion that the present flat rate licence system has the fewest objections to it.' It rejected advertising, sponsorship and subscription. But it was prepared to offer the BBC what it saw as at least a partial solution to squaring the funding circle: more effective marketing of itself and its products. 'The BBC's favourable position has not been exploited anything near as effectively as it might have been.' It should therefore adopt a more aggressive selling policy, exploit its position overseas, perhaps enter into partnerships with the private sector, and in general extend its role in the market in every practicable way. It was precisely the way in which, as it transpired, the BBC itself was thinking.

But in their very next breath, the Select Committee turned their advice into a poisoned chalice. 'Of course,' the report continued, 'if the income from such an extension begins to assume a significant proportion of licence income, the Government would have to take that into account in the annual licence settlements, either by refusing a licence increase or even by reducing the licence fee.' And then the *coup de grace*. If the BBC did indeed discover a new commercial role in any of the suggested ways 'It might be very difficult, if not impossible, to justify the existence of a licence fee at all.' At least there was no pretence that – in return for the effort of a more aggressive, more commercial approach – the BBC would be allowed to keep the fruits of its marketing efforts. It was quite explicit in MPs' minds that the role of commercially generated income was to displace public funding. The BBC could not say it had not been warned.

Strangely enough, the twin themes of globalisation and exploitation of commercial potential had been emerging at the same time as part of a government strategy for the BBC – although not (at least overtly) connected to the licence fee. Government thinking had been stimulated by a sudden realisation that the country's pre-eminence in the cultural industries offered the UK tremendous export opportunities, in a rapidly expanding international market. Back in September, when Peter Brooke had been warning of the possible extinction of a BBC 'dinosaur', he had also underlined the need to sustain British programme production. With the growing international market in broadcasting, he said, 'there should be more opportunities for British broadcasters to sell programmes and services to other countries'.

The notion of 'export potential' had particular resonance for Michael Heseltine who had, until that point, had little contact with the world of broadcasting. But, the self-styled President of the Board of Trade (as he had rechristened the old Department of Trade and Industry) was suddenly very interested. In almost every industry where Britain had held a significant lead, this had been surrendered. Here was a new opportunity, an industry in which Britain still excelled and was widely considered to be the world leader, an industry which could create jobs and might contribute (unusually) to the credit column of the country's balance of payments (although even here the balance had gone into the red over the past couple of years). The rest of the broadcasting industry was fragmented and unstable (due in no small measure to the government's own Broadcasting Act) and in no condition to compete with the international conglomerates such as Murdoch's News International and Berlusconi's Fininvest – let alone the American giants like Time Warner. If Britain was to have any chance at all of fighting in the international arena, the BBC was the only realistic contender.

Suddenly, the prospect loomed of another departmental battle for the soul of the BBC. But unlike the duel of heavyweights in 1988 this one was a lot more unequal, pitching a charismatic figure of enormous stature (and still with prime-ministerial ambitions) against a well-meaning but ineffectual stop-gap. By comparison with the previous fight between Hurd and Young, Heseltine v Brooke was something of a mismatch, and rumours began to circulate about designs which the newly designated Board of Trade might have on the BBC. Once enveloped by a department with little history of concern for the BBC as a cultural institution, it would not be long before the pressures exerted by a single-mindedly commercial Board of Trade started to transform the very essence of the organisation.

If the departmental battle was for the future, the development of a comprehensive commercial strategy was very much for the present. John Birt finished the year with the confidence to tell Ray Snoddy of *The Financial Times* that, 'There is a very, very strong feeling here of achievement.' In line with the Select Committee's recommendation on more effective marketing, he promised that, 'We will greatly increase the amount of money coming into the BBC from our commercial activities chiefly outside the UK.' As the BBC entered 1994, it therefore seemed that an implicit bargain was being struck with no certainty as to the potential consequences. As Peter Koenig wrote in *The Independent on Sunday*, 'The political battle, it turns out, merely cleared the way for the real battle: the tussle in the global marketplace with Rupert Murdoch and the other New Age media barons.' He continued: 'The BBC has won the right to continue as a cultural force in Britain. But to exercise it, it must now compete against American, German and Japanese media conglomerates.'

Over the next few months Bob Phillis, the man brought in to mastermind this global strategy, turned his attention to negotiating the deals and alliances which would be the BBC's ticket to the new world order. For the first time, the BBC was able to turn to the ranks of its own governors for real expertise in this new world. David Scholey, a recent appointment to the board, was a City heavyweight who was Chairman of the merchant bank Warburgs and a director of the Bank of England. He had a detailed understanding of the world of joint ventures and corporate finance in which the BBC had always previously lacked experience. Scholey was joined by another new governor, the banker and novelist Janet Cohen.

On 10 May 1994, Phillis announced an international partnership with Pearson, publisher of *The Financial Times* and owner of Penguin Books and Thames Television. It would give the BBC access to private capital for foreign ventures and would allow Pearson access to the BBC's brand name in their joint activities. To deflect criticism about subsidising essentially private enterprises from public funding – the licence fee – Phillis also announced a new international organisation, BBC Worldwide, consisting of three divisions: BBC World Service, BBC International Television, and BBC Publishing. At the same time he announced the first fruits of that partnership: two new European satellite channels of which one was to be news-and-information-based and the other entertainment-based. Neither channel, Phillis was quick to point out, would be available in the UK. Both parties stressed that this was only the first of a number of initiatives which would stretch to Asia, the Far East, America, and beyond. It was an announcement of enormous significance which, for Phillis, marked out the BBC's future not just as a major international player, but as an organisation in the vanguard of new technology: 'We're talking about a BBC that will indeed lead Britain into a multimedia future.'

But even with such a strategic vision, the schizophrenia which marks all such initiatives within the BBC was never far from the surface. The Managing Director of Enterprises, James Arnold-Baker, had departed earlier in the year to run Oxford University Press, denying widespread reports of a rift with John Birt. After a series of delays, Dr John Thomas, Enterprises' Director of Magazines (responsible for the rapid expansion of the magazines division in the late 1980s) was promoted to succeed him. One of his first acts was to sell off the contract publisher Redwood, and to concentrate magazine publishing on programme-related titles. At the same time, Enterprises had a series of conflicts with the Policy and Planning Unit (by now branded by insiders as the BBC's 'thought police') over activities which, the PPU argued, might be prejudicial to the renewal of the charter. Datacast, a rapidly developing subsidiary which sold information transmission services to business, was closed down as not being a 'core activity', and the Cable and Satellite Division of Enterprises was told not to develop any more deals such as the ones with the satellite channels UK Gold and UK Living. In one case, the PPU announced to Enterprises that it would be briefing them on the Corporation's strategy on new technology after an Enterprises working party had been examining the issues involved for a year.

Throughout the announcement of BBC Worldwide, and in previous speeches and interviews, Phillis had been at great pains to establish that public and private money was to be kept entirely separate. The partnership had been cleared in principle by the Department of National Heritage, and seemed to present no obvious difficulties either in principle or practice. It did, however, return the BBC to the old conundrum of what Liz Forgan had described as 'the tail wagging the dog'. The BBC was now firmly committed to maximising earnings from commercial activities, to the eventual tune of 15 or 20% of licence fee revenue. At what point would this new commercial imperative start to influence the creative process itself, the very heart of Broadcasting House? A month earlier, in a speech to the pro-public service pressure group Voice of the Listener and Viewer, Phillis had assured his audience that commercial activities would only be conducted 'within a clearly defined framework' which would be consistent with existing editorial and programming values. He cited an impressive list of programmes which had benefited from an infusion of co-production money from outside the Corporation, going back to Bronowski's acclaimed *Ascent of Man*, the drama *Tinker, Tailor, Soldier, Spy* and, more recently, *Middlemarch*.

There was, however, a massive difference of scale between money at the margins which the BBC could – if pushed – forego because of its financial strength elsewhere and money which might start to become essential to its survival and stability. Once the revenue stream became significant, it would become harder to resist attractive international offers. The creative compromises need only be small – an adapted script here, a change of location there, a very British joke deleted somewhere else – but they would add up to a rather larger whole. Such co-ventures only work if the subject matter drives the deal, rather than the other way around, as with the BBC's twenty-year retrospective series *Watergate*. But when it does not, it starts to show quickly on screen. Beyond the editorial decisions, there is always the risk that the internal corporate culture will slowly be transformed as a result. As Professor Jay Blumler wrote, following his own studies of American broadcasting culture:

> Along with other imperatives to run a tight financial ship, it could subtly and imperceptibly – yet in the long run decisively – inject a different set of priorities into the organisation's governing ethos, diluting those commitments of service that would have stemmed from a different, earlier and less business-oriented culture.

In truth, there was never an easy choice between commercial expansion, which might endanger core values, and domestic introspection, which would risk gradual decay in the face of competition from powerful international conglomerates. In the first half of 1994, the BBC committed itself to the former.

The risks of playing in the international arena without the financial clout to control satellite distribution were already emerging. The previous autumn Rupert Murdoch had bought the Asian satellite service Star Television (on which the BBC's World Service Television was transmitted to Asia) from the Li family in Hong Kong. Immediately, as elsewhere in the News Corporation empire, he set about dealing with any political factors that might impede his expansion plans. News Corporation sold off the *South China Morning Post*, with its traditional anti-Beijing editorial line – and then started a legal action against the BBC. It alleged that World Service Television had breached the terms of its agreement with Star TV by planning to launch an Arabic language service on a satellite whose 'footprint' overlapped that of Star. That was mere pretext. The motive was to get rid of a television service which irritated the Chinese government, and by March News Corporation had succeeded. In Taiwan, it was replaced by a more lucrative and less controversial Mandarin language pay-movie service; elsewhere in eastern Asia the screens went blank. Sky initially denied that the decision was influenced by politics, but Murdoch was later to admit in an interview with *Esquire* magazine that it had been done to placate the Chinese authorities. 'We said in order to get in there and get accepted, we'll cut the BBC out', Murdoch told the magazine, adding that the Chinese authorities 'hate the BBC'. The BBC was left to pick up the pieces.

At home, meanwhile, there were more familiar problems: in particular, an apparently continuing reluctance in current affairs programmes to do anything that might upset the government. The White Paper, planned for January, was now due for 'late spring' and there was some debate as to when the British spring might formally end. Even with a long consultation period and a government in some disarray, eighteen months was an unusually long time between Green and White Papers. There were those who wondered darkly whether the whole process was not being deliberately extended in order to encourage a little more conformity in political coverage than might otherwise have been the case. As John Birt had made clear in his *Financial Times* interview, the charter review battle was not yet won. Ministers were becoming embroiled in scandals at an alarming rate as the government drifted to new opinion poll lows, and there was growing talk of a major reshuffle. So, just as it had been since Milne's dismissal seven years earlier, journalistic caution was the order of the day.

Two examples, in particular, resurrected questions about the ability of *Panorama* to withstand political pressure created by continuing uncertainty about the BBC's future. On 20 September 1993, an edition was transmitted called *Babies on Benefit*. It was designed to be an analytical approach to the controversial question of 'welfare dependency', in particular to Conservative Party claims that large numbers of young single women were getting themselves pregnant in order to jump the queue for council housing. Right-wing Tories, in particular, were suggesting that this was becoming a widespread practice and were floating the possibility of withdrawing benefits from second or subsequent babies born to single mothers. Others – not just on the left, but from charities and research organisations concerned with these issues – vehemently denied that this was either a widespread or a growing phenomenon and had been horrified by the tone of some public pronouncements. It was, they believed, a blatant attempt to shift blame onto a vulnerable sector of society and whip up public support for the theory that the existence of benefits encouraged people to become 'welfare dependent'.

The *Panorama* in question addressed the issue through two case studies, both of single women living on a Cardiff housing estate. Both cases appeared to endorse the dependency thesis: the women were quite clear about the benefits that would accrue from having children and both had made conscious decisions to have children without being in permanent or even stable relationships. At the same time, the programme drew on evidence from the American state of New Jersey where a policy of restricting welfare benefits to single mothers had been implemented. This, it was said, had produced a significant drop in the number of births to single mothers. The programme used language which would not have been out of place at Central Office, asking whether taxpayers should continue to support this 'burden on society'.

The programme provoked an outcry. It was accused of bias and factual inaccuracy on several counts, with some of the most trenchant criticism coming from surprising sources. When questioning John Birt during the Select Committee hearings, the Conservative MP Alan Howarth said that the programme 'was prejudiced, it pilloried lone mothers in a most unfortunate style, and I believe the programme was unscrupulous with its facts'. He cited a number of inaccuracies which included the incidence of single parent families on the featured housing estate, and the success attributed to the New Jersey policy – this claim had not been supported by those operating the policy. The most serious charge levelled at the programme was that it breached every tenet of the 'mission to explain' doctrine. Although single parenthood was undoubtedly becoming an issue, there was no attempt to place the problem of teenage pregnancies into this wider perspective and give the programme a context for its analysis. The script contained clear indications of apparent prejudice, and the case studies seemed designed to convey an emotional message, not an analytical one. It was exactly the sort of current affairs programme criticised by the Birt–Jay thesis of twenty years earlier. This time, the producer received a personal note from the Director General congratulating her.

Any suggestion that a milder political climate had put a little backbone into the BBC's approach to difficult political stories was dashed on 25 April 1994 by a virtual re-run of the *Sliding into Slump* debacle two years earlier. An edition of *Panorama* was due to be broadcast alleging serious corruption in the Conservative-held local council of Westminster. The same production team had in 1989 revealed how Westminster Conservative councillors, led by Dame Shirley Porter, had sold off council properties in marginal wards to secure a Conservative victory in the 1990 local elections. The subsequent election victory had then been used by Central Office to divert attention from significant losses elsewhere. A district auditor had subsequently been appointed to investigate and, in January 1994, published a scathing interim report, calling the policy 'improper and disgraceful'. Under the government's own rules, if the auditor's preliminary findings were confirmed, ten Tory councillors faced personal surcharges totalling £21.25m.

The *Panorama* team had obtained access to unpublished documents, and was now alleging that the scale of corruption went much further: and that as a result, personal surcharges could now total more than £40m. A provisional transmission date had been set for ten days before the 1994 local elections when, again, the Conservatives were expected to do badly. There had been phone calls from Central Office to put pressure on the programme makers, but this was now an established practice. In the end, it was the BBC hierarchy which decided the programme should be postponed.

The reasons given appeared persuasive: that there were legal problems which still needed to be resolved before the programme went out. It transpired, however, that the problem centred on a legal technicality: whether under section 30 of the Local Government Finance Act it was legal to quote from an unpublished district auditor's report. Since the district auditor had appeared on all the main news bulletins in January to give his interim verdict, and since extracts had been widely circulated in all the newspapers, there was no obvious cause for concern. Any attempt by the government to single out the BBC for injunctions or prosecution on a pure technicality would have been too ludicrous to countenance. Confirmation of the minimal nature of the legal problems came when the programme was finally cleared for transmission (with no serious alterations) on the very afternoon that the Conservatives' election victory in Westminster was declared. By the time it was broadcast, it was history, just like *Supergun* and *Sliding into Slump*. The postponement of the programme was not the result of political partisanship, but another example of excessive caution and a reminder of the political leverage being exacted by the uncertainty of charter renewal. There was certainly no incentive for the government to speed up publication of the White Paper.

It was current affairs, as always, which tended to make the headlines. But current affairs did not define what the BBC was about, and by the middle of 1994, BBC Television seemed to have achieved an unaccustomed position of confidence and stability. Debates about the high ground were forgotten, as unashamedly popular (even populist) programmes aimed at winning viewers were launched with pride. Terry Wogan introduced *Do the Right Thing*, a series on moral dilemmas based on a Brazilian game show. Jim Davidson's *Big Break*, a programme whose populist style would easily have satisfied a Bill Cotton light entertainment schedule, continued to outrate ITV's popular fare on Saturday night. *How Do They Do That?*, an entertainment show which did not receive critical acclaim, was attracting over nine million viewers. Alan Yentob was attacked by ITV executives for introducing a third weekly episode of *EastEnders* on Mondays, thereby demonstrating that the BBC would not be waving its legs in the air in the face of a new commercial edge from ITV. And from the News and Current Affairs Directorate, still reputedly the bastion of hard news and dry analysis, came *Here and Now*, a news magazine programme attempting to reinvent the hugely successful *Nationwide* of the 1960s and 70s. With BBC-1's share of viewing at 33% and climbing in an ever-more competitive atmosphere, there was no better response to those who may have once embraced the market-gap solution.

The previous October, BBC Television's Managing Director Will Wyatt had laid out probably the most eloquent and coherent statement of programming policy that the industry had heard for some time. He dismissed the idea that the Himalayan peaks had ever been an option ('I never even took down an atlas to check where the Himalayas are, as I knew we'd never be going there') but also rejected the full-scale ratings war, underlining the Corporation's commitment to running current affairs, documentaries, and religion in prime time on BBC-1. 'The battle is to bring this mix of programmes to more rather than fewer, to provide something (no, plenty) for every viewer.' Wyatt's preferred geographical metaphor was the English Lake District, 'A place where you don't need breathing equipment to reach the peaks – very British but with overseas visitors; distinct tops, but accessible, risky, testing ridges where your heart may be in your mouth.' The word 'distinctive' was nowhere to be seen. The sense of renewed vigour was enhanced by the continuing process of the Programme Strategy Review, which had already been reaping programme benefits. The most creative ideas emerging from the groups discussing how to implement *Extending Choice* were being poached by Yentob and Jackson and turned into programmes even before a draft of the review had been written. In contrast to the painstaking (and often bureaucratic and political) debates on strategy, tactics and direction, this was an excellent example of cross-fertilisation in a creative environment. It was, in essence, what the BBC is for.

Television's sense of renewal, however, was not being matched in radio. Wyatt's opposite number, Liz Forgan, was not only presiding over some profound changes in network radio, but was still sharing with Yentob the directing of the Programme Strategy Review. While television seemed settled, radio was experiencing real turbulence. Forgan's problem was not just the sheer magnitude of her task after a lifetime spent in press and television. It was also the passionate loyalty which most listeners – and especially BBC listeners – tend to have for their favourite radio stations. As David Hatch was quoted as saying in *The Guardian*: 'You can move a TV programme from Monday to Thursday and no-one gives a hoot, but if you move a radio programme by five minutes there are questions in the House.'

The problem was that, on BBC radio, there seemed to be a lot more happening than just the odd shift of a programme by five minutes. Whatever the need for changes at Radio 1 to re-establish its credibility with young people, the first quarter's listening figures for 1994 showed the station losing another million listeners on top of the 1.5 million who had gone the previous year. Some of these were the inevitable consequence of Virgin, the new national commercial rock station, making further inroads, as well as a growing number of smaller, local commercial stations. But some could be traced directly to the disappearance of Dave Lee Travis and the subsequent falling away of weekend audiences, with a knock-on effect during the week. Matthew Bannister's predecessor as Controller of the station, Johnny Beerling, could not resist the opportunity for some jibes at his old employer. Speaking to the Radio Academy, he reserved particular scorn for organisational changes and a bureaucracy which he described as 'Total control from the centre and very little flexibility or room for manoeuvre – no wonder some have compared it to life under communism.'

Although placing him squarely in the 'old guard' camp, Beerling's comments raised one vital question: given that Producer Choice was designed with the complex interwoven operations of television in mind, was its imposition really vital to the future of radio? The origins of Producer Choice had been in the BBC's statutory duty to contract a proportion of television programmes out to the independent sector, but no such provision had been made for radio. In fact, radio was moving slowly in that direction voluntarily, in order to reap the benefits of some of the independent talent now emerging. But the medium itself – requiring fewer people, no make-up, set design, heavy outside broadcast equipment or the rest of the paraphernalia essential for television – ran on far smaller budgets. The effect of Producer Choice was to generate a large number of transactions for insignificant amounts of money, increasing bureaucracy without generating the efficiency savings claimed for the system in television.

But for listeners, it was programming rather than organisational changes which were causing a mutiny. While Matthew Bannister was revamping Radio 1, two much-publicised changes to Radio 4 underlined Hatch's comments about the sensitivity of listeners. First, it was decided that the panel of one of Radio 4's most enduring programmes, *Gardeners' Question Time*, needed an infusion of younger blood. Its panel members were promptly snapped up *en masse* by the new commercial classical music station Classic FM. It was a great publicity coup for Classic whose target audience was precisely those loyal *GQT* listeners, whom they hoped would defect in droves. Then came a new afternoon magazine programme, *Anderson Country*, fronted by Gerry Anderson and imported from a very successful series in Northern Ireland. It sounded, unfortunately, exactly like the local radio programme it had been and was almost unanimously pilloried by critics and listeners alike.

To add to the pain of Radio 4 listeners, those who preferred reception on long wave were now having to cope with the redirected *Test Match Special*. This national institution – ball-by-ball coverage of England's test matches requiring 50–60 days of airtime a year – had become something of a wandering refugee since the BBC had been forced to give up its AM frequency for Radio 3. It had spent some of its time on Radio 3 FM, some on the new Radio 5, and was now to take over Radio 4 Long Wave on the basis that Radio 4 listeners still had an FM frequency. As the BBC had discovered to its cost, however, there were still large numbers of articulate and influential Radio 4 devotees for whom FM reception was plagued by interference. When plans for a rolling news station had been announced, along with allocation of the long-wave frequency for its use, a very British campaign to 'Save Radio 4 Long Wave' had successfully seen the plan off. Now, those same listeners were going to receive cricket instead of news for some of the time. The realisation did not go down well.

Finally, there had been the resolution of that fifth station. Conceived in the wake of the continuous (and highly successful) radio coverage of the Gulf War, the notion of a rolling news station had been supported by both Checkland and Birt. Amongst the established journalists on Radio 4's news programmes – who were not convinced that news could be stretched throughout the day without resorting to the trivial – this brainchild was soon rechristened 'rolling bollocks'. Once the row about frequencies had broken out, it offered the chance for a radical rethink not just about where the new station should go, but what it should be. Too much had been invested (both financially and morally) to scrap the idea of a news station entirely, but the final solution was a compromise: a joint enterprise of news and sport, with the apposite title of Radio 5 Live. It saved some red faces, but it created a new nightmare for Liz Forgan. Somehow, priorities had to be sorted out in terms of breaking stories, prestigious interviews and resources between 5 Live and the bedrock of BBC radio journalism, Radio 4. As if all that was not enough, all the schools programmes from the original Radio 5 had been diverted to afternoons on Radio 3.

It was a difficult time for Forgan, not of her own making but with its roots mostly in the organisational and strategic changes coming from the top. The problem was that radio, far more than television, is a dangerous medium to change. Audiences are essentially loyal but, if shaken enough, they can desert a station not just for a programme, or for a few days, but permanently. The combination of a number of simultaneous adjustments, an inexperienced hand at the tiller with half her attention diverted elsewhere, and the same morale problems as in television because of uncertain career prospects, all conspired to give the impression of a radio service in permanent revolution. It was not altogether clear that this was serving the listeners' best interests.

In the lull before the eventual publication of the White Paper in July 1994, there were two significant events which illustrated the accumulated tension of the last few years. The Drama Department, after a year of reorganisation under Charles Denton, was thrown into turmoil as Nick Elliott was appointed from LWT as Head of Series. His track record there had been good, with hits such as *Dempsey and Makepeace*, *London's Burning* and *Poirot*. But as a result, Michael Wearing, only recently appointed as BBC Head of Series and Serials, found himself divested of half his department before the projects he had initiated could come to screen. Wearing's credits included *Boys from the Blackstuff* and *Edge of Darkness*, and before his recent appointment he had brought one of the BBC's 1994 successes, *Middlemarch*, to the screen. Three hundred colleagues, including most of the senior figures in the department, signed a petition of support, concerned that the BBC was now trying to chase ratings at the expense of more distinctive material. Their protests were in vain.

The second incident was an indication that the relentless programme of change was taking its toll on staff. The BBC made proposals for changing its pay structure in two important ways. The first was the introduction of performance related pay, under which pay would be linked to a performance appraisal scheme, and a manager would be able to withhold a pay rise from a member of staff if she or he so wished. The second was the delegation of wage and salary negotiations to the separate directorates, and to a local level, as from 1 July. The first had been in favour in the private sector during much of the 1980s, but had become discredited because of the favouritism and sycophancy it encouraged in staff relations with managers, and the disruptive effect on morale and teamwork which inevitably followed; the second meant an end to one of the tenets which underpinned the BBC: a single Corporation with common standards for all staff.

It was the performance appraisal, with its mechanistic and quantifiable indicators, which created the loudest objections. The previous summer, a survey of staff attitudes had revealed widespread distrust of management, and yet those very managers were now being given discretion over pay. The President of BECTU, the ever-quotable Tony Lennon, would have struck a chord with his members when he told the trade paper *Broadcast*, 'The real thorn is the right of managers to withhold pay. That's unacceptable to members, many of whom wouldn't trust managers any further than they could throw them.' The proposals, though, were an inevitable result of the fragmentation of the BBC caused by the implementation of Producer Choice, another way in which values and practices which once were set by the organisation as a whole were now being reshaped by the commercial dictates confronting each separate business unit.

The unions, BECTU and the NUJ, called for strike action, and for the first time in five years there was a significant response from members: well over half in many areas of the BBC. Radio services in particular were hit hard; *Today* was taken off the air, and the newly launched Radio 5 Live was reduced to a skeleton service, with the channel's Controller, Jenny Abramsky, personally driving the studio controls for some of the day. The sense of frustration and anger in the face of successive waves of radical change was reflected in an acronym which started doing the rounds among disillusioned staff: BOHICA. It stood for: 'Bend over – here it comes again.'

On Wednesday 6 July, after several postponements, the White Paper was finally published. The charter was renewed for ten years to 2006. The licence fee was confirmed, at least until 2001 (with a review of the 'formula' in 1996). All the BBC's activities were endorsed, as was its 'across the waterfront' programming policy. All television and radio services were left intact. There was some talk about a clearer definition of the governors' responsibilities and some murmurings about clearer statements of intent for audiences. Far from being a recipe for contraction or break-up, the government's greatest emphasis was reserved for expanding the BBC's commercial activities and 'developing into an international multi-media enterprise'. In tone and content, it was a celebration of the BBC's existence. It could have been written in Broadcasting House.

In the news bulletins and the following day's papers, there followed what amounted to an apotheosis of John Birt: 'Victory for Birt's BBC revolution' (*The Guardian*); 'Birt celebrates victory as BBC escapes intact' (*Daily Telegraph*); 'Birt's BBC is given its reward' (*Independent*); and 'Birt triumphs in battle of the BBC' (*The Times*). Absent from almost every report or feature was the name of Michael Checkland. Absent also was any mention of the changed political circumstances which for over three years had seen the BBC operating with supportive cabinet ministers and with a well-disposed Prime

Minister beset by serious and distracting problems elsewhere.

It was a sweet moment for John Birt and his supporters, but there was a swift reminder of the concessions made to political expediency and the sacrifices endured by staff. In the very same papers which were describing Birt's spectacular victory for the BBC there were reports from a British Medical Association consultants' meeting. The chairman of the consultants' committee described the effect of government proposals to introduce performance related pay and local pay bargaining for doctors. 'How', he asked, 'can you measure the productivity of a psychiatrist treating a severely ill schizophrenic patient?' The following day, senior police officers spoke of a virtual breakdown in relations with the Home Office, following proposals to introduce incentive and performance related schemes to the police service. The obsession with measurement was spreading to all areas of public life. All, apart from the BBC, were resisting.

It was for that very reason that, three days after the publication of the White Paper, the BBC's India correspondent Mark Tully resigned. He cited the new appraisal system; he cited the BMA; he was, he said, not being allowed to speak freely; and he repeated the warnings he had given in his speech to the Radio Academy a year earlier. He was, he said, speaking for large numbers of disaffected and demoralised staff. Even those who gave John Birt all the credit for the BBC's victory knew that Tully was right.

The White Paper did, at least, mark the end of a sustained period of uncertainty going back almost as far as Milne's dismissal. But it still contained the seeds of renewed uncertainty and instability. For the announcement of a ten- rather than fifteen-year charter, suggested by Hussey himself to the Select Committee inquiry, offered only a short-term respite. The reduction in the renewal period, and the review of the licence fee formula, were certain within a short time to catapult the BBC back into the same introspective turmoil that it had experienced for almost five years. It would yet again provide the political leverage – to whichever party might be in power – for subtle influence over BBC output, and in particular its journalism. It meant that the battle for the BBC was not over. It had simply been postponed.

CHAPTER FIFTEEN
'AND WHAT GOOD CAME OF IT AT LAST?'

The White Paper was the culmination of a slow process of rebuilding consensus between Whitehall and Broadcasting House. It raised some intriguing questions about the traumas of the previous decade. Were all the committees, the soul-searching, the consultancy reports, the organisational upheavals, the resignations and confrontations ultimately a futile waste of exceptionally able people which detracted from the creative and cultural purpose of the institution? Or had it been an overdue period of readjustment and modernisation which was essential to revitalise an ailing bureaucracy and – above all – preserve it from a government onslaught?

It was, more than anything, the political environment which had precipitated the battles of the previous ten years. Tension between governments and broadcasters is an inevitable, even desirable, state of affairs and there had been periods of open conflict before. But governmental hostility had never been so sustained or so relentless, never so rooted in a deep-seated philosophical aversion to the public sector. Much of this hostility can be traced back to the single, dominant figure of Margaret Thatcher herself. Except during the Falklands war – when she knew she could count on some frenzied jingoism from backbenchers and supporters in the tabloid press – Thatcher was herself careful not to condemn openly either the BBC itself or its programmes. But she set the tone and parameters of the debate. Every back-bench MP seeking preferment, every Fleet Street editor who craved a knighthood, knew that an excoriating assault on Broadcasting House would receive an approving nod from Downing Street. With or without reforms, the BBC was a soft target.

The question is whether, without major reforms, the soft target would have been a dead duck. Would the BBC, or parts of it, have been privatised if Jeremy Isaacs or Brian Wenham had been appointed as Director General in 1985–6 instead of Michael Checkland – or if internal promotions had continued to fill the top positions and John Birt had stayed at London Weekend Television? Birt would have become a very rich man. But would the BBC have survived with both its TV channels, all five network radio stations and all its regional output intact?

Those who say that the BBC would have weathered the storm, and done so with staff morale and the creative atmosphere in a much healthier state, point to the sheer size and colossal reputation of the institution. Not even Margaret Thatcher was so blind to political reality that she would ignore the possible repercussions of a full frontal assault on such a prestigious body. After all, even she stayed her hand on privatisation of the Post Office and British Rail. The omnipresence of the BBC in people's everyday lives spelt danger for any political meddler. If *EastEnders* suddenly disappeared, or Noel Edmunds was sacked for lack of money, or Radio 1 was transformed overnight into 24-hour talk radio, voters would notice.

Furthermore, the external pressures would have forced change onto anyone's agenda. The successful alliance of independent producers and radical conservatives which pushed an independent quota onto the statute books was irresistible. And once in place, that quota brought with it a brutal logic of staff cuts and transparent costings which any administration would have had to accommodate. Nor would any incoming Director General, even one associated with the 'old guard', want to appear as a mindless successor with no original ideas or strategic imagination. Anyone good enough to get the job would have been astute enough to read the political runes, and set a new course accordingly.

In opposition are those who argue that Thatcher was spoiling for a fight. Yes, she was a canny political animal who – at least during the early 80s – was restrained by wiser voices when it came to some of her more outlandish projects. But the succession of programming catastrophes which had broken around Milne's head in 1985–6 – many of which were deliberately provoked by the BBC's political enemies – had gradually eroded the BBC's public standing. Her lieutenants had done an effective job of chipping away at the esteem and affection in which the BBC was held. There were certainly moments at which Thatcher could plausibly have cast herself as the saviour of a once great but now fading and misguided relic, leading it firmly from the tangled cobwebs of public ownership to the invigorating freedom of private enterprise. Not only would it have been entirely in keeping with a Conservative programme of radical reform, but it would have offered her the opportunity for a grand populist gesture of great electoral appeal: to scrap, or at least significantly reduce, the licence fee, and announce with a flourish the annual £70-odd saving that would benefit every household.

Such a radical action would have become more likely with the gradual dwindling of those who counselled caution. By far the most influential of these, and the man most credited with championing the public service cause in broadcasting, was William Whitelaw. As Home Secretary from 1979 to 1983, he had piloted through Parliament the Broadcasting Act which established Channel 4 on strictly public service principles. He had been elevated to the House of Lords after stepping down at the 1983 election, and continued as Leader of the Lords and Thatcher's deputy until 1988. At the very moment when the Conservative government was in full flower, with its third successive election victory and another three-figure majority, one of its most ameliorative influences withdrew from public office. There were virtually no confidants left to put the case for the BBC in Downing Street.

Any judgement by an incoming Director General would have had to take account of a predominantly hostile press, committed to both the rubbishing of the BBC's reputation and the propagation of the Thatcherite gospel. There were newspapers from Rupert Murdoch's News International stable which had a direct commercial interest in the BBC's demise as their proprietor planned his satellite assault on the country's television screens. That accounted for *The Sun, The News of the World, The Times, The Sunday Times* and *Today*. There were the papers which gave the Prime Minister unstinting support as a matter of course – *The Daily* and *Sunday Express, The Daily Mail* and *The Mail on Sunday*, and *The Daily* and *Sunday Telegraph*. Which left only the struggling *Mirror* papers, *The Independent* and its Sunday paper, *The Guardian* and *The Observer* – together accounting for less than a fifth of total national circulation – to shout for the BBC. It was scarcely an even fight.

Adverse press coverage had implications beyond any impact on public opinion. For it also influenced the governors' perceptions. Even with reforms under way, the constant barrage of articles about waste, inefficiency, bureaucracy, overmanning and extravagance were read, absorbed and regurgitated at Board of Governors' meetings. After eight years of politically inspired appointments, the governors had little compunction in echoing Downing Street's tune. Had Thatcher wanted to mount a full-frontal assault, urged on by the bloodthirsty cheers of Fleet Street's finest, resistance from the governors (with one or two notable exceptions) would not have amounted to much more than a few squeaks of protest.

Under all those circumstances, in the immediate aftermath of Milne's departure, the appointment of a BBC traditionalist in the Milne mould would have done nothing to secure the Corporation's future. While it is impossible to speculate with accuracy, it is a fair conclusion that, in the years 1987 to 1990, real damage would have been inflicted on the BBC had the Checkland–Birt reforms not been instituted in some form. Checkland observed to Birt very early on that if they did not implement change they 'would lose something'.

The relationship between the BBC and the State has always been close, and usually fairly private. But it is not straightforward. The notion that Hussey arrived with sealed orders in his kitbag was never plausible; nor was the idea (widely believed in the BBC in the febrile atmosphere of the time) that John Birt was appointed as an agent of government. But the dynamics of the BBC/government relationship put the Corporation's management in an impossible position. Its future and its funding were being settled by a political process in which all the senior Conservative figures of the day were involved. Yet there was no public consensus about the BBC's role, nor any public definition of its purpose, and the balance of opinion among the politicians shifted with the seasons. It was like playing poker with an open hand against an opponent whose cards were hidden from view and constantly changing.

But there is a supreme irony in what followed beyond 1990. For after three years of redundancies and reorganisation, at virtually the moment when Thatcher gave way to John Major, the BBC quickened the pace. Governors' demands for staff cuts escalated, the Television Resources Review recommended vast sell-offs, the debate on programming seemed to veer towards the 'higher ground' mentality, BBC journalism seemed to become even drier and more analytical, and the Corporation started to gear up for the radical medicine of Producer Choice. At the same time, Michael Checkland was put on notice and John Birt was given the succession, heralding eighteen months of confusion and instability at the top. Instead of being in a perfect position to take advantage of the changing political climate, the BBC increased its own vulnerability. And it is impossible to avoid the conclusion that, over the years that followed, the BBC became a prisoner of a political culture which had been not just superseded but discredited.

An inordinate amount of the BBC's management time was spent second-guessing these swings in the political mood, and then pursuing what it believed were appropriate policies. In the process the department charged specifically with the task, the Policy and Planning Unit, acquired an influence that was generally regarded as baleful. The result was that all facets of the BBC – its programmes, its organisation, its journalism – came to be dominated by this over-arching political agenda. With almost every new reform it introduced, the BBC went at least one step further than was necessary to secure its own survival and one step too far for its own continued health and vitality.

In television, programme strategy gave the impression of lurching from one extreme to the other. Having emerged through the Task Forces, the notion of a BBC which occupied the 'high ground' or even the 'Himalayan heights' was circulating in policy discussions. The latter phrase emerged from the Entertainment Task Force, which was doing what it had been asked to do and thinking the unthinkable. According to one of those closely involved, it was never taken seriously as a strategic option:

> There is a danger of confusing the rhetoric of what goes on with what actually happens ... the high ground was really always there as an option to be knocked down. At no point in the argument on *Extending Choice* did anyone in the BBC ever suggest that we were going down the high ground route.

Unfortunately, the rhetoric *was* taken seriously, not least by the BBC's Chairman. It was taken as a sign, both externally and internally, that the BBC was devoting less attention and resources to nurturing its entertainment tradition. And although entertainment had, by the middle of 1994, been recognised as an explicit part of the BBC remit, it required a number of high-profile statements and higher-profile appointments to drive the message home. Even those closely involved with the BBC's strategic thinking accepted that *Extending Choice* did not enthusiastically embrace the lighter side of television: '*Extending Choice* did not have a language for talking confidently about popular entertainment. It felt embarrassed about it.'

A classic example was the saga of *Eldorado*. In the pursuit of the golden promise of two additional points of audience share, the BBC stopped trusting its instincts. Richard Eyre described it as 'a crisis of faith', arguing:

> There are no clearer examples of working in good faith and working in bad faith than *EastEnders* and *Eldorado*; the first was made in a spirit of innocence, enthusiasm, and energetic commitment; the second was mired in cynicism and the torpor of disaffection.

The same process was at work in radio. The BBC's defence against charges of too much emphasis on high culture in television was, 'Judge us by our output.' And for the most part, even if the popular fare was given less convincing support, the balance of BBC television was never seriously disturbed. The changes to radio, however, came later and were more abrupt. The consequences for audiences were potentially much more dangerous.

Radio 1 certainly needed to recapture its youth and therefore needed an injection of new blood. But the scale of the changes were too much for over two million listeners who were simultaneously being wooed by the plethora of new commercial stations coming on air. The resolution of the rolling news issue bumped off the recently created Radio 5 and its small but growing band of followers. At the same time, cricket fans were being led a merry dance around the airwaves for *Test Match Special*, suffering unaccustomed interruptions for news bulletins and shipping forecasts; and those who were not cricket fans and who only listened to Radio 4 on long wave lost their favourite programmes for over fifty days a year.

The overall impression was of a sudden lurch rather than a gentle touch on the tiller. Radio, far more than television, is a medium which thrives on loyalty, where listeners usually have no more than one or two favourite stations. Even in the age of push-button tuning, once that loyalty is breached it is difficult to bring listeners back to the fold. Alienated listeners become more vulnerable to questions about the need for, or value of, a compulsory licence fee. In radio, too, the BBC seemed to be going faster and further than it needed to.

In journalism the problems were different but the effects were similar. Politicians were becoming more sensitive to the impact of critical stories on an electorate whose declining party loyalties made it more fickle and unpredictable than at any time in modern political history. They were more sensitive than before and even less restrained in the language and tactics of intimidation.

Under these circumstances, and given the structural weaknesses exposed by the Conservative attacks of the mid-80s, it was essential that the BBC put in place a mechanism for ensuring that the highest standards of journalism were adhered to and for alerting managers to difficult programmes at the earliest possible stage of production. But it was also essential that it remain committed to asking awkward questions, and to publishing the answers at the time of their greatest relevance. Its reputation as a torch-bearer for impartiality depended on a sustained commitment, not just to analytical journalism but to vigorous, investigative journalism.

The rigorous process of referral and the painstaking, meticulous way in which scripts were tested down to every last detail went further than just eradicating mistakes. They created an environment in which it became more difficult to suggest – let alone make – a programme which its originator knew from the start would be subjected to intense collective scrutiny. The checking and rechecking of even the tiniest fact meant inevitably that some difficult political stories became watered down or bowdlerised. It was not a deliberately partisan approach to the making of political programmes, but became partisan through the vetting process; the insistence on strict adherence to a rigid process of verification was applied almost exclusively to programmes which challenged Conservative Party policies or Conservative government actions. It was an atmosphere in which the postponement of exemplary current affairs programmes like *Supergun* or *Sliding into Slump* became almost inevitable. Given that each one was pulled at a politically sensitive moment for the government, it was hard to defend the BBC against charges that its journalism was succumbing to political pressure and political expediency.

The best example of the BBC's enthusiasm for going too far, though, is Producer Choice. Internal markets and market testing had become part of the political rhetoric, though it is unlikely that a BBC which had not faced such intense political scrutiny would have embraced them quite so readily. But the process had started in the early 80s, even before internal markets became fashionable. The emergence of Channel 4 and the burgeoning independent sector created a market for every stage of the programme making process which had simply not existed before. There was an industrial logic which dictated that the BBC could not insulate itself from this environment. To become a participant in this market necessitated more accurate and more transparent accounting procedures within the Corporation which – as it happened – fitted well with a mounting concern about accountability in public sector institutions.

But the wholesale transformation which was conceived and introduced within three years, and which seemed to involve attaching a price to virtually every internal transaction, smacked of excess. It conveyed a different message to staff, as even producers who were convinced about the urgent need for new efficiency measures began to fear for the quality of their and their colleagues' work. It seemed to many that the focus on the need for new accounting systems (although it enthused the Corporation's supporters in government) left little room for consideration of its impact on the dynamics of a cultural organisation.

Producer Choice, too, was a symptom of the times. The 80s saw a barrage of theories of management efficiency and organisational change being applied through a growing horde of management consultancies, themselves a symptom of a difficult economic climate and an unfamiliar political one. They were theories which grew out of profit-making, private sector organisations but were being applied increasingly to the public sector: hospitals, local government, universities, even the police force were subjected to the kinds of marketplace language previously reserved for corporate life.

As the BBC sought to update its image and convince those outside that it was determined to change, it embraced some of these theories with a fervour which even their adherents sometimes found baffling. In an institution which depended wholly on the abilities of its staff to function creatively, the importation of management systems devised elsewhere was always going to prove problematic. Given the jargon in which some of the ideas were expressed, they were more likely to be greeted with contempt.

Precisely this point was made with devastating effect by John Tusa, the former Managing Director of External Services, in the James Cameron Memorial Lecture on 14 June 1994. Tusa said: 'Any management theory and practice which does not take into account the human resource becomes a sterile exercise, undervaluing what should be most precious.' Of course there was a need for efficient work practices, but their implementation and measurement had to be set against other criteria:

> For where, in all this reductive numericalism, is the room for creative insights, where is the space for understanding, where the scope for richness of language, boldness of image, the shaft of emotion?

At the heart of his speech was a distinction which an eminent BBC predecessor had made almost exactly 25 years earlier: that cultural organisations are involved in the creation of meaning, and that therefore the standard management techniques of manufacturing or service companies are not helpful. The fundamental distinction was between programmes and products: 'Systems of management control that tend to treat programmes like products can only end up defeating the very activity they claim to protect.' The urgency of this argument was new, but its substance had emerged before. Hugh Greene, BBC Director General from 1960 to 1969, wrote in 1969:

> We . . . look at this question from an angle which is somewhat different from that of many industrialists. Many things produced in industry respond to a predictable universal demand. The products of broadcasting must be as varied as the human beings they serve. Each programme

is – or should be – custom built.

It was the final passage in Tusa's speech – taken from an internal Bush House report – which most clearly spelled out the danger of imposing new management theories on a long-established public institution. The paper had distinguished between an institution's 'ethos' – defined by Tusa as 'its permanent disposition, its true underlying characteristics' – and its 'pathos', defined as 'the overt, often transitory, usually volatile expressions of feelings of the organisation'. The ethos was open to change, but sounds of distress from the pathos warned that the ethos was feeling somehow violated. What really mattered was that it was the staff, rather than management, who were the creators and owners of this ethos:

> Any management that ignores this, that undervalues the basic ethos, or that tries even to reconstruct it without reference to staff who know in their hearts that they embody that ethos in all daily actions, risks an internal psychological schism that will not easily be repaired.

Tusa spoke with the authority of a man who had been both a successful journalist and a successful manager. By 1994 he, like others, saw staff trying to cope with Producer Choice, with the pages of performance indicators, and with short-term contracts. They recognised the notion of a 'psychological schism' in their daily working lives. For the most part, these people were not resistant to change, but to an alien culture which did not seem to help them do their jobs any better. Working for the BBC was becoming a chore.

The shift to short-term contracts was another example of a policy which went too far for the good of the organisation. Once again, the BBC was quick to embrace a new corporate dynamic, the 'contract culture' which saw workers increasingly detached from long-term employment with individual companies and instead selling their services to a number of client organisations. In fact, the nature of John Birt's salary arrangements was cited by Professor Charles Handy as an illustration of the new fashion. Handy described the subsequent row as,

> A dispute symbolic of the times. More and more professionals think of themselves as on a temporary assignment with an organisation. Loyalty goes first to one's team or project, then to one's profession or discipline and only thirdly to the organisation where these skills are practised.

This may be true for the legal, banking or accountancy profession; it may even be true for the medical profession. But loyalty to the BBC remains a powerful source of motivation for many of its staff, who feel a commitment to the institution because of its place in British life; as Handy concluded, 'The BBC was right to be alarmed.' The rhetoric – and the virtues – of public service broadcasting had been almost excised from BBC language during its most difficult periods with the government, and needed to be reclaimed if the BBC was to keep its identity distinct from just any old commercial broadcaster. That was precisely what Will Wyatt did in a speech to a Royal Television Society dinner in November 1993, when he proclaimed:

> Being free of advertisers and proprietors is liberating, it encourages the merry, nimble, stirring spirits to take wing, creates the chance to dream and to surprise, the opportunity to tell any and all the truths.

Wyatt was making a plea for a greater understanding of the audience but he, like Tusa, warned against the invasion of fashionable market language like 'punters', 'product' and 'software'. This was not just semantic pedantry:

> Language is important. Start talking about product – something uniform that comes by the yard – and you'll start thinking about product; start thinking about it and that's what you'll get. Talk about punters and you'll start thinking of people that way; start thinking about them and you'll start treating them that way.

The BBC was still full of people who related to their viewers and listeners as people, who talked about programmes, and who valued their position at the heart of a cultural academy. But they were becoming frustrated by the apparently endless wave of management-led change. The pathos was sending out distress signals.

To some extent, of course, those cries of pain emanating from the organisation may have helped to convince the government that the changes were real. Had Checkland remained Director General until 1994, as he himself had wished, the BBC would have been similar in many respects to the organisation which exists today. Staff levels would probably have been similar. Producer Choice would still have been introduced (probably in a more gradual and less rigid form, and perhaps not applied to radio where it made less sense). And commercial initiatives like World Service Television would have been developed. But the noise level would have been a good deal lower because the style would have been different. And that may have been to the BBC's disadvantage. For even though the Major government was run by people who professed to like the BBC, they were still wedded to the idea of radical reform in the public sector, and to using a combination of sticks and carrots to effect those reforms. Producer Choice was, unarguably, damaging to the BBC's infrastructure, but the protests and internal opposition it engendered were part of the process of winning over the politicians. It was, after all, John Major himself who had once said of his government's economic policies: 'If it isn't hurting, it isn't working.'

Both the speed and the rigid way in which Producer Choice was introduced – and many of the other internal traumas of the BBC in the last few years – stem in large part from the character of the Director General. Many of those who know him perceive a deep personal sense of insecurity. It is difficult to think of the head of another large organisation who would – as Birt did – question a senior colleague as to whether they were pleased to see him appointed to the top job. Or of one who would tell his staff – as Birt did at an *Extending Choice* workshop – that they should have more interest in him as a person.

Birt expressed this insecurity in three ways: first by a need for control; second, by a divisiveness that meant that if you were not for him then you were against him; and third by an unshakeable conviction of his own rightness. In the words of one observer: 'He loves systems. He doesn't want anything to happen in a haphazard way; everything has to happen in a system, the more complex the better.' Much of the new management style was put down to an organisational rigidity which stemmed directly from the Director General.

The divisiveness was expressed within weeks of Birt's arrival, in the form of incessant and insensitive criticism of the work of experienced BBC journalists, followed by the import of cohorts of LWT journalists who were inevitably distrusted. The same process was seen again in the development of Producer Choice, where anyone who harboured misgivings about the way it was implemented came to be regarded as an enemy of change itself. Since the large majority of the staff fell into this category, it was not surprising that morale was low.

Those on the right side of the divide were succoured by Birt's unwavering sense of certainty. As one colleague observed, 'John is always right. He is a most remarkable man, so able to be right about everything.' His ITV colleagues said as much when the BBC appointed him; one told a member of the Board of Management, 'He'll go on and on and on until you have to say "Fuck off".'

At the same time, some of the values which Birt brought with him made a more positive impact. In daily news reporting, there had been a feeling in some parts of the BBC that its news values were being defined more in terms of what the competition (ITN) was doing than by reference to its own objectives. The result was a news service which many thought was placing undue emphasis on murder, courtroom and royal stories. Under Birt's direction, a new policy emerged which was based on a conviction that, in the words of one senior manager,

> A public service broadcaster ought to have a set of news values founded on significance. . . . BBC news should be trying to make the judgment – which is subjective judgment – on how significant is this development or event for our viewers and listeners. That ought to be the test.

The public service emphasis on comprehensive news provision was reinforced by the opening of news bureaux in continental Europe, an initiative which was long overdue. Birt also ensured that a range of equal opportunity initiatives (under the banner of 'Opportunity 2000') were given a high profile.

His personality was a mixed blessing to the BBC. Only someone with his sense of certainty would have had the determination and resolve to push through the reorganisation of news and current affairs – which was clearly necessary – in the face of almost universal hostility and universal vilification. Again, his systematic approach was invaluable in the period leading up to the White Paper. 'Only John would have had the patience for the endless papers and the endless meetings', a colleague was quoted as saying. The other side of the coin was his mechanistic view of the world, which led him to see the BBC as a giant system which needed tighter control, just when other creative organisations were concluding instead that they got the best results from looser structures. Again, in formulating Producer Choice, the detail which was imposed hampered its effectiveness. And at a more profound level, the implementation of such a large-scale change needed a management that was able to listen and to respond, rather than one which was obdurate in its belief that there was no alternative.

Birt's problems were compounded by a stiffness in large groups which predated his BBC days. He could not display the diplomatic skills of Ian Trethowan, or the manifest devotion to the BBC of Alasdair Milne, or the down-to-earth style of Michael Checkland. He had come in, as an outsider from a small organisation, facing enormous hostility, at a time when the BBC was about to enter the most precarious period in its history. It would have been a battle of survival for the most charismatic and inspirational leader, and few would have emerged unscathed or with an enhanced reputation. Some would have given up. But even his friends worried about Birt's reluctance to mix with the people on whom the BBC's reputation depended. One suggested that he should take some time out to watch programmes being made and chat casually to those involved in order to get informal feedback about problems. Birt's response was that, 'It is not an effective use of management time.'

His lack of ease with the staff was matched by a lack of ease with the press. Throughout his BBC tenure, John Birt has distrusted the press and the press have – mostly – reciprocated. This has meant that the hostile coverage which BBC affairs have often received, due in part to sheer editorial malevolence (and some PR incompetence), has been magnified by a withdrawn chief executive who, in the words of one media correspondent, 'alienates the vast majority of the press and makes no effort at all'. The manifest lack of sympathy for the Director General did not help his cause.

This was especially bad news, for the press had become fascinated by the media. Specialist correspondents are as old as newspapers themselves, and many have long and honourable traditions – some journalists have devoted their careers to reporting sport or politics or crime. But there emerged during the 80s a new breed of specialist reporter, the media correspondent. And media correspondents needed something to write about.

The BBC has been fair game ever since Chamberlain stepped in to persuade Reith to retire. What changed during the 80s was the sheer number of column inches devoted to the Corporation. As Will Wyatt observed in his RTS speech, 'The BBC seems to obsess everyone else in the broadcasting industry and all those who write about it: no detail is too small, no passing reference too insignificant.' Liz Forgan was said by *The Guardian*'s Anne Karpf to be 'stunned by. . . the enormous attention given to her every utterance'. Running the modern BBC has, for its senior managers, come to resemble living in a goldfish bowl.

There have been a number of reasons. With the removal of restrictive practices and the arrival of new technology, there are more pages to fill than there were ten years ago. The media industry has also provided a commercial opportunity: as one of the few expanding areas, there was valuable recruitment advertising to be had, which in turn required a dedicated editorial section. In 1984, *The Guardian* blazed a trail by introducing a Media section on Mondays. Within a few years, every broadsheet newspaper had media pages once a week, and even the mid-market papers had media correspondents.

Then there was the growing proprietorial interest in things media-related. The prospect of multi-channel television and more opportunities for investment alerted newspaper owners – previously precluded from any stake in television – to the possible financial pickings. With proprietors becoming interested in the changing media landscape, no editor could go wrong in appointing a specialist reporter in the field. Finally, particularly in the 'heavies', media stories offered a lighter read to leaven the mix. For the rest, as Clive James observed, 'To goad the BBC is a rewarding sport in itself. It makes a tabloid feel like a heavyweight.'

The BBC was an obvious target simply because it was so big, and so everpresent. BBC programmes were familiar, and BBC presenters were famous. Increasingly, so were BBC senior staff (although rather more reluctantly). Programme disasters like *Eldorado* or rows between 'supremos' like Grade and Birt were fun because everyone knew the names. The combination of show business, politics and money was irresistible. And, of course, the BBC was public property. It could not object because it only existed courtesy of the licence payers who read the newspapers which were publishing the stories.

The consequence was stories which, first, concentrated on 'problems' (otherwise they would not be stories) and, second, focused on personalities. Writing about changing trends in sports journalism, Matthew Engel noted that, after the 1970s, came 'the arbitrary and brutal world of "victim journalism", led by *The Sun*, with England managers, captains and chairmen of selectors the chief targets'. To that list could be added Prime Ministers and BBC Directors General. Public figures in all walks of life are now subjected to the kind of scrutiny which only certain types of personality can comfortably cope with: either those whose skeletons have already been torn from their cupboards (which qualified Terry Venables as the manager of the English soccer team) or the showman with a ready quote and easy access.

In the full glare of the media, and in the absence of a public consensus about the purpose of the Corporation, the BBC's strategy, in the shape of the Task Forces and *Extending Choice*, was to set out to do the government's job for it. It was a lengthy procedure, which Michael Checkland introduced in order to involve BBC staff – rather than just management – in the process of moulding the BBC's vision of its own future. It was explicitly designed to be a 'bottom up' rather than a 'top down' operation.

The statement of public purpose which has resulted is not a million miles from the original Reithian statement. In the words of one insider, 'The language of *Extending Choice* is slightly different but we're really talking about entertaining, informing and educating – it's the same fundamental public purpose.' Perhaps the process of the exercise was more important than its results; perhaps it was necessary both to lift institutional self-confidence and to reassure political masters that some deep thinking was in hand. Perhaps its achievement is that we can still, after the social and political upheaval, talk about Reithian values without attracting ridicule.

What is certainly true is that the essential nature of the creative process – what promotes it, what stifles it, how to improve it, how to make it happen – is as much a mystery now as it was when Reith first took control of the British Broadcasting Company. In 1975, the BBC Chairman Michael Swann in tandem with three of his top managers commissioned Professor Elihu Katz of the Hebrew University of Jerusalem to prepare an 'agenda for new projects of social research in the field of broadcasting'. One of these was about the management of creativity. Katz recommended a 'sort of review' which would 'attempt a sociological reconstruction of Great Moments in the history of creativity at the BBC'.

It was the kind of idea which professionals would probably have dismissed as academic extravagance, but which might have informed the managerial questions being addressed nearly twenty years on. Part of the answer was given by Michael Grade in 1988:

> The only successful programmes you ever see on television anywhere in the world . . . are the programmes that come out of some lunatic's obsession with a particular idea and their ability to carry it out.

The lunatics, in other words, need an asylum. Some of them may want to work inside it, others from outside, but they need the structural support (and money) to be able to pursue their obsessions. As well as financial security and organisational stability, therefore, the asylum needs pockets of anarchy and impulse so that the lunatics can indulge their whimsies. By the middle of 1994, against all the odds, the asylum was still standing. The only question was whether, after all the years of upheaval, the BBC was still a place which was able to let its lunatics loose.

CHAPTER SIXTEEN
GAZING AT THE STARS

Predicting the future of the BBC is a hazardous activity. In September 1991, less than a year ahead of the publication of the Green Paper on the BBC, Richard Hooper of the British consultants PA predicted in the trade magazine *Television Week* that the renewal of the BBC's charter would be based on four main precepts: first, the staged replacement of the licence fee by subscription over eight years; second, a much greater freedom to gain sponsorship revenue; third, a continuing ban on advertising on BBC-1 and BBC-2; and fourth, the privatisation of 51% of BBC Enterprises. One out of four is not bad.

Hooper's article, at the height of the so-called 'Himalayan' debate, argued that 'The BBC has to stop thinking of itself as a "wall-to-wall" provider of all television and start thinking of which market niches it should dominate.' It cited *The Financial Times* and *The Economist* as examples of organisations which had combined commercial success with quality and upmarket positioning, and observed, 'The idea that you necessarily lose quality and independence and public service obligations when you embrace Mammon will be seen as quaint by the mid-1990s.'

It is easy to single out one forecast and poke fun. But Hooper's prediction is revealing because it exemplified the narrow track along which the BBC debate has run for the past decade. Two themes in particular stand out. The first is the market, and how the market defines not just the BBC but also its hinterland. The second is technology, and the inevitability of an all-embracing, interactive, multi-channel society which so enchanted the National Heritage Select Committee and continues to enthral its Chairman. In its wake, say the evangelists of this media revolution, will come unavoidable decline for the BBC and the certain demise of the licence fee. Marketplace arguments and technology arguments combine to produce the apparently irresistible conclusion that in the new televisual world a public broadcaster – even one the size of the BBC – will become irrelevant. But both arguments are fallacious.

The problem with a market approach to broadcasting is that the peculiar economics of the industry make it certain that the market will fail. Broadcasting is a 'public good', meaning that consumption by one person has no impact on the ability of others to consume exactly the same good. My decision to listen to or watch a programme has no effect on your opportunity to watch or listen to the same programme. The cost of transmission is the same whether the audience is twenty thousand people or twenty million; the marginal cost of supplying each new viewer, and the price to them of the programmes, is zero. Because customers typically undervalue such public goods, the private sector tends to under-supply them.

Secondly, the market does not work well where information or experience is being sold. Because people are loath to buy the unfamiliar, the marketplace, if left to itself, will not supply new experience. Neither *Monty Python's Flying Circus* nor *Blackadder* were immediate hits because viewers needed time to get used to their idiosyncratic humour. Commercial channels in a truly competitive market cannot afford to take risks or build audiences slowly. To do so will threaten guaranteed ratings from tried and tested formats.

Third, advertising-funded stations are not selling programmes to viewers, but viewers to advertisers. This has a number of unfavourable consequences for viewers and listeners. It means that low-spending groups, like the elderly, the young or the unemployed, who hold little interest for advertisers, will be ignored. Audiences like those for Radio 2 (the over-fifties) or those for downmarket quiz shows are of interest to too few advertisers to make them commercially viable. The assumption that advertisers' interests are always congruent with those of viewers and listeners is demonstrably untrue: television viewing is at its highest on Christmas Day and over the holiday period which follows. By then, most shops are closed, presents have been exchanged, and the consumer spending spree which precedes Christmas is over. Advertisers have less interest in reaching people, so a commercial channel has less interest in scheduling its strongest programmes or highest rating films. It is now accepted that ITV effectively concedes the Christmas period to the BBC, and in doing so short-changes the viewing public.

Perhaps the most vital flaw in the market approach centres around questions of content and scheduling. As new channels and stations proliferate, there will be no shortage of specialist offerings, apparently catering for every conceivable age, taste and interest. But limited revenues and competitive pressures will inevitably have an impact on the variety and quality of programming. Radio 3, with its emphasis on new work in both music and drama, is a prime example of a station which could not exist in the marketplace without making drastic changes to the volume and type of original material. In 1993–4, for example, Radio 3 broadcast 2,500 hours of live music – almost half its total output. Each year it plays around 14,000 titles including the works of 225 living British composers. Devotees of the market philosophy point to the advertising-funded Classic FM as proof that classical music radio can survive in the marketplace. But Classic fulfils a different function from Radio 3: its broader appeal, small revenue base and dependence on the attractive audience profile of its listeners make it a wholly different cultural animal.

Exactly the same argument applies to Radio 1, the prime target of free marketeers urging 'privatisation'. How, they ask, can a popular music station which could run very profitably in the private sector be justified as part of the public service remit? The answer, as with Radio 3, is the content: 1,500 titles played each week compared to around 500 on commercial stations; 300 new bands recorded each year 'in session'; regular in-depth news bulletins rather than thirty-second soundbites; discussions and documentaries on issues relevant to young people (such as jobs or drug addiction).

In a more competitive world, the culture and style of an advertising-funded pop station is ever more vulnerable to the commercial demands of advertisers. Liz Kershaw, a BBC DJ who did a stint on commercial radio, described in *The Guardian* her experience of meeting the sponsors of a show she was guesting on:

> What I'd never appreciated was the extent to which the advertisers may exercise their financial muscle in dictating the editorial content of programmes. . . . I now see that a couple of big-wigs who might know a lot about fries and fat content but not a lot about pop and programme content can dictate the output of a [commercial] radio station.

Matthew Bannister, Radio 1's new Controller, has also worked in the commercial sector and knows its constraints:

> You go in, you have no producer; you have a computer screen which throws up the running order; you can't play anything else because they don't give you any CDs; you press the computer screen to play the CD; if you drop an ad you're in deep trouble; if you don't identify the station at every other link, if you don't keep the links to eleven seconds, you're fired. . . . We will never be like a commercial station in the way we operate.

In television, the same argument applies to programmes rather than channels. In the arts, commercial channels will tend to favour the safer, higher-rating approach of big-name interviews or performances. Less time is devoted to operas, art or the more obscure performers which can – nevertheless – attract over a million viewers.

In children's programmes, the commercial imperative means more involvement from advertisers and more formats intended to launch new characters or concepts which can subsequently be marketed as a commodity. The emphasis is on merchandising, rather than challenging and stimulating the young. In drama, too, commercial requirements can dictate the direction of the creative process. In a study of commercial pressures on American programme making, one producer told Professor Jay Blumler how 'The amount and timing of advertising have formative implications for programme content . . . climaxes and artificial cliff-hangers must be regularly built [in] . . . so that viewers will be motivated to stay tuned.'

Finally, in current affairs, the pressure on ratings and the high cost of investigative reporting inevitably shifts the emphasis to 'softer' areas like crime and money, and to human interest stories featuring the aristocracy or royalty. The tougher political stories, the miscarriages of justice, or the stories about government or corporate incompetence are squeezed out. Even before the new London weekday ITV franchise-winner, Carlton, went on air, its Director of Programmes, Paul Jackson, declared his unashamedly populist vision. He told *The Daily Telegraph* in May 1992: 'If *World in Action* were in 1993 to uncover three more serious miscarriages of justice while delivering an audience of three, four or five million, I would cut it. It isn't part of the ITV system to get people out of prison.'

The market approach also influences scheduling. Current affairs, arts, educational and news programmes are all squeezed out of peak time as they rate lower than movies or adventure series. Many of these programmes will attract three, four, or five million viewers – more than the number of people buying *The Sun* each day – but their preferences are subordinated to those of the majority. Recent moves by ITV to have the evening news bulletin – *News at Ten* – moved out of peak time have so far been rebuffed by the Independent Television Authority. It is almost certainly a temporary reprieve.

A non-commercial channel can afford to cater for everyone's tastes at a time when people can watch. David Docherty, the Head of Research and Strategy for BBC Network Television, underlined the BBC's position at the 1993 Manchester Broadcasting Symposium:

> The BBC is committed body and soul to offering viewers range and diversity, and that will not change. By range I mean that we guarantee to have factual programmes as well as entertainment in prime time, regardless of the pressure. By diversity I mean that within each season the BBC will schedule and commission fresh and adventurous programmes as well as established stars and formats, regardless of the market. The licence payer pays the BBC to give them not just what they want now, but to experiment with what they might want in the future.

It is no longer possible to expect that sort of language from a commercial television executive.

The irony is that, until very recently in the UK, it was possible. Both ITV in 1955, and Channel 4 in 1982, were established by Act of Parliament with strong public service obligations. Moreover, ITV's monopoly of advertising revenue allowed the ITV companies to commit themselves wholeheartedly to delivering their public service obligations. Some, like Granada, sometimes did it better than the BBC. The 'feather-bedding' which so angered Mrs Thatcher may have been good for the staff of ITV companies, but it was also good for viewers. This system was undermined by the 1990 Broadcasting Act which introduced the auction system for ITV licences – thus diverting millions of pounds from programmes to the Treasury – and set up Channel 4 as a separate company to compete for advertising revenue. As the new system came into operation in 1993, the effects could be seen almost immediately and have continued to be evident ever since: more populist (and fewer peak time) current affairs programmes, and drama with a heavy reliance on recognised stars.

This is not to argue that the market approach produces bad programmes or schedules; simply that the pressures of outright competition have consequences, in every area of radio and television, which are unfavourable to some viewers and listeners. The BBC's output is dictated by different priorities which reflect different funding and organisational pressures. Even free-market advocates (like Professor Peacock) concede the principle of market failure, but apply it only to certain 'elitist' programme areas. This is a mistake. Competitive commercial broadcasting entails some market failure across all programme areas in radio and television. The BBC is the antidote.

Underlying all the arguments about the market approach is a more fundamental, almost philosophical view, of what broadcasting is for. It is clearly more than just a series of television channels or radio stations. It has a profound social function which it is impossible to measure in terms of a conventional discussion about the marketplace. In particular, the market has nothing to say about the quality of goods which the individual can choose from, claiming only that a range of goods will exist because the market will provide them. As the conservative British political thinker, John Gray, has argued in *Beyond the New Right*, it is not enough that the individual has choice:

> Autonomy, if it is to be meaningful and valuable, requires not only capacities for choice on the part of the individual but also a span of worthwhile options in his or her cultural environment. In the absence of this, autonomy wanes, and the lives of individuals become the poorer, however many choices they make.

Gray's argument involves the concept of 'inherently public goods' – cultural goods which enable us to make such choices – and, elsewhere, he has compared broadcasting to 'the streets and parks of a well-ordered city in the classical European tradition'. As he explains,

> Streets and parks are not public goods in the technical terms of economic theory. They can be viewed as, and may indeed become, private consumer goods, paid for by those who use them, and designed to exclude those who do not pay. When this happens, however, a great public good is lost – that of city life itself. . . . The point is not that market mechanisms are inappropriate in urban policy, but that they need a framework of public provision if they are to make their full contribution to well-being. Analogously, the broadcast media are not solely in the business of supplying news or entertainment as commodities. They are doing their bit towards the renewal of the common culture.

If the BBC was looking for new language to justify a continuing presence, it could do worse than quote 'the renewal of the common culture'.

If the discourse of the market dominated discussion of broadcasting in the 1980s, then a discourse of technological inevitability has come to dominate that of the 1990s. A high-tech world of 500 television channels is envisaged, in which set-top computers will make our decisions for us, and create a 'Me-tv' environment. In such a world, we will no longer be mere viewers; instead our television set will be a computer-driven gateway to an electronic world in which we can shop, bank, order films, and maybe communicate with each other electronically. This is the vision of the new barons of the electronic age, and can enthuse Rupert Murdoch and News International as much as Bill Gates and Microsoft. It can excite even Labour MPs, as the Select Committee on National Heritage demonstrated in its report in 1994. It is a world in which the BBC, say its opponents, has no place. For how can one public organisation with two television channels justify the cost of an annual licence fee when so much else is available? It is a wholly misleading vision, based on a series of misunderstandings about the pace of technological change and the way individuals react to new technology.

It is an area which is overrun by numbers – in particular the number of homes and the proportion of the time they spend viewing particular channels – and for this reason the discussion can seem abstract. But the numbers have meaning because they determine the ground on which British broadcasting policy will be debated over the next – critical – ten years.

By the middle of 1994 there were between 2.5 and 3 million UK house-holds (out of 22 million) receiving satellite channels via a satellite dish. A further 600,000 households could receive multi-channel television via cable, around one in five of those whose homes are passed by cable. This is likely to grow rapidly as the cable companies fulfil their franchise requirements and lay their cables past about twelve million homes by the year 2000. At the same time the number of satellite subscribers is likely to creep upwards, though the rate of increase has been steadily declining.

Given the slow growth rate of satellite dish sales and the competition from cable, it is unlikely that satellite homes will exceed four million by the turn of the century. Assuming a generous connection rate for cable, rising from one in five to one in three, there will also be around four million homes connected to cable. In the year 2000, then, a total of around eight million homes will be taking multi-channel services, less than 40% of the British total.

Evidence from existing multi-channel homes in the UK and the United States – where the process is more advanced – tells us a lot about likely view-ing habits when people have a multiplicity of choice. In the UK, viewers in multi-channel homes spend around two-thirds of their time watching the four terrestrial services; in the US, the share of the three main networks is about three-fifths. Even on the most generous assessment, then, by the year 2000 the national share of the four terrestrial channels will still be 84% (down from 94% in 1994). That is hardly a giant step down the digital superhighway. It is entirely reasonable to expect that the BBC's share of that national audience will still be comfortably above one-third. Equally, in radio, new stations will reduce the numbers listening to the BBC, but its range across five national stations and 39 local stations will almost certainly maintain its audience at over a third of all listeners.

Moreover, subscribers to satellite channels regard them as discretionary expenditure. Cable households will cancel their subscription if they get bored with the service or if money is tight. Satellite owners, too, stop paying their subscriptions despite their investment in a dish and decoder. Those eight million households will therefore be a floating population, whose expenditure will fluctuate, making revenue for new satellite channels unstable and unpredictable. At the same time, even the more stable advertising revenue for ITV and Channel 4 is being threatened by new communications and marketing opportunities, and by an increasing scepticism on the part of big advertisers about the value of television airtime. The decision by Heinz to divert product advertising from television to direct marketing may presage a large-scale defection with disastrous consequences for advertiser-dependent channels.

Digital compression will increase the number of channels available, although the so-called '500-channel universe' is a long way off. Some services might be able to deliver 150 channels to some viewers in the UK by the end of the decade, but most of these will provide a range of services which are very different from conventional television: both video-on-demand and 'near-video-on-demand' (with movie start times ten or fifteen minutes apart) will be as much a challenge to video shops and existing movie channels as network television; there will be shopping channels (classified ads or supermarkets), interactive quiz channels, and channels for closed business groups. These will take time from other activities (like shopping trips or reading newspaper classifieds) rather than watching television. Apart from the absence of direct competition, there will be significant consumer barriers to new technology take-up: in particular, money. As Joe Ashton pointed out to his National Heritage Select Committee colleagues, ten million homes have no wage earner. Terrestrial television is popular because it is cheap: according to the consultancy London Economics, watching BBC programmes costs the viewer 5p per hour, compared to 14p for satellite channels and 43p for video rentals. It is also simple. In a world where many people still despair of tuning their radio or programming their video, that is a powerful attraction.

Finally, much of the discussion about new technology confuses audience share and audience 'reach'. A channel's share can be small (both BBC-2 and Channel 4 hover around the 10% mark), but that does not mean that only 10% of the population watch them. Reach – the proportion of the audience which uses a channel over a given period of time – is a more accurate yardstick of a

channel or station's presence in people's lives. In a given week almost everyone will tune to BBC-1 at least once, and 90% will watch BBC-2. Even among
homes with satellite television, 90% will tune to BBC television. Reach is a
better justification than share for a licence fee levied on all households in a
multi-channel world.

In the public arena, then, discussion of the BBC has been dominated by the
assumption that the supply of broadcasting will increasingly be taken over by
the market, that public provision will be marginalised, and that the opportunities for the market to provide such services will be amplified enormously by
technology. The main ground on which the BBC chose to fight its case for
charter renewal was that of value for money rather than the inherent value of
public broadcasting. Such a tactic was probably necessary in the political climate of the 1980s, but the result has been a debate which always starts from
the BBC's likely income, and then moves to the range of services which the
BBC can afford to supply. In the 1990s, when the political climate is changing, there is a danger that this argument could become self-fulfilling; that the
BBC will mistake this tactical response for a strategy, and doom itself to a
future of wearying skirmishes about penny-pinching while the Corporation,
and its value as an institution, withers on the vine.

This conflation of purpose and delivery has marked much of the last
decade. As Anthony Smith has observed:

> Public service, the BBC, and the universal licence fee are no longer an
> accepted, unarguable, trinity. The debate about public service is thus
> both a discussion of the validity of a principle and an inquest into the
> stewardship of the BBC, and the two, having been placed together upon
> an agenda, are now impossible in practice to separate.

Or almost impossible; for the division between those who call into question
the concept of public broadcasting, and those who only wish it to be more efficient, is the fault-line which has run through the government's attacks on the
BBC over the last decade. The right-wingers who advised Thatcher in the
early and mid-80s wanted to see an end to the principle of the thing, and it was
this antipathy which drove inquiries such as the Peacock Committee; more liberal Conservatives, such as Hurd and Mellor, deflected their zeal by shifting
the terms of the debate onto management and efficiency. It is possible to date
precisely the defining moment of this elision between the two; Douglas Hurd's
speech to the House of Commons during the debate on the Peacock
Committee's report, in which he ruled out the introduction of advertising but
imposed the independent production quota, appears with hindsight to have
been an adroit defence of his personal belief in the principle of public service
broadcasting.

Hurd no doubt understood what he was doing, but the ambiguity between
purpose and delivery has continued to bedevil the BBC. Ostensibly the BBC

management has been pursuing a twin-track strategy, under which initiatives such as the Task Force reviews and *Extending Choice* have been designed, apparently, to argue the public case for public broadcasting, while the internal apparatus of Producer Choice has been constructed to deliver (and be seen to be delivering) an efficient and measurable public service. However, the two initiatives do not have equal weight. The impact of Producer Choice has been inexorably to drag the values of the market into the BBC's internal culture along with the attendant market disciplines. In contrast, for all the paraphernalia of the *Extending Choice* workshops, these public arguments about the value of the BBC as an organisation simply do not carry the same weight. Producer Choice is present in the BBC's daily working life, whereas *Extending Choice* is a day of rhetoric away from the office or the warehouse.

It is not surprising that the one feels more important in the new model BBC than the other, or that staff continue to be suspicious of the intentions of their senior management. For all that the BBC management attempted to portray the strikes against performance related pay and local bargaining as a traditional dispute over conditions of service, it would be more accurate to see them as a dispute about the future of the BBC. A BBC is being constructed in which relationships, between and within departments, are economic; in contrast, in the traditional BBC, all individuals perceived themselves as part of the whole. Once fractured, the sense of the whole would be impossible to recreate, which will further deepen suspicions about motive.

In truth, it is not enough for a public broadcaster merely to be efficient, transparent and accountable, because purpose is the key. The point is to be better at delivering the public goods – the social purpose – for which they are responsible. As Greg Parston of the Office for Public Management has put it,

> For the BBC . . . management change must be fashioned and tested not by objectives of efficiency and accountability, but by the very purpose of public broadcasting itself: by how well those arrangements help inform the national debate, express British culture and entertainment, create opportunities for education and communicate between the United Kingdom and abroad. . . . The real test of management changes is the extent to which they contribute to the production of social results, not the degree to which they work as individual strategies to make the BBC more efficient, more distinctive, or more accountable. A more accountable BBC that does not create opportunities for education is not effective; a more efficient BBC that does not deliver the value of public service broadcasting is a contradiction in terms.

This is a vision of a BBC which is not just a broadcaster, but an instrument of public life, a disinterested national institution which provides a universal service, and in doing so enables us all to participate fully as citizens in our increasingly fragmented society. It is this vision which is articulated by John

Gray in his critique of the free market.

Only a comprehensive public broadcasting service such as the BBC can hope to articulate the common national culture. It is worth noting the obverse truth – that market-led services are unlikely to give the full expression to the diversity we harbour among us if they are not complemented by public service broadcasting. . . . There is a danger that in the 90s, policy will be guided by fetishes and dogmas inherited from the 80s, such as the dogma of economism . . . with its neglect or incomprehension of the importance of cultural goods or of the role of national institutions in giving body to the national culture.

Inevitably, this returns us to the question of funding. Once the need and purpose of this national public institution is agreed, it still remains an expensive proposition. Where should the money come from? One of the reasons for the Thatcher government's hostility to the BBC was the way in which it was funded. The licence fee is a flat-rate household charge on the reception of a television signal, which is different from a tax only in that the revenue is 'hypothecated', or paid directly to the BBC. Evasion runs at 8% (whether this is seen as high or low seems to depend on the critic's view of the licence fee) and the detector vans have been variously described as a 'bespoke policing function' or – in an American magazine – 'state-sponsored TV storm troopers'. Its disadvantages are that it is regressive in effect (poor households pay the same as rich ones), it is anti-consumerist (payment is not contingent on using BBC services), and it is anti-democratic (the licence fee payer gains no voice in the organisation in exchange for his or her money).

It does, however, have a number of advantages. It is resilient and sufficiently predictable (political finagling notwithstanding) to enable the BBC's management to plan the service. This is important in a world where the impact of new technology and the fall-out from the Broadcasting Act are creating a fiercely competitive broadcasting environment in which more channels and stations will be chasing fluctuating revenue. Financial instability will be compounded by corporate instability as new strategic alliances are forged and unforged by companies desperate to stay in touch with the media 'revolution'. The problem of fairness is mitigated by the disproportionately high use made of television by those on low incomes. There is an inbuilt process of redistribution since those on high incomes – who tend to use BBC services less – effectively subsidise the less well off.

The only public funding alternative would be direct taxation. This would have both fiscal and political consequences. It would put around a penny on the basic rate of income tax or half a percentage point on VAT; and, as with the ABC in Australia, it would make the BBC even more vulnerable to political influence. In an atmosphere of spending cuts and sacrifices, it would be impossible to plead a special case for broadcasting against – say – health or education spending. The experience of direct funding around the world – in Canada and the USA as well as Australia – is that money is progressively removed from a state-funded public broadcaster which, in turn, is forced into an evermore compromising relationship with its paymasters.

But while the principle of a licence fee system can stand up to scrutiny, its mechanics now pose a serious threat to the BBC's survival. One of the reasons the licence fee has stood the test of time is the natural growth of revenue it has afforded over the years: first, through increasing take-up of television as new transmitters were built and the medium became more popular; and second with the gradual switch to colour sets which required a more expensive licence. There are no further identifiable sources of growth. Even with the licence fee pegged to inflation, as it is until the end of 1996, there will still be a squeeze on expenditure (the cost of labour rises faster than inflation when the economy is growing, and broadcasting is a labour-intensive industry). There is only so much that efficiency savings can do.

Given this funding squeeze, the BBC is confronted with a series of difficult questions. If it does nothing, it is faced with death by a hundred slow cuts – or at best, organised retreat. It needs to find ways of reducing its expenditure or increasing its revenue. The latter is not easy, and the former not attractive. When it comes to cutting services, every pundit has a favoured candidate (usually selling off Radios 1 and 2), but the only way to make real inroads is to cut back on television. Adam Singer, Vice-President of the American cable company TCI (and son, incidentally, of the former BBC executive Aubrey Singer), tried to make a virtue of necessity by suggesting the BBC could auction off BBC-2 and use the proceeds to pay for BBC-1. This would have two effects: first, it would create a valuable opportunity for a new media player (like TCI, perhaps?) to gain access to part of the terrestrial network; and, second, it would remove from the BBC the central pillar of its success. For if there is one single policy decision in the last seventy years which has guaranteed the BBC's survival in a more competitive world, it was the Pilkington Committee's recommendation in 1962 to give the third terrestrial TV channel to the BBC. The ability to run minority and innovative programmes at peak viewing times on one channel in tandem with popular programmes on another, as well as the cross-scheduling flexibility for major sports and news events, have given the BBC a rare and priceless flexibility. Reduced to a single television channel, it would rapidly fade into insignificance. Applying our analysis of the market failure argument must mean that the BBC must continue to operate across the waterfront. The question has been posed in eloquent terms by the former BBC executive Brian Wenham: how many corners should the cornerstone cover? The answer – even in the 1990s – is all of them.

If there are to be no significant expenditure cuts, the spotlight falls on the other side of the equation: how to raise additional revenue? One suggestion was proposed in a paper written for the think-tank Demos by Ian Hargreaves, who was recruited by John Birt as Controller and then Director of News and Current Affairs before rejoining *The Financial Times* as Deputy Editor. He argued for moving the BBC into the private sector, under new ownership (possibly employee-controlled), and under a set of financial arrangements which would include advertising. This would, in his view, 'liberate the BBC', enabling it to move away from reliance on the licence fee over a number of years and become a truly international competitive force.

His argument falls into a familiar trap of assuming that the private sector always liberates while the public sector always constrains. It contrasts vividly with Will Wyatt's declaration that 'being free of advertisers and proprietors is liberating', and returns us again to our definition of market failure. There are any number of 'liberated' private media corporations who are free to compete for all sources of commercial revenue. But in a number of ways – the need to placate advertisers, the relentless concentration on numbers – the cultural effect can be stifling rather than liberating. To transfer the BBC to the private sector would be to remove at a stroke its fundamental distinguishing characteristic – that it is subject to different pressures from a private company, that many talented people find in it a creative freedom which is missing from the private sector, and that this is reflected in the programmes offered to viewers and listeners. For most of those working within the BBC, Hargreaves's liberation would be an imprisonment.

It is therefore ironic that, even though the funding and structural solution is anathema, the BBC has adopted much of the Hargreaves approach to commercialism and international expansion. BBC Worldwide, announced by the Deputy Director General Bob Phillis in the middle of 1994, is designed to earn revenue for the BBC abroad – from programmes and even channels – by exploiting the BBC's 'brand-name'. Phillis's stated objectives are hugely ambitious: for the BBC to generate through its commercial operations another 15–20% of revenue. Historically, the BBC has not been very good at commerce, and even some private sector ventures which have been launched by aggressive entrepreneurs have proved far from lucrative. CNN International, for example – the one service which is comparable to World Service Television – has on CNN's own figures only recently broken even. Others claim it is still running at a loss. Even operating at the highest level of efficiency, to generate an additional 20% of *net* revenue requires a much larger gross income. It so happens that the Task Force on 'The BBC as Entrepreneur' calculated in 1991 what it would mean: for a commercial division to contribute 20% of BBC income, it would need a turnover of around the same size as the licence fee revenue, and would be making profits equivalent to half of the entire Marks and Spencer group. The effect would be to create a huge parallel organization; not so much (as Liz Forgan once warned) the tail wagging the dog, as another dog trying to squeeze itself into the kennel.

Such a strategy has important political and cultural consequences. If it is successful, it is naive to expect politicians simply to ignore this extra revenue stream and continue to raise the licence fee. The National Heritage Select Committee was blunt – and honest – about its attitude to new income; it would be an opportunity to peg the licence fee at its present level, and perhaps even reduce it. At the same time, a more powerful, aggressive and commercial BBC will start to anger the private sector players as they find their own expansion plans thwarted by this hybrid organization with an unfair advantage. Other media conglomerates – and not only News International – will see their own empires threatened and will lose no opportunity to vilify the new-look commercial BBC through their newspaper columns. For the BBC, it will be a re-run of the late 1980s, this time without a friend in sight.

Ultimately, of course, an aggressive commercial strategy has an obvious conclusion. The bigger it becomes, the more it challenges private vested interests, and the more opprobrium levelled at the licence fee, the more likely it is that those counselling the privatisation option will have their way. It will be a simple argument: if it looks like a commercial company, then there is no reason to insulate it from the competitive pressures which real commercial companies have to endure in the marketplace. The combination of political and corporate self-interest will become an irresistible force. A strategy designed to preserve the BBC from the privatisers will deliver it to them on a plate.

These are the long term dangers of the new commercial strategy. In the short term, it brings in its wake real cultural dangers which could irrevocably alter the Corporations's ethos. Both the economic and cultural risks of aggressive commercialism were elegantly put in an editorial in the British magazine *Sight and Sound* in June 1994:

> The central illusion of the whole strategy. . . is the belief that the world of multi-channel television is panting to pay big money for British programming. The global television market is highly skewed. . . . The big terrestrial channels in each country will continue to take most of the audience. And in many countries these bigger players are actually increasing the domestic content of their programming. On the other hand the international trade in programming that does go on is overwhelmingly an export trade by the United States. . . . Most countries mix US products with their own national production; third countries scarcely figure.
>
> In such a lop-sided international market, the niche British television can reasonably contend for will be limited and keenly contested. So the BBC will not get anywhere near its new targets for international revenue unless it cuts some corners. If drama is to be commissioned with a serious eye to overseas sales potential, we are going to get more period pieces set in country houses, as the BBC trades on its unique selling point as the audio-visual arm of the British heritage industry. And if a

serious effort is made to increase the amount of co-production money, we will find rather more American heiresses just happening to get involved in the storylines. These are not the editorial priorities of public service.

The importance of domestic programmes for the BBC is underlined by the poor ratings performance of even American programmes for almost the last decade. No imported TV programme has been watched by fifteen million viewers since an episode of *The A-Team* shown on ITV in February 1984 (since when some 1,500 British-made programmes have topped the fifteen-million figure), and the last time an American show made even a seasonal top ten was *The Equalizer*, also on ITV, in autumn 1986. *Dallas*, which once terrified the defenders of British culture, ended its final run buried on a Sunday afternoon schedule. The only two foreign programmes to make a dent in British ratings are the Australian soaps *Neighbours* and *Home and Away*. Even these are consistently outperformed by the home-grown *Coronation Street* and *EastEnders*.

It is therefore highly questionable whether a public broadcaster – whose primary task is to serve its domestic audience and reflect their lives – can also operate effectively in the global market. As the *Sight and Sound* editorial suggests, one objective or the other eventually gives; and if the strategy were successful, the world-beater thus created would be less sensitive to the needs of the domestic viewers and listeners whose licence fees first built the BBC's resources, skills, and reputation. If the purpose of the BBC is to give all its licence paying citizens the opportunity fully to participate in the public life of the nation – the common and cultural life as well as the political life – this should be the criterion to decide the basis for its future strategy – even if the price to pay is depriving the rest of the world of the BBC's presence. Ideally, we should all support the principle of a BBC determined to broadcast impartial news to China without making the craven political compromises of Rupert Murdoch. But, ultimately, such projects will distract from domestic priorities which are more consonant with the BBC's history and tradition.

However, such a strategy almost certainly leaves the BBC with the unenviable task of finding ways of creating a political consensus around the idea of a higher licence fee – that is, increasing it above the rate of inflation. The work of Ehrenberg and Mills suggests that viewers and listeners are willing to pay significantly more than they do for their existing BBC services, yet curiously this is an option the BBC seems reluctant to air. (In *Paying for Broadcasting*, sponsored by the BBC 'as a contribution to public debate about the future of one of Britain's most successful industries', raising the licence fee faster than inflation is the one possibility never countenanced.) There may be a fear of getting to the psychological barrier of the £100 licence fee too soon, but this is a marketing problem; cable and satellite customers pay far more but do so in bite-sized monthly instalments. £8.50 per month seems more acceptable than £100 per year, and initial evidence suggests that the BBC's recently introduced system of monthly payment is having some effect on evasion.

The problem is that such a strategy involves the BBC turning itself on its head. Its links with the State – and explicitly with the government of the day – mean that it is more accustomed to conducting its political discussions through the channels of Whitehall and Westminster, rather than through mobilising its users. It is revealing that even in the language of *Extending Choice*, and the subsequent audience surveys announced by the Corporation, viewers and listeners are referred to in the language of consumerism and the marketplace, rather than as social beings or citizens. The BBC's lack of engagement with the public processes of politics is a far greater threat to its legitimacy as a public broadcaster than the iniquities (real and imagined) of the licence fee mechanism. The result is that although the BBC was, in the 20s and 30s, regarded as an examplar of a new type of public organisation, it now risks being lumped in the public mind with the plethora of unelected and unresponsive quangos which are one of the most corrupting legacies of the Thatcher years.

This is partly a direct result of its public and constitutional status, which borders on the arcane: from the Royal Charter, negotiated every fifteen years or so, after dialogue with the government rather than Parliament, to the ill-defined relationships between the government and the governors and between the governors and management, to its poorly defined public purpose, all is left open to interpretation. The consummate political skill (or compromise) of John Reith in the mid-1920s, which left him with great individual scope to set the objectives and the purpose of a fledgling organisation in a fledgling industry, is no basis for public broadcasting policy seventy years later.

Paradoxically Channel 4, created sixty years after the BBC, offers a more appropriate model for the BBC. Channel 4's public purpose, its celebrated 'remit', has been enshrined in law after due parliamentary discussion and process. If a statutory framework is good enough for one minority television channel, it should be good enough for the 'cornerstone' of British broadcasting. An Act of Parliament would specify the range of programme areas expected from a public broadcaster, pre-empting any discussion about 'high' or 'higher' ground. It would set public objectives on training, on research, on innovation. It would set in law the duty of the BBC to scrutinise and challenge public policy – in programmes like *Zircon* or *Sliding into Slump*.

Almost more important than the contents of the Act itself would be its constitutional implications. Under the charter, the BBC's constitutional relationship is with government, not Parliament. It must go cap in hand to whatever secretary of state or prime minister is currently in office, and lives in fear of being saddled with a cabinet master who opposes its very existence. The fear this can instil was vividly demonstrated during the spring and summer of 1994, as dates for publication of the BBC White Paper came and went with disturbing regularity. It was known that John Major was planning a major cabinet reshuffle for his beleaguered government, and the tension in Broadcasting House was palpable: what if the new National Heritage minister was an ambitious neo-Thatcherite, desperate to prove his credentials to the Conservative right? As it was, the Chancellor (and Conservative moderate) Kenneth Clark made a point of attending the relevant ministerial meetings on the BBC himself, rather than delegating it (as he might have done) to his Thatcherite junior Michael Portillo.

An Act of Parliament would remove such uncertainties. It would eliminate the now semi-permanent state of preparation for the next charter review, a process which – under the present system – will now be starting again within three to four years. Perhaps most significantly of all for a public body operating in a mature democracy, it would allow for proper democratic debate on the BBC's role through our elected representatives. There would be real political accountability through the due process of Parliament, rather than simulated accountability via ministerial whim. An Act of Parliament would be a political benchmark which, as with Channel 4, would offer the BBC a visible means of support in testing times, and its licence payers a means of assessing the Corporation's role in upholding our public culture.

Part of this new statutory foundation would be a carefully delineated role for BBC governors which would define precisely the nature of their 'trusteeship' and the limit of their responsibilities. In a seminar in March 1994, Sir Kenneth Bloomfield, the Northern Ireland Governor since 1991, set out four influences which he believed determine how governors act: the statutory framework; custom and practice; the prevailing working environment (governors behave differently in times of perceived crisis); and powerful personalities, who can 'take the disputed ground'. Given the vague and ill-defined nature of the first two factors, there have been vast tracts of disputed land which have always made the BBC vulnerable to powerful personalities on the governing board. In an atmosphere of almost permanent crisis over the last ten years, those blurred lines of responsibility have done immense damage to the BBC's stability. New guidelines were issued at the end of 1993 to try to clarify the confusion, but they remain guidelines. There is still plenty of scope for politically motivated, or incompetent, or power-hungry individuals to seize the reins and interfere with management issues if they are so inclined. An Act of Parliament would provide a clear and transparent division of responsibilities.

A vital element of this definitional process would be a new and more open mechanism for selecting the Chairman and governors, to discourage the systematic political favouritism of the last fifteen years. Nominations could be invited from relevant public bodies like the Consumers Association, National Consumer Council, regional Arts Councils, the CBI and TUC. There should be open scrutiny by the National Heritage Select Committee, who have not so far covered themselves with glory but do at least represent a balance of parliamentary opinion. Candidates for the Board who are patently ignorant, prejudiced, or incompetent are more likely to be exposed, and answers to questions would be a matter of public record. More than anything, it would be a transparent process rather than an inscrutable system of patronage and political point-scoring.

It is hard, in the 1990s, to encourage people to believe once again in the value of public institutions. But the aggressively pro-market policies pursued in the 1980s combined with rapid technological and social change have created a social fragmentation which make such institutions more necessary than ever. The BBC is, uniquely, an independent social institution which everyone experiences in their everyday life – unlike, say, the Arts Council or even the National Health Service. It is probably therefore the most important public institution in Britain (Anthony Smith has described it as 'second only to Parliament as an instrument of our political life'). In the face of such sweeping change, it is possible to argue that the licence fee is a tax on citizenship, which should be set (preferably by an agency independent of the government) at whatever level is required to enable the BBC to fulfil its statutory public duty. In organisational terms, if the BBC is to survive, it will need to re-create itself – as in its early years – as a pioneering form of public organisation. The apostles of these new forms will not be the economists and accountants who have driven the dry arithmetic of Producer Choice, but (as Geoff Mulgan has suggested) the new management thinkers whose work prizes ethos, imagination, federalism, and learning. 'Far from replacing a monolithic bureaucracy with a classical market [television professionals] may find that there are a multiplicity of ways of running a broadcasting system, and that few of the best ones fit a classic blueprint.' In other words the BBC requires a different approach and different thinking from the derivative, accountancy-based management-speak of the 1980s.

If the political will is not yet there, it is not impossible that the continuing wave of Second World War fiftieth anniversaries, which has been rolling through the years since 1989 will – as it reaches the British post-war settlement – coincide with a shift in political mood which forces a re-examination of the role of public institutions in our public life. There is a real need and real desire for such a review. As John Gray has written, 'The political task of the age . . . is reconciling the subversive dynamism of market institutions with the human need for local rootedness and strong and deep forms of common life.' There are positive signs in some of the community-based language coming from the new Labour Party leader Tony Blair, language which is not wholly alien to a resurgent Tory left. There are also signs that the development of new technologies is most dynamic when (as with the explosion of the Internet) they foster communication rather than consumption.

It is for these reasons that the battle for the BBC, the battle for the idea of a public broadcasting organisation, which has raged over the past decade, is important; for it is a battle about the forms of our public life, and therefore our society. The story told in this book is of a series of defensive engagements, fought out in Whitehall and White City, in which the BBC's form has been pummelled almost out of shape, but appears, so far, to have survived with its core intact. The battle which is about to begin is a more difficult one, for to survive beyond the charter period which begins in 1997 will require a public battle for the hearts and minds of all of its constituents, rather than for a handful of civil servants and ministers. As with so much else in the modern BBC, this is a problem with long-standing antecedents. Fifteen years ago, the Director General Charles Curran wrote:

> What will remain a problem for my successors is the process of convincing the public and their representatives, the politicians, that the price which is paid for a superb public service is, by any standard, absurdly low. The BBC has to sell itself, not simply as a bargain but as excellence within the reach of everyman.

Richard Eyre tells the story of Tom Clarke, a dramatist who had written for the BBC since the early days of television. Clarke described the BBC as a cross between the Church and the Post Office, but still remained optimistic that it could retain the vigour it had when he first started to write for it. Towards the end of his life, he had had a lively exchange of letters with John Birt about BBC drama. As Eyre recounts,

> His life-long view of the BBC's bureaucracy was triumphantly vindicated when, after a meeting with the Director General, and more correspondence, he received a letter from an *apparatchik* which began, 'I am sorry that you feel our television drama is disappointing'. To which Tom replied, 'Let me say that "your" television drama is also mine'.

The next battle for the BBC will be to transform the Corporation from 'your BBC' to 'our BBC'. That will be the real battle for survival.

CHRONOLOGY

1922   The British Broadcasting Company is formed by a group of radio manufacturers. John Reith is the first Director General.

1923   Sykes Committee rejects advertising as means of funding BBC.

1926   The Crawford Committee recommends that the BBC becomes a public corporation. During the General Strike, Reith forbids the Labour Party leader Ramsay MacDonald and the Archbishop of Canterbury to broadcast.

1927   The BBC becomes the British Broadcasting Corporation, formed under Royal Charter. Reith gets a knighthood.

1928   Staff numbers exceed 1,000 for the first time.

1932   BBC moves to Broadcasting House in Portland Place, central London.

1936   The BBC launches the world's first public television service. The first programme includes a discussion about books between T.S. Eliot, Somerset Maugham and Rebecca West.

1946   Radio licence doubles, from 10/- to £1. Combined radio and television licence introduced, cost £2.

1950   First televised report of general election results. Beveridge Committee recommends indefinite charter period and that the BBC retains monopoly of broadcasting. Minority report (by Selwyn Lloyd) recommends introduction of commercial television and radio.

1953   Live coverage of the Coronation is watched by twenty million people. First edition of Panorama broadcast.

1955   ITV goes on air.

1956   The Suez crisis. In the face of government pressure, the BBC allows the Labour Party a right to reply which criticises the invasion.

1958   Numbers of combined TV/radio licences exceed radio licences for the first time (8m against 6.5m). Staff numbers top 15,000.

1960   Hugh Carleton Green becomes seventh Director General.

1962   Pilkington Committee report condemns poor quality of ITV and recommends that third channel should go to BBC. Charter extended for two years to July 1964. Z-Cars and That Was the Week, That Was go on air.

1963   Dr Who first broadcast.

1964   Staff numbers exceed 20,000. Match of the Day first broadcast. BBC-2 is launched.

1967   Radios 1, 2, 3 and 4 go on air.

1968   Hugh Greene resigns as Director General. McKinseys recommend reform of BBC's management and financial structures.

1971   Radio-only licence abolished. Yesterday's Men broadcast.

1974   Labour returned to power. Abolishes ministry of Posts and

Telecommunications and transfers responsibility for broadcasting to the Home Office; sets up Annan Committee to examine future of broadcasting. BBC staff numbers exceed 25,000.

1977 Annan Committee reports in March: recommends that fourth television channel be run by an Open Broadcasting Authority on a publishing model; endorses licence fee as means of funding BBC; criticises BBC current affairs for 'feebleness' and 'palsy'. Ian Trethowan becomes ninth Director General in October; Alasdair Milne promoted to Managing Director, Television. Colour TV licences exceed black and white for the first time.

1978 Secretary of State for Northern Ireland, Roy Mason, accuses BBC of being propaganda outlet for IRA, reminds it that charter and licence fee are due for renewal.

1979 Charter extended for two years until July 1981. Margaret Thatcher becomes Prime Minister. Irish National Liberation Army spokesman interviewed by Tonight. Panorama crew films Provisional IRA at village of Carrickmore.

1981 **July** Sixth charter granted for fifteen-year term (to December 1996).

August William Rees-Mogg succeeds Mark Bonham-Carter as Vice-Chairman.

December Alasdair Milne chosen as next Director General.

1982 **May** Conservative MPs lambast Chairman George Howard and Director General-elect Alasdair Milne for the BBC's coverage of the Falklands war.

August Milne succeeds Trethowan, becoming tenth Director General.

November Channel 4 goes on air as publisher-broadcaster.

1983 **June** Conservatives win second term in office.

August Stuart Young succeeds Howard as Chairman.

1984 **January** Maggie's Militant Tendency broadcast.

September Michael Grade returns from America to become Controller, BBC-1. Staff numbers peak at over 29,000.

1985 **March** Peacock Committee set up to examine the financing of the BBC.

May Michael Checkland appointed Deputy Director General. 'Black Spot' committee set up to identify savings.

August Real Lives: At the Edge of the Union postponed by governors, causing one-day strike by journalists. Shown in October.

1986 **April** All commercial activities brought under BBC Enterprises.

June Michael Grade promoted to BBC TV Director of Programmes.

July Peacock Committee report decides against advertising on the BBC, but recommends a quota for independent production. Independent producers' 25% Campaign starts in earnest.

August Joel Barnett succeeds William Rees-Mogg as Vice-Chairman. Chairman Stuart Young dies.

September Rows over The Monocled Mutineer and Falklands Play.

October   A libel case by two Conservative MPs against Maggie's Militant Tendency is settled out of court. BBC Daytime launched. Conservative Party delivers report accusing BBC News of unbalanced coverage of the bombing of Tripoli in April. Marmaduke Hussey appointed Chairman.

November   Douglas Hurd announces independent production quota of 25%. Licence fee frozen at £58 until April 1988. Celebrations of BBC TV's Golden Jubilee shunned by Margaret Thatcher.

December   Douglas Hurd tells Alasdair Milne he wants action on independent quotas.

1987   **January**   Governors ban Secret Society programme Zircon. Police raid offices of BBC Scotland to seize tapes of the series. Alasdair Milne dismissed as Director General. Superchannel satellite station launched.

February   Michael Checkland appointed eleventh Director General.

March   John Birt joins from LWT as Deputy Director General with responsibility for the BBC's journalism.

May   Conservative Party wins third election under Margaret Thatcher.

July   Birt announces creation of News and Current Affairs Directorate and closure of Lime Grove.

September   Downing Street seminar on broadcasting. Policy and Planning Unit set up under Patricia Hodgson.

October   Jonathan Powell is appointed Controller, BBC-1 and Alan Yentob Controller, BBC-2.

November   Michael Grade resigns; becomes Chief Executive, Channel 4.

December   Newsnight given fixed start time, provoking row between BBC TV and Current Affairs Directorate. The government announces that future licence-fee increases will be linked to inflation.

1988   **April**   Bill Cotton, Managing Director, Television, retires. He is succeeded by Paul Fox. Death on the Rock broadcast by Thames Television.

May   Launch of three (of four) specialist current affairs programmes.

June   Rupert Murdoch announces launch of Sky Television. Tumbledown shown. Douglas Hurd says BBC should move towards subscription funding in speech to Coningsby Club. Home Affairs Select Committee report on broadcasting urges caution in changing BBC funding ahead of charter renewal.

July   Ian Phillips joins as Finance Director.

August   ITV pays £44m for rights to Football League matches for four years.

September   Zircon finally shown.

October   Home Office announces order banning broadcasters from interviewing or broadcasting speech by individuals associated with a range of Northern Irish groups, including Sinn Fein.

1989 **February** Sky launches four-channel satellite TV system.

May Series of strikes begins over pay.

August Rupert Murdoch gives MacTaggart Lecture at Edinburgh Television Festival.

1990 **January** Funding the Future Committee recommends axing new buildings for radio and news and current affairs planned for the White City site.

February Centre for Policy Studies report advocates Public Service Broadcasting Council.

March Checkland announces plans for World Service Television.

April Launch of BSB.

July BBC seeks private investment for World Service Television. BBC-1 share of viewing falls below 34%.

August Radio 5 starts broadcasting.

November Broadcasting Act, which creates auction for ITV licences, becomes law. Margaret Thatcher steps down as Prime Minister. The satellite TV station BSB merges with Sky after weeks of secret talks.

1991 **January** Gulf War. John Major praises BBC news coverage. Panorama's Supergun programme is postponed by John Birt. Launch of night-time BBC Select.

March Sadler Report criticises extent of on-screen BBC promotion of magazines.

April Hussey reappointed Chairman for five years, and Lord Barnett Vice-Chairman for two. BBC licence fee set at less than the rate of inflation following report by accountants Price Waterhouse. First Producer Choice pilot scheme starts in Television and Film Services, Ealing. Task Forces announced, results to be drawn together by Charter Review group.

July John Birt appointed Director General-designate, to take over in March 1993. Checkland to remain as Director General for another eighteen months.

October World Service Television launched. New ITV licensees announced after auction.

November Television Resources Review unveiled. Proposes closure of six regional studios.

December Michael Checkland knighted.

1992 **March** Panorama's Sliding into Slump programme pulled by Samir Shah, head of weekly programmes. It is shown after the general election.

April John Major wins election. New Department of National Heritage, under David Mellor, takes responsibility for broadcasting from the Home Office.

May Deal with BSkyB wins BBC Premier League football highlights.

July Mellor resigns after revelations of an affair with an actress. He is replaced by Peter Brooke. Eldorado is launched. Checkland announces plan for 24-hour rolling news service on radio. £25m overspend uncovered, and doubles during course of inquiry.

August Michael Grade attacks BBC management in speech at Edinburgh Television Festival.

October Michael Checkland criticises BBC governors and the Chairman at a meeting of the Royal Television Society.

November Green Paper published. The BBC's own document, Extending Choice, follows two days later. At its launch, John Birt says BBC TV's audience share could fall to 30% by 2000.

December Michael Checkland stands down as Director General. Jonathan Powell resigns as Controller, BBC-1.

1993 **January** John Birt becomes twelfth Director General. New ITV licensees start broadcasting. Bob Phillis appointed Deputy Director General (from ITN); Liz Forgan appointed Managing Director, Radio (from Channel 4).

February The Independent on Sunday reveals John Birt's 'freelance' tax status. Ian Phillips leaves.

March Senior management, and senior journalists, have letters supporting Birt published in The Times. Alan Yentob succeeds Powell as Controller, BBC-1. Yentob scraps Eldorado; last episode scheduled for July. John Birt describes old BBC as 'vast command economy' in Fleming Lecture.

April Producer Choice is launched throughout BBC.

June BBC-1 share of viewing falls to below 29%.

July Mark Tully attacks BBC management in speech to Radio Academy. Yentob tells Radio Academy that BBC may be 'super-serving' ABC1 viewers.

August At Edinburgh Television Festival, Dennis Potter describes Hussey and Birt as 'a pair of croak-faced Daleks'.

November Licence fee to be increased in line with inflation, but BBC to reduce £200m overdraft to zero by end of charter period.

December Select Committee on National Heritage publishes report on BBC recommending more aggressive commercial approach.

1994 **March** Launch of Radio 5 Live (news and sport station).

May Series of one-day strikes against performance-related pay proposals and other changes to working conditions. Bob Phillis announces international partnership between BBC and Pearson.

July White Paper published on renewal of charter after repeated delays. Mark Tully resigns. Stephen Dorrell replaces Peter Brooke at National Heritage Department in reshuffle.

BIBLIOGRAPHY

Adam Smith Institute, *The Omega Report: Communications Policy*. London: Adam Smith Institute, 1984.

Keith Anderson, 'The Management and Organisation of BBC Television's Programme Making Process' in Richard Paterson (ed), *Organising for Change, The Broadcasting Debate 1*. London: British Film Institute, 1990.

Stephen J. Ball, 'Management as Moral Technology' in Stephen J. Ball (ed), *Foucault and Education: Disciplines and Knowledge*. London: Routledge, 1990.

Eric Barendt, 'Legal Aspects of BBC Charter Renewal' in *Political Quarterly*, Vol 65, No 1, 1994.

Steven Barnett, *Games and Sets*. London: British Film Institute, 1990.

Steven Barnett (ed), *Funding the BBC's Future*, BFI Charter Review Series vol 2. London: British Film Institutute, 1993.

Steven Barnett and David Docherty, 'Purity or Pragmatism: a Cross-Cultural Perspective on Public Service Broadcasting' in Jay Blumler and T.J. Nossiter (eds) *Broadcasting Finance in Transition: a Comparative Handbook*. Oxford: OUP, 1991.

BBC, *Extending Choice*. London: BBC, 1992.

BBC, *Producer Choice*. Unpublished, 1993.

BBC, *Responding to the Green Paper*. London: BBC, 1993.

BBC, *Turning Promises Into Realities*. Unpublished, 1993.

Richard Belfield, Christopher Hird and Sharon Kelly, *Murdoch: The Great Escape*. London: Warner, 1994.

BFI/BAFTA, *Commission of Inquiry into the Future of the BBC,* London: British Film Institute, 1993.

Jay Blumler, 'The Increasing Self-Commercialisation of the BBC: Profit or Peril?', in Steven Barnett (ed), *Funding the BBC's Future*. London: BFI, 1993.

Roger Bolton, *Death on the Rock (and other stories)*. London: W.H. Allen, 1990.

Mihir Bose, *Michael Grade: Screening The Image*. London: Virgin, 1992.

Will Bracken and Scott Fowler, *What Price Public Service?* London: Adam Smith Institute, 1993.

Asa Briggs, *The BBC Governors*. London: BBC, 1979.

Asa Briggs, *The BBC: The First Fifty Years*. Oxford: OUP, 1985.

Tom Burns, *The BBC, Public Institution and Private World*. London: Macmillan, 1977.

Carnegie Commission, *A Public Trust: a Report on the Future of Public Broadcasting*. New York: Carnegie Commission, 1979.

Peter Chippindale and Suzanne Franks, *Dished!* London: Simon & Schuster, 1991.

Michael Cockerell, *Live from Number 10*. London: Faber, 1988.

Tim Congdon *et al, Paying for Broadcasting*. London: Routledge, 1991.

Richard Crossman, *The Crossman Diaries*. London: Jonathan Cape, 1979.

Charles Curran, *The Seamless Robe*. London: Bodley Head, 1979.

James Curran and Jean Seaton, *Power Without Responsibility: the Press and Broadcasting in Britain* (4th edition). London: Routledge, 1991

Andrew Davidson, *Under The Hammer*. London: Heinemann, 1992.

Jonathan Davis, *TV, UK*. Peterborough: Knowledge Research, 1991.

Department of Trade and Industry, *Enquiry into Standards of Cross Media Promotion* (The Sadler Report). London: HMSO, 1991.

David Docherty, *Running the Show – 21 Years of London Weekend Television*. London: Boxtree, 1990

Andrew Ehrenberg and Pam Mills, *Viewers' Willingness To Pay (A Research Report)*. London: Broadcast, 1990.

Matthew Engel, 'An Unmanageable Surfeit of Sport' in *British Journalism Review*, Vol 5, No 1, 1994.

Harold Evans, *Good Times, Bad Times*. London: Weidenfeld & Nicolson, 1983.

Richard Eyre, 'The Odd Couple?', keynote address in *The Odd Couple?: Broadcasting and the Arts Conference Speakers Notes*. London: The Arts Council, 1992.

Richard Eyre, 'Dreaming of Hollywood', speech at the Edinburgh International Television Festival 1993. Unpublished.

FACT Magazine, *BBC Special Edition*. London: PACT, 1993.

Bob Franklin, *Packaging Politics: Political Communication in Britain's Media Democracy*. London: Edward Arnold, 1994.

Graham Fuller (ed), *Potter on Potter*. London: Faber, 1993.

Alex Fynn and Lynton Guest, *Out of Time*. London: Simon and Schuster, 1994.

Nicholas Garnham, 'The Broadcasting Market and the Future of the BBC' in *Political Quarterly*, Vol 65, No 1, 1994.

Grace Wyndham Goldie, *Facing the Nation: Television and Politics 1936–1976*. London: Bodley Head, 1977.

Peter Goodwin and Wilf Stevenson (eds), *Responses to the Green Paper*, BFI Charter Review Series vol 6. London: British Film Institute, 1993.

Andrew Graham and Gavyn Davies, 'The Public Funding of Broadcasting' in Congdon *et al, Paying for Broadcasting*. London: Routledge, 1991.

John Gray, *Beyond The New Right*. London: Routledge, 1993.

John Gray, 'Cultural Diversity, National Identity and the Case for Public Service Broadcasting in Britain', in Wilf Stevenson (ed) *All Our Futures*. London: British Film Institute, 1993.

Damian Green, *A Better BBC*. London: Centre for Policy Studies, 1990.

Hugh Carleton Greene, *The Third Floor Front: A View of Broadcasting in the Sixties*. London: Bodley Head, 1969.

Sir Douglas Hague, *Transforming the Dinosaurs*. London: Demos, 1993.

Denis Hamilton, *Editor-in Chief*. London: Hamish Hamilton, 1989.

Charles Handy, *The Empty Raincoat*. London: Hutchinson, 1994.

Ian Hargreaves, *Sharper Vision*. London: Demos, 1993.

Robert Harris, *Gotcha! The Media, the Government and the Falklands Crisis*. London: Faber and Faber, 1983.

Sylvia Harvey and Kevin Robins (eds), *The Regions. The Nations and the BBC*, BFI Charter Review Series vol 5. London: British Film Institute, 1993.

Home Affairs Committee, *3rd Report. The Future of Broadcasting*. HMSO, 1988.

Home Office, *Report of the Committee on the Future of Broadcasting* (Chairman Lord Annan). London: HMSO, 1977.

Stuart Hood, *On Television*. London: Pluto 1980.

Stuart Hood and Garrett O'Leary, *Questions of Broadcasting*. London: Methuen, 1990.

Chris Hopson, *Reforming The BBC*. London: European Policy Forum, 1992.

Chris Horrie and Steve Clarke, *Fuzzy Monsters*. London: Heinemann, 1994.

David Housham (ed), *The Television Book 1993*. London: Edinburgh International Television Festival, 1993. (Includes text of Michael Grade's MacTaggart Lecture, 1992.)

Marmaduke Hussey, 'Chairing an Institution', in *Mission and Strategy in the Public Sector*. Office for Public Management Conference Paper 2, 1989.

Bernard Ingham, *Kill The Messenger*. London: HarperCollins, 1991.

Jeremy Isaacs, *Storm Over Four*. London: Weidenfeld & Nicholson, 1989.

Clive James, *The Dreaming Swimmer*. London: Jonathan Cape, 1992.

Rosabeth Moss Kanter, *When Giants Learn to Dance*. London: Simon & Schuster, 1989.

Elihu Katz, *Social Research on Broadcasting: Proposals for Further Development*. London: BBC, 1977

Hilary Kingsley and Geoff Tibballs, *Box of Delights*. London: Macmillan, 1989.

Stewart Lansley, *After the Goldrush*. London: Random House, 1994.

John Lawrence and Robert Lawrence MC, *When The Fighting Is Over: Tumbledown*. London: Bloomsbury, 1988.

Michael Leapman, *The Last Days of the Beeb*. London: Allen & Unwin, 1986.

James McDonnell, *Public Service Broadcasting: A Reader*. London: Routledge, 1991.

McKinsey & Co, *Creating Value in the New Entertainment Industry (Part 2)*. Unpublished, 1991.

McKinsey & Co, *Public Service Broadcasters Around The World* (A McKinsey report for the BBC). London: BBC, 1993.

Marshall McLuhan, *Understanding Media*. London: Routledge & Kegan Paul, 1964.

Leonard Miall, *Inside the BBC*. London: Weidenfeld & Nicolson, 1994.

Ronald Millar, *A View from the Wings*. London: Weidenfeld & Nicolson, 1993.

Nod Miller and Cresta Norris (eds), *Life After The Broadcasting Bill* (Proceedings of the 20th University of Manchester Broadcasting Symposium). Manchester: Manchester Monographs, 1989.

Nod Miller and Rod Allen (eds), *And Now For The BBC. . .* (Proceedings of the 22nd University of Manchester Broadcasting Symposium). London: John Libbey, 1991.

Nod Miller and Rod Allen (eds), *Broadcasting Enters The Marketplace* (Proceedings of the 24th University of Manchester Broadcasting Symposium). London: John Libbey, 1994.

Stephen Milligan, *What shall we do about the BBC?* London: Tory Reform Group, 1991.

Alasdair Milne, *DG: The Memoirs of a British Broadcaster*. London: Hodder & Stoughton, 1988.

David Morrison and Howard Tumber, *Journalists at War*. London: Sage Publications, 1988.

Geoff Mulgan and Richard Paterson (eds). *Reinventing the Organisation*, BFI Charter Review Series vol 4. London: British Film Institute, 1993.

Rupert Murdoch, *Freedom in Broadcasting*, The MacTaggart Lecture 1989. London: News International, 1989.

James Naughtie, 'Paper Tiger', in *Edinburgh International Television Festival Programme 1989*. London: EITF, 1989.

National Heritage Committee, *2nd Report. The Future of the BBC*. London: HMSO, 1993.

Greg Parston, 'Public Service, Public Management and the BBC' in Geoff Mulgan and Richard Paterson (eds) *Reinventing the Organisation*, London: British Film Institute, 1993.

Dennis Potter, *Waiting For The Boat*. London: Faber, 1984.

Dennis Potter, *Seeing The Blossom*. London: Faber, 1994. (Includes text of 1993 James MacTaggart Memorial Lecture.)

John Ranelagh, *Thatcher's People*. London: Fontana, 1992.

St Catherine's Conference Report No. 35, *The Future of Broadcasting in Britain*. Windsor: King George VI and Queen Elizabeth Foundation, 1992.

Colin Seymour-Ure, *Press and Broadcasting Since 1945*. Oxford: Basil Blackwell, 1991.

Andrew Sharp, paper to 'Interactive Cable in the Next Three Years' conference, London : London Economics, 1994. Unpublished.

Colin Shaw (ed), *Rethinking Governance and Accountability*, BFI Charter Review Series vol 3. London: British Film Institute, 1993.

William Shawcross, *Rupert Murdoch: Ringmaster of the Information Circus*. London: Chatto & Windus, 1992.

Anthony Smith, 'The Future of Public Service in Broadcasting', in Wilf Stevenson (ed) *All Our Futures*, London: British Film Institute, 1993.

Anthony Smith, *Books to Bytes: Knowledge and Information in the Postmodern Era*. London: British Film Institute, 1993.

The 25% Campaign, *The 25% Campaign*. Unpublished, 1986.

Michael Tracey, *The Production of Political Television*. London: Routledge, 1978.

Michael Tracey, *A Variety of Lives: a biography of Sir Hugh Greene*. London: Bodley Head, 1983.

Ian Trethowan, *Split Screen*. London: Hamish Hamilton, 1984.

John Tusa, *A World in Your Ear*. London: Broadside Books, 1992.

John Tusa, 'Programmes or Products – the Management Ethos and Creative Values'. Text of James Cameron Memorial Lecture. London: City University, 1994 C.G. Veljanovski and W.D.Bishop, *Choice By Cable*. London: Institute of Economic Affairs Hobart Paper 96, 1983.

Cento Veljanovski (ed), *Freedom in Broadcasting*. London: Institute of Economic Affairs, 1989.

Brian Wenham (ed), *The Third Age of Broadcasting*. London: Faber.

White Paper on Broadcasting, *Competition, Choice and Quality*. London: HMSO, 1989.

White Paper, *The Future of the BBC: Serving the Nation, Competing Worldwide*. London: HMSO, 1994.

Charles Wood, *Tumbledown*. London: Penguin 1987.

Hugo Young, *One of Us*. London: Macmillan, (1989).

INDEX